# Our Musicals, Ourselves

## A SOCIAL HISTORY OF THE AMERICAN MUSICAL THEATRE

John Bush Jones

*Brandeis University Press*

Published by University Press of New England

Hanover and London

Brandeis University Press

Published by

University Press of New England, 37 Lafayette St., Lebanon, NH 03766

© 2003 by Brandeis University Press

Printed in the United States of America

5  4  3  2  1

LIBRARY OF CONGRESS CATALOGING-IN-PUBLICATION DATA

Jones, John Bush.
Our musicals, ourselves : a social history of the American musical
theater / John Bush Jones.
p.  cm.
Includes bibliographical references (p.   ) and index.
ISBN 1–58465–311–6 (cloth : alk. paper)
1. Musicals—United States—History and criticism. 2. Musical
theater—United States—Social aspects. I. Title.
ML1711 .J65 2003
782.1'4'0973—dc21          2003000240

Every effort was made to contact the current copyright holders of the works cited in this volume. Any mistakes or oversights will be corrected in future editions.

"All Kinds of People" by Richard Rodgers and Oscar Hammerstein II
Copyright © 1955 by Richard Rodgers and Oscar Hammerstein II
Copyright Renewed
WILLIAMSON MUSIC owner of publication and allied rights throughout the World.
International Copyright Secured All Rights Reserved Used by Permission

"America" from *West Side Story* by Leonard Bernstein & Stephen Sondheim
© Amberson Holdings LLC & Stephen Sondheim. Renewed. By Permission of the Leonard Bernstein Music Publishing Company LLC.

(*list continues on p. 384*)

*Our Musicals, Ourselves*

To my son, Carson Jones, who, like me, saw his first musicals at age five with his father, and who (like his dad) has never lost his love of them.

# Contents

# Foreword

## Sheldon Harnick

I am part of a generation of theatre writers whose sensibilities were shaped by the Great Depression and World War II. With those experiences in our backgrounds, it was natural for us to want to address serious issues in our work. We enthusiastically followed the footsteps of writers who had created such issue-driven musicals as *Show Boat, Pins and Needles, Of Thee I Sing, Lost in the Stars,* and *South Pacific.* Although much of my own work dealt with romantic or comedic subjects, musicals like *Fiorello, Tenderloin, The Rothschilds, A Wonderful Life,* and *Dragons* did not shy away from voicing serious social and political concerns.

Yet we realized that whatever serious statements we wanted to make had to be presented in the most entertaining way possible. Had we written a commandment for the creators of Broadway musicals, it would have been "Enlighten if thou canst, but entertain thou *must.*" For me, E. Y. Harburg and Burton Lane's *Finian's Rainbow,* with its witty, elegant lyrics and wonderful music, represented the best that "serious" musical theatre had to offer. It proved that a trenchant story line need not hamper entertainment value. Indeed, *Fiddler on the Roof,* the most serious of my musicals, has also been the most successful.

When I began writing for the musical theatre, I firmly believed that what I chose to put onstage had the potential of changing people's lives. I wrote from the belief that plays and musicals can foster in their audiences a feeling of shared community, thereby combating personal isolation and fear. In theatrical settings, people become receptive, and important lessons about life can be genially imparted from the stage.

Given the ever-increasing complexity of today's world, we wonder about our nation's place in the global community. We need to know ourselves better in order to better understand where we "fit" in the geography of the twenty-first century. More than ever, we need to examine our attitudes and beliefs and look honestly at ourselves as individuals and as citizens of a great nation. To do this, we must understand how we've developed as a people and as a country in the past one hundred years. One of the most diverting places to reconstruct this history is in the Broadway musical. Because these entertainments, generally speaking, are deliberately concocted to appeal to the broadest possible segment of the population, they have much to tell us about ourselves and our culture.

Since my own goal in much of my work has been to "hold a mirror up to nature," I tend to be a bit condescending toward musicals whose sole aim is to amuse patrons. But, as John Bush Jones shows, even light entertainments can reveal a social or political slice of life. And the same is true of Broadway's many revivals, which, like all musical theater, convey the assumptions, biases, aspirations, and racial and sexual attitudes of the time in which they were first written and staged.

*Our Musicals, Ourselves* excavates cultural information from dozens of shows, first-run and revivals, serious and frivolous, over the course of the twentieth century. Jones, interpreting musicals through a historical lens, enables us to see them with new eyes. More importantly, he teaches us to see them not simply as vehicles of transient pleasure but as social documents that tell us who we were and who we are — as individuals, as members of a community, as citizens of a nation. In my view, such awareness is necessary to help us see more clearly where we're going early in the twenty-first century.

# Acknowledgments

Like the writing and staging of any musical, this book has been a collaborative effort. Therefore, the next few pages are intended in some small way to show my appreciation to those people "behind the scenes" who helped bring this book to fruition. I start with Dr. John Hose, Executive Assistant to the President of Brandeis University, since the book really started with him. Discovering that no book took my approach to teaching about American musicals in their context of history, society, and culture, John suggested that I turn the way I teach about musical theatre into a book about how musicals reflect, critique, or otherwise interface with the times in which they are written and produced. John's suggestion was a good idea waiting to happen—for me, resulting in over five years of the happiest and most exciting research and writing of my academic career.

I owe very special thanks to the physicians, nurses, and support staff of The Miriam Hospital in Providence, Rhode Island, and especially my pulmonologist, Dr. Charles B. Sherman. Together they brilliantly diagnosed and pulled me through a rare critical illness in the summer of 2000, just as I was starting the first draft of the final chapter. To say that I owe the hospital and Dr. Sherman more than I could ever repay would just prompt jokes about my health insurance provider, so I will simply say that I owe them all my life.

As cornerstones of the historian's work, libraries and other repositories of information deserve mention along with their personnel. I am especially grateful for the generous assistance of Steven B. Lavallee and the staff of the circulation department of the John D. Rockefeller Library, Rosemary Cullen and the staff of the John Hay Library (special collections), and Carol Tatian and the staff of the Virginia Baldwin Orwig Music Library, all at Brown University; Darwin Scott, Creative Arts Librarian of the Brandeis University Libraries; the staff of the Rhode Island State Law Library; the Reginald Allen Gilbert and Sullivan Collection of the Pierpont Morgan Library; and, so useful for their "popular" books not housed in most university libraries, the Providence Public Library system and the public libraries of Cranston and Pawtucket, Rhode Island. Lisa C. Long, former Brandeis University Archivist, pointed me to the materials surrounding the world premiere there of Leonard Bernstein's *Trouble in Tahiti*; and, as a close friend and an historian herself, Lisa was an invaluable reader of early drafts and a source of encouragement throughout. And while not librarians or archivists, Tara Faircloth, the Non-Equity Licensing Agent at Music Theatre International, and Charlie Scatamacchia, Manager of Professional Licensing at the Rodgers and Hammerstein Organization, each provided from their companies' records invaluable statistics about productions of certain musicals subsequent to their original New York runs.

People too can be repositories, and I have been able to tap the expertise or personal experience of a large and varied array of them. Among the most valuable are those writers and composers of musicals who took the time to spend some time with me, whether in correspondence or on the phone—Martin Charnin, Tom Jones, Joe Masteroff, Stephen Sondheim, Joseph Stein, Dale Wasserman, and, especially, Sheldon Harnick, for putting me in touch with most of the others and for graciously agreeing to write the foreword to this book. Thanks too to two men intimately conversant with the intricacies of *Hair*'s legal battles: John C. Johnson, Archival Assistant in the Department of Special Collections at Boston University, for sharing with me the summary of his interview with Attorney Gerald Berlin, and Attorney Berlin himself for spending more than forty-five minutes with me filling in yet more details of *Hair*'s byzantine wanderings through the court system.

The other "living repositories" include academic colleagues, friends, my son, and a number of former students, each an invaluable collaborator for his or her special knowledge of some area of musical theatre or social history. Among my colleagues at Brandeis, Professors Jonathan Sarna and Sylvia Barack Fishman, both of the Department of Near Eastern and Judaic Studies, shared their knowledge and insights respecting twentieth-century American Jewish culture. Members of the Department of American Studies all, Professors Joyce Antler, Jacob Cohen, Thomas Doherty, and Stephen J. Whitfield recommended valuable source material on American social history and gave me excellent feedback when their department invited me to present my work-in-progress at one of their monthly seminars. From Brown University, Professor Karl Jacoby, a specialist in Western American history, guided me toward material for the historical background of *Oklahoma!*

Three longtime friends, all musicians—voice teacher and vocal coach Claudia Novack, musical director for many shows I have directed Jonathan Goldberg, and concert pianist Judith Lynn Stillman—each lent me (a decided non-musician) their very different kinds of musical expertise. My son,

Carson Jones, a New York screenwriter with numerous theatrical connections, and my former student Erika Karnell, late of the Gage Group, a New York talent agency, both provided me with up-to-the-minute and often "insider" information about a number of recent musicals. The contributions of other former students have been varied, starting with Gavriel Z. Bellino, who, upon graduating, gave me a present of the second edition of Gerald Bordman's *Chronicle*, my continual source of information—and occasional aggravation. David Chmielewski's research paper for my theatre history course guided me in my own work on Marc Blitzstein's *The Cradle Will Rock*, and Devorah Bondarin shared the intimate knowledge of Kurt Weill's *Street Scene* she acquired from being in a production of it. Equal thanks to self-proclaimed *Hair* "groupie" Danielle Borenstein for putting me in touch with John C. Johnson and, through him, Gerald Berlin, to Jessica Lichtenfeld for sharing her research findings on African American theatre, and to Theresa D. Cedrone, who possesses a familiarity with the post–Tim Rice works of Andrew Lloyd Webber I could never hope to achieve.

Invaluable were the efforts of four men and a woman who went way beyond just telling me where to seek reprint permissions by often doing the legwork for me, personally putting my requests before the permissions holders: Charlie Scatamacchia of the Rodgers and Hammerstein Organization, Sargent Aborn of Tams-Witmark, Richard Salfas of Music Theatre International, Brad Lohrenz of Samuel French, and Hope H. Taylor.

Finally, my most profound debts of gratitude are owed to two exceptional people in my life, one personal, one professional. Not just my thanks but my love goes out to my most precious friend Babzi, whose uncommon sensitivity, caring, generosity of time and self, and just plain being there helped get me through some very rough spots when the final rounds of revisions coincided with an unexpectedly trying time for me, medically and emotionally. And, finally, my almost inexpressible thanks to someone I owe more than I can articulate for navigating this book to completion. Throughout the writing, she was my strongest ally and toughest critic, my gadfly and sounding board, cheering section and chopping block—my personal Maxwell Perkins, so to speak—friend and executive editor at University Press of New England, Phyllis Deutsch.

J.B.J.

*Our Musicals, Ourselves*

# Introduction

I t all started in Philadelphia. In 1767, David Douglass's seasoned American Company tried to present *The Disappointment*, the first known musical written on these shores. But four days prior to the opening, the Philadelphia city fathers informed the good citizens of the town that the show would not go on, since it contained "personal reflections, [and] is unfit for the stage" (Bordman 2; Brockett 263). Thus began, if a bit ignominiously, a centuries-long, multidimensional relationship between musical theatre and American society. To be sure, censorship such as this is just one way in which American public life has interfaced with American musical theatre, but such clashes of values have also been particularly visible and dramatic, as in the events surrounding the first production of *The Cradle Will Rock* and the legal battles of *Hair*.

Most often, however, this book concerns a more subtle interchange: that between social and political values and their expression on the musical stage. As a form of popular entertainment for fairly broadbased audiences, throughout the twentieth century musicals variously dramatized, mirrored, or challenged our deeply-held cultural attitudes and beliefs. And those musical plays that sought not just to entertain but also to advocate a point of view hoped to move the audience to see things their way. In a very real sense, then, this social history of the musical stage examines musicals both *in* history and *as* history during the twentieth century—as theatrical vehicles that intended to transform, not just report, the tenor of the times. Even shows that contain little content of social relevance—those I call "diversionary musicals," which have always comprised the majority of all professionally produced musicals in the United States—these too are important, if only to raise the question of why certain decades delivered more "mindless fluff" than others.

Any book about musicals that isn't merely a chronology is likely to leave some popular favorites out. Because this is a social history of musicals, I focus almost exclusively on shows that in some way spoke to the issues, achievements, and, often, the anxieties of their particular era. By and large, I restricted my selection to musicals that seem to have been *consciously intended* to have contemporary social relevance. I spend more time with lesser-known musicals like *I'd Rather Be Right* and *Lost in the Stars* than with blockbusters like *My Fair Lady, Hello, Dolly!*, or *42nd Street*. The appendices catalogue the most popular diversionary musicals by their periods in order to provide the broader musical theatre context for the socially conscious musicals I discuss.

Unlike movies, radio, and television, the musical stage as an institution and the shows written and produced for it have not been fully examined in their historical context. Prior chronological booklength studies of musical theatre have almost exclusively focused on the development of the shows themselves, with little or no reference to their social setting. The single exception is Gerald Bordman's monumental and in many ways invaluable *American Musical Theatre: A Chronicle*, with its occasional historical notes preceding the year-by-year cataloging of the shows themselves. But given Bordman's stated goal of inclusiveness, his capsule discussions of the shows are rarely long enough to contain in-depth historical analysis. Other chronological surveys of Broadway (and sometimes off-Broadway) musicals, from Cecil Smith's early *Musical Comedy in America* (1950) to Denny Martin Flinn's *Musical!: A Grand Tour* and Kurt Gänzl's *The Musical: A Concise History* (both 1997) and beyond, tend to be slick and/or highly selective. Other than such chronological histories and biographies or critical studies of individual composers, authors, lyricists, and directors, there are primarily two sorts of books on musicals: those that are "show specific" and those largely ordered by topics or a special subject rather than chronology. In recent years, show-specific volumes have proliferated to include, among many others, three different books on the making of *A Chorus Line*, Max Wilk's fiftieth-anniversary tribute to *Oklahoma!*, and "coffee table" picture books about shows like *Phantom of the Opera, Miss Saigon*, and *Titanic*. Representative of books on musicals that are topic- or special subject-oriented are Richard Kislan's *The Musical*, Ken Mandelbaum's delightful treatment of flops *Not Since Carrie*, Mark Steyn's recent *Broadway Babies Say Goodnight: Musicals Then and Now*, and, for me the most valuable of all, Stanley Green's composer-by-composer *The World of Musical Comedy*. Informed, literate, and humane, Green's reasoned and judicious insights are as valuable today as when he wrote them.

I use the term "musical" here to refer to both "book shows" (musicals with a plot or story) and "revues" (anthologies of separate and usually unrelated songs, dance numbers, and comedy routines). Also, too, I use "show" only as synonymous with "musical" (never with "play"). Finally, "musicals" here refers only to those shows professionally mounted for commercial production in New York both on and off Broadway (and, in the early decades of the century, Chicago). Excluded are American operas, except those such as *Porgy and Bess* and some by Gian-Carlo Menotti and others that were written specifically for Broadway production and Broadway audiences. Also, with few exceptions, British and other imported musicals that played on Broadway are not treated here. Mainly, I deal with musicals by American composers, lyricists, and book writers. Although this history is essentially chronological, I disrupt strict chronology to discuss the musicals according to themes, genres, subject matter, ethnicity, and other logical groupings that reflect how related shows in each period interfaced with the world beyond the theatre.

Who were the audiences for Broadway shows in the twentieth century? While such demographics are difficult to plot, twentieth-century audiences for New York musicals were generally white and middle class, though not necessarily extremely affluent until late in the century and after. Skyrocketing ticket prices have made Broadway audiences much more elitist than in previous decades. From the turn of the century through World War II, most musicals priced some seats at some performances low enough so that even people of modest means could afford to attend — and attend regularly. After the war ticket prices escalated, doubling between 1945 and 1960. In 2001, *The Producers* set a new precedent by regularly charging $100 for orchestra seats. Even the TKTS half price booth in Times Square doesn't provide much relief; half price of a $100 ticket is still $50.

One result of these soaring prices is that audiences have become wealthier and older. With fewer young people exposed to musicals (see chapter 5), the potential audience for musical theatre has begun to shrink. Furthermore, African Americans only comprise a significant portion of Broadway musical audiences for black-oriented shows, whether by black, white, or mixed-race creative teams. Therefore, with certain ethnic and "radical" exceptions (such as *Hair*), socially relevant shows have mirrored the concerns and lifestyles of middle Americans, their primary audience. The reality of commercial theatre dictates that, no matter how brilliant or artistic, if a show doesn't interest or entertain its audiences, it won't run long enough to make back its investment.

In this history, however, I generally discount such financial concerns when evaluating the success or failure of shows. Instead, I judge the success of musicals on audience appeal alone, usually as indicated by the length of their runs. In many cases (*Milk and Honey* and *Follies*, to name just two), musicals have had impressively long runs, entertained many thousands of spectators, and still lost money. Generally speaking, to be considered a success a Broadway musical needs to play far more performances than an off-Broadway one, although prior to World War I and for sometime thereafter, hit status was generally accorded to Broadway shows that played but a hundred times.

Generally speaking, what makes a musical succeed is simple (if vague) enough: something about a show captures the public imagination, and people swarm to see it. It's harder to say why a show fails. I sometimes think it all comes down to what my father, a pragmatic Chicago theatre owner, once told me. In my early teens I asked him why a show I really liked had bombed. To my seemingly naive question, Dad gave what for him was the obvious answer: "Nobody bought tickets." Still, as a work of historical analysis this book does speculate about the failure of a number of musicals. There are a few documented cases of external factors forcing musicals to close, such as a newspaper strike preventing enough advertising and publicity to keep a show open; the departure of a star that audiences particularly came to see (Liza Minnelli in *The Act*); or the terrorist attack of September 11, 2001, which caused a sharp drop in New York tourism. But such demonstrable extrinsic causes are rare. More often something intrinsic to the show makes it flop. Sometimes a musical simply isn't very good or very well performed, but some creditable shows with very talented casts also fail (*Let 'Em Eat Cake*, the 1956 *Candide*, and *Pacific Overtures*, among many others). The reasons for musicals failing are complex and varied, some historically grounded, others coming down to simply a matter of taste.

Of course, American musical theatre and Americans' taste for it were not born fullblown at the turn of the twentieth century. But in the 1800s, and with few exceptions such as the minstrel show (see chapter 1), most musical entertainments on the American stage were either imports or imitations of British and European comic opera, operetta, or rudimentary musical comedy, and they had little influence on musicals after 1900. These shows, beyond the scope of this history, have been treated extensively elsewhere (see, for example, Bordman 1–170). Nonetheless, one nineteenth-century import virtually alone laid the groundwork for the twentieth-century American musical: Gilbert and Sullivan's *H. M. S. Pinafore*.

## Pinafore *Fever*

For years after its arrival here in 1878, *Pinafore* achieved a nationwide popularity for a musical unprecedented up to that time. That popularity fostered an American audience for musical theatre, while the show itself became a model for the form, content, and even intention of American musicals ever since, especially socially relevant musicals.

*Pinafore* was the third collaboration of British comic opera writers W. S. Gilbert and Arthur Sullivan in conjunction with producer Richard D'Oyly Carte, then lessee of London's Opéra Comique theatre. The story, an example of what we will come to know and love as the "boy meets girl, boy loses girl, boy gets girl back" formula, was hardly innovative. Ralph Rackstraw, a common sailor, is in love with Josephine, daughter of the *Pinafore*'s Captain Corcoran (and she's in love with Ralph). But Josephine's father has arranged for her to marry Sir Joseph Porter, First Lord of the Admiralty. All seems hopeless when, into this formula, Gilbert injects his trademark devices of deliciously inverted logic and love of the absurd. He resolves the conventional plot through one-time nursemaid Little Buttercup's revelation that she accidentally switched Ralph and Corcoran as babies, so that (nonsensically, of course) Ralph is now the Captain (and a suitable match for Josephine), while Corcoran is demoted to the rank of common seaman.

Within just months of its London opening on May 25, 1878, at the Opéra Comique, *Pinafore* became the musical theatre rage of the English-speaking world, but its beginnings did not seem so auspicious. *Pinafore* opened with two strikes against it. First, in the euphemistic words of Gilbert and Sullivan scholar Leslie Baily, reviews in the London daily press ranged from "very kind" to the *Daily Telegraph*'s hostile "A frothy production destined soon to subside into nothingness." Second, a rare spring heat wave in London kept audiences away from the Opéra Comique, a stuffy, ill-ventilated old wreck of a theatre. The stifling heat made sitting through *Pinafore* enough of an ordeal that nightly receipts quickly dropped below £100 and, by July, "down to £40 and less" (Baily 131).

The innovative Carte rescued *Pinafore*, at the same time convincing increasing numbers of middle-class Londoners that attending the theatre was not disreputable, as many believed it to be. (The "family show" quality of Gilbert and Sullivan's musicals would have much the same effect in the United States toward removing the "taint" of theatregoing.) Carte persuaded Sullivan to add Hamilton Clarke's "brilliant arrangement of *Pinafore* selections" to the programs of more "serious" music he would conduct for the Promenade Concert series at Covent Garden Opera House (Baily 134; Goldberg 214). Encored twice at its first performance, the *Pinafore* medley was repeated nightly throughout the Promenade series. Long before radio and TV talk shows to hype one's work, Carte's ploy of getting "respectable" concertgoers to hear *Pinafore*'s tunes proved effective in getting them into the theatre as well. By the end of August every performance was selling out. Ultimately *Pinafore* played at the Opéra Comique a full seven hundred times. Moreover, in the days when people made their own music around the parlor piano, "music shops sold 10,000 copies of the piano score in one day" (Baily 134).

On November 25, 1878 — exactly six months after *Pinafore's* London premiere — the Boston Museum offered Americans their first stateside glimpse of Gilbert and Sullivan's nautical opera. To say the response was enthusiastic would be an understatement. Productions of *Pinafore* spread literally across the country in no time at all, to San Francisco by December 23 and to Philadelphia by the first week of 1879 (Bordman 46). New York was a bit slow on the uptake; the Standard Theatre presented its version on January 15, 1879. It is customary to refer to these and the many other American *Pinafores* as "pirated" productions, since none of them remunerated Gilbert, Sullivan, or Carte with as much as a shilling. But before international copyright, these lucrative productions weren't actually piracies — opportunistic, perhaps, but not illegal. (Years later, Gilbert — an attorney himself — would argue for international copyright protection for dramatic authors.)

Loose copyright laws also allowed the bizarre practice of competing productions of *Pinafore* to run simultaneously in a single city. Such productions often resorted to gimmicks to bring in an audience. Not more than a week after the Standard opened its rendition of the show, the Lyceum premiered what has since been called "the transvestite *Pinafore*," with a nautically clad young woman as Ralph Rackstraw and six-foot-plus George K. Fortescue in drag as a more than usually massive Little Buttercup.

If novelty was one goal, "authenticity" was another. Although Americans could buy the libretto and piano-vocal score in London (and not long after in the United States as well), Sullivan's orchestrations and the London costume and set designs remained the exclusive property of the composer and of Carte's Comedy Opera Company. It was not, therefore, uncommon for American producers to send the theatrical equivalent of industrial spies to London to sit night after night at *Pinafore*, surreptitiously sketching the designs or transcribing orchestral parts. American impresarios went to almost any length to capitalize on the *Pinafore* craze.

As the craze mounted, so did the number of productions. Depending on one's source, at one time or other between three and eight *Pinafores* competed in New York City (Bordman 46; Baily 146). (Try to envision modern-day Broadway peppered up and down with rival showings of *Phantom of the Opera*!) The *Dramatic Mirror* for May 3, 1879, noted that since January 15, *Pinafore* had played in "eleven major houses — Wallack's, the Fifth Avenue, the Standard, the Globe, the Olympic, Niblo's, the Lyceum, the Academy of Music, Tony Pastor's, the Germania, and the Windsor" (Bordman 46). Soon there was an all-black *Pinafore*, an all-children's company, and German, Yiddish, and other foreign-language productions in ethnic and immigrant enclaves around the country. *"Pinafore* Fever" spread nationwide. One San Francisco company toured at least as far as Tombstone, Arizona. In the summer of 1879, Providence, Rhode Island applauded an outdoor performance on a mock-up ship anchored offshore in a lake, to which Sir Joseph, his sisters, cousins, and aunts were actually rowed for their first entrance. In fact, before Gilbert, Sullivan, and Carte arrived in New York on November 5, 1879, to mount their "authorized" *Pinafore* at the Fifth Avenue Theatre on December 1, over one hundred fifty separate productions had played in the United States since the first American *Pinafore* less than a year before.

The *New York Herald* called America's nearly faddish love affair with *Pinafore* "the greatest craze—or lunacy." As with twentieth-century entertainment fads from rock bands to blockbuster films, in the wake of the good ship *Pinafore* came parodies, spin-offs, advertising slogans, and what much later would be called licensing merchandise. At the theatre that bore his name, impresario Tony Pastor mounted, along with the actual *Pinafore*, the parody *T. P. S.* [Tony Pastor's Ship] *Canal Boat Pinafore*; and, while the musical was running at Philadelphia's Broad Street Theatre, audiences could also catch the spoof *Shadboat Pinafore* at the 11th Street Opera House a few blocks away (Bordman 47). Not to be outdone, the enterprising San Francisco Minstrels mounted *His Mud Scow Pinafore*, peopled with such characters as Captain Cork-onion and Little Buttertub. Printing presses in Boston, New York, and Chicago spewed out staggering quantities of the complete piano-vocal score as well as sheet music of the show's most popular songs and arrangements for dancing. Meanwhile, on urban sidewalks street "musicians" cranked their barrel organs, endlessly churning out tunes from *Pinafore* to the delight or aggravation of passersby.

*Pinafore* products abounded. Just as modern Americans can purchase posters of favorite movie stars, models, and rock idols, once *Pinafore* came to Manhattan fans could buy photographs of performers (in costume) from nearly any of the competing productions. Not long after, products expanded from souvenirs to include items of leisuretime or practical utility. A *Pinafore* card game sported color drawings of the characters and was played rather like "Old Maid." Girls owned Little Buttercup dolls, and their mothers wore dresses depicting scenes from the show. Housewives could accessorize their dining tables with handsome cut-glass "celery glasses" and other tableware featuring the musical's characters in relief. And in the world of commerce, *Pinafore*'s catchphrases as well as characters graced newspaper ads and full-color trade cards (like baseball cards but advertising a product). In short, *H. M. S. Pinafore* launched the first media blitz in the United States, long before radio, television, and the Internet.

Why did *Pinafore* so capture the hearts of Americans, and how did it influence future American musicals? The immediate answer to the first question is simple: *Pinafore* is rattling good entertainment. In its own day *Pinafore* was arguably the most all-around satisfying piece of musical theatre entertainment the United States had yet seen, homegrown or imported. It had (and its continuing popularity confirms it still has) everything a musical-theatregoer could ask for. An engaging and even relatively suspenseful story is populated with varied and well-drawn characters who speak and sing witty, literate, and often outrageously funny dialogue and lyrics. Also, *Pinafore* has a musical score that, no matter how "operatic" in places, has plenty of tunes for the audience to go away humming, not to mention its colorfully romantic set and costumes.

Yet *Pinafore*'s mass appeal in the United States arose equally from a kind of cultural misunderstanding. Even more than British parliamentary politics and some absurd aspects of British naval life, Gilbert's main target of satire was the tradition of English classbound marriages. In Victorian England it was socially acceptable only for men and women within the same class to marry. Or, if class lines were to be crossed, a man could properly marry a woman beneath his class, but a woman could not marry beneath hers. While the phrase "love levels all ranks" is uttered repeatedly in *Pinafore*, that was not Gilbert's own position or belief. In nearly all his comic operas Gilbert was a fairly conservative satirist, in the sense that he ultimately advocated maintaining the status quo. With brilliant irony, in *Pinafore* Gilbert's spokesman for preserving class propriety is the repulsive Dick Dead-eye, the apparent villain of the piece. Against all others, Dick argues against a common seaman like Ralph marrying his Captain's daughter. And yet Ralph does, seemingly proving (if one isn't quite awake) that love indeed levels all ranks. But it doesn't. In the deliciously phony logic of Gilbert's legalistic mind, the union becomes acceptable only through the absurd second-act revelation of Buttercup's inadvertent switching of the infants who grew up to be Captain Corcoran and Ralph Rackstraw. Now, as adults, that switch effectively (if preposterously) makes Ralph the Captain of the *Pinafore* and demotes Corcoran to lowly deckhand—as if their status in adulthood was preconditioned by their babyhood. Now that Ralph's social class is higher than Josephine's, there is no impropriety about their marrying, British class distinctions are preserved, and, as Gilbert set out to show, love definitely *does not* level all ranks.

That was what Gilbert intended but apparently not what Americans saw.

American audiences likely missed the irony implicit in the baby switching that actually *preserved* class distinctions, instead reading in *Pinafore* an affirmation of the allegedly American "classless" democratic society in which a common sailor actually marries a woman of higher social rank. I would further suggest that audiences in 1878 and the years following were primed to see the ending of *Pinafore* that way through their familiarity with Horatio Alger's boys' books, currently in vogue. Alger's heroes rise to wealth, status, and the right girl not through their diligent application of the American work ethic alone. Also abetting the hero is a fair bit of luck, twists of fortune, and plain old coincidences. Granted, the turn of luck in *Pinafore* happens preposterously faster than in Alger's stories, but the two are alike in kind if not in duration, since each, in the eyes of American audiences, appeared to be a confirmation of American "classless" democracy in action.

Speaking of ironies, Gilbert and Sullivan wrote *Pinafore* in part as a defense of the British class system, but the show became this country's first nationwide hit musical partly because Americans saw it as a love story advocating for classless egalitarian marriages. *Pinafore* also demonstrated that a musical can treat significant social issues and still be eminently entertaining. Ever since *Pinafore*, numerous American musicals have dealt with contemporary social issues, whether comically or seriously, and most without sacrificing their entertainment value. Playwright Albert Innaurato observes the ties between social relevance and American musical theatre in the decades just following *Pinafore*: "Featuring stock characters straight out of American mythology, satirizing class difference and full of song-and-dance numbers, the earliest lighthearted musicals emerged at the turn of the century . . . a very tumultuous moment in American history. Theater must be a paradox to succeed, and this was ferocious fluff, deadly uproarious political theater that was also tons of fun" (27).

In addition to creating a taste for musical theatre in the United States, *Pinafore* also influenced the writing of subsequent American musicals. Because of its unparalleled success, Gilbert and Sullivan's comic opera format had its American imitators, most notably, of all people, John Philip Sousa, best known for his marches. His early comic opera *The Smugglers* (1879) owed a great deal of its structure and content to *Pinafore*, which Sousa had conducted for a New England tour (Bordman 65). Less well-known now, but in his own day a prolific and popular writer of Gilbert and Sullivan–style comic operas, Philadelphia's Willard Spenser capitalized on "things Japanese" in *The Little Tycoon* (1886), opening shortly after the American success of *The Mikado*. *The Little Tycoon* had a healthy run in Philadelphia before doing nearly as well in New York (Bordman 85–86). Only one other of his comic operas ever reached Manhattan, but Spenser's shows had extravagantly long runs in Philly and were staples of touring companies until about 1912 (86).

Far more important is Gilbert and Sullivan's enduring impact on the content and shape of twentieth-century American musicals. Gilbert used the ancient romantic plot formula (see chapter 1) of "boy meets girl, boy loses girl, boy gets girl back" in all but two of his musicals with Sullivan (*Utopia, Limited*, and *Princess Ida*), regardless of each show's satiric thrust. With few exceptions but as many variations as librettists could dream up, this formula became the nearly universal plot of all American book musicals until about 1960 and even beyond. And, too, the tremendous audience appeal of Gilbert's satire gave later American writers the green light to include socially conscious material in their shows—at least those writers of more than purely diversionary entertainment.

*Pinafore*'s other influence on American musicals over time had to do with form and structure. In reference to the rash of *Pinafore* productions from 1878 to 1880, Gerald Bordman rightly observes that "American theatregoers were exposed to a rare, but not new, kind of musical theatre in which book, lyrics, and music combined to form an integral whole" (47), or what today we generally call the "integrated musical." What is hard to explain, however, is why this demonstrably popular model was largely ignored by American musical theatre writers and composers during the last decades of the nineteenth century and the first two or three of the twentieth. Instead, most writers just churned out slapdash shows in which the songs had little to do with story and characters; group song and dance was just an excuse for splashy production numbers; and much of the humor was so gratuitous it seemed as if some vaudeville comics had just wandered onto the stage.

There is no question that the model of Gilbert's libretti and Sullivan's scores influenced the American writers who developed this kind of integrated show. It is patently evident in Jerome Kern and Guy Bolton's Princess Theatre Shows (see chapter 1), in Kern and Oscar Hammerstein 2nd's *Show Boat* (chapter 2), and even, though in more veiled ways, in Rodgers and Hammerstein's *Oklahoma!* (chapter 4). The G&S model is most explicitly apparent in George S. Kaufman and Morrie Ryskind's deliberate modeling of *Of Thee I Sing* and *Let 'Em Eat Cake* on the minute particulars of Gilbert and Sullivan's comic opera plots, characters, and incidents, not to mention the inherent satire (chapter 3); Kaufman and Ryskind's direct "Americanization" of Gilbert and Sullivan had no successors. No matter how late in coming, there is little doubt that the pioneers of the American integrated musical had in mind (even if at the back of it) Gilbert and Sullivan's methods for making script, score, and production elements form an integrated whole. If they accomplished nothing else in America but providing a model for integrated musicals and demonstrating that musicals can address contemporary social and political issues without sacrificing entertainment value, these two lasting influences qualify Gilbert and Sullivan as the primary progenitors of the twentieth-century American musical.

# 1

# Patriotism, Xenophobia, and World War I

*"The Good Years"*

Decmber 31, 1899: It was New Year's Eve, a small but gala evening of theatre in Manhattan. Lillian Russell dazzled a packed house in Weber and Fields's *Whirl-i-gig* at their newly renovated Music Hall. Audiences heard Victor Herbert's music in both *The Singing Girl* at the Casino and *The Ameer* at Wallack's—not yet his great scores of later decades, but better than anything else Broadway had to offer. At the Manhattan Theatre, the electrifying Anna Held stopped the show singing "I Wish I Really Weren't, But I Am" in *Papa's Wife*, an amalgamation of two French musicals commissioned and produced by her young husband Florenz Ziegfeld. And over at the Fifth Avenue Theatre, the Boston Cadets presented *Three Little Lambs*, the second show they had brought down to New York. *Lambs* was the 1898 musical *The Queen of the Ballet* rewritten to have the hero travel to Puerto Rico, a territory acquired by the United States following the Spanish-American War in that year. These five shows— all with respectable runs—were the total of Broadway's musical offerings.

At midnight, countless Americans welcomed the new century. Of course they were a year early. The new century wouldn't turn "twentieth" until the first day of 1901. A *New York Tribune* editorial for January 2, 1900, remarked, "No new century began yesterday. Avoid all delusions on that head. But those who had to date anything . . . '1900,' . . . felt something momentous had happened to the calendar" (qtd. in Lord 2).

A year later, Broadway had less to offer than in 1899. True, there were seven musicals playing on New Year's Eve 1900, but most were fairly inconsequential and had quite short runs. The only two long-running American-made hits were essentially musical revues, not book musicals— *Fiddle-dee-dee*, the annual Weber and Fields offering, and something called *The Giddy Throng*. While the English import *Florodora* (11/12/00) had yet to catch fire as the runaway hit it would become, the New York production eventually outstripped its original London engagement (which was unusual for British shows early in the century). With its run of 505 performances, it became just the second musical in American history to top the 500-performance mark; the first had been *A Trip to Chinatown* (11/9/91), with a then-remarkable run of 657 performances.

*Florodora's* story is typical of the melodramatic musical plots of the day. A young woman named Dolores owns Florodora, an island in the Philippines, along with the proprietary rights to the perfume produced there. A dastardly entrepreneur named Gilfain tries to wrest from her the rights, but Dolores, aided by her fiancé Frank and his comic sidekick Tweedlepunch, foils him. Not the stuff of a hit show in itself, which is why most writers on musical theatre credit the American success of *Florodora* first to the enormous popularity of a single song, "Tell Me Pretty Maiden," and second to its singers, the "Florodora Girls"—a female sextet with each member "weighing 130 pounds to an ounce, five feet four inches tall, long-waisted, willowy, and either brunette or redheaded" (Smith 78). A matching sextet of young men got much less attention. Attractive showgirls aside, the popularity of this English show may be partly attributed to its setting in the Philippines, which, along with Puerto Rico, became a U.S. possession after the Spanish-American War.

Pride in these territorial acquisitions was just one index of the optimistic mood of the United States from the turn of the century to World War I (Cooper xiv)—and with good reason. In 1900, only Russia and Canada were larger geographically, and the U.S. economy was the most vital in the world. American steel production was over ten million tons, and 167,000 miles of railroad tracks crisscrossed the country. Per capita income at the turn of the century was estimated at $569, far outstripping second-place Britain (Cooper 3).

The possibilities of U.S. industry seemed limitless. The airplane and the skyscraper appeared in rapid succession, prompting newspapers and magazines "to devote much of their space to accounts of inventions, massive construction projects, and faster, more comfortable travel" (Cooper 137). Most of all, the swift development of mass production made the automobile—formerly the plaything of the rich—affordable to middle-class Americans. The popular press pointed with pride to how the new technologies, and especially the motorcar, were the tangible symbols of America's expanding economy and its corresponding rise as a world power.

### Techno-Pride

The automobile, in fact, took center stage in musical theatre productions. Woodrow Wilson's odd 1905 public pronouncement notwithstanding—that motorcars represented "a picture of arrogance of wealth" to farmers and the working class (qtd. in Lord 117)—cars on stage were never intended to denigrate people who could afford such wondrous technology. Instead, audiences were meant to marvel at the ingeniousness of the autos themselves, and, when cars figured large in the plots of book musicals, to delight in how these French/German-invented but American-perfected contraptions helped the hero or heroine foil the villain and win the prize.

Of all Broadway producers, Florenz Ziegfeld gained a singular reputation not just for his "glorification of the American girl" but for featuring in his annual revues and other shows the latest inventions, fashions, and news items. In *Papa's Wife* (11/13/99), he had the spectacular singing sensation Anna Held make an equally spectacular exit in an 1899 model motorcar. By 1908, taxis were already ubiquitous on the streets of New York, so his 1908 *Follies* contained a taxicab number, with twelve showgirls dressed as cabs, sporting lighted signs, meters, and headlights. A year later Ziegfeld moved to airplanes. Celebrating the Wright Brothers and their successors, Ziegfeld's 1909 edition featured Lillian Lorraine, "the *Follies*' first incontestable dazzler," singing "Up, Up in My Aeroplane" while circling above the audience in a miniaturized aircraft—mercifully secured to a sort of monorail track (Bordman 250). For the opening of the Panama Canal, Ziegfeld and his designers created an elaborate production number in 1913. While José Collins sang "Panama" surrounded by showgirls, a mock-up warship was raised in the newly completed canal locks—an obvious tribute both to America's technology and to the United States as a power in world affairs.

Not just single numbers in revues but full-length book musicals sometimes celebrated motorcars (and motorboats!). Between January 1906 and September 1910, five such shows opened—four in New York, one in Chicago. Based on the Vanderbilt family's offer of a cup to auto race winners in 1904 and 1905, *The Vanderbilt Cup* (1/16/06) was an immediate hit, with a run of 143 performances. *The Auto Race* (11/25/07), with its spectacular staging in the mammoth 5000-seat Hippodrome, ran 312 times. *The Girl at the Helm* (9/5/08)—obviously the motorboat show—held its own for five months in Chicago but never played New York, while *The Motor Girl* (6/15/09), with the Paris race as its setting, managed only ninety-five laps on Broadway. But *The International Cup* (9/3/10), which fictionalized the New York to Paris auto race and threw in a yachting race for good measure, packed the vast Hippodrome 333 times.

The essentials of all these shows are the same. In each, an American race driver—twice a man, three times a woman—wins the race, its prize, and her or his true-blue American sweetheart while thwarting the dastardly doings of a (sometimes foreign) villain. The shows all featured real motorcars (or boats) on stage in simulated races, with the passing scenery zipping by to the extent allowed by theatrical technology of the day. Still, what drew audiences to the auto and motorboat musicals was not the machines alone but the marriage of man or woman *and* machine triumphing over adversity, thereby scoring not only a personal victory in competitive sport (and love) but also a symbolic victory for American pluck, sportsmanship, and technology.

### America's Boosters: Teddy Roosevelt and George M. Cohan

Pre–World War I America boasted a remarkable number of strong personalities. In politics, there were "The Great Commoner" William Jennings Bryan and Wisconsin Senator "Fighting Bob" LaFollette; in jurisprudence, Supreme Court Justices Oliver Wendell Holmes and Charles Evans Hughes; in manufacturing, Andrew Carnegie, John D. Rockefeller, and Henry Ford; in finance, J. Pierpont Morgan; in what we now call social activism, Jane Addams and Carry Nation; in journalism, H. L. Mencken and William Randolph Hearst; and in the theatre, those pioneering producers David Belasco and Florenz Ziegfeld. This impressive roster also includes president/politician Theodore Roosevelt and writer/performer/director George M. Cohan, two men surprisingly similar despite vast differences in family background. More than the others, TR and George M (their frequent sobriquets) captured the public imagination as embodiments of the spirit of the age.

Teddy Roosevelt was president of the United States from 1901 to 1909. According to historian Francis Russell, "Roosevelt at the end of his first term could claim to be the most popular man in the country. . . . [His] new term would make him not only the most dynamically popular president since Andrew Jackson but the most conspicuous public figure in the world" (348, 358). Yet TR's popularity—and strong personal influence on crafting the upbeat mood of America—began long before his presidency. Prior to becoming William McKinley's running mate and then succeeding him to the presidency upon McKinley's assassination, Roosevelt's political service had included stints as a New York state assemblyman, New York City police commissioner, assistant secretary of the Navy, and governor of New York. In each public office, TR cultivated his reputation for outspokenness, for handling problems swiftly, and for emphasizing the moral basis of whatever decisions he made. In addition to his political career, two other ventures established Roosevelt in the public imagination. In 1883, he bought a Wyoming ranch, working it so effectively that he overcame the hostility of the local "cowboys," who had distrusted him as a bespectacled Eastern tender-foot. Then, during the Spanish-American War, TR recruited that ill-assorted cavalry troop known then and ever after as the "Rough Riders," so called for their daring, if reckless, charge up San Juan Hill. The troop consisted of those selfsame cattlemen, along with Teddy's Ivy League cronies from his college days. This foolhardy but publicity-rich gambit elevated TR to the stature of a national hero.

TR's popularity and public image of aggressive self-confidence escalated throughout his presidency. His words became household expressions. He coined the term "muckraker" for a ruthlessly thorough investigative reporter, and, best-known of all, he often quoted a West African saying that embodied his approach to problem solving: "Speak softly and carry a big stick, and you will go far" (see Lord 82, Cooper 50).

Following his own advice, Roosevelt usually got the job done. Whether he was initiating the government's series of successful antitrust suits against railroads and other monopolies in 1902, intervening to end the 1907 bank panic, brokering the Russian-Japanese peace agreement in 1905 and the Moroccan crisis the following year, or negotiating the treaty that gave the United States the right to build and control the Panama Canal, what the public saw in TR's actions was not just a reflection of American accomplishments but an impressive incarnation of American manhood in action.

Still, whatever TR achieved, "so overwhelming was Roosevelt's personality that it tended to dwarf his accomplishments" (Russell 338). His larger-than-life bravura, along with his singular appearance, made him the inevitable subject of countless political cartoons caricaturing his features — the thick, round glasses, the droopy moustache, the incredibly toothy grin. Even in political cartoons, TR was caricatured as a Wyoming cowboy, a Rough Rider, or a big-game hunter (another of his pastimes). Given the often vituperative nature of the genre, these cartoons are remarkable for their affectionate good humor; clearly, much of the popular press shared the public's admiration for TR.

This good-humored treatment of Teddy extended to the popular musical stage. While TR was never the starring president in a full-length musical — for that, the world would have to wait until 1937, when George M. Cohan starred as FDR in I'd Rather Be Right — Teddy was nevertheless the subject of a number of songs and sketches in the revues and musicals of his day. The first of these was in The Duke of Duluth (1905). The musical was mostly a showcase for the comic skills and outlandish costumes of Nat M. Wills, a popular singing comedian. The Roosevelt routine was a song called "Strenuous," based on TR's admonition that Americans lead a strenuous physical, mental, and moral life. Wills, on horseback (it's not clear if this was a stage horse or a real one), costumed and made up to look like Roosevelt right down to the teeth, sang a rather inflated encomium of TR's personality and accomplishments, to wit: "Let our Teddy bite the Isthmus: He can cut it through by Christmas" (Bordman 212), referring to the just-concluded Panama Canal treaty.

Ziegfeld first put TR on stage in his third *Follies* (6/14/09). Out of office for several months, Roosevelt was still in the public eye. On a year-long African safari with his son, the great conservation president, who created more national parks and monuments than all presidents before him combined, killed some three thousand animals (Russell 373). Ziegfeld, always looking for a current event worth staging, created a hunting number. Harry Kelly impersonated Roosevelt while the showgirls paraded in cute animal suits, so eager to be bagged by this illustrious hunter that "[a]n amiable lion allowed the President to shoot at him, accommodatingly holding a large target between his paws" (Smith 91–92).

This same edition of the *Follies* included a more extensive and serious tribute to TR. Called "The Greatest Navy in the World," the pageant featured a harbor backdrop "variously interpreted as New York and Hampton Roads [Virginia]" (Smith 92), in front of which paraded the Ziegfeld showgirls, dressed to represent the various states. Each wore on her head a miniature replica of one of the battleships in the U.S. fleet. When the stage lights were dimmed, the ladies threw switches concealed in their costumes, thereby lighting up the portholes and "searching spotlights" in their nautical headgear. The overall effect suggested that the entire fleet had appeared on stage (Baral 47). Nothing here overtly says "Theodore Roosevelt," but contemporary audiences surely knew they were viewing Ziegfeld's spectacular tribute to what Edward Wagenknecht calls the "most spectacular gesture of his administration," sending the sixteen battleships of the Great White Fleet around the world (329). TR himself had watched the ships steam out of Hampton Roads on December 16, 1907, embarking on a noncombative mission variously interpreted as a goodwill cruise and a display of U.S. naval power. After circumnavigating the globe, the Great White Fleet—their hulls literally painted white—returned to the United States on February 22, 1909, just under four months before Ziegfeld's theatrical tribute. Twice more Ziegfeld featured Roosevelt-related segments in his *Follies*. In 1910, the showgirls "paraded as Rough Riders" to welcome Roosevelt back from his safari. Then, in 1912, TR and incumbent President Taft appeared in a sketch to joke about "income tax, trusts, the Philippines, tariff reform, and Cuba" (Ziegfeld 48, 239).

A. E. Campbell describes Roosevelt as "cocky, pugnacious, forthright, physically active, morally courageous—and not, perhaps, over-sensitive" (8).

These adjectives apply equally to George M. Cohan, in many ways TR's musical-theatre equivalent, whose career flourished during the same years as Roosevelt's. Cohan was a phenomenon—granted, thanks to his temperament, sometimes a less than popular one, but still a phenomenon. He acted, he sang, he danced. He wrote, directed, and starred in numerous musicals (and plays), which he usually produced or co-produced with his partner Sam Harris. Short of stage design, George M did it all. And he did it very well. Even critics who objected to the brash, slangy style of his shows admired his skill. According to the *Dramatic Mirror* in 1906, "Perhaps the true secret of Mr. Cohan's unprecedented success, too permanent for mere theatrical luck, consists in his admirable stagecraft. In the art of presenting musical comedy, Mr. Cohan is apparently without a peer" (qtd. in Smith 86).

According to the scant and ambiguous historical records, George Michael Cohan was born to Irish-American parents in Providence, Rhode Island, on either July 3 or July 4, 1878. Cohan himself chose to believe he had been born on Independence Day, a belief that both shaped his sentiments about the United States and deeply influenced his musicals. In the words of one (very appreciative) Cohan biographer:

There was a mystique, a self-created mystique, in which he identified himself indelibly with everything elemental to American life. This he could not have done in quite the way he did had he known he was born on the 3rd of July. From his earliest days he was, he said, profoundly "impressed with the fact that I had been born under the Stars and Stripes, and that has had a great deal to do with everything I have written. If it had not been for the glorious symbol of Independence, I might have fallen into the habit of writing problem plays, or romantic drama, or questionable farce. Yes, the American flag is in my heart, and it has done everything for me." (McCabe 2)

There's a good bit of the showman in Cohan's words, but they do describe his approach to playwriting and songwriting. As musical theatre historian Stanley Green wryly put it, "Everything that Cohan had written before 1906 had featured only himself, his family, and the American flag" (24). Cohan's family consisted of father Jerry, mother Nellie, sister Josie, and George himself, who toured the vaudeville circuits as The Four Cohans. And, as Green pointed out, once George discovered his abilities as a playwright and tunesmith, he tailor-made his early shows as vehicles for the Cohan clan.

Cohan also tailor-made his musicals for an audience looking for something fresh, vigorous, and celebratory of America. Most book musicals were still either European imports or American-written clones of British musical comedy or continental comic opera and operetta. George M pioneered what became the essentials of the form, tone, and national character of American musical comedy for decades to come. Between 1901 and 1911, Cohan wrote and opened eleven musicals on Broadway: *The Governor's Son* (2/25/01), *Running for Office* (4/27/03), *Little Johnny Jones* (11/7/04), *Forty-Five Minutes from Broadway* (1/1/06), *George Washington, Jr.* (2/12/06), *The Talk of New York* (12/3/07), *Fifty Miles from Boston* (2/3/08), *The Yankee Prince* (4/20/08), *The American Idea* (10/5/08), *The Man Who Owns Broadway* (10/11/09), and *The Little Millionaire* (9/25/11). After these ten years as composer, lyricist, and author, Cohan didn't write another book show until *Little Nellie Kelly* in 1922. In the meantime he mostly performed, produced, and directed, writing only non-musical plays and musical numbers for revues.

*Little Johnny Jones* was not just Cohan's first Broadway triumph; it is, of all his musicals, also archetypal Cohan in its script and in its sentiments. Cohan's usual plot formula goes back at least to the third or second century B.C. Roman Plautus and even to the fourth-century B.C. Greek New Comedy writer Menander, but George M gave it a thoroughly American spin. The plots of the early Cohan musicals are convoluted and melodramatic, but they invariably include the ancient "boy meets girl, boy loses girl, boy gets girl back" formula. Connecting each major literary genre to a season in his *Anatomy of Criticism*, Northrop Frye describes this formula as "The Mythos of Spring" (163–86). According to Frye, from the ancient Greeks onward, the Mythos of Spring, with its connotation of renewal and growth, has shaped the structure of most romantic comedy. This "boy meets girl" paradigm was the main storyline of most American musicals until the late 1950s.

The particulars of the formula are simple enough. In the ancient Greek and Roman models, a young man from a respected family falls for a young woman who is totally unacceptable, usually because she is a slave or courtesan (or both). The young man's romantic quest is further complicated by the fact that the girl (if a slave) has already been sold, or contracted for sale, to someone else, and/or an older man (sometimes the boy's own father) is lusting after her. With the help of a family slave much cleverer than himself, the boy forestalls the sale of the girl and/or her assignation with the older man. A happy turn of events ultimately reveals that she is the long-lost daughter of a respectable family, allowing the two to marry. (This Plautine silliness is perfectly and accurately realized in the world of musical theatre in *A Funny Thing Happened on the Way to the Forum* [5/8/62].)

Almost two thousand years later, in the *commedia dell'arte* of the Italian Renaissance, Shakespeare's romantic comedies, and Moliere's comedies of manners, the girl-as-slave element is updated—usually she's the object of an arranged marriage. In Gilbert and Sullivan's mid-to-late Victorian comic operas—the most immediate prototypes of twentieth-century American musicals—a young man is normally blocked from achieving his romantic desires because, variously, an older male authority figure also lays marital claim to the girl, or an unacceptable older woman lays claim to the boy himself. Characters that throw up obstacles to the romantic and marital union of the boy and girl (Frye's "blocking figures") are integral to the "boy meets girl" plot formula.

George M. Cohan transformed this timeless Mythos of Spring by making the young lovers' goals, as well as the circumstances preventing their union, completely consonant with and reflective of a firmly established American mythos, often called the "American Dream." When *Little Johnny Jones* opened in 1904, most Americans viewed the United States as a land of opportunity, where anyone could succeed by dint of hard work and perseverance. Horatio Alger had popularized this myth in his stories of young men rising, through their own merits and efforts, from humble beginnings to positions of wealth, status, fame, and happiness. In the musical, the eponymous Johnny Jones, a jockey, is engaged to San Francisco heiress Goldie Gates. Given his low social position, Johnny doesn't want to be viewed as a man marrying a woman for her money. The "blocking figure" here is not a character trying to come between Johnny and Goldie but rather Johnny's manly pride, his need to show that he can make it on his own and prove himself worthy of his intended. He plans to ride in the British Derby, win the purse, and thus clear the way financially for an acceptable marriage. Although he loses the race, Johnny triumphs by foiling a number of second-act villains. In the end he wins Goldie's hand.

Cohan repeated this story pattern in all but two of his pre–World War I musicals. In four—*George Washington, Jr., The Talk of New York, The Yankee Prince,* and *The American Idea*—the blocking element to the young people's happiness is parental and usually has to do with social class. The hero's ultimate triumph over family objections—his own family's or the girl's—advocated romantic love while reinforcing the notion that there are no class barriers in the United States. Cohan believed that real Americans marry for love, not money, and that feelings, not fortunes, unite people. At the end of *Forty-Five Minutes from Broadway,* Mary, a housemaid, becomes sole heir to a wealthy man. The show's hero, Kid Burns, loves her, and she him, but Mary is wary that Kid just wants her fortune like her other shady suitors. She asks whether he'd still marry her if she were poor, and he assures her he would. So Mary tears up the will, and the two go off together, poor but happy. From *Little Johnny Jones* forward, Cohan's "boy meets girl" formula incorporated popular homespun truths about self-made men, social mobility, and marriages based on love. Cohan's Americanization of the "boy meets girl" motif, together with his breezy dialogue, contemporary characters and stories, music based on current popular songwriting, and energetic displays of fashionable dance styles, became the basic components for the writing and staging of musical comedy well into the 1940s. But in his own day, Cohan's songs, above all, expressed his flag-waving patriotism. People nationwide sang Cohan's tunes, which few heard on Broadway, since most of his pre-War musicals had fairly short New York runs. Only three of the eleven broke the magic 100-performance mark for a hit back then—*The Talk of New York* (157), *The Man Who Owns Broadway* (128), and *The Little Millionaire* (192). Cohan often toured his productions to help recoup expenses.

Cohan's earliest patriotic ditty dates from his first Broadway show, *The Governor's Son*, in 1901. Called "Yankee Doodle Doings" and sung by himself, it prefigured his later, much more popular flag-wavers, but it failed to catch on with the public. His first big chauvinistic crowd-pleaser was "The Yankee Doodle Boy" (still a perennial favorite and still popularly but erroneously known as "I'm a Yankee Doodle Dandy"), first performed by Cohan as the title character in *Little Johnny Jones*. There is one line that specifically refers to a plot point, Johnny riding in the Derby—"Yankee Doodle went to London / Just to ride the ponies"—a line most people have been singing ever since without a clue as to what it means. But other lines are strongly autobiographical:

> I'm a Yankee Doodle Dandy,
> Yankee Doodle do or die—
> A real live nephew of my Uncle Sam
> Born on the Fourth of July.

In lyrics like these, lines of dialogue, and, indeed, entire characterizations (whether he played the roles or not), Cohan created fictional stage personages that were also projections of his own intensely personal vision of America and what it stood for. This synchronicity of real and stage personas is best seen in the title character of *George Washington, Jr.* The George of the title (played by Cohan) is George Belgrave, son of the Anglophilic Senator Belgrave, who insists his son marry Lord Rothburt's daughter. But young George loves a homegrown American girl and so disinherits himself from his father, taking the name George Washington, Jr., as the ultimate display of his patriotic roots. At one point in the show, an old Civil War veteran appears with a particularly battlescarred Stars and Stripes, impelling George to sing the rouser originally titled "You're a Grand Old Rag." Because some people found "Rag" an offensive reference to Old Glory, Cohan was pressured to change the title and relevant lyrics to "Flag," even though he meant "Rag" as a tribute to the military encounters this particular specimen had endured. "You're a Grand Old Flag" became the first song written specifically for a musical to sell over a million copies of sheet music. It's a toss-up whether this or World War I's "Over There" (not written for a musical at all) is Cohan's all-time most popular patriotic tune.

Patriotism is manifest in many Cohan lyrics and melodies that make no specific reference to cultural icons or national symbols like Yankee Doodle or the Stars and Stripes. A good case in point is "Give My Regards to Broadway," which, like "The Yankee Doodle Boy," Cohan sang in *Little Johnny Jones*. For George M, if the United States was the hub of the universe, Broadway was the heartbeat of America. The song is pure paean to the sassy, brassy center of show business—totally positive and upbeat, without any of the wry (or worse) winks at Broadway's seamy underside in later songs like Harry Warren's "Lullaby of Broadway," Frank Loesser's "My Time of Day," or Stephen Sondheim's "Broadway Baby." Cohan's tribute to Broadway resounds more like a patriotic anthem.

So too with what might be called George M's "Irish melodies." For Cohan, the spirit of Ireland thrived in the large Irish-American communities in New York, Boston, and his native Providence. To be Irish in America was, for him, to be an American with a proud ancestral heritage. Accordingly, he wrote songs like "Mary's a Grand Old Name" from *Forty-Five Minutes from Broadway*, "Harrigan" from *Fifty Miles from Boston* (a tribute to Edward Harrigan of the Harrigan and Hart musical theatre duo), and "Nellie Kelly, I Love You" from Cohan's postwar *Little Nellie Kelly*. These numbers' lyrics extolled the Irishness of the title characters, while the melodies fused an Irish lilt with American flair, trading on popular song-forms of the day, such as the "waltz clog" rhythm for "Nellie Kelly" (most familiar in "The Sidewalks of New York"). *New York Times* critic Brooks Atkinson observed that "Cohan's songs, both words and music, were sublimations of the mood of their day. They said what millions of people would have said if they had Cohan's talent." Later, also in the *Times*, lyricist and librettist Oscar Hammerstein, 2nd noted more precisely that "never was a plant more indigenous to a particular part of the earth than was George M. Cohan to the United States of his day. The whole nation was confident of its superiority, its moral virtue, its happy isolation from the intrigues of the old country, from which many of our fathers and grandfathers had migrated" (both qtd. in McCabe 51).

Of course, George M did not have a patent on patriotism in musicals. Julian Edwards's score for *When Johnny Comes Marching Home* (12/6/02), a musical treating the Civil War "with surprising compassion for both sides," contained the patriotic anthem "My Own United States," which was met with "fervent applause" every night of the show's seventy-one performances (Bordman 187). *The Silver Star* (11/1/09) was a thinly plotted star vehicle to showcase dancer Adelaide Genee, who in one number wore a soldier suit and danced while waving an American flag (253). *America* (8/30/13), a Hippodrome spectacular, was one of several musicals about the building of the Panama Canal and dastardly (usually foreign) plots to steal the plans. A dubious musical genre at best, this particular example periodically interrupted chasing the thieves to present lavishly staged tableaux from American history (289). Between its spectacle and its patriotic appeal, *America* played 360 times.

Cohan tends to be remembered for his upbeat patriotism, but his shows also reflect the xenophobia of their time. In the early years of the twentieth century, the American people evinced contradictory attitudes toward foreigners and foreign affairs. On the one hand, the U.S. victory in the Spanish-American War and the subsequent acquisition of Puerto Rico, the Philippines, and Hawaii, coupled with Teddy Roosevelt's rise to the presidency, reinforced a largely pro-imperialist stance. Almost diametrically opposed to the sabre-rattling of Roosevelt-inspired imperialism was a powerful isolationism based on a distrust of all things foreign. This isolationism surfaced in response to TR's brokering of the Russian-Japanese peace agreement and the Moroccan crisis in 1905 and 1906, with many Americans voicing strong disapproval of the United States meddling in what they perceived as the internal affairs of foreign nations (see Wagenknecht 330, Russell 364).

More generally, there was great pride in the notion that the United States had severed ties with its British and European forebears, defined itself as a country with its own national character, and, in the process, become a major world power. The United States of Roosevelt and Cohan was proud, smug, and willing to denigrate foreign countries as a way of expressing its own superiority. This attitude often peppered the dialogue and even formed the basis for entire plotlines in some of Cohan's musicals. A single exchange of dialogue in *Little Johnny Jones* says it all. Shortly before the end of act 1, a group of American young women is gathered on the dock at Southampton to sail from England back to the United States. One of the ship's officers asks, "What makes the Americans so proud of their country?" To which one young lady replies, "*Other* countries" (qtd. in McCabe 60).

### The "Euro-Title" Shows

If imperialism, isolationism, and xenophobia made Europhobes of many Americans, some U.S. citizens remained Europhiles—mostly the rich in search of titled marriages for their daughters. According to *McCall's* magazine, by 1903 there were fifty-seven such matches between the American plutocracy and the European aristocracy, and the number continued growing up until the war years (see Lord 265). Both President Roosevelt (in public statements) and George M. Cohan (in three musicals) railed against this practice as being not very "American." But Cohan was not the first to write shows critical of title-seeking parents. The earliest was *The Tourists* (8/25/05), with book and lyrics by R. H. Burnside and music by Gustave Kerker. Here Dora Blossom's father is out to find a nobleman for her to marry, although she is in love with John Duke of Plymouth, Massachusetts (note Burnside's choice of the Mayflower landing spot). John, passing himself off as the Duke of Plymouth, eventually gets the girl. In Cohan's own *George Washington, Jr.* (2/12/06), George's father insists he marry the particularly snooty daughter of an English lord. In the end, of course, young George marries the American girl of his choice. *The Girl behind the Counter* (10/1/07) was an imported musical that Edgar Smith totally rewrote both to reflect strong American values and to serve as a star vehicle for Lew Fields. Fields played a father who, in various disguises, helps his stepdaughter marry the American man she loves rather than the English nobleman her mother chooses for her. In 1908, Cohan attacked titled marriages twice. In *The Yankee Prince* (4/20/08), a wealthy and snobbish Chicagoan (played by Jerry Cohan) takes his daughter (played by Josie Cohan) abroad to find a suitably titled husband for her. Of course she falls in love with American Percy Springer (played by George M himself) and manages to marry him. Less than six months later Cohan opened *The American Idea* (10/5/08), in which two rival Brooklyn millionaires go to Paris to find French counts for their daughters; but the young ladies find two Brooklyn boys abroad who, disguised as nobility, win the love and the hands of the girls.

After Cohan's two shows in 1908, other musicals took up the theme with new variations and complications. An impoverished English nobleman in *A Broken Idol* (8/16/09) pursues an American woman for her wealth but drops her like a hot rock when he learns she has lost her fortune; she then marries the newspaperman she had loved all along. With music by Victor Herbert, *When Sweet Sixteen* (9/14/11) tells of Mrs. Hammond, who, in order to gain a place in society, demands her daughter, Victoria, marry the Laird of Loch Lomond. But Victoria's father wants her to marry his old friend (in both senses) Jefferson Todd. Victoria pretends to go along with this because she's in love with Todd's secretary, Stanley Morton, and Stanley and she finally do get together. Perhaps the oddest variation occurs in *Betsy* (12/11/11), in which an American widow is threatened with losing her inheritance unless she remarries another American. She accordingly weds Jasper Malone, even while planning to divorce him so she can have the titled Englishman she really wants. But by the end of the show she has grown to love Jasper and sends the earl packing. The last Euro-title show was *The American Maid* (3/3/13), with music by John Philip Sousa. It was a throwback to the earliest specimens of this strange subgenre of musicals: an American manufacturer wants his daughter to marry a duke, but she's in love with an American, whom she marries by the finale. The fad for these shows did not survive the Great War, which greatly transformed relations between the old world and the new.

## The Gunboat Musicals

If the Euro-title shows expressed America's isolationism and perhaps a fear of foreign contamination, the gunboat musicals celebrated U.S. sabre-rattling abroad by the U.S. Navy. With the exception of the first of the ten gunboat shows that played between 1902 and 1907, the plots are absolutely homogeneous, save for coloring details. An American gets impossibly entangled in foreign affairs in a (usually) imaginary country, and all seems hopeless until the proverbial eleventh hour—or, literally, in the theatre, around eleven o'clock—when he or she is rescued by the arrival of the good ol' U.S. Navy—never the army, at this time a shabby, ill-trained affair compared to the nation's mighty naval forces. Also, except for anyone who becomes the love interest of an American character, foreigners in the gunboat musicals are portrayed as barbaric, bloodthirsty, or buffoonish (or all of the above)—whether they are Asians, Pacific Islanders, or Latin Americans.

The first of these shows, *The Sultan of Sulu* (Chicago 3/11/02; New York 12/29/02), boasted a book and lyrics by prolific librettist and playwright George Ade, who was also an outspoken anti-imperialist. Because of this leaning, Ade's musical differs from the subsequent gunboat shows in that much of it spoofs the foibles of American governmental institutions, when the Navy arrives to inform the king of a new U.S. possession that changes must be made on his island to conform with the U.S. constitution (Bordman 188). In this respect Ade's plot sounds like a spin-off, if not rip-off, of Gilbert and Sullivan's *Utopia, Limited* (1893), in which Gilbert lampooned everything from parliament to the stock exchange when some Englishmen try to make British institutions work on a South Sea island. But whatever Ade's source, *The Sultan of Sulu* sent the same signals as the later last-minute-rescue gunboat shows: the United States is a power to be reckoned with, and American political values and institutions are superior to everyone else's. The show was also a hit; following a very long run at Chicago's Studebaker Theatre, it ran 192 times in New York. (Chicago at the time was America's "Second City" for theatre, especially musicals; in fact, eight of the ten gunboat musicals premiered there.)

The plots of the remaining nine gunboat musicals are stupefyingly similar. The story of the first, except in details, pretty much encapsulates the rest. General Hardtack in *The Runaways* (5/11/03; 167 performances) uses his winnings on a horse to ship "the entire cast of 160 to the Island of Table d'hote," where he is immediately made king. But Hardtack finds the honor untenable, since to be king he must marry the former king's widow or die. Finally, as Gerald Bordman whimsically puts it, "The American navy, which seems to have spent much of its time behind the footlights, comes to the rescue" (192). *The Yankee Consul* (2/22/04; 115 performances) simply moved a similar situation to a Latin location called Puerta Plata (199–200). *The Isle of Spice* (8/23/04; eighty performances) cruised back to the South Pacific and is singular only in that the American in need of rescue is a woman. Teresa is a tourist about to be forced to marry the island king Bompoka. Fortunately U.S. sailors arrive and are mistaken by the islanders for sun gods; Teresa winds up not with Bompoka but with Lt. Harold Katchall, U.S.N. *The Royal Chef* (9/1/04) — same plot, different locale — played twenty-three weeks in Chicago but bombed after seventeen showings on Broadway.

Conversely, *The Sho-Gun* (10/10/04) was a genuine Broadway hit, playing 125 times. It was one of just two gunboat musicals in which the general locale, Korea, was real, though its specific location, the capital city of Ka-Choo, was the purely imaginary setting for another tangled plot by *Sultan of Sulu* playwright George Ade. But the essential story of an entangled American — this time a chewing gum magnate caught in sticky situations who gets rescued by the navy — remained the same as in the others (Bordman 204). Japan was the setting for *Fantana* (1/14/05 after a Chicago tryout), the most successful of the gunboat shows with 298 performances. *The Duke of Duluth* (9/11/05), which contained the Teddy Roosevelt "Strenuous" number, wasn't so fortunate, capsizing after twenty-four. After weak showings by *The Press Agent* (11/27/05) and *The Grand Mogul* (3/25/07), the gunboat genre finally, utterly, and perhaps mercifully, sank.

The common denominator of all the gunboat musicals was a chauvinistic patriotism that married positive exhibitions of U.S. naval intervention in foreign affairs with negative portrayals of foreigners, particularly non-Europeans. This treatment of foreigners carried over from the gunboat shows to other musicals as well. The primary target of such slurs was Japan and the Japanese people, in part because Japan was perceived as a potentially threatening new world power with its own imperialistic ambitions, and in part because of massive Japanese emigration to the United States (primarily the West Coast) at the beginning of the twentieth century. Tens of thousands of Japanese on U.S. soil posed a threat to the American labor force and became an easy target for minority-bashing. Indeed, in 1906 TR had to cope with an outbreak of "anti-Japanese agitation on the Pacific Coast . . . much promoted by the labor unions in their hostility toward Japanese laborers" (Russell 364). Less than two years later, *Funabashi* (1/6/o8), a conventional musical love story, made little use of its Japanese setting, and its script's references to Japan were "half-respectful, half-condescending" (Bordman 239). The plot involved the love affair of an American naval officer, so the show saw fit to include one rousing song of the "our imperialism is better than your imperialism" variety called "The Girl behind the Man behind the Gun."

More directly insulting was a very successful Chicago musical called *The Girl at the Gate* (9/1/12). Its complex plot focused on an American captain of the engineers on the Panama Canal project falling for a lovely Japanese spy and carelessly letting her steal the fortification's plans. The show was also peppered with such openly racist dialogue as:

> *Strawl:*   They're bright alright but they don't remain servants! There's only
>              one thing worse than a Jap!
> *Tiffany:*  What's that?
> *Strawl:*   Another Jap!
>              (qtd. in Bordman 279)

Future Broadway playwright Marc Connelly wrote the lyrics for the lavish, $20,000 amateur production *The Lady of Luzon* (Pittsburgh 6/2/13), another musical denigrating the Japanese. The enormously intricate plot traded on America's fear of the so-called "Yellow Peril" (Japanese) making incursions into the Philippines (Bordman 287). That such fears and anti-Japanese sentiments filtered down from the professional to the amateur musical stage — from New York and Chicago to such a place as Pittsburgh, never a major theatre town — illustrates how widespread Japan-bashing had become in the theatre.

*African American Musicals before World War I*

It was not, of course, just foreigners and the foreign-born who were subject to racial slurs in the first decades of the twentieth century. In the concise summary of one historian, "throughout the entire period, black Americans suffered segregation, discrimination, disenfranchisement, racist political demagoguery, and racial violence that nearly always went unpunished and often won applause from whites" (Cooper xiii). Show business contributed to reinforcing stereotypes of African Americans. For countless whites, images of American blacks approximated the caricatures developed in nineteenth-century minstrel shows. White comfort in these minstrel show depictions made it difficult, if not impossible, for black entertainers to present themselves as anything but "happy-go-lucky darkies." Generally, to succeed a black performer had to conform to and, hence, perpetuate the stereotypes of his race created by white performers and endorsed by white audiences. Because the minstrel show's deleterious effects on black musicals and performers lingered well into the twentieth century, a brief overview of minstrelsy is in order.

*Blackface Minstrelsy*

Robert C. Toll's assertion that from the 1840s to the 1890s the indigenous minstrel show "remained the most popular entertainment form in the country" is absolutely incontestable ([v]). At its inception, blackface minstrelsy was exclusively a white, urban, male, Northern phenomenon. While there had been white blackface solo performers (notably Thomas D. Rice, famed forever for the notoriety of his "Jim Crow" song and dance) as well as group entertainments of various kinds, the first recognizable minstrel show per se opened in New York City in February 1843. The Virginia Minstrels, a four-man troupe that included the eminent Dan Emmett, were so successful that they toured their show to England. After that they went their separate ways but left in their wake "a minstrel-mad public and a bevy of imitators that reshaped American popular entertainment" (Toll 31).

In 1846, E. P. Christy, leader of the most prominent of the burgeoning troupes, gave the minstrel show its "distinctive form" (Brockett 371). In the first part, sometimes called the "concert," the cast sat in a semicircle, the Interlocutor (emcee, in effect) in the upstage center seat, and the "end men" Tambo and Bones (players of the tambourine and bones respectively) obviously at either end. These three exchanged comic banter between the musical numbers. Part 2, the "olio," was a series of unrelated songs and specialty performances (Brockett 371–72). A third part not credited to Christy evolved during the 1850s; it was a "one-act skit . . . almost invariably . . . set on Southern plantations" and packed with a potpourri of songs and dances interlaced with bits of dialogue (Toll 56). This three-part form remained constant from the early days of a handful of players to the mammoth troupes of a hundred or more after 1870 (Brockett 372).

After 1855, blackface minstrelsy ceased to be an exclusively white phenomenon. There were not, of course, mixed-race companies. But from the debut of the Mocking Bird Minstrels in Philadelphia during 1855–56, exclusively African American troupes flourished alongside existing white ones, ultimately numbering about 120 such companies (Toll 275–80). These black troupes, like the white ones, performed primarily for audiences of white, urban Northern males. At first, only the end men of all-black troupes regularly blacked up with burnt cork "as a comic mask" (200), but later it was not unusual to see entire casts of black men in blackface, their stage personae grotesque caricatures of their true racial identity.

What made minstrel shows so popular? Throughout its entire history, blackface minstrelsy's "images of Negroes [were] shaped by white expectations and desires and not by black realities" (Toll [v]–vi); yet those images underwent a shift in the first few decades of the minstrel show's existence. Early on, the Virginia Minstrels and other white troupes claimed to be "authentic delineators of black life" and, according to Toll, did create some "plausible black characters" (40, 38). At the same time, however, they were laying the groundwork for stereotypes and caricatures of African Americans that would endure in the white American consciousness well into the twentieth century.

What first caught the imagination of blackface minstrelsy's urban audiences was "the promise of satisfying white Northerners' growing curiosity about blacks and especially slaves at a time when slavery was becoming a national controversy. . . . Northerners did not know what slaves were like, [but] they believed or wanted to believe that black slaves differed greatly from free, white Americans" (Toll 34). This audience expectation led to the ever-growing presentation of "differences" in minstrel show character types, differences that turned to exaggeration, caricature, and stereotyping. Before the 1840s were over, many minstrel shows presented the dichotomous picture of "ludicrous caricatures of blacks" against the sentimental "idealized world" of the agrarian South extolled in the Stephen Foster songs the minstrels so heavily employed (37).

In the pre-Civil War North, minstrel shows served the dual purpose of allaying fears and confirming prejudices and differences. The active presence of abolitionists has given the lingering impression to many later Americans that the North was a liberal and welcoming environment for blacks. In truth most Northerners considered the abolitionists "radicals" and the "great majority of Northerners were in favour of slavery and distrustful of blacks, or at best apathetic to both," until sometime after the Fugitive Slave Law was re-enacted in the Compromise of 1850 (C. Rice 309). During this time the minstrel show helped calm fearful Northern audiences by presenting "nonthreatening images of Negroes as harmless curiosities" (Toll 42), and, in so doing, it created and solidified a number of demeaning comic stereotypes.

A brief catalogue of the caricatured physical and behavioral characteristics is instructive in showing the ways the minstrel show was especially damaging to white Americans' impressions of blacks. Very often, not only did minstrel shows disseminate images and attitudes already existing in the public consciousness but in fact *minstrelsy was their very point of origin.* According to minstrel caricature, the generalized African American had an outsized, gaping mouth, usually smiling, thick lips, gleaming white teeth, bug eyes, and wooly hair; he also had huge feet and walked with a gangly, shuffling gait—his body always in motion, even sitting down, ever ready to break into song and dance. The Southern plantation "darky" was slow, stupid, superstitious, and gullible, although hardworking for his white "massa'," whom he loved with unqualified devotion and loyalty; also, the plantation "coon" could work all day and still sing and dance all night. The Northern urban black dandy was an ostentatiously flashy dresser, a fast-talking con artist out to dupe his slow-witted Southern brothers, a womanizer, and a gambler with a pair of dice in one pocket and a dangerous straight-edge razor in the other. Before the Civil War, minstrelsy's depictions of Northern free blacks in particular "served not only as ego-boosting scapegoats for whites but also as confirmation that Negroes could not play a constructive role in a free society and did not 'belong' in the North" (Toll 71). As the creator, not just the disseminator, of so many negative images of American blacks, "Minstrelsy was the first example of the way American popular culture would exploit and manipulate Afro-Americans and their culture to please and benefit white Americans" (51).

The only positive effect of all-black minstrel troupes on the nineteenth-century African American community was to make room as never before for large numbers of blacks to be employed, and often well compensated, in the white-dominated entertainment industry. Yet the price they had to pay for this was high. Even during Reconstruction and on to the end of the century, white audience expectations remained white audience expectations. The caricatures and stereotypes had become so ingrained that black

entertainers had to serve the paying white customers these "comic" portrayals as well as the singing and dancing. Accordingly, once the black troupes
established themselves and became as popular as the white, "black minstrels
in effect added credibility to these images by making it seem that Negroes
actually behaved like minstrelsy's black caricatures" (Toll 196). In a word,
the black entertainers — especially wearing blackface makeup — were enact-
ing caricatures and stereotypes of their own authentic selves. But that's what
audiences wanted to see, or, as Toll frankly puts it, " 'Acting the nigger' was
precisely what whites expected blacks to do" (202), and that's precisely what
this employment opportunity *forced* them to do. And these stigmata carried
forward into the twentieth century, when more opportunities became available for blacks in the entertainment world.

### Black Musicals and Mainstream Broadway

As other varieties of black musical entertainment supplanted the minstrel
show, musical theatre "became one of the few avenues of black mobility in
a white world" (Woll xiv). Most of the new black shows were revues or
vaudeville — though their origins were in minstrelsy, they were broader in
the scope of their material and tone. These productions — *The Creole Show*
(1890), *The Octoroons* (1895), *Oriental America* (1896), and, most notably,
*Black Patti's Troubadours* (1896) — were primarily touring shows with only
limited runs in New York. Though these revues were conceived by white
impresarios and still contained their share of racial humor and "coon songs,"
they nevertheless gave more latitude to the talents of black performers than
had minstrelsy. *Black Patti's Troubadours* was especially memorable for
showcasing the operatic talents of Sissieretta Jones, "dubbed Black Patti by
*Clipper* magazine after the Italian singer Adelina Patti" (Woll 5). But racial
stereotypes still prevailed in shows written as well as performed by American
blacks.

This was true even of the first two book musicals written and composed
by blacks, both in 1898, the landmark year in which black musicals were
first produced for Broadway's virtually all-white audiences. After success as
a song and sketch writer for *Black Patti's Troubadours*, Bob Cole teamed
with Billy Johnson to write the full-length black musical comedy *A Trip to
Coontown*. (Cole would later go on to collaborate with the far more prominent J. Rosamond Johnson and, briefly, with his brother, the even more
distinguished James Weldon Johnson.) After business dealings with several
white producers and managers turned sour, Cole skirted such associations
altogether by creating an all-black production company for *Coontown*.

When it opened at the Third Avenue Theatre on April 4, 1898, *A Trip to Coontown* won the distinction of being "the first full-length musical comedy written, directed, performed, and produced by blacks" (Woll 12). While such a thing would not happen again for some time, African Americans had entered the business and managerial side of mainstream New York theatre, setting a precedent for future ventures. Although *Coontown* was ostensibly a book musical, its plot was mostly an excuse to explore "one of New York's ethnic enclaves" (Woll 12), allowing numerous specialty acts to entertain the audience. In this respect it broke no new ground. The show was crowded with stereotypes of the citified con man, the gullible old "plantation darky," and the shuffling comic tramp, not to mention a liberal dose of coon songs with titles like "All I Wants Is Ma Chickens" and "I Wonder What Is That Coon's Game." In the last analysis, *Coontown* was little more than the minstrel formula held together by the thinnest of plots. What white audiences saw in *Coontown*'s brief run at the Third Avenue Theatre, and again at the Grand Opera House after the show returned from touring, was another comfortable recycling of white-created stereotypes of American blacks.

The same can be said for *Clorindy, the Origin of the Cakewalk*, an entertainment created by two men destined for distinguished careers in their fields: composer Will Marion Cook and poet Paul Lawrence Dunbar. They ostensibly wrote *Clorindy* in one night: "Cook and Dunbar barricaded themselves in the basement of a house near Howard University. Equipped with beer, whiskey, a T-bone steak, but no piano, they finished the songs and libretto for *Clorindy* by early the next morning" (Woll 7). Dunbar's lyrics would remain intact, but his script was finally scrapped. Dunbar found Cook so exasperating that he vowed never to work with him again, a vow he would break more than once.

What remained of *Clorindy* when it opened on July 5, 1898, at Ed Rice's Casino Roof Garden was not, then, really a book show at all. It was just Cook and Dunbar's songs and dance numbers, with no script whatever, making it impossible to know what the story was to have been. The title and Cook's intention "to explore the cakewalk craze" and to "set [the show] in Louisiana of the 1880s" (Woll 7) only suggest that the book musical would have somehow dramatized the southern black origins of that nationally popular dance. But what all-white audiences saw at the Roof Garden was a cast of thirty to forty accomplished black performers in a plotless series of songs and production numbers. On opening night the star, Ernest Hogan, was called back for ten encores of his song "Who Dat Say Chicken in Dis Crowd," and at the finale the audience rose and cheered (Woll 9–

10). The strong white response to this black show let it run through the rest of the summer (Bordman 159).

For Cook's second effort he managed to talk Dunbar into writing the lyrics again, but he wrote the book himself. *Jes Lak White Fo'ks* played at the New York Theatre Roof Garden in the summer of 1899 and "expressed Cook's personal philosophy in a one-act operetta." When Pompous Johnson finds a pot of gold, he uses his money "jes lak white fo'ks" to enter high society and arranges his daughter's marriage to an African prince—all of this reading like a black version of the Euro-title shows but predating them by several years. The prince turns out to be a fraud, the daughter marries her real sweetheart, and Johnson stops acting "jes lak white fo'ks" because "an honest American Negro will . . . make the best living for his daughter." The moral: blacks should not try to emulate white customs and culture but should look for happiness within their own cultural traditions (Woll 10).

With music and lyrics again by Cook and Dunbar, *In Dahomey* (2/18/03) was the first full-length book musical written and performed entirely by African Americans to play a major Broadway house, the New York Theatre. It was also one of the most successful starring vehicles for the great song-dance-comedy team of George Walker and Bert Williams. But the characters they played, the songs they sang, and the comedy they performed only perpetuated the white audience's expectations of black stereotypes. Indeed, the particularly light-skinned Williams wore blackface, as he would throughout his distinguished career. So startling was the idea of an all-black show in a mainstream Broadway theatre that the *New York Times* reported rumors of a potential "race war" on opening night (Woll 38; Bordman 190); fortunately, no such thing occurred. But the *Times* reviewer did observe a vivid image of segregation in theatres at the time, noting that "the footlights drew a 'sharp color line' in the theatre—the only blacks on the main floor of the house were James Vaughn, the conductor, and the ushers" (Woll 38).

*In Dahomey* was a hit with white audiences and critics in New York and, later, London, but the show provoked at least one instance of backlash from the African American community. Not long after *In Dahomey* closed, Albert Ross, a black business professor at a Midwestern university, wrote to Walker and Williams, "complaining that they 'held the old plantation Negro, the ludicrous darky, and the scheming grafter up to entertain people'" (Woll 40). In their reply, published in *Variety* on December 14, 1907, Walker and Williams delineated the paradoxical position of black writers and performers of the time. Pointing out that black entertainers were "entirely dependent on white audiences and critics for their livelihood, . . . [they] had to keep in mind the expectations of those audiences." While admitting that they portrayed the expected white stereotypes of African Americans, Walker and Williams still took pride in the fact that their shows were written and performed by blacks and gave employment to a large number of black entertainers (Woll 41–42).

The following year Cook composed the music for *The Southerners*, also at the New York Theatre (5/23/04), a conventionally melodramatic musical that was singular for being the first interracial musical on Broadway. Yet even in this respect the production had its ironies, not the least of which was Caucasian blackface entertainer Eddie Leonard playing the role of Uncle Daniel, an old slave. Still, for the big cakewalk number *The Southerners* employed a "chorus of real live coons" (*New York Times*, 24 May 1904, qtd. in Woll 11). Anticipation of racial tension ran even higher than with *In Dahomey*, but according to the *Times* critic, "[H]ere were scores of blacks and whites mingling. . . . [T]he spirit of harmony reigned. The magician was discovered on inquiry to be the Negro composer Will Marion Cook, who all alone had succeeded in harmonizing the racial broth as skillfully as he had harmonized the accompanying score." The show may have struck a blow for mixed-race casting, but, with little going for it save Cook's music, it closed after thirty-six showings.

Two years later Cook and Bert Williams composed the score for another Walker and Williams musical, this time without Dunbar. Jesse A. Shipp and Alex Rogers wrote the book and lyrics of *Abyssinia* (2/12/06), which portrayed African and, to some extent, black American characters in ways radically different from the comic stereotypes of earlier black musicals. One cannot help wondering whether Walker and Williams, despite their public apologetics, took some of Professor Ross's criticism to heart. And yet, noble as the enterprise was, its realistic and dignified depiction of Africans and American blacks was bound to come under attack from other quarters— and it did. The lone negative review of *Abyssinia* criticized Walker and Williams precisely for abandoning the familiar stereotypes and creating "a white man's show acted by colored men, whereas to be entirely successful it should have been a colored men's show acted by themselves" (*Theatre Magazine*, April 1906, xiv, qtd. in Woll 46). Caught between objections from both the black and white communities, it seemed that African American creative artists of the day couldn't win for losing. The public wasn't buying *Abyssinia*, and the show folded after thirty-one performances (Bordman 219). For *Bandanna Land* (2/3/08), Walker and Williams returned to more "traditional" material, and the production played eighty-nine times. This was the team's last show together—Walker fell ill during the run and died in 1911.

The experiment of non-stereotypical black musicals for white Broadway audiences continued briefly but not too successfully with two shows by Bob Cole and J. Rosamond Johnson as both the composing/writing team and starring performers. Predictably, their efforts were met by the same objections *Abyssinia* had encountered. *The Shoo-Fly Regiment* (8/6/07) tells of a Tuskegee Institute graduate who against his girlfriend's wishes gives up becoming a teacher to fight in the Spanish-American War. After typical complications and a successful attack on the enemy in the Philippines, the young man comes home and marries the girl. The plot (minus Tuskegee Institute) suggests this show could have been about whites as easily as blacks. In fact, the young black characters were written and portrayed as courageous and intelligent, a far cry from the stereotypes harking back to minstrelsy. The show also contained romantic and sentimental love songs and scenes, hitherto "taboo in black shows, since it was assumed that romancing would offend white audiences" (Woll 23). *The Shoo-Fly Regiment* closed after just fifteen performances.

In Cole and Johnson's *The Red Moon* (5/3/09), a Native American chief abducts his daughter from her black mother with whom she lives, but she is rescued by two city blacks. The musical score was universally praised; the book was not. The team toured the show for nearly a year, perhaps some compensation for just thirty-two performances in New York.

*The Shoo-Fly Regiment* occasioned a response from the critic for *Theatre* remarkably similar to the attack on Williams and Walker the previous year: "[The] colored authors have much to learn before they can instruct or entertain our public. They may reach a certain standard, but, for the present, such performances are futile. If they are to advance, they must advance in a direction of their own. In the direction of imitation they will accomplish nothing, or nothing that is their own" (*Theatre Magazine*, September 1907, n.p., qtd. in Woll 24). Beneath this circumlocution the writer is saying that blacks should "continue to write shows of a minstrel nature and leave modern musicals to white authors" (24).

After the spate of creativity from the late 1890s to about 1910, the field of black musicals for mainstream white audiences lay fallow until after World War I. The reasons are many and complex (see Woll, chapter 4), but not least among them were the deaths of some of the most creative writers and performers—Ernest Hogan, Bob Cole, and George Walker; the defection from musical theatre to explore other pursuits by Will Marion Cook, James Weldon Johnson, and J. Rosamond Johnson; and Bert Williams's breaking the color bar of white musical theatre.

After Walker's degenerative illness kept him from performing, Williams unhappily went solo for the first time in sixteen years, starring in *Mr. Lode of Koal* (11/1/09). Recognizing Williams's unique talent, Flo Ziegfeld signed him for the *Follies of 1910* (the edition that also thrust Fanny Brice upon Broadway). Bert Williams thus became the first and only black in the *Follies*—performing in seven more editions through 1919—until 1931, when the team of Buck and Bubbles appeared (Woll 48; Ziegfeld 45). Yet even as a Ziegfeld headliner, Williams blacked up for his performances and, as a black, "found himself barred from most hotels while the show was on tour" (Woll xiii), one of the cruel ironies of show business success that would haunt black performers well into the century.

### Over There Over Here—America Awakens to the Noises of War

On June 28, 1914, the shots fired in Sarajevo woke up Europe, but smug, isolationist America continued to snooze. U.S. journalists dismissed or ignored the assassination of some archduke in some place no one ever heard of: "As the Grand Forks, North Dakota, *Daily Herald* put it, 'To the world, or to a nation, an archduke more or less makes little difference'" (Lord 333). Then, on July 23, Austria issued its ultimatum to Serbia: comply with its demands by 6:00 P.M. on July 25, or Austria would invade Serbia herself. Still dozing, "The Muskogee, Oklahoma, *Daily Phoenix* gave it ten lines on page six. And lest it seem unfair to take such a small paper, the mighty Chicago *Tribune* didn't mention it at all" (Lord 338). Even at the end of July, the mobilizations of the European powers seemed like make-believe to most Americans (Russell 381). When told of Germany's August 4 entry into Belgium, President Wilson himself called the war "a distant event, terrible and tragic, but one which does not concern us closely" (qtd. in Churchill 17).

Right up to U.S. belligerency nearly three years later, the general American position was insularity and, officially, neutrality. Still, as late as April 2, 1917, when asking Congress for a declaration of war against the Central Powers, Wilson cited among his stateside goals "the enforced loyalty of all Americans in a cause to which many were indifferent or openly hostile" (Kennedy 14). The federal government accordingly launched widespread publicity campaigns promoting Liberty Loans, the draft, Victory Gardens, and just plain patriotism. On April 6, Wilson signed the declaration of war. Inspired by that event, within twenty-four hours George M. Cohan had written "Over There," the war years' most popular song and arguably more effective than some of the government programs in getting Americans behind the war effort (Churchill 44–45; McCabe 137–38).

Cohan's stirring flag-waver aside, Broadway was lukewarm toward the war, at least initially. From the summer of 1914 to the Armistice in 1918, only a few straight plays and fewer book musicals treated the war. But the spectacular revues incrementally included more and more patriotic and war-related numbers. In the two and a half years from the summer of 1914 to the U.S. declaration of war in 1917, only seven musical productions touched on the war, six of them revues. But during the comparatively brief nineteen months of American involvement from April 1917 to November 1918, Broadway saw a total of nine such shows, one book show and eight revues. The number of revues (compared to book shows) that contained war-related songs or scenes — some quite grimly serious — suggests that while Broadway producers wanted to keep audiences mindful of the war, they also kept the tone of the shows as a whole light and entertaining. Hence, the norm remained one or two war-related numbers in revues, except for one special case toward the end of the war.

## The War in Revue

Revues had included patriotic tributes as far back as "Song of the Navy" in Ziegfeld's *Follies of 1908*, but the events of the summer of 1914 inspired flag-waving that focused squarely on the war, even before our boys went "over there." *Dancing Around* (10/10/14), the 1914 Winter Garden extravaganza, featured Al Jolson, a fixture of most Winter Garden revues since 1910. As usual performing mostly in blackface, Jolson sang two war-related songs, both interpolated into the Sigmund Romberg/Harry Carroll score for the revue. Jack Judge and Harry Williams's "It's a Long Way to Tipperary" became a standard of World War I song repertoire, but Jolson's performance of "Sister Susie's Sewing Shirts for Soldiers" as an incremental singalong made a special impact. The mere fact that this song appeared in an October 1914 revue speaks volumes about the political inclination of the mainstream, allegedly neutral, audience. In 1914, "Sister Susie" obviously wasn't sewing shirts for U.S troops that weren't "over there"; what's more, no one really suspected they ever would be. Susie was stitching for the French and British forces. By having more and more people join each chorus, Jolson could work the audience up to a mood of patriotic enthusiasm for both the Allies and our American girls helping their cause.

Jolson's efforts notwithstanding, it took the sinking of the *Lusitania* by a German U-boat in May 1915 to get America's attention and keep the war before Broadway audiences. In 1915, too, Flo Ziegfeld hired the gifted Austrian-born Joseph Urban as his scenic designer. Together they created "America," the big patriotic sequence in the *Ziegfeld Follies of 1915* (6/21/

15). The number focused on America's armed forces and was more militant in tone than most of Ziegfeld's earlier patriotic tableaux. With its set painted in "a riot of Urban reds, whites, and blues," "America" was a large-scale production number in which performers represented either branches of the armed services or allegorical figures. Featured dancer Ann Pennington and George White, new to the *Follies* that year, depicted the navy, May Murray and Carl Randall the army. Presumably hovering *over* these proceedings, Kay Laurell personified the Dove of Peace, and "[t]o top the production of this patriotic flash, Justine Johnstone, one of Ziegfeld's most beautiful girls, posed as 'Columbia.' It was flag-waving—but Ziegfeld style" (Baral 57). At one point during all this, Bernard Granville sang "We'll Build a Little Home in the U.S.A.," welcoming "a hundred thousand refugees" (Bordman 308). A comic number, "My Little Submarine," was both a paean to American technology and a racy suggestion that a snug little sub is the best place for what a later generation would call "makin' whoopee." But the *Lusitania* sinking just two months before the *Follies* opened may have tainted the song with an unintended irony.

A year went by before another Broadway show addressed the war. The *Ziegfeld Follies of 1916* (6/12/16) featured a convincing recreation of a North Sea naval battle. Without live actors, using just scenery and special effects, "a war vessel appeared to be moving along in the ocean. A zeppelin and airplanes flew over the ship and beyond it. The ship sank, but a submarine emerged to take its place" (Ziegfeld 244). *The Passing Show of 1916* (6/22/16) at the Winter Garden was produced by the Brothers Shubert, who, according to one biographer, lived by the credo that the theatre is "a machine that makes dollars" (Stagg 128). It's therefore no surprise that, in addition to patriotic displays, "the excitement on front pages of the dailies convinced the Shuberts that more topicality would pay" (Bordman 315). That timeliness materialized as comic sketches featuring such notables as Republican presidential candidate Charles Evans Hughes; President Wilson, just renominated for another term; past president Teddy Roosevelt, an outspoken advocate of U.S. intervention in the war; and Mexican revolutionary Pancho Villa.

The patriotic spectacle in the 1916 *Passing Show* was made possible by a variation on the treadmill, a piece of stage machinery in use since the late nineteenth century for such effects as horse racing or the chariot race in the original stage adaptation of *Ben Hur*. These sets of treadmills were laid in the stage parallel to the curtain line, so the audience viewed *in profile* horses galloping, chariots careening, or motorcars racing, in an illusion that they were traveling from stage right to stage left or vice versa. The illusion was reinforced by a moving painted panorama, cranked in the proper direction to make it appear that scenery was flashing by the speeding horses or vehicles. The patriotic sequence in *The Passing Show* featured a cavalry charge. What was new for this effect was that the treadmills were laid from downstage to upstage, so that horses and riders would be viewed *head on* and appear to be charging right into the audience (Bordman 315). That a 1916 revue represented the war as a cavalry charge is of more than casual interest. Most of the Allies (especially France) went into the war with their outmoded, nineteenth-century, romantic ideas of war pretty much intact, still believing in personal valor, *élan*, heroism, and sacrifice (see Kennedy 178–82). By 1916, all but a few diehard idealists among the Allies must have had the romantic stuffing knocked out of them when faced daily with the gritty reality of trench warfare and the horrifying new technologies of the automated German army, such as machine guns. But in June 1916, the United States had not yet entered the war, and its depiction on Broadway often emphasized the dramatic and romantic. It's also worth reiterating that the U.S. Army was still one of the smallest and worst prepared among the world's major powers, "with the cavalry still its strongest arm" (Churchill 57–58).

One more revue with patriotic content opened prior to the declaration of war on April 6, 1917. Important for the collaboration that created the show, *The Century Girl* (11/6/16) was co-produced by "New York's two finest producers of musicals," Florenz Ziegfeld and Charles Dillingham, who engaged two of Broadway's best composers, Irving Berlin and Victor Herbert, to write the score. The revue included two patriotic sequences. "Uncle Sam's Children" was another refugee melting-pot number, and "When Uncle Sam Is Ruler of the Sea" celebrated America's naval supremacy (Bordman 318).

Once the United States was in the war, Ziegfeld really outdid himself in the patriotic tableau department. Although published accounts differ in details, it is absolutely clear that Ziegfeld pulled out all the stops for the *Ziegfeld Follies of 1917* (6/12/17). The title of the song "I'll Be Somewhere in France" doesn't just suggest the loneliness and displacement of the American soldier abroad; the vague "somewhere" seems to allude to—perhaps comments on—the strict censorship recently imposed on everything related to the war, including letters home from U.S. soldiers. More in the line of general patriotism, Victor Herbert composed a rousing number titled "Can't You Hear Our Country Calling."

But the most prolonged and spectacular flag-waving was a finale so extravagant it "required two scenes" (Ziegfeld 245). Part one of this elaborate tableau was a trip through U.S. history from the Revolution to the present. It began with Paul Revere's ride, using a treadmill for a white horse and a rider impersonating the Boston patriot. Then along came George Washington and Abraham Lincoln, followed soon by Woodrow Wilson. Not only did the popular imagination view Washington and Lincoln as two of the country's greatest presidents; each was also associated with a "heroic" war. Putting Wilson in such good company was a powerful endorsement of the president and of the "rightness" of America's intervention. The actor playing Wilson reviewed a troop of showgirls dressed in the red, white, and blue of the Continental Army during the Revolution while performing precision drills "in front of a painted eagle" (Ziegfeld 245) as the orchestra played "The Star Spangled Banner." When the audience rose to their feet, a gargantuan Old Glory unfurled above them in the theatre's auditorium. Also, dispersed about the stage, some of Ziegfeld's showgirls posed as icons of Americana; "ever an experimenter with feminine nudity, [Ziegfeld] had reached the point where he dared show one of his statuesque showgirls with a breast exposed. The patriotic tableau gave him an excellent opportunity to do this, for who would dare criticize it on any grounds?" (Churchill 108). And apparently no one did.

Part 2 of the finale dispensed with the human element entirely in favor of scenic splendor and effects. A fleet of battleships appeared far upstage, moving through the night toward the audience. As they approached the footlights, the ships seemed to get bigger and bigger, and just as they reached the edge of the stage the scene blacked out and ended (Ziegfeld 245). No text was needed for this vivid display of U.S. naval power.

Other revues jumped on the Ziegfeld/Shubert bandwagon in creating visual imagery related to the war. The Hippodrome spectacular *Cheer Up* (8/23/17) revealed—beautifully if grimly—a cornfield turning into a poppy field (Bordman 324), red poppies already the universal symbol for combat deaths. The year's Winter Garden extravaganza *Doing Our Bit* (10/18/17) included a scene of a troopship carrying the entire chorus, men and women alike, dressed in military uniforms. Not to be outdone, a revue opened at the end of 1917 whose very title was the familiar battle cry of trench warfare, *Over the Top* (12/1/17). Starring the ravishing Justine Johnstone, the show also featured a spectacular visual recreation of American aircraft attacking a German trench (328).

Six months later it was Ziegfeld's turn again. The *Ziegfeld Follies of 1918* (6/18/18) was packed with war-related material—far more than any one revue before it. But other kinds of songs and sketches showcased this edition's stars Will Rogers, Eddie Cantor, W. C. Fields, and dancer Ann Pennington. The 1918 *Follies* also introduced another dancer who would ultimately eclipse the diminutive (four feet eleven inches in heels) Miss Pennington, the nearly as petite (five feet three inches) Marilyn Miller. Still, despite this constellation of stars and their specialty material, the plethora of numbers about the war and America in Ziegfeld's 1918 annual led Allen Churchill to declare it a show "the theme of which was patriotism" (172). No fewer than five patriotic songs or scenes have been documented. One particularly pugnacious number was titled "You Keep Sending 'Em Over and We'll Keep Knocking 'Em Down," while Irving Berlin contributed two war songs, one a "plaintive little love song" called "I'm Gonna Pin a Medal on the Girl I Left Behind" (Baral 75), the other "Blue Devils of France," featured in the revue's most spectacular war-oriented production number, "Forward Allies," treated in detail below. For sheer stage spectacle Ziegfeld presented three tableaux that referenced the war, two direct, one more oblique, but all visually stunning.

The *Follies of 1918* opened with a tableau of sorts that put the war in serious and immediate, if symbolic, perspective. After the overture, the curtain opened to reveal a darkened stage. As the lights came up, the audience could see an enormous revolving globe with Kay Laurell, draped as the "Spirit of the Allies," perched on top. With Laurell looking down on it, the globe revolved to show all of Europe burning (Ziegfeld 247). A pretty heavy way to open an annual revue, especially one known for hilarious comedians and beautiful women, but apparently audiences bought it; they kept the show running until just about the Armistice. Richard and Paulette Ziegfeld point out that choreographer Ned Wayburn's intricate production number "Aviators' Parade" "was *part* of the first-act finale" (247; italics supplied). Given what went on in just Wayburn's contribution, that must have been one long finale! The stage was empty until "a silk tent was pushed up through a trap door. One by one forty-eight chorus girls, wearing gold aviator outfits and silver trench hats, emerged from the tent and alternately went right and left. After marching in precise formations, the women gradually disappeared the way they entered" (247). But the *pièce de resistance* of the patriotic scenes had to be "Forward Allies," one of many tableaux designed for Ziegfeld over the years by Ben Ali Haggin. The "Blue Devils of France" number was part of the larger scene as a tribute to the French military unit of that name. Lillian Lorraine and a chorus of girls in uniforms based on those of the Blue Devils sang the Berlin song. The tableau itself was an astonishing blend of war imagery. As Allen Churchill describes it, "Actors in battle dress stood frozen in the act of tossing grenades, bayoneting cringing Huns, and charging Over the Top. Completing this tableau were . . . Follies Girls as Red Cross nurses, waifs in war-torn undress, and goddesses of war. Dominating the vivid scene was Miss Kay Laurell representing the Spirit of the Allies, her costume in enough disarray to expose one . . . breast" (172).

Three more revues with numbers touching on the war opened before the Armistice—one of them conventional, the others anything but. The conventional *Passing Show of 1918* (7/25/18) is notable only for containing a rare sketch about war efforts on the homefront, in this case War Savings Stamps. A spoof of the biblical Salome in which she asks for the head of the kaiser—and gets it—is indicative of the more usual level of humor in *The Passing Shows* (Smith 108). The other two revues were unusual for Broadway because they were performed by more or less amateurs and because all the performers were members of the armed forces; these were camp shows, transferred from the drab world of the cantonments to the glittery Great White Way. On May 30, *Biff! Bang!*, a rather slapdash offering by sailors from the Pelham Bay Naval Training Station, opened for sixteen performances. If it didn't meet with much critical or popular success, the naval revue at least paved the way for a second camp show to reach Broadway, this one capturing the public imagination. The show performed by the men of Camp Upton was called *Yip Yip Yaphank* (8/19/18) after the camp's location at Yaphank, Long Island. Actual soldiers acted and sang the show's sketches and songs, most dealing with the life of new recruits. But what made this camp show noteworthy is that all of its music and lyrics were by Corporal Irving Berlin, who also performed "Oh, How I Hate to Get Up in the Morning," not just the hit of the show but one of the most popular songs of the war, far outlasting *Yip Yip Yaphank*'s thirty-two performances (Bordman 333; Churchill 91, 171–72). What is singular about *Yaphank* as a revue entirely about army life, written and performed by soldiers, is that it was lighthearted, funny, and sometimes satirical, whereas war-related revue numbers written and performed by civilians most often were serious, even solemn occasions of patriotic display.

### The War in Book Musicals

With the proliferation of revues, it's easy to forget that there were also a lot of book musicals on Broadway during the war. But almost none focused on military life or anything else of topical interest. Over the nearly four years and four months of the war, just three book shows touched on soldiering, and only the extrinsic historical interest of each makes them worth mentioning. The score of *Her Soldier Boy* (12/6/16) was a collaborative effort between Sigmund Romberg and Emmerich Kalman. Hungarian-born Romberg by then was a U.S. citizen and one of Broadway's most prolific songwriters; Kalman, a distinguished Austrian composer of operetta, still lived in Vienna, capital of one of the Central Powers. Before the war, a few Kalman operettas had been imported and adapted for Broadway, and there was actually some hope that the Romberg-Kalman piece would "ride above international animosities" (Bordman 318). Apparently it did for a while; Broadway audiences showed up 198 times. *Her Soldier Boy* told of a soldier posing as his buddy killed in battle "so the buddy's family would be spared the painful truth" (318). In a vintage musical comedy ending, the soldier marries his buddy's sister, and the young man presumed dead rejoins his family after being just missing in action.

Broadway didn't see another book show about the military for well over a year, and when it did, it didn't see it very long. Not even Jerome Kern's music could save *Toot-Toot!* (3/11/18) from becoming a forty-performance flop. The war was mere background for the story of Lt. Harry Malloy, who was determined to marry his girlfriend as soon as he got orders to be shipped out. The couple spends most of the show trying to find a minister to marry them on the train taking Malloy to his base. They do, and he does, and that's about it.

The most militaristic thing about *The Girl behind the Gun* (9/16/18) was its title. Except that our hero is a soldier on leave, the show was just another innocent bedroom farce set to music. The soldier decides to visit his "god-mother" instead of his wife, which pleases the former, who wants to use him to make her husband jealous, and upsets the latter, who starts flirting with an army colonel. Of course all resolves happily, with the proper couples together, as if they were ever seriously apart. The score wasn't one of prolific Ivan Caryll's best, but critics uniformly praised the witty book and lyrics by Guy Bolton and P. G. Wodehouse and the performances of popular musical theatre stars Donald Brian and Wilda Bennett. With all that going for it, this fluff with the military title ran 160 times, closing long after the war itself did. It also didn't hurt business that President and Mrs. Wilson, "who liked frothy entertainment," attended the show on October 11, 1918. At the end of act 2, Wilson mounted the stage and turned intermission into an impressively successful Liberty Bond rally, raising $750,000 in bonds (Churchill 193–94).

Two other war-focused musicals showed up on Broadway with too little too late—after the Armistice. *Atta Boy* (12/23/18) was another all-soldier revue that looked humorously at army life but survived just twenty-four outings (Bordman 337). *Come Along* (4/8/19) was a drab, heavy book show about a nurse traveling to France in wartime, only to find she must care for her wounded lover; it played just forty-seven times. These shows' short runs suggest that for Broadway audiences once the war was over, it was *over*.

*Topical and Diversionary Musicals during the War*

Of roughly 135 Broadway revues and book shows between the Austrian ultimatum and the Armistice, only one book musical, *Ladies First* (10/24/18),
treated a topical subject other than the war. Numerous issues could have
provided grist for the revue sketch mills, if not for full-length musicals, but
the musical stage all but shunned such matters. And it's not as if audiences
were so occupied with the war that nothing domestic concerned them.
During the war years, issues like Prohibition and the Woman Suffrage
Movement were on the minds of many Americans. It could even be argued
that the prospect of the United States going dry or of women having the
vote affected more lives than did the war.

In 1916, "dry" groups like the Anti-Saloon League and the Women's
Christian Temperance Union helped elect a Congress sympathetic to the
prohibition of alcohol. The Senate proposed the Eighteenth (Prohibition)
Amendment just before the Fourth of July 1917, and the House gave its
approval in December. From January 8, 1918, when Mississippi became the
first state to ratify Prohibition, it took only a year for thirty-five more states
to do the same, making the amendment law. Those twelve months were
filled with intense publicity and lobbying of state legislatures by the Pro-
hibitionists, aided by charismatic Billy Sunday's cross-country preaching of
his notorious but effective "Booze Sermon." Prohibition went into effect on
January 17, 1920. While the battle over Prohibition's pros and cons raged
during the war years, the musical theatre was silent on the subject. The
first documented revue sketch about it was in the *Ziegfeld Follies of 1919*,
and Prohibition and bootlegging became central to a book musical only in
1926.

The Suffragists had to wait longer to achieve their aim than the Prohi-
bitionists. The Suffrage Amendment passed Congress in the summer of
1919, and the requisite number of states ratified it as the Nineteenth Amendment by August 18, 1920. While the Woman Suffrage Movement was strong
in the prewar years, opposition to women having the vote, let alone holding
public office, was often stronger, sometimes virulent. That virulence showed
itself once in a New York musical. The very title of *The Never Homes* (10/
5/11) reflects male America's primary objection to women entering public
life. The women of Lilydale take over the entire town. One young man,
"neglected by his political mother," sets fire to their house, and the whole
town burns down because the firewomen are too busy redecorating the fire
station: "Besides it's sort of damp today, and it wouldn't be good for the
horses to go out." The women are hauled into court, order is restored, and

the men run the city again (Bordman 272). Its reasonably decent run of ninety-two performances suggests the show appealed to the prevailing attitude of the primarily male audiences of the time.

During the war, however, such Suffragist organizations as Carrie Chapman Catt's enormous National American Woman Suffrage Association carried out a very vocal and visible crusade for the vote for women, even finding ways to capitalize on the war, patriotism, and democracy in support of their cause. Thanks to their efforts, President Wilson himself "unequivocally harnessed the spirit of the war for democracy to the cause of woman suffrage, telling the Senate in 1918 that the vote for women 'is vital to the winning of the war' " (Kennedy 284). During the war the Woman Suffrage Movement stirred up enough interest in the musical theatre world to produce one book show, and it was a 164-performance hit. In *Ladies First* an elderly "suffragette" convinces her niece to run for mayor against the niece's own boyfriend. Since she adores her young man, she doesn't much mind when she loses the election (Bordman 336). The musical's tone reflects the shifting national mood. Unlike the ugly stance taken against women in politics in *The Never Homes* seven years earlier, *Ladies First* was sympathetic to the Women Suffrage Movement, as was a steadily increasing percentage of the (male) population and their representatives in Washington.

With topicality at a premium in the war years, what was the nature of most Broadway musicals? It was what it has been throughout the twentieth century: diversionary, light, sometimes entirely escapist entertainment. Americans from 1914 to 1918, daily exposed to war news and, once the United States entered the conflict, to the daily casualty list, faced a grim reality. While the unadorned fact of the war cannot alone account for the preponderance of diversionary musicals — they are always with us — it helps explain the virtual absence of topically relevant shows after the first fourteen years of the century produced so many. Generally speaking, wartime audiences went to musicals not to be reminded of but to forget their concerns.

### The Princess Theatre Shows

While Broadway audiences continued to enjoy the "boy meets girl" formula shows, a small group of musicals in a very small theatre was staging a quiet revolution. These were the Princess Theatre Shows, so named for the theatre in which all but one played, a tiny 299-seat house on West 39th Street on the very fringe of the theatre district. The Princess Theatre Shows are *Nobody Home* (4/20/15), *Very Good Eddie* (12/23/15), *Oh, Boy!* (2/20/17), *Leave It to Jane* (Longacre Theatre, 8/28/17, because *Oh, Boy!* was still

running at the Princess), and *Oh Lady! Lady!!* (2/1/18). These shows shared
Jerome Kern as composer, Guy Bolton as book writer, and variously Philip
Bartholomae or P. G. Wodehouse as provider of some of the lyrics. This
team created not just a series of delightful small-scale musicals but a revolutionary philosophy for the crafting of musical plays. As articulated by
Bolton, "Our musical comedies . . . depend as much upon plot and the
development of their characters for success as upon their music, and because they deal with subjects and peoples near to the audiences. . . . In the
development of our plot . . . we endeavor to make everything count. Every
line, funny or serious, is supposed to help the plot continue to hold. . . . [I]f
the songs are going to count at all in any plot, the plot has to build more
or less around, or at least, with them" (qtd. in Bordman 330). One of the
most forward-looking composers in the history of the musical, Kern put this
more succinctly: "It is my opinion that the musical numbers should carry
on the action of the play, and should be representative of the personalities
of the characters who sing them" (qtd. in Bordman, *Kern* 149). What Bolton
and Kern were describing, and what they and their compatriots were writing, was a rudimentary form of what in later years has generally come to
be called the "integrated musical" (or, sometimes, "seamless musical").

The concept of the integrated musical is similar to Richard Wagner's
ideal of the *Gesamtkunstwerk* or "master art-work" (sometimes loosely translated and conceived of as "Total Theatre"). Here all elements of theatrical
production—the sung word, the spoken word, vocal music, orchestral music, stage movement, choreography and dance, sets, costumes, and lighting—all work collaboratively to give the musical play auditory and visual
expression and thereby communicate it to the audience. This ideal led
Wagner to call the works he wrote, composed, and staged "music-dramas"
(not operas), a term that emphasized their collaborative and balanced nature. The musical play itself is therefore of overarching importance, with
the individual elements of composition and production—music, lyrics,
story, characters, ideas, and point of view—all harmonizing to present it to
the audience.

The Princess Theatre Shows took some steps in this direction. Bolton's
books told plausible tales about believable characters who spoke like everyone else (if perhaps a bit wittier and funnier). Their songs grew naturally
from the exigencies of plot and character, and even jokes in the dialogue
related to the story (yet it would be many years before dance was fully
integrated into musicals to convey story and character). Even though Gilbert
and Sullivan had integrated the elements of their comic operas, no one had
done so for the American musical in a significant way until Kern and Bolton's Princess Theatre experiments. Yet they were ahead of their time. Even

Kern and Hammerstein's 1927 *Show Boat*, generally regarded as the first large-scale integrated Broadway musical, had no immediate influence. It would take until 1943 for Rodgers and Hammerstein's *Oklahoma!* to provide an ongoing model and inspiration for integrated musicals, which became the normative form for American musicals for the rest of the century (see chapters 4–6 especially). For all of their experiments in musical theatre *form*, Kern and Bolton's Princess Theatre Shows were real crowd pleasers, since their content, as in most other musicals, was just diversionary fluff.

## Operetta — A Casualty of War

With few exceptions, diversionary fluff was the order of the day for book musicals from the turn of the century through World War I and beyond. Before the Great War, the opposing Europhobic and Europhilic sentiments within the American public found their way into musical theatre with perplexing and contradictory results. The same audiences that wildly embraced the lavish flag-waving tableaux in Ziegfeld's *Follies* and sang George M's rousing chauvinistic tunes mostly spent their money to see operettas. From 1900 to 1914, and especially from 1907 on, most book musicals to achieve long runs, critical success, and substantial financial profit were European imports or American "operettas with a distinctly European bias" (Bordman 287). The content and style of these operettas virtually defined diversionary fluff. Musical comedies mostly had contemporary settings, colloquial dialogue and lyrics, and music based on the latest dance crazes or Tin Pan Alley styles of songwriting. Operettas on the other hand usually took place in a romanticized past and/or fictitious country and had artificially elegant dialogue and lyrics and a lush, romantic musical score largely descended from Johann Strauss Jr. and the Viennese waltz tradition. Most operetta plots concerned a cloyingly sweet love story and traded on unabashed sentimentality as opposed to the lighthearted, racy tone of musical comedy.

From 1907 forward, the ratio of Central European imports to American-written shows (including the imitations of mittel-European operetta) increased each season, peaking in the theatrical year of 1913–14. Of the thirty-four musicals on Broadway, thirteen were imports from Vienna or Germany, two revivals of older shows, eight revues, and only eleven new American book musicals, a number of them in the style of Old World operetta. And most of the American-written clones throughout the period had actual Old World connections, their composers often foreign-born and foreign-trained musically. Gustav Luders and Gustave Kerker came to the United States from Germany; Ludwig Englander from Vienna; Ivan Caryll from Belgium;

Karl Hoschna and Rudolf Friml from what is now the Czech Republic; Victor Herbert from Ireland; and, just making his Broadway debut as the war clouds loomed, Sigmund Romberg from Hungary. Small wonder the scores of so many American shows had a distinctly European and—except for Herbert's—specifically Central European flavor.

Prior to 1907 most imported musicals came from England and France. In that year, however, the importation of Franz Lehar's almost archetypal Viennese operetta *The Merry Widow* (10/21/07) shifted the geographical center. Its phenomenal Broadway run of 416 performances inspired U.S. producers to crank out ever-increasing numbers of *Merry Widow* clones. According to Gerald Bordman, "For seven years all the best works offered by American composers were in this . . . style that we would now brand 'operetta.' Those writers who could not or would not write in this gay, sweeping Central European idiom met with increasing disappointments. Native musical material was still presented regularly but it often seemed intimidated by the cavalier elegance of the Viennese school" (230).

The outbreak of hostilities meant less theatrical output in England and France, which in turn reduced the number of shows imported from London and Paris. Musical comedy thus became almost exclusively the product of American librettists, lyricists, and composers—often naturalized American composers, but American nevertheless. Still, for some time into the war, most operettas remained Central European importations—translated and adapted, of course, and in many cases "Americanized," but still exuding the Old World in three-quarter time. But after the banner season of 1913–14, there was a drastic downward slide annually in both the number of operettas on Broadway and the percentage they represented of all musicals produced. Finally, by winter 1917, Broadway entirely banished European operetta from its musical stages until nearly a year after the Armistice.

The cause of this about-face in audience preference had little to do with taste and everything to do with politics and patriotism. As the war persisted, Broadway audiences and producers became, in a sense, "silent partners" in the escalating and often irrational manifestations of anti-German (and, by extension, anti-Austrian) sentiment that swept the United States almost as virulently as the killer influenza epidemic of 1918.

Anti-German sentiment ran the gamut from the ludicrous to the unspeakable. Restaurants renamed sauerkraut "liberty cabbage" and hamburgers "liberty sandwiches," and many beer halls stopped serving pretzels (Kennedy 68; Churchill 167). Breweries with German names like Schlitz, Blatz, and Anheuser-Busch experienced a dramatic slowdown in sales. Walking a dachshund raised suspicion, and German shepherd owners risked being arrested as spies (Churchill 167–68). Super-patriots pressured school districts into dropping German from the language curriculum; the California State Board of Education damned German as "a language that disseminates the ideals of autocracy, brutality, and hatred," while one Iowa politician charged that "ninety percent of all the men and women who teach the German language are traitors" (qtd. in Kennedy 54). Libraries trashed and burned their holdings of German literature, while actors and opera singers with German-sounding names had trouble getting work. One Manhattan minister titled a homily "The Prussian Is a Moral Imbecile." A foreign accent could get a man fired from his job, and rabidly patriotic workers forced others with "foreign-sounding" names to kneel or crawl across the floor and kiss the flag. At the hysteria's farthest reaches there was vigilantism and the lynching of German-Americans (Churchill 165–67).

It was in this context that audiences and producers progressively exiled Viennese operettas and their American cousins. In 1913–14, producers mounted more than a dozen Central European imports and their American clones, but in 1914–15 that number dropped to four, never rising higher than six during any year of the war. Also, ticket sales for such shows decreased after the summer of 1914, indicative of "a palpable distaste for even the most harmless Austro-Hungarian operetta" (Bordman 297).

Producers risking Central European operetta tried their best to disguise its origins. When they didn't, the results were disastrous. On March 3, 1917, the *Dramatic Mirror* noted that to succeed, Austrian operettas had to be "so largely Americanized . . . that they lost most of their Viennese atmosphere" (qtd. in Bordman 315). Such Americanizing accounts for the success of *Miss Springtime* (9/25/16) and *Her Soldier Boy* (12/6/16), both revised beyond recognition from their Old World originals. Conversely, Oscar Straus's *My Lady's Glove* (6/18/17) was presented pretty much intact, save for some interpolations by Romberg, and folded after sixteen performances (Bordman 323). Yet, just a month later, Romberg, finally composing in his own musical idiom, wrote what is considered his first outstanding score for *Maytime* (8/16/17), based on a Viennese story, *Wie Einst im Mai*, but totally Americanized by librettists Rida Johnson Young and Cyrus Wood. Moreover, the Shuberts so scrupulously kept the show's origins out of theatre programs and sheet music that *Maytime* became "the year's overwhelming hit" (324).

In winter 1917, operetta's last waltz ended on Broadway with a strange and terrible irony. Franz Lehar's stylish and melodic *The Merry Widow* had been largely responsible for starting the operetta vogue in 1907. Now it was Lehar's *The Star Gazer* (11/26/17) that locked operetta out of New York theatres for the remainder of the war and then some. That those shrewd theatrical businessmen, the Shuberts, thought to produce a Viennese operetta in 1917 seems odd, but they did. Perhaps they thought changing the locale from Austria to New England would help. It didn't. Audiences weren't buying, and the show's pitiful eight-performance run was enough to keep any more operettas off the boards until nearly a year after the Armistice (Bordman 327–28; Smith 95).

## Goodbye, Vienna — Hello, Broadway!

With fewer theatres occupied by Central European operettas during the war, there was more room for shows by American composers, lyricists, and librettists, or, at the very least, greater opportunity for songs by young, unknown American talent to be interpolated into other writers' shows. Indeed, the catalogue of new American, including naturalized American, talent whose songs were first heard on Broadway during the Great War reads like a who's who of what many consider the golden age of Broadway songwriting—the 1920s and 1930s.

Taking these newcomers' Broadway debuts in rough chronological order, Hungarian immigrant Sigmund Romberg began mainly as a staff writer for the Shuberts, composing interpolations or doctoring up scores for other people's shows. His first full score came just before the war in *The Whirl of the World* (1/10/14), but, other than his triumphant *Maytime*, Romberg would not succeed in his own European idiom until a string of hits in the 1920s. Since around 1907, Russian immigrant Irving Berlin had had considerable luck as a Tin Pan Alley songwriter, also interpolating numbers into musicals not his own. In 1911, he became instantly famous with "Alexander's Ragtime Band," but not until the war years did Broadway make room for *Watch Your Step* (12/8/14), the first show with all Berlin music and lyrics. Audiences heard Cole Porter's sophisticated words and music via his interpolations in *Hands Up* (7/22/15) and *Miss Information* (10/5/15) and, soon after, in his first full score for *But See America First* (3/28/16). For a single number in *The Passing Show of 1916* (6/22/16) called "The Making of a Girl," Romberg teamed with the still (but not for long) unknown George Gershwin. And about nine months after the Armistice, well into the run of *A Lonely Romeo* (6/10/19), a lone interpolation called "Any Old Place with You" first thrust the melodic wit and wisdom of Richard Rodgers and Lorenz Hart upon a public undoubtedly unprepared for such outrageous yet perfectly plausible rhymes as "I'll call each dude a pest / You like in Budapest" and the now classic "I'll go to hell for ya, / Or Philadelphia" (Hart and Kimball 12).

This is not to suggest that these luminaries would have never written for the American musical theatre had European operetta not disappeared from Broadway. But the historical facts argue that the doors to the musical stage may have opened to them much later had there still been a glut of Old World waltz-time romances on Broadway during the war. And removing those operettas out of earshot of the theatregoing public doubtlessly induced them to listen sympathetically to idiomatically American music. That new American music, in productions that mostly flaunted style over substance, would mirror and express the lifestyle of the postwar 1920s.

# 2

# The Musicals of the Roaring Twenties

### Prosperity

The 1920s, a decade characterized as both prosperous and frivolous by numerous writers on the period, fostered hundreds of "mindless" musicals—diversionary shows intended purely as entertainment. Recent historians David A. Shannon and William E. Leuchtenburg—as well as Frederick Lewis Allen, whose 1931 classic *Only Yesterday* offers a contemporary's look at the 1920s—agree that the main feature of the period was unprecedented economic growth and increased prosperity for most Americans. Shannon, in fact, dubs the '20s "the dollar decade." Although Shannon criticizes Allen's work for affecting subsequent histories "with a kind of nostalgia" for "what were actually superficialities" and for putting "an unusual emphasis upon the bizarre and transitory aspects of the 1920's" (85), Allen's immediate take on the '20s is especially valuable for illuminating how the decade saw *itself*.

For many Americans (farmers were among the notable exceptions), 1923 to late 1929 were "years of unparalleled plenty" (Allen 121). According to Leuchtenburg, the staggering growth of the automobile industry, spurred by new technologies, initiated a second industrial revolution. "In 1900, there had been an annual output of 4,000 cars; by 1929, 4,800,000 automobiles were being produced in a single year, and Americans were driving more than 26 million autos and trucks" (185). As the auto industry boomed, so did steel, rubber, and petroleum manufacture, developments that underwrote dramatic expansion in the building trades. Construction of both single- and multi-family dwellings was at an all-time high, and buildings of commerce and trade grew ever taller. The skyscrapers appearing on the urban landscape were "as certain an expression of the ebullient American spirit as the Gothic cathedral was of medieval Europe" (183).

In the realm of high finance, the stock market of the mid-'20s gave cause for optimism. Stock prices generally rose in the years of "Coolidge Prosperity" and crescendoed, along with runaway speculation, between March

1928 and the summer of 1929. People who had never heard of a "margin" or tried to read a ticker tape invested life savings in securities, convinced the good times would last forever.

The Coolidge administration's hands-off policy helped spur economic growth. As Allen remarks with characteristic humor, "Almost the most remarkable thing about Coolidge Prosperity was Calvin Coolidge." "Silent Cal" was "a meager-looking man, a Vermonter with a hatchet face, sandy hair, tight lips," whose speeches and autobiography were characterized by "uncompromising unoriginality" (Allen 137, 138). But business gained from Coolidge's belief "that by asserting himself as little as possible and by lifting the tax burdens of the rich he was benefiting the whole country — as perhaps he was" (140).

## Getting and Spending: The Rise of Consumerism

The spectacular growth in business and commerce and the development of technologies geared to mass-market production made available a vast range of consumer goods. In this heightened consumer economy, installment purchases became the norm, enabling ordinary Americans to purchase not just necessities but specialty goods as well. Spending was celebratory: when Henry Ford announced the Model A early in 1928, "500,000 people made down payments without having seen the car and without knowing the price" (Leuchtenburg 187). With consumerism came hype. Ad men switched from extolling a product's virtues to emphasizing its effect on the buyer's looks or status. This new approach to selling products ranging from laundry soap to sporting goods to automobiles suggests a link between spending and the narcissism that underscored much of what people saw on the Broadway musical stage in the 1920s.

## Leisure Time and Leisure Pursuits

In the 1920s, more Americans than ever before had both discretionary income and increased leisure time. World War I and the postwar expansion of the economy created additional jobs for women — ten million of them were at work by 1930. In exchange for the rigors of punching a time clock, the "new woman" enjoyed more independence, more free time, and more money in her purse. Men too, with shorter working hours and bigger paychecks, were also on the lookout for ways to spend their money.

No one had to look far. Even before the talkies appeared in 1927, Hol-

lywood churned out silent films at an incredible rate; "in 1922, movie theatres sold 40 million tickets every week; by 1930, the average weekly attendance was 100 million" (Leuchtenburg 196). By 1922, three million homes
had radios and "the sale of sets was already a $60 million industry. Seven
years later $852 million worth of radio sets were sold" (196). With a speak-
easy on nearly every city block, Prohibition made alcohol not just enticingly
illegal but extremely easy to find (if in varying degrees of toxicity).

Both participatory and spectator sports caught the public imagination as
never before. Golf had far and away the most participants—an estimated
two million, playing on five thousand golf courses around the United States
and spending about half a billion dollars annually on the game (Allen 156).
Along with country clubs, "[t]ennis clubs were multiplying" (60). And those
who didn't play sports watched—baseball, boxing, horseracing, but, beyond
all the rest, college football. According to Allen, "More Americans could
identify Knute Rockne as the Notre Dame coach than could tell who was
the presiding officer of the United States Senate" (156–57), and Leuchtenburg notes that by the end of the 1920's "college football had become a
major industry, with gate receipts each year of over $21 million" (195). So
had boxing. When 91,000 spectators watched Jack Dempsey knock out
"Gorgeous" Georges Carpentier in the fourth round at Jersey City on July
2, 1921, "the country had seen the first 'million dollar gate'" (195).
Horseracing, always popular with a certain set, gained a much greater following thanks to Man o' War's victories in 1920 (Allen 60). In baseball,
Babe Ruth became a national hero, and by 1925 the World Series began to
see record-breaking crowds (156).

Even things that weren't spectator sports came to resemble them in the
thrill-seeking '20s: the sensational Hall-Mills murder trial of 1922; the Sacco
and Vanzetti case, which lingered from their arrests in 1920 to their exe-
cutions in 1927; Clarence Darrow and William Jennings Bryan going head
to head in the 1925 Scopes trial; Lucky Lindy making his nonstop hop from
Long Island to Paris in 1927. Such events held the public captive with good
reason: "Genuine public issues, about which the masses of the population
could be induced to feel intensely, were few and far between" (Allen 142).
Moreover, as early as Harding's inauguration in 1921, "[t]he nation was spiritually tired. . . . Sick of Wilson and his talk of America's duty to humanity,
. . . they hoped for a chance to pursue their private affairs without governmental interference and to forget about public affairs" (Allen 94).

Allen concluded that while most sensational events that caught the public's attention "were quite unimportant from the traditional point of view
of the historian," nevertheless "that such things could engage the hopes and
fears of unprecedented numbers of people was anything but unimportant"

(141). " 'Happy,' they might have said, 'is the nation which has no history — and a lot of good shows to watch' " (142). Falling in with that mood, Broadway gave people what they wanted: well-packaged, upbeat entertainment.

### Prosperous Broadway

The 1920s were boom-time on Broadway. In the words of one theatre historian,

> After the Armistice of 1918, the pleasure-seeking, prohibition-despising, boom-rich American public enabled the musical theatre to revel in a decade of luxury and wastefulness and irresponsibility such as it had never known before and will probably never know again in our time. Money was available to produce anything with the slightest prospect of success, and audiences were lenient, easily amused, and generous with their patronage. . . . [P]eople were making money faster than they could spend it. . . . For one mad, magical decade, the Broadway theatre could afford to produce as many musical shows as it wanted to, and to market them at box-office prices that the audience could pay without feeling any pinch. (Smith 125)

Indeed, from the season of 1919–20 to 1929–30, Broadway produced a larger total number of musicals than in any other eleven-year period. Single-season figures for new musicals and revues reached heights never again replicated. And, except in 1923–24, more hit shows opened each year than at any other time in the musical's history (see appendix A).

### Mirroring the Audience

Except for a few shows that in small ways spoke to current events, trends, or issues, in the 1920s the sole purpose (other than making money) of virtually all musicals in relation to their audiences was diversionary entertainment. The production of book musicals was unique, since from 1924 to 1929 operetta and musical comedy peacefully co-existed as crowd pleasers on Broadway. Operettas (principally by Sigmund Romberg and Rudolf Friml) continued to be set in exotic locales, removing audiences from familiar settings into realms of make-believe. But musical comedies, set mainly in the contemporary United States and featuring mostly Tin Pan Alley–type music, mirrored their audiences' lifestyles and the good-time spirit of the decade. While these shows were pure entertainment, they also reflected the audiences' quality of life in the Roaring Twenties. Since Broadway theatregoers then — at least those in the best orchestra seats — were prosperous and pleasure-seeking, what they mostly saw looking back at them from the musical stage were the cheeriest aspects of their own daily lives.

### Topical Shows: Prohibition, Bootlegging, and the "Florida Musicals"

In the '20s, the treatment of even potentially serious issues was more often playful than satirical. Revues began taking potshots at Prohibition even before the Eighteenth Amendment went into effect on January 16, 1920. In the *Ziegfeld Follies of 1919* (6/19/19) Bert Williams sang two songs lamenting the coming dry spell and happily suggesting ways to circumvent it: Irving Berlin's "You Cannot Make Your Shimmy Shake on Tea," and "The Moon Shines on the Moonshine" with lyrics by Howard Rogers and music by Robert Hood Bowers. In John Murray Anderson's *Greenwich Village Follies* (7/15/19), Bessie McCoy Davis sang "I'm the Hostess of a Bum Cabaret"; and in *Scandals of 1920* (6/7/20), George White's annual before he began attaching his name to it, a comic dialogue sketch set in an airship spoofed Prohibition (Bordman 341, 350).

Once the public learned to cope with it as a fact of life, Prohibition became a source of fun in book musicals. Regarding *Oh, Kay!* (11/8/26), with music and lyrics by George and Ira Gershwin and a book by Guy Bolton and P. G. Wodehouse, Gerald Bordman's words are apt: "The story *had a good time* with Prohibition and bootlegging" (418; italics supplied). The show's story of a dead-broke duke who has "turned to rum-running to keep in pocket money" (418) took a back seat to some Gershwin songs destined for immortality, including "Maybe," "Do, Do, Do," "Dear Little Girl," "Clap Yo' Hands," and the classic "Someone to Watch Over Me." Audiences for *Oh, Kay!* had fun circumventing Prohibition 256 times. The only other '20s book show with Prohibition central to its plot was *Bye, Bye Bonnie* (1/13/27). It ran just 125 performances, most likely because Albert Von Tilzer's score was fairly pedestrian and the show's Cinderella storyline had become equally so by 1927. Bonnie is secretary to teetotaling Noah Shrivell of Shrivell Soft Soap. When he is jailed for "buying booze for his customers," Bonnie helps free him and get him elected to Congress as an anti-Prohibition candidate. Bonnie and her boss thus actually take advantage of Prohibition to rise socially, politically, and financially.

Except for Prohibition, the only national issue that became the stuff of Broadway book musicals in the 1920s was the Florida land boom of 1925. In the mid-'20s, South Florida experienced "the most delirious fever of real-estate speculation" the United States had seen in ninety years. Miami grew from a population of 30,000 in 1920 to 75,000 in 1925, when it became "one frenzied real-estate exchange. There were said to be 2,000 real-estate offices and 25,000 agents marketing house-lots or acreage" (Allen 205, 206). This came about in part because "not only the man of wealth, who headed for Palm Beach and Boca Raton, but the man of moderate income decided to winter in Florida" (Leuchtenburg 184). It was not the deflating land values but two massive hurricanes that made the land boom go bust in 1926. Nonetheless, "resorts were strung from Jacksonville to Key West" (184), and the lure of South Florida as a vacation (and, later, retirement) spot would stay.

While the Florida land grab filled the headlines and fed the fantasies of Americans seeking cheap land in a balmy clime, Broadway launched three "Florida musicals" late in 1925. Of the three, two simply capitalized on this latest public mania by making Florida the setting for plots that could have taken place anywhere. *Florida Girl* (11/2/25) was a sort of musical comedy thriller that starred Vivienne Segal as Daphne, a woman detraining in Coral Gables while unaware that there were smuggled diamonds in her shoe. From there, for forty performances, the show became a convoluted chase to recover the diamonds and, presumably, Daphne's shoe (Bordman 406). Except for its potential audience appeal, the Florida locale was equally irrelevant to *Tip-Toes* (12/28/25), but Guy Bolton and Fred Thompson's book and George and Ira Gershwin's music and lyrics kept it playing 194 times. The story dealt with a vaudeville trio stranded in Palm Beach, but the simple and irrelevant plot (see Bordman 408) could as easily have taken place in Pocatello, Idaho.

Only the Florida musical sandwiched between these two was about the frenzy of land speculation — sort of. What it was *really* about was a lot of hilarious silliness. *The Cocoanuts* (12/2/25) was "two and a half hours of nonsense Irving Berlin and George S. Kaufman (aided, without public credit, by Morrie Ryskind) provided for the Marx Brothers . . . with Groucho as a rapacious, unethical Florida hotel owner and real estate developer" (Bordman 408). The musical's plot is too labyrinthine to recount, but Berlin provided some "Florida-based" songs: "Florida by the Sea," "A Little Bungalow," and "Monkey-Doodle-Doo." Of the three Florida shows, *The Cocoanuts* ran longest: 377 performances.

### The Cinderella Shows

The numbers say it all: out of some 463 musicals and revues over eleven theatre seasons, just five book shows (that's 1.08 percent) took as even their tangential context a specific national issue or event of social, political, or economic significance. These miniscule numbers and percentages reinforce

Leuchtenburg's conclusion that the decade's interest in politics was "at its lowest ebb" in fifty years (81), and Allen's observation that what was significant and fascinating about 1920s America was its fascination with the insignificant. Eschewing explicit topicality, far more shows picked up on broader trends in American society for their plots or settings. While such shows were intended and attended as diversionary entertainment, their inclusion of so much that was familiar in the daily lives of audiences may very well have helped account for their popularity.

Most musical comedies continued the boy meets girl, boy loses girl, boy gets girl back formula popularized by George M. Cohan earlier in the century—but with a decidedly '20s spin. In the "Cinderella musicals" of the early 1920s, a working-class girl (almost always Irish-American!) works as a maid, shop girl, or secretary. Through marriage and/or good business sense, she ultimately obtains not only the man of her dreams but wealth and elevated social status. In a few shows, she achieves theatrical stardom as well. The 1920s spin is the gender of the protagonist, reflecting the increasing number of women entering America's workforce. The storyline also differs from the prewar Euro-title musicals in which a girl rejects not just aristocracy but wealth in favor of a poor but honest American boy. Our '20s heroines almost always go for the gold as well as the guy (frequently synonymous). And the "Irishness" of most of these female protagonists suggests that the Cinderella musicals let recent immigrants see that they too could make it in America.

All but one Cinderella show was named for the protagonist, proclaiming the era's focus on "the new woman." Cinderella's rise from rags to riches got off to a roaring start with Harry Tierney and Joseph McCarthy's *Irene* (11/18/19), the runaway hit of 1919–20 that gave the world the timeless "Alice Blue Gown" and ran for 670 performances. The title character is "poor shop girl" Irene O'Dare (Bordman 345), who goes from running an errand at the Marshalls' Long Island estate to falling in love with their son Donald; he in turn gets her work as a fashion model and, once both the O'Dares and the Marshalls lay aside their prejudices about mingling social classes, marries her. That, in a word, became the plot pattern of the ensuing Cinderella shows. *Irene*'s immediate successor, *Mary* (10/18/20), played a solid 219 performances and was another of "the best loved and best remembered of the decade's shows" (Bordman 355), mostly for its Louis Hirsch score, featuring the hit song "The Love Nest," and George M. Cohan's fast-paced direction and choreography (Cohan did not write the show). Mary is secretary to the mother of Jack Keene, a young man who dreams of building affordable "portable houses" in Kansas. Jack's scheme fails, but he returns east to Mary, who has been fending off a slew of suitors, announcing that oil was discovered on his land; in the end Mary happily marries Jack and his money.

Though the run of *Sally* (12/21/20) fell short of *Irene*'s by precisely one hundred performances, the show was still a triumph, both for its Cinderella title character and its impressive artistic and production team. Produced by Florenz Ziegfeld with sets by Joseph Urban, *Sally* boasted a book by Guy Bolton, ballet music by Victor Herbert, a score by Jerome Kern (most remembered for "Look for the Silver Lining"), and a cast that featured Leon Errol, Walter Catlett, and "the entrancing Marilyn Miller as Sally" (Bordman 356). Sally begins as a poor dishwasher at the Elm Tree Alley Inn in Greenwich Village, where she meets Blair Farquar, "scion of the Long Island Farquars." She turns out to be a remarkable dancer, and by the end of the show Sally has become not just Mrs. Blair Farquar but (in a bit of self-promotion by Ziegfeld) a star of the *Ziegfeld Follies*.

These three hits led off the Cinderella cavalcade, but the parade of similar shows marched along for another three years or so. *The O'Brien Girl* (10/3/21) is "sweet little Irish stenographer Alice O'Brien . . . who receive[s] a windfall of $800" that she blows on a vacation in the Adirondacks, where she magically meets and gets engaged to her own Prince Charming—164 times (Bordman 366). *Good Morning, Dearie* (11/1/21), assisted by a Jerome Kern score, was a 265-performance hit. "Society's" Billy Van Cortlandt falls in love with working-class couturiere's assistant Rose-Marie and, after appropriate complications, marries her. Unlike her Cinderella predecessors who married into wealth, the title character of *The Gingham Girl* (8/28/22) shows the enterprising spunk of the new '20s "working girl." John Cousins leaves Mary Thompson, literally a "gingham-garbed girl," in smalltown New Hampshire to seek success in New York. Fearing she will lose him to big-city philandering, she follows. But, more importantly, like a musical comedy prototype of Mrs. Fields, Mary starts up and runs a big, moneymaking cookie company. This time, the young man comes back to the girl and *her* dough (372). Audiences admired Mary's pluck an impressive 422 times.

If *The Gingham Girl*'s self-starting heroine was forward looking, George M. Cohan's *Little Nellie Kelly* (11/13/22) was something of a throwback, as might be expected of a show so comparatively late in Cohan's career. Nellie, a department store clerk and police captain's daughter, rejects wealthy Jack Lloyd in favor of the "simple wise-cracking Irish ways" of Jerry Conroy. On that point Bordman says it all: "In the glittering twenties, when prosperity made material acquisitions more readily obtainable and clever advertising made them universally desired, Cohan often held to the earlier American dream that love outweighed riches" (376). Throwback or not, the show ran 274 performances.

*Glory* (12/25/22) wasn't so lucky. The "daughter of the village ne'er-do-well"—whose name really is Glory and, unlike the other Cinderellas, who seems to be unemployed—finds love, marriage, and money when a former town resident who made good in the city returns, falls in love with her, and helps her win "a popularity contest" (377), which the show's sixty-four performances failed to do. Not even Noble Sissle and Eubie Blake's songs could save *Elsie* (4/2/23) from theatrical oblivion after forty showings, its by now predictable story that of a struggling young actress "winning the acceptance of Harry Hammond's rich, snobbish family" (378). Nor could that stellar operetta composer Rudolf Friml do any better for *Cinders* (4/3/23; thirty-one performances). Starting with its title, *Cinders* traded most directly on the fairy tale. Cinders is a waif "who was discovered in an ash can and who has grown up dreaming of being a jazz-age Cinderella" (378). She is sent to deliver a gown to a wealthy woman but absconds with it so she can crash a charity ball, where she meets that very woman's son; they fall in love and . . . you know the rest.

The silliest Cinderella show title has to be *Helen of Troy, New York* (6/19/23), but then the book was by two of the cleverest, sometimes silliest, playwrights of the period, George S. Kaufman and Marc Connelly. This show depicted a woman's ingenuity in the workplace. The latter-day Helen is Helen McGuffey, a stenographer at a shirt-collar factory who gets sacked when the c.e.o. finds out his son is in love with her. Helen goes off and invents a better collar, "which she sells to a rival house. Her former company is forced to merge and she wins the heir apparent" (Bordman 379). The show played 191 times. *Mary Jane McKane* (12/25/23) is another "poor Irish secretary" whose story reads like a shameless rip-off of *Helen of Troy, New York*. Like Helen, Mary Jane "loses her job when her boss's son . . . shows interest in her" and goes "into business with the son when his father fires him" too (383). Despite the tired plot, a refreshing score by relative newcomer Vincent Youmans and a book co-authored by a young Oscar Hammerstein, 2nd kept the show running 151 times. In *The Rise of Rosie O'Reilly* (12/25/23), George M. Cohan tried to blend his favorite marry-for-love and the more up-to-date marry-for-love-*and*-money brands of the Cinderella story, but the show managed only eighty-seven Broadway outings before touring. Rosie sells flowers under the Brooklyn Bridge and falls in love with "Bob Morgan, a wealthy man-about-town." "Papa Morgan cuts Bob off at the pockets" but finally relents. Bob regains his wealth, "though Rosie clearly would have taken Bob even if he had never been restored to his fortune" (Bordman 383; *Best Plays* 23–24 375).

With *Plain Jane* (5/12/24) and its shopworn story of a "tenement waif" and her boyfriend competing with the boy's father's business, the clock struck midnight for the decade's Cinderellas, at least on the musical stage (Bordman 385). But the Cinderella shows had made their point: not just young men but young women of the day were on the make in the world of business as well as romance.

### Leisure-Time Musicals

While the musical comedy Cinderellas were having a ball, their real-life counterparts could afford the comparative luxury of seeing them, thanks to shorter working days and weeks and higher wages. While orchestra seats for evening, and especially weekend, performances were out of reach for shop-girls and secretaries, even such hits as *Hitchy-Koo of 1920* and *Sally* advertised balcony seats for Wednesday and Saturday matinees for as little as fifty cents. Toward the end of the period, tickets to see Marilyn Miller in *Rosalie* and Eddie Cantor in *Whoopee* could be had for just a dollar.

Indeed, the 1920s was one of the last decades of the century when ticket prices rose so slowly that the incomes of working-class and middle-class Americans could more than keep up with them. Indicative are the price scales for two of the biggest hits in 1929. Sigmund Romberg's *The New Moon* and De Sylva, Brown, and Henderson's *Follow Thru* jointly advertised "Evenings at 8:30 — ORCH. (EXCEPT SAT.) $5.50 and $4.50 — BALC. $1 to $4.40," prices not markedly higher than in 1920 (*New York Times*, 26 May 1929). It only stands to reason, then, that from start to finish, '20s musicals periodically celebrated the lifestyles not just of the rich and famous, or even just the rich, but also of the newly affluent and reasonably prosperous kinds of people who made up a large part of these shows' audiences. That some of these celebratory musicals rank among the biggest hits of the 1920s is ample indication that their audiences loved to watch themselves at play.

The world of sport provided the setting or context for most of the "leisure-time musicals," while their plots remained almost invariably the tried-and-true boy-meets-girl formula. And it's hardly an accident that the sports on display in these shows were those that were drawing the biggest crowds in the 1920s, either as spectators or participants. In addition, many of these musicals featured some of the day's biggest stars or had scores by some of the best and brightest composing and writing talent.

The first leisure-time musical, *Honey Girl* (5/3/20), was a show about horseracing with the horse's name as its title. It seems hardly coincidental that it opened the very year Man o' War was breaking track records, capturing the public imagination, and, effectively, turning the "sport of kings" into mass entertainment. Sustained by a strong book and at least serviceable music and lyrics by Albert Von Tilzer and Neville Fleeson, not to mention a race with real horses on treadmills, "*Honey Girl* ran well into the next season" (Bordman 349). Another horserace show, *Red Pepper* (5/29/22) — again named after the horse — barely cleared the starting gate. A vehicle for the routines of blackface duo McIntyre and Heath, the show seemingly had little going for it except a lot of extravagant — extraneous — scenery (371).

It took a while for Broadway to catch up with the public's passion for boxing, which began on Independence Day 1919, when Jack Dempsey knocked out six-foot-six-inch champion Jess Willard at Toledo (Allen 3). Enthusiasm rose to a fever pitch with Dempsey's Jersey City victory over Carpentier in 1921. Only late in 1923 did prizefighting first appear in a Broadway musical, and then in a show that wasn't even wholly American. *Battling Buttler* (10/8/23), a London smash, came to this country in a version rewritten for the United States and starring Charles Ruggles; the show was a knockout, with 288 performances in its initial season and a run extending well into the next (*Best Plays* 23–24 330, 444; Bordman 381).

Horseracing and boxing had more than their share of spectators, but in the '20s golf had the most actual participants. According to Allen, "More men were playing golf than ever before. . . . The ability to play it had become a part of the almost essential equipment of the aspiring business executive. The country club had become the focus of social life in hundreds of communities" (156). With golf no longer just for the rich but becoming the sport of Everyman or at least Everybusinessman, *Kid Boots*, the first golf-and-country-club musical, swung onto the fairway on December 31, 1923. The sumptuous production, guided by Flo Ziegfeld, Mary Eaton's looks, charm, and dancing, and the infectious starring performance of Eddie Cantor, let *Kid Boots* play through the season with 192 performances and continue into the next. Golf's popularity and the popularity of *Kid Boots* help explain *Top-Hole* (9/1/24), another country-club show, opening just nine months after *Kid Boots*. This low-budget musical played 104 times in the small Fulton Theatre (Bordman 390–91).

Then it was off to the races again! Horses and treadmills aside, what really sustained *Big Boy* (1/7/25) was Al Jolson's bravura performance as Gus, the stable boy who rides the title character to a Derby victory. He also finally introduced "California, Here I Come" to Broadway audiences, having first sung it in the 1921 tour of *Bombo*. Whatever the merits of the book or the rest of the score, Jolson alone should have guaranteed a long run, but his poor health forced *Big Boy* to close after forty-eight shows (Bordman 398). Well again, Jolson was back in the saddle on August 24, 1925, for 120 more laps.

A kind of racing that typified the sillier excesses of the Roaring Twenties, the six-day bicycle race was the subject of *The Girl Friend* (3/17/26). The musical had a thin but clever book by Herbert Fields and a totally triumphant score by relative newcomers Richard Rodgers and Lorenz Hart, headlined by the Charleston-inspired title song and what would become the perennially popular anthem to marital bliss, "The Blue Room." And, no, unlike the horseracing shows, the title isn't the name of the hero's bike. It refers to his actual girlfriend and trainer, the pair played by the popular dancing team, real-life husband and wife Sammy White and Eva Puck. With such strong writing and performing talent, *The Girl Friend* was a winner, weathering a slow start at the box office to stay the course for a near sell-out run of 103 performances (Bordman 410–11).

The last four leisure-time shows all had songs by B. G. "Buddy" De Sylva, Lew Brown, and Ray Henderson. With an impressive string of scores for revues and musicals from 1925 to 1930, they were "the only successful long-term three-person collaboration in American musical theatre history" (Jones, "DeSylva" 490). The precise way De Sylva, Brown, and Henderson worked remains a mystery, but each partner so often contributed to every aspect of a song that their "specific credits for lyrics or music were seldom listed" on theatre programs, sheet music, or phonograph records (Green 132). The archetypal college football musical *Good News* (9/6/27) was the first De Sylva, Brown, and Henderson leisure-time show and also their biggest hit, with a run of 557 performances.

Archetypal, too, was *Good News* of the decade's musical comedy style and of the decade's style itself, a quality of the show often remarked on by writers on musicals. "*Good News* was probably the quintessential musical comedy of the 'era of wonderful nonsense.' The decade's jazzy sounds, its assertive, explosive beat, its sophomoric high jinks were joyously mirrored in a hilarious, melody-packed evening" (Bordman 427; see also Smith 151–52; Mordden, *Make Believe* 127–30; Gänzl 183). Operative in Bordman's description is "mirrored," not "spoofed" or "parodied" or "satirized." Earlier, Cecil Smith had erroneously claimed the intention of De Sylva, Brown, and Henderson in all their sporting musicals to be satire, which "[by] refraining from digging very deep into the subjects they treated, . . . managed to avoid alienating any of their patrons" (152). But it was topicality, not satire, that made *Good News* and its three successors so congenial to patrons who recognized and had fun with reflections of themselves (or their college-age offspring) on stage. It also aided these shows' longevity that De Sylva, Brown, and Henderson had an uncanny knack for writing songs that were both immediately popular and destined to become standards. *Good News* alone produced the title song, "Lucky in Love," "Just Imagine," and "The Best Things in Life Are Free." The show-stopping dance number "Varsity

Drag" became "the last popular variation to appear in the period's Charleston craze" (Bordman 428).

The trio had also written the previous Charleston-based dance sensation "Black Bottom," which Ann Pennington premiered in *George White's Scandals of 1926*. The song was a hit, but Pennington's flashy performance sparked the "Black Bottom" dance craze, "which rivaled the Charleston" of several years before (Green 135; Ziegfeld 308). It was the original theatrical choreography of these two De Sylva, Brown, and Henderson song-and-dance numbers that ignited two of the most popular social dance fads among America's youth in the '20s. The third had been "Charleston" from *Runnin' Wild* in 1923.

Popular social dances originating in Broadway dance routines were unique to the Roaring Twenties. The Broadway performances of "Charleston," "Black Bottom," and "Varsity Drag" taught the precise steps, wiggles, shakes, and shimmies that distinguished each dance from the others and made rages of them all. According to choreographer Agnes De Mille, "with them dancing became the property of the young. Anyone over thirty simply could not stand up to the demands of these dances. The older generation just pushed around in a friendly hug and got drunk sitting in cars" (19).

Granted, two of these dances had a long history prior to their Broadway incarnations, but it was a very localized, even parochial, history. "Charleston" and "Black Bottom" originated among urban Southern blacks narrowly and specifically in the coastal regions around Savannah, Charleston, and New Orleans (see Stearns 110–112 for a concise history of both dances). Rarely did these dances get beyond those communities. Just prior to the debut of James P. Johnson and Cecil Mack's still familiar "Charleston" in *Runnin' Wild*, Broadway had heard and seen "The Charleston Dancy" in *Liza* (1922) and "Charleston Cut-Out" in *How Come?* (1923), but neither caught on. It took the specific Johnson/Mack tune as performed by a male chorus called "The Red Caps" to a breathtaking accompaniment of hand-slapping and finger-snapping for the "Charleston" to take off and become the number one dance sensation of the '20s. Conversely, "Varsity Drag" was totally original from tune to choreography to execution; yet it, too, quickly found its way from the stage to America's dance floors.

Two things stand out about this phenomenon. First, Broadway not only launched the popularity of "Charleston" and "Black Bottom" but also implemented the crossover of African American vernacular dance forms to the ballrooms of white America (one via an all-black show, the other via a very mainstream white one). And even after the crossover occurred, black as well as white younger Americans continued to engage in these recreational dances. Second, all three dances reflect a pattern of influence virtually inverse to that in the show choreography of all other periods. If appropriate, Broadway choreographers incorporate in their work popular dance forms of the day, often raising them to a higher level of theatricality or "art"—the most obvious example being Jerome Robbins's dances for the Dance at the Gym sequence in *West Side Story* (1957). Rarely do such dances then return to the recreational dance floor more popular than before because of their theatrical appearances. But the 1920s saw three major dance crazes in just four years go directly from Broadway to ballroom—peculiar, perhaps, but reflective of the period. If Americans of the '20s were the thrillseeking folks the social historians say they were, here was a chance for them to take a piece of theatre home with them.

*Good News* was still playing when De Sylva, Brown, and Henderson traded on the country's passion for boxing in *Hold Everything* (10/10/28). A cast featuring Jack Whiting, Ona Munson, Betty Compton, Victor Moore, and Bert Lahr in the role of a slap-happy pugilist that rocketed him to stardom, along with another strong score with hits like "To Know You Is to Love You" and "You're the Cream in My Coffee" kept the show on its feet for 413 performances (Bordman 443; Green 137). And *Good News* was *still* running when the intrepid trio offered up *Follow Thru* (1/9/29), their musical tribute to golf—billed, in deliciously silly word play, as "A Musical Slice of Country Club Life" (Bordman 447). A rather unusual plot picked up on the trend of women getting into the swing of athletic pastimes. Two young ladies vie for the Bound Brook Country Club's women's championship and for the affection of one particular young man—making the show's story a rare instance of girl meets boy, girl loses boy, girl gets boy back. The cast was not as distinguished as that for *Hold Everything*, but the tap routines of newcomer Eleanor Powell in the minor role of Molly "earned her several encores every night" (447). Highlighting the typically robust De Sylva, Brown, and Henderson score were "[You Are] My Lucky Star" and "Button Up Your Overcoat." All in all, *Follow Thru* had enough going for it to do just that 401 times, driving it well past the stock market crash in late 1929.

The last De Sylva, Brown, and Henderson leisure-time show—in fact the last of their three-way collaborations entirely—*Flying High* (3/30/30) chronologically belongs to the Depression era. But thematically its place is here as the continuation and finale of the trio's musicals about recreational pastimes. Its subject was aviation, a long-time fascination of the American public recently fueled by the exploits of Charles Lindbergh and Amelia Earhart. Despite the increasingly bad news on Wall Street and a less than sparkling De Sylva, Brown, and Henderson score, *Flying High* stayed aloft for 347 performances thanks to the attractive performances of Grace Brinkley and Oscar Shaw as the romantic couple, Kate Smith's show-stopping "Red Hot Chicago," and Bert Lahr's portrayal of an inept airplane mechanic who breaks the world record for time in the air because he doesn't know how to land (Bordman 459; Green 137–39). After *Flying High* the genre of leisure-time musicals came to an end. For too many Americans the Depression meant too much leisure time — not by choice — and too little money.

### Backstage Musicals

The nation's love affair with Broadway climaxed in 1927–28, when about fifty-one musicals were produced, and that was just the tip of the theatrical iceberg. The total number of plays and musicals mounted that season was in the vicinity of three hundred (Brockett 495), a figure never before achieved and never since equaled. With theatrical production and attendance at an all-time high in the 1920s, it's not unreasonable to suggest that such savvy producers as George Lederer, Lew Fields, and Florenz Ziegfeld figured audiences might also want to see plays (and, especially, musicals) *about* the theatre (especially musicals). They and others produced a number of such self-referential show biz shows — generally called "backstage musicals" — but with the advent of the talkies in 1927, the genre was commandeered almost exclusively by Hollywood, only rarely to return to Broadway.

Just as the boy-meets-girl formula was the archetypal musical comedy plot for decades, the "chorus-girl-or-other-unknown-takes-over-for-the-prima-donna-and-becomes-a-star-overnight" story so rapidly and repeatedly became the focus of backstage musicals on both stage and screen as to become a cliché, so much so that in later years it could be successfully parodied in *Dames at Sea* (12/20/68) and made the object of nostalgia in the stage remake of the Warner Brothers' classic 1933 backstage musical *42nd Street* (8/25/80), with Harry Warren's score augmented by his hits from other Hollywood films.

*The Girl in the Spotlight* (7/12/20), produced by George Lederer and with music by Victor Herbert, was the first such show. The title character was Molly Shannon, who lives in the same boarding house as aspiring opera composer Frank Marvin. Molly memorizes Frank's music as she listens to him rehearse it; "[w]hen the leading lady of Marvin's opera refuses to perform, Molly goes on in her place. She becomes a star and Mrs. Marvin" (Bordman 351). The show played only fifty-six times, but the prototypical backstage musical plot was born. *Poor Little Ritz Girl* (7/28/20), produced by Lew Fields, nominally had a score by the fledgling team of Rodgers and

Hart—nominally, since after the Boston tryout Fields scrapped more than half of their songs in favor of numbers by Sigmund Romberg and Alex Gerber. *Ritz Girl* was just marginally a backstage musical, since its focus was on a chorus girl's falling in love with a rich young man whose apartment she had sublet, not on her meteoric rise to stardom. Still, the show gave audiences plenty of chances to see "backstage" scenes of rehearsals and the like for 119 performances.

*Sally*'s rise from dishwasher to Ziegfeld girl has already been noted as a specimen of Cinderella musicals. It was the last show biz show of 1920, the year's biggest hit, and, at 570 performances, one of the decade's longest running musicals. After *Sally* the backstage musical took a nearly five-year intermission, and when it came back, *Merry, Merry* (9/24/25) took an unusual turn. Eve Walters comes to New York to be a chorus girl. (Another part of the archetypal plot, especially in Hollywood, is the fresh, innocent heroine just arrived in New York from some rural locale.) Eve falls in love with Adam Winslow, not wealthy or socially prominent, just a nice ordinary guy. She gives up her theatrical ambitions out of her love for Adam and her disillusionment with show biz because of the "greedy, dishonest attempt of her roommate and fellow chorine Sadi LaSalle . . . to extort money from a stage-door Johnny" (Bordman 406)—a rare triumph of purity and innocence over ambition for this period, and refreshing enough to keep the show open 176 times. Note, too, how in this genre the "good" girls and the "bad" girls can be spotted just by their names, on a scale from simple (Eve Walters) to exotic (Sadi LaSalle).

In that tradition, devious burlesque diva Violet Wilding and her partner Jacob Perlstein hoodwink George Weston into backing a hopeless Broadway musical in *Footlights* (8/19/27). George loses his cash but also loses his heart to sweet Hazel Deane, a minor player in the show, and together they leave the wicked city for George's hometown (Bordman 427). The backstage setting was a flimsy excuse for "the crudest form of burlesque" and "cheap vaudeville" acts that filled over half the evening. *Footlights* went dark after forty-three nights. Another "excuse for variety turns"—and a thirty-one-show flop—was *White Lights* (10/11/27), which returned to the standard backstage formula, showing how "a society girl named Polly Page" defies both parents and corrupt managers to become a nightclub star, and, of course, to marry the man of her dreams (431).

Finally, Ziegfeld tried one last backstage musical as Hollywood was on the brink of virtually monopolizing the genre. Typical of The Great Ziegfeld, the lineup of writers and performers for *Show Girl* (7/2/29) was remarkable. George and Ira Gershwin did the score, with additional lyrics by Gus Kahn. Dixie Dugan, "a harder, pushier young lady" than Sally, whose rise from "pretty unknown" to "Ziegfeld stardom" the plot depicted, was the soon to be legendary Ruby Keeler. The cast also featured Harriet Hoctor, Eddie Foy Jr., and Clayton, Jackson, and [Jimmy] Durante. In the pit, no less, was Duke Ellington and his orchestra. No one could ever accuse Ziegfeld of doing things by halves. But for all it had going for it, *Show Girl* managed only 111 performances (Bordman 452–53).

Overall, the backstage musical was not especially successful on stage. Yet with the advent of sound in *The Jazz Singer* in 1927 and throughout the 1930s, show biz sagas were a popular and profitable motion picture genre. Perhaps the Broadway stage was just too familiar to New Yorkers for them to be intrigued by the supposed machinations of theatrical life, whereas folks across the country (many of whom would never get closer to Broadway than in a movie) were spellbound by what they took to be the glitter, romance, and even gutsy wheeling and dealing of the theatre world as dished up to them by Hollywood.

### Black Musicals

Along with farmers, the vast majority of African Americans did not reap the fruits of Coolidge Prosperity. For blacks in the entertainment field, however, the African American musicals of the 1920s produced some positive changes in employment and income, and, for black audience members, more equal treatment with whites. After almost a decade-long absence from Broadway (see Woll, chapter 4), black shows returned in strength starting in 1921, something the theatre world took immediate notice of. Even before the real rush of black revues and musicals starting later that year, when the *Ziegfeld Follies of 1922* opened on June 5, Gilda Gray introduced "It's Getting Dark on Old Broadway," a song not, as Richard and Paulette Ziegfeld would have it, about blacks "moving beyond Harlem and closer to Broadway" (254), but about the proliferation of black entertainment in midtown:

> Pretty choc'late ladies
> Shake and shimmie ev'rywhere
> Real dark-town entertainers hold the stage,
> You must black up to be the latest rage.
>
> Yes, the great white way is white no more,
> It's just like a street on the Swanee shore.
> It's getting very dark on old Broadway.
>                         (qtd. in Woll 76)

The pioneering *Shuffle Along* (5/23/21) was, for good *and* ill, the most influential show both written and performed by blacks in the early decades of the twentieth century. And, with its run of 504 performances, it was also the most successful. Black shows created as well as played by blacks have been few. In fact, since the late 1920s, with only occasional exceptions, most musicals and revues tailored for African American performers have been written by whites. Still, most of these white-written shows for all-black or predominantly black casts gave African American performers both employment and the chance to play realistic, non-stereotypical characters. The list of such shows is distinguished and long, from *Porgy and Bess* (1935) and *Cabin in the Sky* (1940) in the earlier years to *Dreamgirls* (1981) and *Once on This Island* (1990) later in the century.

*Shuffle Along*'s Flournoy Miller and Aubrey Lyles wrote the book (and played the leads), Eubie Blake the music, and Noble Sissle the lyrics. In the *chorus* were future greats Adelaide Hall, Josephine Baker, and Paul Robeson! But the producers who took the risk of this black show almost on Broadway were white (see Woll chapter 5 for a full production history). "Almost" on Broadway, since *Shuffle Along* was booked into the 63rd Street Theatre, only marginally in the theatre district. With typical wit and a lot of pride, Eubie Blake later explained, "It was really off-Broadway, but we caused it to be Broadway. . . . It was the price of the ticket that mattered. Our tickets cost the same as any Broadway show. That made it Broadway!" (qtd. in Woll 62).

Nearly all the critics loved the show, although they largely ignored its most enduring number, "I'm Just Wild About Harry." They mostly praised other numbers in Blake and Sissle's up-to-the-minute score, especially the title song, "In Honeysuckle Time," "I'm Craving for That Kind of Love," and, rather remarkably, "Love Will Find a Way." Not remarkable because "Love Will Find a Way" isn't worthy of praise—it is, as arguably one of the most gorgeous love duets in the entire Broadway canon—but remarkable because the song was a sincere love song performed by persons of color, an occurrence up to that time virtually taboo. Previously, love songs sung by blacks had to be comic or parodic for white acceptance. Here a romantic love song between blacks was made riskier yet as the first-act closer! But the audience returned after intermission. Blake's reaction to the first-nighters' enthusiasm is poignant: "The proudest day of my life was when *Shuffle Along* opened. At the intermission all those white people kept saying: 'I would like to touch him, the man who wrote the music.' Well, you got to feel that. It made me feel like, well, at last I'm a human being" (qtd. in Woll 62–63).

If Blake had his emotional side, he had his analytical side as well. He was a composer with real savvy who knew how to write a theatre score for audiences of any color:

The successful song writer of today must be something more than a mere juggler of harmonious sounds. He must be a student of what the public wants—a sort of psychologist. The mushy, sobby, sentimental love songs of twenty or more years ago would not be at all popular today. Nor would the semi-martial music of songs popular during the United States' participation in the war make a hit now. What the public wants today are lively, jazzy songs, not too jazzy, with love interest, but without the sickly sentimentality of a generation ago. (qtd. in Woll 69–70)

Blake and Co.'s musical comedy made history in several ways. Most obviously, since black musicals were usually large-cast shows, *Shuffle Along* and its successors provided steady, well-paying work for large numbers of African American performers on the mainstream New York stage. This employment afforded a real opportunity for numerous blacks to achieve true recognition, even stardom, in a theatre world dominated by whites both on stage and in the audience. Further, the success of *Shuffle Along* "legitimized the black musical. It proved to [white] producers and theatre managers that audiences would pay to see black talent on Broadway. As a result, *Shuffle Along* spawned a series of imitators, and black musicals became a Broadway staple" (Woll 59). And audiences were paying the same top dollar ($3.00) for the best seats to black shows as they were for other musicals.

Show business employment and recognition for African Americans aside, *Shuffle Along* had its most significant social impact on the other side of the footlights. Six months into the run, by *Variety*'s sampling in November 1921, 90 percent of the audience was still white, but, dramatically, on opening night "colored patrons were noticed as far front as the fifth row" (qtd. in Woll 72). *Shuffle Along* had broken the color barrier and "marked the beginning of the end of segregation in New York's legitimate theatres. With each succeeding black show produced during the 1920s, seating restrictions gradually disappeared" (Woll 73). As with all New York shows, the box office for *Shuffle Along* "controlled the seating patterns," but no longer were persons of color confined to the balcony: "Two-thirds of the orchestra was reserved for whites, and blacks were seated in the remaining third" (72).

Still, for all its positive effects, *Shuffle Along* unfortunately continued to depict blacks as comical, mostly negative caricatures. Except for breaking the love song taboo,

Its comedy of malapropisms and black chicanery tended to reinforce existing stereotypes rather than change them. Thus as *Shuffle Along* became the model for all black musicals of the 1920s, it also set certain boundaries as well. Any show that followed the characteristics of *Shuffle Along* could usually be assured of favorable reviews or at least a modest audience response. Yet, if a show strayed from what had become the standard formula for the black musical disastrous reviews became almost inevitable. . . . [I]n the 1920s . . . black authors and composers prepared shows within extremely narrow constraints. (Woll 78)

Once again, here are the lingering influences of minstrel shows, even those written and performed by blacks. The only significant differences were that by the 1920s most male performers no longer wore blackface — though Miller and Lyles continued to black up throughout their careers — and women played more leading roles.

Allen Woll's remarks are more than born out by *Deep Harlem* (1/7/29), a sort of revue of "black history from Africa, to American slavery, to Harlem" (Woll 129) that was the only black-written musical with totally authentic and serious content throughout; it "opened on Monday and folded on Saturday" (Bordman 447). And yet, while more "conventional" black shows proliferated, none came near the mark of success set by *Shuffle Along* either in quality or length of run, including another by Sissle and Blake themselves. In just the three years following *Shuffle Along*'s triumph, New York saw *Put and Take* (1921); *Strut Miss Lizzie, Plantation Revue, Oh Joy!,* and *Liza* (all in 1922); *How Come?* and *Runnin' Wild* (1923); and *The Chocolate Dandies* (1924), a Blake and Sissle effort that ran just ninety-six performances. Many of the same critics who had faulted only the rather shabby sets and costumes in *Shuffle Along* (see Woll 71) complained that *The Chocolate Dandies* was too lavishly mounted (Bordman 391), suggesting a racially biased view that black shows *should* in fact be shabby and not try to emulate white Broadway's scenic opulence. Of the remaining shows in this spate of black musicals, only two were even moderate hits, the rest running a month or so at best. With 169 performances, *Liza* was the most successful black show of 1922–23, and *Runnin' Wild*'s 213 performances in 1923–24 made it a hit by anybody's standards at the time (*Best Plays 23–24* 446).

No black musicals opened in 1925, but they returned in force with *My Magnolia* in 1926; *Bottomland, Africana,* and *Rang Tang* in 1927; and *Keep Shufflin'*, another Miller and Lyles show, in 1928. In this same period, to the great benefit of black actors' employment and positive images of African Americans for white audiences, there appeared a series of quite remarkable non-musical plays written by prestigious white playwrights specifically for all-black or mostly black casts. Only the production of the first of these, Edward Sheldon and Charles MacArthur's *Lulu Belle* (1925), was a bit peculiar. The arguably brilliant but equally quirky producer/director David Belasco cast persons of color in all the supporting roles but had prominent white actors in blackface playing the leads in this tale of a Harlem prostitute (Mordden, *Make Believe* 137). But in the three far greater plays to follow, racial identity was preserved, as was respect for the dignity of blacks as individuated human beings, not racial stereotypes. All large-cast and long-running plays, Paul Green's *In Abraham's Bosom* (1926), DuBose and Dorothy Heyward's *Porgy* (1927), and Marc Connelly's *The Green Pastures* (1930) marked the first sustained opportunity for numerous non-singing black actors to perform on Broadway, but the way had surely been paved for their acceptance by the black musicals that came before.

As salutary as they were in employing black actors and allowing them to portray fully realized characters, these white-written plays were harbingers of a change that, with few exceptions, would forever alter the artistic autonomy of black revues and musicals. From the outset most producers of such shows had been Caucasian, but the books, revue sketches, lyrics, and music had nearly all been by African Americans. But as Woll astutely observes, "[I]t became increasingly difficult to mount new black musicals without the support of the traditional financial methods for Broadway shows. One consequence of black artists losing financial control would be the loss of creative control" (78).

That is precisely what began to happen with *Plantation Revue* in 1922, continued with *Dixie to Broadway* (10/29/24), and became virtually the norm with the phenomenal success of *Blackbirds of 1928* (5/9/28), all thanks to the backing and personal vision of white Jewish producer/director Lew Leslie, a man whose name is almost synonymous with the black revue in the late '20s and '30s. As early as *Plantation Revue*, Leslie had the white team of Roy Turk and Russell Robinson write the score. In *Dixie to Broadway* the sketches were by Walter De Leon, Tom Howard, Sidney Lazarus, and Leslie himself, with music and lyrics by George W. Meyer, Arthur Johnston, Grant Clark, and Turk again — all Caucasians. Headlining the all-white creative efforts of Leslie's *Blackbirds of 1928* were the dazzling lyrics and music of Broadway newcomers Dorothy Fields and Jimmy McHugh, who sang and danced the revue through a spectacular 518 performances and produced two standards, "Diga Diga Doo" and "I Can't Give You Anything but Love" (Bordman 438–39). While Leslie was giving black talent plenty of chances to perform (boasting "a full hundred" in the company of *Blackbirds* alone [Mordden, *Make Believe* 143]), opportunities for black writers and composers decreased to less than few and far between.

Only once did Leslie hire a black composer and lyricist, in the persons of Eubie Blake and Andy Razaf. They wrote most of the score for Leslie's first revue in the tradition of the self-proclaiming nomenclature of Florenz Ziegfeld, Earl Carroll, and George White — *Lew Leslie's Blackbirds* (10/22/

30). Why Leslie otherwise hired white creative talent rose from his vision as a self-styled expert on the relative writing abilities of whites and blacks. His fundamental creed, proclaimed in the early 1930s, was that white song-writers "understand the colored man better than he does himself. Colored composers excel at spirituals, but their other songs are just 'what' [white] songs with Negro words. The two greatest Negro songs now sung were written by white men—'Ol' Man River' and 'That's Why Darkies Were Born'" (qtd. in Woll 97). Leslie went on to pontificate about white expec-tations of black shows: "Americans think of Negro revues in terms of fast dancing and swing songs. They seem to prefer the traditional Negro co-median with the burnt cork make-up, big shoes and a razor, who plays craps and steals chickens" (124–25).

Because of such remarks, it's difficult to agree with popular arts writer Ethan Mordden that the Jewish Leslie mounting so many all-black shows was "a case of the minorities advancing each other's cause" (143). Although Leslie's revues depicted Northern urban blacks, much of the humor came from variations on such timeless (by then, one would think, timeworn) sketches as the timid "darky" spooked in a graveyard, the razor-toting sharper at a craps game, and chicken-stealing. In the 1920s, Harlem's population continued to swell from the continuing northern migration of Southern blacks that began before the turn of the century. Further, the New York black community was defining its own cultural identity. Accordingly, Les-lie's "nonthreatening images" (Toll 42) of blacks would have had the same comforting effect for white audiences in the '20s and '30s as they had in the days of minstrelsy, allaying fears of a vigorous black community just uptown.


## Show Boat

Oscar Hammerstein, 2nd and Jerome Kern challenged white audiences by writing a mixed-cast musical in which African American performers played three-dimensional, sympathetic characters. This "breaking of the rules," along with its other singular features of form and themes, made *Show Boat* (12/27/27) the one musical of the 1920s that qualifies as serious entertain-ment—entertainment with a mission. *Show Boat's* innovations also in time made it a major influence on the form of future book musicals as well as a classic in the canon of American musical theatre. Even today, *Show Boat* remains a model of the quality composers and librettists can produce when they look upon their work as true theatre, even art, not just as a property for making money.

As with most breakthroughs and classics, the true greatness of *Show Boat* was only recognized over time, yet the dean of *New York Times* critics, Brooks Atkinson, in a Sunday review on January 18, 1928, clearly foresaw the show's future status by referring to it as "one of those epochal works." The unsigned writer of the opening night review in the *Times* was a bit more loquacious, saying that *Show Boat* has "about every ingredient that the perfect-song-and-dance confection should have," but then going on to state, somewhat negatively, that the show is "crammed with plot which simply must be explained," so that "exposition slowed down the first few scenes."

What the *Times* critic must have meant was "incident," not "plot," since Hammerstein trimmed the sweeping, decades-long narrative of Edna Ferber's novel down to a few relatively simple storylines. In fact, the main plot of Magnolia and Ravenal is simplicity itself. In the 1880s, riverboat gambler Gaylord Ravenal meets and falls in love with Magnolia, daughter of Parthy Ann and Cap'n Andy Hawkes, skipper of the show boat *Cotton Blossom*. Magnolia and Gaylord marry, have a daughter named Kim, and, several years later, swamped by gambling debts, Ravenal leaves his wife and child. Magnolia and, subsequently, Kim make show business careers for themselves, and in the final scene set in 1927 (not in the novel) the elderly Magnolia and Gaylord fortuitously and implausibly meet for a final embrace, most likely Hammerstein's contrivance to appease contemporary sensibilities demanding some sort of "musical comedy" happy ending.

The secondary, less conventional plot concerns the downward slide of Julie, a woman of mixed race victimized by society and, ultimately, by her own self-destructive inclinations. The third story is purely the stuff of musical comedy fluff: Frank and Ellie, the *Cotton Blossom*'s song and dance team, are happily in love, happily married, and happily find a new career in vaudeville when the days of the show boats are no more (see Kreuger 28–48 for a *minute* scene-by-scene summary). All these goings-on of the white characters are set against the lives of Queenie, Joe, and the other blacks. They, like "Ol' Man River" himself, provide a kind of resigned, stable grounding and anchor for the lives of the whites that always seem to be in turmoil and in flux. Like William Faulkner's Dilsey in *The Sound and the Fury*, it can be said of *Show Boat*'s blacks that "They endured."

Whether audiences recognized the serious intent of the show or simply saw a lavish Ziegfeld-produced extravaganza is impossible to know. Ziegfeld's own posters called *Show Boat* a musical comedy, and the daily *Times* reviewer used that term at least twice. Brooks Atkinson gave *Show Boat* the more fitting label "musical play." Audiences so taken with the alternately lush and playful Kern/Hammerstein score may have barely noticed that this musical dared to dramatize serious social issues from miscegenation to compulsive gambling to spousal desertion. Further, these issues force crises that Hammerstein skillfully condensed from Ferber's epic novel into the narrower confines of a musical play.

Ravenal's gambling addiction drives the story of him and Magnolia. His habit causes him to leave her for long periods, until finally, in act 2, scene 2, Magnolia discovers he has left her for good. In this, the main plot, two serious issues work in a causal relationship: Ravenal's compulsive gambling has resulted in debts so profound that deserting his wife and child seems the only solution.

But *Show Boat*'s depiction of an antagonistic world goes much farther than this. In the principal subplot, the fortunes of Julie and her husband Steve, the leading lady and man on the *Cotton Blossom*, begin their downward turn in the very first scene. Steve, a jealous and protective husband, scuffles with Pete for making advances on his wife. By scene 3, Pete is out for revenge, openly asking Frank whether it's illegal "in this state for a white man to be married to a nigger wench" (qtd. in Kreuger 32). The seemingly white Julie in fact has an unspecified degree of African American blood, in those days making her marriage to the Caucasian Steve enough for a miscegenation case in the South. Things come to a head in scene 4, when Steve and Julie escape arrest only by a highly theatrical ruse: he cuts her and swallows some of her blood. Steve can thus declare in front of witnesses that he's a man "that's got Negro blood in him" (qtd. in Kreuger 35). Nevertheless, fearing retaliation directed at the *Cotton Blossom*, Steve and Julie pack up and leave the showboat. Sometime later, Steve deserts Julie and disappears from the play. But years later Julie reappears, much changed from her former self. While Hammerstein considerably softened her "ultimate degradation as a lady of the streets" in the novel (Bordman 434), she is still very much on the skids. In act 2, scene 3, Julie appears as a washed-up singer rehearsing in a Chicago nightclub, "considerably older and sadly worn . . . wearing too much make-up, and her hair . . . dyed red," periodically taking "a drink from a pint flask she keeps in her handbag" (Kreuger 43–44). In Julie's story, Hammerstein has embedded three social issues: racial bigotry, spousal desertion, and alcoholism.

The way the two plots handle spousal desertion is of special interest. Mixed-race Julie just gives up. Clearly quite dependent, she had identified herself entirely in terms of her man and becomes hopelessly lost without him—a sadly perfect scenario for the character who sings "Can't Help Lovin' Dat Man" in act 1 and "Bill" in her only second act appearance. White Magnolia, on the other hand, is not only a survivor but, as Atkinson observed, one of the first characters, if not *the* first, in an American musical to grow, mature, and strengthen as the exigencies of the plot make demands upon her. It could be argued that *Show Boat* depicts the white woman as a strong survivor and the mixed-race woman as a self-destructive victim, but it is more plausible to think that Hammerstein, always a liberal thinker, is condemning not Julie but the society that ostracizes her. Magnolia, on the other hand, becomes a successful entertainer and raises Kim to be a successful performer herself—all without a man around the house.

In addition to tackling serious issues like bigotry, spousal desertion, and alcoholism, *Show Boat* was the first large-scale, successful integrated musical on Broadway. Jerome Kern finally realized his ideal—begun over a decade earlier in the Princess Theatre Shows—of creating a musical in which song and dialogue work together to reveal the characters and tell their story (see chapter 1). Only a critic with Brooks Atkinson's sharp eye and sense of theatre history could have seen that something important was happening and praise Kern for it: "In providing 'Show Boat' with a full complement of 'song hits' Mr. Kern has not violated his sense of the fitness of things." While indeed *Show Boat* is packed with more hits than should probably be legal in a single show—"Ol' Man River," "Make Believe," "Can't Help Lovin' Dat Man," "You Are Love," "Bill," "Why Do I Love You?" and even the novelty number "Life upon the Wicked Stage"—each of these songs, and all the rest in Kern and Hammerstein's bountiful score, is a direct, logical extension of the action or dialogue, divulging aspects of character, furthering character relationships, helping move the story along, or, at the very least, establishing the ambiance of a scene (as in the second act's Columbian Exposition sequence).

For *Show Boat*, Kern collaborated with Oscar Hammerstein, who, in his later career with Richard Rodgers, would virtually "invent" the modern integrated musical. Some of Hammerstein's hallmarks appear as early as *Show Boat*. Just two brief examples: first, Hammerstein (and Kern) understood the magical power of compression that a melody and its lyrics can have for moving a story forward more quickly than dialogue can. Such a "musical scene" occurs in act 1, scene 1 when only a few alternately charming, playful, and sincere stanzas of "Make Believe" are enough for Magnolia and Gaylord to fall in love. Somehow the music makes this love at first sight perfectly plausible. (For Hammerstein's later growth in constructing such a scene, compare "Make Believe" with the full-length "If I Loved You" sequence and its similar placement, to identical effect, in *Carousel*.) Second, as early as *Show Boat* Hammerstein understood the dramatic and emotional power of the reprise. A reprise is simply the repetition of a song after its initial appearance, whether with the original or revised lyrics, and whether sung by the same or different character(s). Historically, reprises most often have been used to beat a song into an audience's consciousness in order to sell sheet music, records, or CDs. While even Hammerstein and Rodgers may be guilty of this in their innumerable reprises of "Some Enchanted Evening" in *South Pacific*, Hammerstein's sense of the theatrical power of the reprise was usually right on the money. An early instance occurs in the often overlooked act 2, scene 4 of *Show Boat* in which Ravenal, after writing his farewell letter to Magnolia, goes to say goodbye to eight-year-old Kim at St. Agatha's Convent School. Offering her an optimistic belief system, Ravenal sings not a new song but, appropriately and poignantly, "Make Believe" with altered lyrics. The dramatic and emotional effect is stunning. An audience cannot help recalling that this is the same song that ignited Magnolia and Ravenal's love. Here he repeats it to their daughter, shortly before deserting both of them. Hence, two critical moments in their lives are powerfully linked by repeating a single song. Miles Kreuger has even noted a kind of chilling irony in this reprise: "When one considers how seriously both Gay and Magnolia have been hurt by the song's philosophy of fantasying as a way to obtain life's goals, it is grimly ironic that Ravenal is now offering the same advice to his own daughter" (45).

There are other ironies about *Show Boat* as well. First, in a musical of otherwise scrupulously authentic mixed-race casting, the original Queenie — the main female African American character — was played not by a black woman but by white Tess Gardella, a popular blackface entertainer who performed so consistently as "Aunt Jemima" that Ziegfeld's programs credited Aunt Jemima, not Gardella, as playing Queenie. Ziegfeld was obviously going for some measure of star power rather than racial authenticity.

Second, *Show Boat* was a hit by anybody's standards — 575 performances, not to mention touring companies. The first of three film versions was in 1929, and Ziegfeld himself mounted a revival in 1932 for 181 performances in which Broadway first experienced Paul Robeson as Joe, singing "Ol' Man River." (Contrary to legend, Jules Bledsoe created the role in 1927, not Robeson.) After *Show Boat*, Kern continued to compose and Hammerstein to write throughout the 1930s, sometimes together. Why, then, were there no other integrated musicals like *Show Boat* (not even by Kern and/or Hammerstein) for another sixteen years? Audiences had to wait until 1943 for *Oklahoma!* to finally establish the integrated musical as the norm for musical theatre writing and production in America. *That* is the inexplicable irony. The intervening years poured forth a veritable deluge of musicals brimming over with topical satire and social issues after the virtual drought of the 1920s, but none were in the Kern/Hammerstein mold for *Show Boat*. The American musical stage would have to wait out the Great Depression and half of World War II for the full flowering of integrated musicals depicting concerns of real significance to contemporary audiences. It would be worth the wait.

## ✻ 3 ✻

# Coping with Depression

### The Crash and the Great Depression

Stock prices began plummeting on October 24, but it was the Stock Market Crash of October 29, 1929, that effectively ended the Roaring Twenties. By the closing bell on that infamous Tuesday, 16,410,030 shares were traded, a record not broken for another thirty years. According to Frederick Lewis Allen, "the value of stocks listed on the Exchange had dropped fourteen billion dollars" and what happened triggered "near-panic in other markets—the foreign stock exchanges, the lesser American exchanges, the grain market" (253). And stocks continued to fall throughout the early 1930s. Although pinpointing the precise causes of the Crash is difficult, as historian Edmund Stillman sees it, "The Great Bull Market had been sustained for months, even for years, on dreams and promises of wealth. It was a jerrybuilt structure, a slapdash creation of admen's hard sell, stock pushers' fraud and near fraud, business self-complacency, do-nothing government, economic nationalism, high tariffs, and an unregulated market place. It could not last, and it did not last" (158–59).

Following the Crash the United States was plunged into a depression that lasted a decade, despite the early optimism of President Herbert Hoover and his cabinet (Allen 257). Not surprisingly, business and industrial employees felt the pinch sooner and harder than employers and professionals. By the spring of 1930, "White-collar workers began to take salary cuts, laborers to find discharge slips in pay envelopes. The city felt the shock first. Initial symptoms were not ostentatious: postponement in buying that new car, or breaking ground for a new home; surrender of small apartments by young couples moving in with parents; a drop in pleasure travel and theater attendance" (Wecter 16).

But it wasn't long until joblessness became a national disease. "Hoovervilles," the packing-crate shantytowns that were home to many of the jobless, dotted cities' vacant land as early as 1932. Southern sharecroppers and tenant farmers, white and black, headed north in the (usually erroneous) belief that there was work in the cities, while hundreds of thousands of "Okies" trekked west from the Dust Bowl, following the equally elusive dream of agricultural employment in California's Imperial Valley. Wages of the still-employed plummeted: "Factory girls in Chicago in 1932 were earning an average of twenty-five cents an hour . . . in New York a top-flight executive secretary was paid sixteen dollars per week, down from forty-five dollars only three years earlier" (Stillman 159). By March 1933, unemployment hit fifteen to sixteen million. Starting in the mid-1930s, the Works Progress Administration (WPA) and other New Deal agencies put eight million people back to work; "many a wife whose husband had been jobless soon came to say in effect, 'We aren't on relief any more—my man is working for the government' " (Wecter 96).

Many Americans hit bottom not just financially but psychologically: "Unkempt hair and swarthy stubble, shoulders a-droop, a slow dragging walk, were external signs of inner defeat often aggravated by malnutrition. Joblessness proved a wasting disease" (Wecter 32). And those symptoms were genuine; a Michigan county administrator attuned to "the psychological value of job relief" reported men assigned CWA work " 'weeping for sheer happiness.' With their initial pay checks many went straight to the barber for their first professional haircut in months, and during the weeks that followed their appearance mirrored the further stages in the recovery of self-respect" (75).

Respecting self-respect, "[t]he most memorable symbol of the great unemployment, and of pride in facing it, came to be the apple" (19). Or, more precisely, it was the apple sellers who started appearing on urban sidewalks in the fall of 1930 when the International Apple Shippers Association "offered to sell the fruit on credit to the jobless, to retail at five cents apiece. By early November six thousand apple sellers had taken their stand on the sidewalks of New York, and the idea soon spread elsewhere." The most moving images of the jobless trying to preserve some semblance of dignity are the photographs of apple sellers, clean-shaven as possible, wearing shirts and collars, suits, overcoats, and hats that have seen better days but are still remarkably clean, pressed, or brushed. And, proudly, the face in the photo seems to be saying, "It may not be much, but I'm still in business."

As was the United States generally. Contrary to later popular imagination, the Depression did not reduce all Americans to a mere subsistence economy; people still working, even at reduced wages, could keep bread on the table and a roof over their heads and still have a bit left over for recreation. For instance, the Broadway season of 1929–30 shows that the immediate effects of the Crash on musical theatre production and attendance were minimal. Although Gerald Bordman speaks of a "precipitous decline" in the number of musicals mounted in 1929–30, in point of fact that season's thirty-four isn't such a drastic drop from the previous pre–Crash season's forty-two. Indeed, many Americans continued spending pretty freely not just on theatre tickets but on other leisure-time luxuries: tickets to the movies and sporting events, sporting goods and bicycles, radios — lots of radios, "four million families buying them in the abysmal years 1930–1932" (Wecter 229). Sales of other home entertainments escalated, no doubt because, like radio sets, after the initial purchase price the entertainment would be free. Jigsaw puzzles, card playing, and board games — especially "Monopoly" — gained new popularity. Across the country people managed an occasional night at the picture show, an afternoon at the ballpark, a round of miniature golf or the real thing on one of the new public courses with their affordable daily fees (Wecter 219). And in cities like New York and Chicago enough of the still-employed bought tickets to the living stage, including musicals, to keep that stage alive. The shows went on — if less lavish and fewer in number than before — because audiences still came.

### The Depression Hits Broadway

And yet the Depression dealt the musical theatre some very serious blows. The most extravagant productions and producers were hit earliest and hardest. Charles Dillingham, producer of the spectacular and almost always long-running Hippodrome revues, began to fall first and fell the longest. On March 30, 1930, Dillingham staged a concert/vaudeville featuring Maurice Chevalier, Eleanor Powell, and Duke Ellington's Cotton Club Orchestra. The show boasted high-powered talent but no scenery apart from draperies (Bordman 459). On February 9, 1932, again without sumptuous sets, Dillingham presented Maurice Chevalier in a one-man show (475). Finally, in 1934, the program for Leonard Sillman's *New Faces* listed Dillingham as producer as a courtesy but in fact he "was destitute and dying" (488). Theatre owner and producer Arthur Hammerstein's theatrical downfall was as swift as Dillingham's was protracted. Just before Christmas 1930, Hammerstein opened *Ballyhoo* in his namesake theatre as a vehicle for W. C. Fields. The show's losses plunged him into bankruptcy, even costing him the theatre he so loved (466).

Similar if less spectacular fates awaited the other once-great producers of glittery revues. Earl Carroll mostly lost property; by scaling back the size of his shows, and even for a time changing his venue from New York to Hollywood, Carroll continued to mount his slightly salacious revues at a profit. His *Vanities* for 1931 managed 278 nights almost against the odds of playing to the 3,000-seat auditorium of his new state-of-the-art, art-déco Earl Carroll Theatre. But the theatre passed quickly from Carroll to Ziegfeld, who renamed it the Casino, and then to producer George White. Still, Carroll had better luck than some. The Depression had depleted the taste and capital for revues, so he turned his annual show into *Murder at the Vanities* (9/8/33), a book musical that was just a revue with a plot, allowing for specialty acts and parades of semiclad showgirls. It ran six months. His *Sketch Book* for 1935 was Carroll's last New York show in the '30s, running 207 times. After that, he successfully took the *Vanities* to his Hollywood dinner theatre. Carroll returned to New York in 1940 for one last edition, which played only twenty-five times (Bordman 519).

In 1932, "Financial difficulties prevented [George] White from mounting a lavish *Scandals*," so he produced the less expensive *George White's Music Hall Varieties* (11/22/32). White hoped that tickets at $2.20 top (usual then was $3.30 to $4.40) would bring playgoers into the huge Casino, but they didn't (Bordman 480). On February 14, 1933, White ended his producing career with Sigmund Romberg's *Melody*, with sets that would prove to be the incomparable Joseph Urban's last. *Melody* lingered on seventy-nine times. Shortly thereafter the cavernous theatre became a Woolworth's.

Although facing personal bankruptcy, The Great Ziegfeld stayed afloat for a time. The last *Ziegfeld Follies* bearing both his name and his personal touch opened July 1, 1931; the Depression and the waning taste for lavish revues held its first-rate cast and material to a respectable, if not brilliant, 165 performances. In the midst of personal bankruptcy proceedings, Ziegfeld was still respected enough to raise capital for what proved to be his theatrical swan-song—the first Broadway revival of *Show Boat* (5/19/32). By Depression standards the revival was a hit, but Ziegfeld would never know that; he died, almost destitute, on July 22, 1932, two months into *Show Boat*'s six-month run. After his death, the *Ziegfeld Follies of 1934* and *1936* billed "Mrs. Florenz Ziegfeld" (Billie Burke) as producer, but the Shuberts were the real power and money behind the revues. According to Bordman, the widowed Ms. Burke's "only real interest in the show was the possible profits that might help pay her late husband's debts" (486).

As the Shubert Corporation, Lee and J. J. Shubert imported mittel-European operettas, backed American imitations, produced many other revues and book shows, and owned numerous theatres—controlling a vaster empire than any single producer. Yet the Depression almost wiped them out. They survived largely by being incorporated and using the law to save their corporate necks. Foster Hirsch lays out all the Shuberts' chicanery during the Depression in *The Boys from Syracuse* (163–68). To illustrate

the Shubert way of doing things, suffice it to say that, with the full cooperation of the courts, Lee (representing a new corporation) contrived to be
the only bidder at the bankruptcy auction of the Shubert properties!
Through this maneuver he bought back his own bankrupt company (which
retained a book value of $12.5 million) for the minimum bid of $400,000 —
and managed to squeeze brother J. J. out of the business to boot.

Not only did the big producers and theatrical extravaganzas collapse,
more modest musical theatre suffered as well. The Crash of '29, the Great
Depression, and the success of "talking pictures" caused a steep drop in the
number of musicals and revues produced during the 1930s. Money was
tight, and the production of commercial theatre, musical and otherwise,
depends on investment capital. While the season of the Crash, 1929–30,
produced thirty-four new musicals — the lowest number in eleven seasons
(Bordman 451) — by the dismal years of 1933–34, the number of new musicals dropped to thirteen. Only twice again in the twentieth century would
the number once more reach twenty — an irreversible, decades-long drop in
musicals produced annually since the plush days of the '20s.

The Depression affected the New York stage in other ways as well. According to Wecter, "Two thirds of Manhattan's playhouses were shut in
1931, . . . eight out of ten offerings in the 1932–33 season failed, and
thousands of actors faced penury. In 1932, in desperate hope of a job with
the 'talkies,' no less than twenty-two thousand registered with Hollywood
casting bureaus" (261). Not just actors headed west; so too did composers
and lyricists. Buddy De Sylva left first, in 1930, soon followed by Rodgers
and Hart, the Gershwins, Jerome Kern, Vincent Youmans, Cole Porter,
Irving Berlin, and others. Almost all returned to Manhattan and the Broadway musical stage by the mid-1930s or shortly thereafter. But the theatre
closings would prove to be a permanent long-term effect of the Depression
on Broadway. As Oscar Brockett dryly notes, "In the 1920s, Broadway had
eighty theatres and presented about 218 productions each year . . . about 45
were new musicals. In the 1990s, Broadway had 35 theatres and presented
just over 30 productions each year" (573–74). The shrinking volume of plays
and musicals produced in later decades can't be blamed solely on the Depression, but it did jumpstart the decline.

## Depression Economics and Black Musicals

In the earliest years of the decade — the worst of the Great Depression —
black musicals managed to weather the hard times, at least in terms of the
number of them produced. According to Allen Woll, "More black musicals

and revues appeared in the early 1930s than at any time since the golden age of the early 1920s" — six in 1930–31, and five the season after (135–36). There were several reasons for this, all of them economic. Apart from Lew Leslie's extravaganzas, from the late 1920s forward black revues focused primarily on musical talent instead of elaborate physical production. The effects of this were twofold. First, since these shows resembled theatrical versions of nightclub acts, out-of-town tryouts were rarely needed; they tried out in local New York nightspots, thereby eliminating expenses associated with touring. Second, since sets and costumes were minimal, production costs were low. Following the demise of his costly, elaborate *Lew Leslie's Blackbirds* (10/22/30) after fifty-seven shows, even Leslie used "no chorus, and no fancy scenery," just "a mere black backdrop" for *Rhapsody in Black* (5/4/31: Bordman 464, 468; Woll 136).

Low labor costs made black shows attractive to producers during the Depression. Except for stars like Ethel Waters, most African American entertainers were willing to work for lower salaries than whites. The big problem with steady work for black performers was that most of the early '30s black musicals were flops with very short runs. With 111 performances, *Brown Buddies* was the longest running black book show, Lew Leslie's *Rhapsody in Black* the longest running revue with eighty. So while the plethora of African American musicals employed large numbers of black entertainers, they employed them only briefly. What's more, the black shows of the early '30s were essentially derivative of *Shuffle Along* or the black revues of the 1920s. By the early 1930s, such fare had become passé in the eyes of critics and the public alike. And, as in prior decades "experimentation [by black writers of black shows] was frowned upon" by most critics (Woll 156). But at mid-decade a highly experimental musical written by whites for a nearly all-black cast ushered in a new era of black-performed, if not always black-written, musicals for mainstream Broadway.

## Porgy and Bess

Even future classics struggled to break even in the Depression, and George Gershwin's *Porgy and Bess* (10/10/35) was no exception. The Theatre Guild failed "to retrieve its $50,000 investment" despite the opera's 124 performances and a post-Broadway tour (Bordman 495). Still, the very nature of the project made *Porgy and Bess* socially important. In the dreary years of 1935–36, the production provided fairly long-term employment for a large number of African American singer/actors, especially ones with operatic training and experience for whom work was always more scarce than for musical comedy types. With about twenty black principals and a huge chorus (plus four minor white roles), *Porgy and Bess* probably provided steadier work for more African American performers in the mid-'30s than did the total of short-lived black revues in the Depression's earlier years. While it could not match the length of employment enjoyed by the cast of about forty African American actors during the phenomenal 640-performance run (plus national tour) of Marc Connelly's *The Green Pastures* (2/26/30), nevertheless *Porgy and Bess* did its share to keep black performers working. Between these two commercial ventures and the productions of the Negro Theatre Unit of the Federal Theatre Project, there were more African Americans working in the New York theatre in the mid-1930s than at any time before. And perhaps more to the point, they were working in plays and musicals that did not convey stereotyped images of blacks.

From the start *Porgy and Bess* stirred controversy. Unclear whether it should be reviewed as an opera or a conventional musical, most major New York papers sent two critics to the opening—the music critic and the drama critic. The result was generally disastrous since "[m]ost music critics disliked the show's musical comedy elements, and the drama critics abhorred its operatic tendencies" (Woll 171). Brooks Atkinson in particuticular blasted the fact that recitative replaced spoken dialogue for everyday speech. What none of the critics grasped was George Gershwin's vision of using the idioms of folk and popular song as the basis for a musical play that was operatic in form thanks to its sung-through nature.

Whereas white reviewers mostly questioned the opera's artistic merits, a few black critics challenged it on social grounds, chiefly leveling the charge of stereotyping against Gershwin for what he was trying to pass off as "Negro music" and against librettists Ira Gershwin and DuBose Heyward for drawing caricatured types rather than real human beings (see Woll 172–73). But if one examines what the Gershwins and Heyward were really up to, it becomes clear that both their intention and the result were as far from stereotyping as possible. In fact, in adapting DuBose and Dorothy Heyward's 1927 *Porgy*, also produced by the Theatre Guild, the three collaborators transplanted that five-act prose play's specific brand of realism into an all-sung music-drama for Broadway.

That brand of realism was naturalism, the literary and theatrical movement whose principles were first fully articulated and strenuously advocated by the French philosopher, novelist, playwright, and critic Emile Zola in the 1870s. Zola argued that the playwright must be as objective an observer of the human condition as the scientist is of natural phenomena. This objectivity will reveal fundamental patterns in human affairs that the writer must depict without editorializing. According to Zola, the playwright/investigator will discover that human beings behave as they must. This is the central tenet of the nineteenth-century philosophical/scientific position known as determinism, upon which naturalism is based. Although human beings have free will, the capacity for choice, and a conscience, these are weak compared to the more potent forces of heredity and/or environment. Therefore, an individual's actions, choices, and behavior are ultimately conditioned or *determined* by heredity, environment, or both. Although the playwright strives for objectivity, a naturalistic play takes a socially responsible stand by dramatizing that "at least partial responsibility for undesirable behavior [has] to be accepted by the society that has allowed adverse hereditary and environmental factors to exist" (Brockett 427).

The Gershwins and Heyward carried over into their opera nearly all of the naturalistic elements of the Heywards' play. Most immediately striking is the physical setting of Catfish Row, the Charleston, South Carolina, black enclave in which nearly all the action takes place. The courtyard set's minute, realistic detail of squalor combined with faded Southern charm reveals from first rise of curtain the effect such a cramped, impoverished environment has on its inhabitants. Such realistic detail pervades all aspects of the opera. Some critics perhaps saw stereotypes in *Porgy and Bess* because naturalistic writing leans toward drawing characters in fairly broad strokes in order to stress the force of heredity or environmental factors over the weaknesses of individual personality traits. And, admittedly, the operatic adaptation somewhat compounded this tendency. In the naturalistic "slice of life" framework of the five-act original, the Heywards took their time in the leisurely dialogue and action to draw subtle, complex portraits of even secondary characters—Maria, the cook shop woman, for one. Because so much of the lengthy play was compressed to accommodate George Gershwin's musical score, many such subtleties and complexities diminished, making some of the opera's characters appear more stereotypical than intended.

Rich and full as the opera remains, the plot of *Porgy and Bess* is absolutely straightforward and linear. During a crap game near the start of the show, Crown, dockworker and part-time pimp, kills Robbins, one of the men of Catfish Row. As he flees, Crown abandons "his woman" Bess, and the crippled beggar Porgy takes her in. Porgy and Bess fall in love. By renouncing drugs and prostitution, Bess allows the good Christian ladies of Catfish Row to accept her into the community. Later, Crown returns to reclaim Bess, but Porgy kills him. When the police take Porgy away just to identify the body, the neighborhood drug dealer Sportin' Life convinces Bess the police actually suspect Porgy of murder. He tempts her with cocaine, promises her the "high life," and takes her off with him to Harlem. At the final curtain Porgy returns and resolves to find Bess.

While the effects of environmental conditioning can be seen in the lives and actions of all of the persons in *Porgy and Bess*, it is most fully dramatized in the story of the title characters. After Crown flees in the first scene, a dramatic change occurs in both Bess and Porgy. While the play makes more of this than the opera does, Porgy, though a good person at heart, is also a self-pitying, misanthropic recluse; his love for Bess and hers for him (a material change in his environment) opens his heart and turns him into a generous member of the community. Bess's case is even more dramatic. As "Crown's Bess," she was a prostitute addicted to "happy dust" (i.e., cocaine) and shunned by all the "Gawd fearin' ladies" of Catfish Row. Living with Porgy in close proximity to these good women, Bess becomes an accepted part of their world. Although these character changes suggest people *can* fight negative conditioning, *Porgy and Bess* concludes on a mostly deterministic note. Late in the action, when the police take Porgy away, Sportin' Life preys on Bess's superstition (wounds bleed in the presence of the murderer) and her latent addiction to cocaine. Try as she might, she cannot overcome her negative conditioning.

The almost identical endings of both the play and the opera suggest that American writers of naturalism cannot wholly commit to its worst-case scenario prognosis. When Porgy returns from police custody, he finds his beloved Bess has gone. Calling for his goat cart, he rides off with absolute conviction that he will get to New York and find "his woman," thereby confirming his own resiliency of spirit. In the play, however, that ending is profoundly ambiguous. Is it uplifting and affirmative, expressive of Porgy's indomitable will? Or, conversely, is Porgy off on a fool's errand, a doomed exercise in futility? The Heywards let spectators interpret that ending as they choose.

In the opera, while the action is absolutely the same as in the play, George Gershwin's brilliant musical scoring completely resolves the ending's ambiguity. Returning to Catfish Row to find Bess isn't there, Porgy, in one of the opera's most musically moving moments, asks his neighbors, "Oh, Bess, oh where's my Bess," sung in the hauntingly plaintive key of C-sharp minor. Moments later, after learning Bess has gone with Sportin' Life, and determined to find her, Porgy again rides out, but now singing the thrillingly upbeat "Oh, Lord, I'm on My Way." This song's melodic line and rhythm (but not tempo) are very similar to "Where's My Bess," but its key is E major, the relative major key to the previous number's C-sharp minor. This dramatically conveys through music alone the shift from a mood of hopelessness to one of, if not triumph, at least affirmation. The ambiguity is thereby eliminated and resolved. The opera's finale opens an escape hatch from the hold of environmental determinism, affirming that people have the strength, will, and resilience to rise above oppressive social conditions.

### Cheering Up the Audience

The majority of musicals in the 1930s were scaled-down versions of the feel-good shows of the 1920s, and many attracted audiences for two hundred performances or more despite economic hard times (see appendix B). Book shows still tended to depict the carefree living and leisure pursuits of Americans at home or abroad, but these musicals no longer mirrored most of their spectators' lives. In the dark days of the Depression, the kinds of shows that had recently reflected their audiences' lifestyles suddenly became true escapist entertainment, recalling perhaps the lives their viewers once lived (nostalgia always being a powerful draw), or, conversely, letting spectators imagine what life would be like when the Depression ended. The revues, less lavish than in the '20s, still featured star talent, musical numbers, stylish dance routines, sketch comedy, and, in some, the inevitable, endless parades of gorgeous showgirls. The longest-running musical of the 1930s, indeed of all time when it ended performance 1,404, was *Hellzapoppin* (9/22/38), a vehicle for vaudevillians Olsen and Johnson with a workmanlike but undistinguished Sammy Fain score.

The presence of at least nine intentionally optimistic songs in shows between February 30, 1930, and November 26, 1932, suggests that some songwriters were doing their bit to cheer Americans during hard times. The roster of these songs is impressive: most were written by first-rate composers and lyricists and introduced by major stars; over half of the numbers became standards of American popular song. To name just the most enduring of the nine, in 1930 Broadway first heard Ruth Etting perform Harold Arlen and Ted Koehler's "Get Happy," Harry Richman sing "On the Sunny Side of the Street" by Dorothy Fields and Jimmy McHugh and also "Fine and Dandy" by Kay Swift and Paul James. In 1931, Fred Astaire sang and danced Arthur Schwartz and Howard Dietz's "New Sun in the Sky" and Ethel Merman belted out Lew Brown and Ray Henderson's "Life Is Just a Bowl of Cherries." Irving Berlin's "Let's Have Another Cup of Coffee" debuted in 1932, as did Vincent Youmans's "Rise 'n' Shine," another Merman show-stopper.

Along with the purely escapist musical comedy fluff and the chin-up songs, New York's musical stages offered a few lightly topical diversionary musicals—topical in that they referenced current events or issues, but not satirical in that they did not comment or have a strong point of view on such matters. Bootlegging, for example, was treated humorously in four musicals that opened between June 1930 and February 1931, but none after that, although Prohibition wasn't repealed until December 5, 1933. *Change Your Luck* (6/6/30) was a black show that began with the premise that Evergreen Peppers, town undertaker, might do better for himself in the moonshine trade. But the plot dried up early on, and the dancing and specialty numbers weren't enough for more than a two-week run (Bordman 460; Woll 141). In *The New Yorkers* (12/8/30), with a book by Herbert Fields and score by Cole Porter, New York sophisticate Alice Wentworth falls for "the murderous bootlegger, Al Spanish. Miss Wentworth is from Park Avenue where, in the show's most famous line, 'bad women walk good dogs' " (Bordman 465). The show struggled through 168 unprofitable performances. Harold Arlen's first full score was heard in *You Said It* (1/19/31), in which a campus racketeer helps the dean's daughter avoid getting caught at some extracurricular bootlegging (466); the college highjinks and Arlen's score kept the show going 192 times. Finally, a three-week flop called *The Gang's All Here* (2/18/31) was a comic Romeo and Juliet affair in which the son and daughter of rival Atlantic City bootleggers help reconcile their gangs (467).

Had *The Little Racketeer* (1/18/32) been written in the early 1920s, it would have been just another Cinderella musical. But in 1932 its premise of "Dixie, a street urchin who pretends to fall asleep in fashionable cars hoping their owners out of pity will give her a few dollars" poignantly underscored the plight of the Depression-era's homeless (Bordman 474). Otherwise the show was absolutely conventional. One car's wealthy, handsome owner finds her and takes her in. "They soon fall in love, and Dixie is assured of a big car all her own," but the public slammed the door on her after forty-eight performances.

*Face the Music* (2/17/32) was a show biz show in which the wife of a New York cop on the take backs a musical. Moss Hart's inspiration for the book was the recent Seabury investigation into graft among the NYPD, but it remained just that—an inspiration, not a direct target of Hart's wicked asides about police corruption. One song in Irving Berlin's score was gently satiric of the collapse of America's economy. Standing alone, "Let's Have Another Cup of Coffee" is just one more of those ubiquitous "cheer up, things will get better" songs catalogued earlier. But when sung in an Automat restaurant by the likes of New York's Astors and Vanderbilts, dressed in morning suits and evening gowns for "the regular five-cent dinner" (Bordman 475, Smith 164), the song speaks to its historical moment. Berlin's song wryly echoes lyrics from five pre-Crash songs also of the chin-up genre: Nacio Herb Brown and Arthur Freed's "Singin' in the Rain," Kern and

Wodehouse's "Till the Clouds Roll By," Kern and De Sylva's "Look for the Silver Lining," De Sylva and Louis Silver's "April Showers," and Sammy Fain, Irving Kahal, and Francis Wheeler's "Let a Smile Be Your Umbrella." Berlin amalgamated key cheery phrases from these songs and for good measure ended with sharply topical lines aimed at the diminishing fortunes of Rockefeller and the undiminished optimism of Herbert Hoover:

> Why worry when skies are gray?
> Why should we complain?
> Let's laugh at the cloudy day.
> Let's sing in the rain.
> Songwriters say the storm quickly passes.
> That's their philosophy.
> They see the world through rose-colored glasses.
> Why shouldn't we?

> Just around the corner there's a rainbow in the sky.
> So let's have another cup o' coffee and let's have another piece o' pie!
> Trouble's just a bubble, and the clouds will soon roll by.
> So let's have another cup o' coffee and let's have another piece o' pie!
> Let a smile be your umbrella,
> For it's just an April show'r.
> Even John D. Rockefeller
> Is looking for the silver lining.
> Mister Herbert Hoover says that now's the time to buy.
> So let's have another cup o' coffee and let's have another piece o' pie!
>                                                        (Berlin 50–53)

## A Milieu for Satire

The social ferment of the Depression gave the musical theatre something to sing about. Historically, Aristophanes wrote most of his satiric comedies (musicals, actually) during the Peloponnesian War, a time of great political, economic, and military difficulties for ancient Athens. And when Gilbert and Sullivan wrote their satiric comic operas, the conservative propriety of Victorian England's starched-linen and crinoline social fabric was coming apart at the seams. In a word, periods of societal turmoil and discontent provide far more material for satiric comedy than the Babbittlike complacency of Coolidge/Hoover Prosperity. The milieu of the Depression was more than just the impetus for satire to emerge as a dominant mode of the period's musicals; the conditions of the times also fed the stance of most musical satires. Capitalism's seeming collapse inspired an increase in left-leaning sentiments, a tendency that led to a spirit of social inquiry, commentary, and criticism in many musicals of the Depression years. It also accounts for the fact that the point of view of all the satirical musicals ranged from liberal to far left. Although most satiric book shows kept the core boy-meets-girl romantic plot, these were musicals of real substance that allowed book and lyric writers to pen much more than inconsequential fluff.

## Satirical Shows of the Early '30s: *The Kaufman, Ryskind, Gershwin Collaborations* — Strike Up the Band

*Strike Up the Band* (1/14/30), the earliest satiric musical of the Depression era, had its first abortive but still important incarnation back in 1927. Approached by producer Edgar Selwyn to collaborate with George and Ira Gershwin, George S. Kaufman drafted a libretto with an "antimilitarist" theme and a hilariously silly plot. Horace J. Fletcher, an American cheese magnate, offers to finance a war against Switzerland when the Swiss balk at Congress's 50 percent tariff on imported cheese (Goldstein, *Kaufman* 132–33). Kaufman's antiwar sentiment reflected that of much of America at the time. But despite the humor of Kaufman's book and a strong Gershwin score, 1927 audiences weren't buying. *Strike Up the Band* closed with significant losses in the second week of its Philadelphia tryout.

Despite the flop, Selwyn wouldn't let go. Kaufman had become "[t]horoughly tired of the script" and happily let Selwyn turn it over to Morrie Ryskind for rewrites (171). Partly because Ryskind kept Kaufman's themes while softening his trenchant satire, and partly because of timing, the revised *Strike Up the Band* had a solid run of 191 performances — helped by a Gershwin score that included the stirring title song, "Soon," and "I've Got a Crush on You." Ryskind replaced Kaufman's Swiss cheese with chocolate and made the war a dream from which the chocolate czar awoke, Scroogelike, completely reformed. And in 1930 the show's satire had more immediacy than it had in 1927; life was almost imitating art. When the show opened, Congress was hotly debating what became the Hawley-Smoot Tariff, which Hoover signed about a month before the musical closed. The Hawley-Smoot Tariff levied such outrageously high import duties on foreign goods it's a wonder most of Europe — let alone Switzerland — didn't go to war with the United States (see Allen, *Since* 37; Stillman 180–81; Leuchtenburg 110).

Nearly everyone remarking on this musical even in passing has seen special significance in the first of what would be three Kaufman/Ryskind/Gershwin shows. To Cecil Smith, "The miracle of *Strike Up the Band* was its ability to present its argument without losing its good nature. . . . It was the first real token of liberalism and a social conscience in the American musical theatre" (154). Gerald Bordman wrote of the 1927 original, "It was the very sort of thing Gilbert and Sullivan might have contrived had they been children of the jazz age," and of the final version,"[i]n its willingness to face important social issues *Strike Up the Band* broadcast a new era in stage musicals" (457).

## Of Thee I Sing

Bordman's Gilbert and Sullivan analogy is even more apt for the second, arguably best, and certainly best known of the Kaufman/Ryskind/Gershwin musical satires, *Of Thee I Sing* (12/26/31). It became both the first Broadway musical to be published as a hardcover book for popular readership and the first to win the Pulitzer Prize for drama. Its plot, from the ridiculous premise to the preposterous logic of its resolution, could have come from W. S. Gilbert. And, in a sense, it did. George S. Kaufman was practically weaned on Gilbert's verse and the comic operas he wrote with Arthur Sullivan (see Goldstein, *Kaufman* 13, 17) and retained a lifelong love for them. Writers on musicals have generally agreed that *Of Thee I Sing* is a "barbed, witty look at American political institutions" (Bordman 473). And yet, while some of the one-liners are topically pointed, most of the actual story is less a satire on current American politics than a silly spoof of the workings of American democracy in general — often in the manner of a preposterous Marx Brothers romp. The show preserved the "good nature" of the final version of *Strike Up the Band*.

The plot is as far removed from real Washington politics as Gilbert and Sullivan's *The Mikado* is from the real Japan. Bachelor John Wintergreen is running for president. He has no platform and no girlfriend, let alone spouse, a clear disadvantage since Americans prefer their presidents married. All Wintergreen has is a committee and a campaign song. The Ira Gershwin lyrics give a friendly nod to recent U.S. immigrant populations and their role in electing public officials. The song alternates "Wintergreen for President!" with the couplet "He's the man the people choose — / Loves the Irish and the Jews" (Kaufman and Ryskind, *Of Thee* 4). Small wonder, since two key players on Wintergreen's campaign team are Francis X. Gilhooley and Louis Lippman! These two, along with committeemen southern senator Robert E. Lyons, western senator Carver Jones, and newspaper publisher Matthew Arnold Fulton (who behaves like a stage version of William Randolph Hearst), agree that Wintergreen's platform should be simply "Love," but to make this plausible he needs a bride. Another nonentity who hangs around the campaign committee without anyone ever much recognizing him is Alexander Throttlebottom, initially the vice-presidential candidate and later the vice-president in fact. The committee hits on the idea of an Atlantic City beauty contest to pick Miss White House. The winner gets Wintergreen as the prize and, should he be elected (which of course he is), the role of first lady. Louisiana's entrant, Miss Diana Devereaux, wins, but in the meantime John has fallen in love with one Mary Turner, a genuine working girl employed by the election team. He's fallen for her not because of her beauty, brains, talent, or go-getting drive (all of which she has), but because Mary bakes "the best darned" corn muffins. Kaufman and Ryskind's Mary is a remarkably fleshed-out character. She is bright, clever, and candidly outspoken in what was still a man's world, at the same time remaining charming and feminine. In a word, an exemplar of the new woman of the '20s and '30s, as seen when she and John first meet:

MARY
Nonsense! Every girl can cook.
WINTERGREEN
[*Scornfully*]
Every girl can cook—can *you?*
MARY
I certainly can!
WINTERGREEN
Then what are you doing here?
MARY
[*Right back at him*]
I'm holding down a job! And I can cook, and sew, and make
lace curtains, and bake the best darned corn muffins you ever ate!
And what do you know about that?
(Kaufman and Ryskind, *Of Thee* 62–63)

As if choosing a political bride by a beauty contest weren't ludicrous enough in the Gilbert and Sullivan scheme of things, the first-act finale is Kaufman and Ira Gershwin's explicit nod to *The Mikado's* act 1 closing. The scene is the dual inauguration and wedding ceremony of John and Mary (compare the betrothal of Nanki-Poo and Yum-Yum). Into the midst of this silly solemnity crashes Diana Devereaux, claiming her right to John as the beauty contest winner (just as Katisha crashes in to claim Nanki-Poo). Diana demands justice; John just wants Mary and her muffins. Asked to decide, the Supreme Court votes unanimously for corn muffins over justice. Diana, like Katisha, leaves, but vows she'll be back. No idle threat, since there's still the whole second act in which to deal with her.

Act 2 finds John and Mary snugly ensconced in the White House, or they would be snug if not for Diana's threats and the French ambassador's claim that

> She's the illegitimate daughter
> Of an illegitimate son
> Of an illegitimate nephew
> Of Napoleon!
> (Kaufman and Ryskind,
> *Of Thee* 151–52)

President Wintergreen could be facing a breach-of-promise suit, divorce, impeachment, an ugly international diplomatic incident, and/or war with France. It doesn't make matters any simpler when we discover the first lady is pregnant. When all seems hopelessly tangled, true to Gilbert's manner of resolving a preposterous situation through fallacious but seemingly watertight logic, Kaufman and Ryskind have Wintergreen solve the dilemma: "It's in the Constitution! When the President of the United States is unable to fulfill his duties, his obligations are assumed by—'The vice-president!' Throttlebottom chimes in, 'I get her!' " (213). So Diana has herself a husband (and vice-president), John and Mary have each other, Mary has twins, and Broadway audiences have a lot of goodnatured laughs at the expense of some foibles of the American political system for 441 performances.

   The story and characters made for good fun, silliness, and even a bit of farce, but it was individual lines of dialogue and a prolonged visual joke in act 1 that carried the show's specifically topical satire. During the balloting, about a dozen absurd election returns were projected along with appropriate graphics, while the pit-band played rousing campaign music. Among the more pointed were:

LEXINGTON, KENTUCKY
Wintergreen . . . . . . . . . 27,637
Light Wines and Beer . . . . . . . 14
Straight Whiskey . . . . . . 1,850,827

ROME, ITALY
127 Election Districts give:
Wintergreen . . . . . . . . . . . 0
Mussolini . . . . . . . . . 828,638

NEW YORK, N.Y.
First Returns from Wall St. Give:
Wintergreen . . . . . . . . .192,000
Radio. . . . . . . . . . . . . 5¾
Goldman, Sachs . . . . . . . . 2⅛
(Kaufman and Ryskind, *Of Thee*
92–95 *passim*)

More real than funny, this doesn't much exaggerate Wall Street's continuing nosedive.

The ongoing bank panic was the subject of an even more brutal joke in act 2. *Of Thee I Sing* opened the day after Christmas in 1931. In 1929, there had been 659 bank closings; 1,352 banks failed in 1930; and in 1931, 2,294 shut their doors for good (Leuchtenburg 256), bringing the total by the show's opening to roughly 4,305. In act 2, scene 1, Wintergreen and his secretary Jenkins are seen with "*a wooden board, covered with electric buttons. A long wire is attached to it.*" Apparently this gadget allows John to ceremonially "open" everything from expositions to speakeasies at the push of a button:

> JENKINS
> All ready, Mr. President. Time to press a button.
> WINTERGREEN
> So early in the morning?
> JENKINS
> Opening of the International Corn Growing Exposition. Button No. 1. . . . Ready. . . . Press.
> WINTERGREEN
> [*Presses button, then laughs*]
> Say, Jenkins, I never will forget the time I reopened the Bank of United States by mistake.
>
> (Kaufman and Ryskind, *Of Thee* 129)

Shortly before Christmas 1930, the Bank of the United States fell. With its 400,000 depositors, this was the worst bank failure in American history. To New Yorkers, this was the bank that had "held the life savings of thousands of recent immigrants, [and its failure] affected a third of the people of New York City" (Leuchtenburg 256).

By comparison, the remaining topical asides are tamer and funnier but equally pointed, taking aim at farm surpluses, Hoover's proposal for an international moratorium on war debts (Allen, *Since* 47), speakeasies, unemployment, and phonograph records losing sales because of radio's popularity. One moment of commentary deserves special notice both because of its placement—dramatically, at the very end of a scene—and because its tone is serious. Wintergreen and his vice-president are talking:

> THROTTLEBOTTOM
> Couldn't you make a speech instead? Then they'd *have* to listen.
> WINTERGREEN
> No, no! You've got to be careful about speeches. You only make a speech when you want the stock market to go down.

THROTTLEBOTTOM
What do you do when you want the stock market to go up?
WINTERGREEN
[*Fairly falling on his neck*]
Oh! wouldn't I like to know!
(Kaufman and Ryskind, *Of Thee* 169)

Wintergreen's curtain line clearly shows Kaufman and Ryskind's sympathy with millions of Americans who, like Wintergreen, looked forward to better days, but who had no immediate solutions for the present hard times.

## Let 'Em Eat Cake

The last of the Kaufman/Ryskind/Gershwin shows was as big a failure as the first two were successes. *Let 'Em Eat Cake* (10/21/33), *Of Thee I Sing*'s legitimate heir and genuine sequel, could muster only a dismal ninety performances. Opening-night critic Brooks Atkinson called the musical's mood "bitter" and charged that the writers' "hatreds have triumphed over their sense of humor" (Bordman 485; Smith 162). Most later writers on musicals have seemingly just jumped on the Atkinson bandwagon, attributing the show's failure to its overtly hostile tone. As Cecil Smith wrote, "Kaufman and Ryskind made the mistake of letting their bitterness find too plain an expression" (162; see also Mordden, *Better* 117; Goldstein, *Kaufman* 220; Green 95). But in fact, other than Atkinson, the press was kind, though not as enthusiastic as for *Of Thee I Sing* (Goldstein, *Kaufman* 221).

A close reading of *Let 'Em Eat Cake* belies the almost universal charge of bitterness. Specifically targeting real situations at home and abroad, the satire is edgier than in *Of Thee I Sing* but is neither vituperative nor personal. In fact, the sharper satire of *Let 'Em Eat Cake* is contained in a story brimming with the same kinds of whimsy and Gilbertian absurdity that had made a success of *Of Thee I Sing*. If reasons for *Cake*'s failure are to be found, they must be sought elsewhere.

First, purely in terms of musical comedy conventions, *Let 'Em Eat Cake* contained no boy-meets-girl love story, and musicals with no love interest rarely succeeded until much later in the century. Second, the show's approach to its satire was rather scattershot. As Ira Gershwin himself remarked years later, "If *Strike Up the Band* was a satire on War, and *Of Thee I Sing* one on Politics, *Let 'Em Eat Cake* was a satire on Practically Everything" (qtd. in Bordman 485). Finally there was the mood of the world at large and American audiences in particular. Though affected by the deepening Depression and the international crises of the early 1930s, Kaufman, Ryskind, and Ira Gershwin's approach to the show's humor and satire had not changed nearly as much as the historical context. Looking back on the failure of *Let 'Em Eat Cake*, Ryskind blamed the mood of the age. Between the Depression at home and the Nazis' ascendancy in Germany, American audiences by 1933 "had begun to see international politics as no laughing matter" (Goldstein, *Kaufman* 221).

The musical opens on Wintergreen's re-election campaign against John P. Tweedledee, who could be Wintergreen's bland, generic twin. The electorate opts for Tweedledee. John is out of work and John and Mary are out of a home. With the Twentieth Amendment ratified on February 6, 1933, setting an earlier inaugural date for presidents, the couple has to vacate the White House sooner than planned: "Well, we can't stay here after January 20th. They even pulled *that* on us. Instead of March 4th it's January 20th. Six weeks' salary gone to hell!" (Kaufman and Ryskind, *Let* 34).

At this point virtually all published summaries misinterpret a major point of the satire. These accounts make it appear that Wintergreen, a sore loser, immediately stages a revolution to set himself up as dictator, while in fact revolution and dictatorship are afterthoughts based on pragmatic necessity. What actually happens is that a beautiful blue shirt Mary made for him inspires the ex-president to go into business, making and retailing one exclusive product, the Mary Blue Shirt, with corporate headquarters consisting of a storefront on Union Square, New York City. John's partners are his cronies Jones, Gilhooley, Fulton, Throttlebottom, and Lippman (who, as the Jew in the bunch, seems to know a lot about the garment trade). The idea of going into business turns out to be better than the reality. Soon Wintergreen & Co. are producing more Mary Blue Shirts than they can sell. Only near the first act finale, in the kind of inverted Gilbertian logic Kaufman so loved, does the idea of revolution even occur to the gang. If you can't unload a surplus of monochromatic shirts, the only thing to do is stage a revolution: "Italy—black shirts! Germany—brown shirts! America—blue shirts! By God, if the American people want a revolution we can give it to them! We've got the shirts for it!" (Kaufman and Ryskind, *Let* 73–74).

Plans are made to get the army on Wintergreen's side, since the revolution will need military support. The idea of revolution doesn't sit well with John's longtime ally General Snookfield, who was recently elected to the Union League Club, a conservative, exclusive men's club. Kaufman and Ryskind aren't afraid to point to the club's exclusivity: "LIPPMAN: What *is* this Union League Club? I never heard of it. JONES: You wouldn't know, Louis. They don't allow your people" (95). The problem is solved when Throttlebottom, whose uncle is a waiter at the club, convinces its ancient membership to wear the blue shirts on the pretext that the revolution is the one against the British a couple of centuries back. With the Union League Club now backing revolution, the army gets on board. Act 1 ends triumphantly for Wintergreen, with the revolution's banner hoisted on the White House flagpole—a white field emblazoned with a blue shirt.

Act 2 opens with Wintergreen in full dictatorial regalia being dictatorially regaled by repeated shouts of "Saluta!"—the signature cheer of Mussolini's Fascisti—and then in song. (In 1933, the Italian dictator still seemed a far less serious threat than Adolph Hitler.) The central event of act 2 is a baseball game between the nine Supreme Court justices and representatives of nine member countries of the League of Nations, the stakes being double or nothing on the repayment of war debts from World War I. (The emissary of a tenth country, Finland, also shows up, and pays up—a very topical hit, since Finland was in fact the only country to pay off all interest payments, if not its loan, in full and on time [Perrett 19, note].) The umpire for the ballgame is Throttlebottom. When a controversial call goes against the Supreme Court, poor Throtty is sentenced to die by the guillotine, a gift to the United States from France. The scene of the would-be beheading is another in the tongue-in-cheek manner of W. S. Gilbert; at the eleventh hour, Mary enters with the wives of John's associates to save the day. Each woman is wearing a different Paris evening gown of the latest and most gorgeous design. Mary urges the wives to abandon the sartorially challenged revolution, which confines fashion to blue shirts. Preferring the latest fashions, they do so. Their husbands follow, and, thanks to more Gilbertian "logic," Throtty becomes president. Silly though it may be, the plot resolution reflects American individualism (different gowns for different women) as opposed to the conformity required in totalitarian dictatorships (uniform blue shirts—or black, or brown).

The satire in *Let 'Em Eat Cake* must be viewed in the context of Roosevelt's extended New Deal Honeymoon. The hundred days had long since passed. And yet, although Kaufman and Ryskind were naming names and penning some blisteringly funny remarks about current issues and personalities, they left the president and his programs completely alone. The show joked about deposed National City Bank czar Charles Mitchell's tax evasion, about the seemingly indestructible longevity of Senator Borah, about the Daughters of the American Revolution having nothing better to do than overthrow Culbertson's rules for contract bridge. But it would be four more years before George S. Kaufman would have explicit fun with FDR's presidency in a musical, and he would do so with his later and long-term collaborator Moss Hart. Yet even then their satire of the president and the New Deal would be in the spirit of lighthearted entertainment.

*A Topical Song and Satiric Revue: "Brother, Can You Spare a Dime"*
*and* As Thousands Cheer

Perhaps the most grimly and universally realistic song in a 1930s revue was
E. Y. Harburg and Jay Gorney's "Brother Can You Spare a Dime." Cheerless though it was, the song's popularity far outlasted its debut in the seventy-seven performances of the revue *Americana* (10/5/32), becoming
through its portrayal of joblessness a kind of anthem to the plight of America's unemployed. But it was more than that; for contemporary audiences,
it sharply alluded to one of the worst public embarrassments of the decade—the rout of the "Bonus Army" from Washington, D.C., two months
earlier.

In summer 1932, between fifteen and twenty thousand veterans of the
Great War, victims of the Depression's hard times, came to Washington
demanding *immediate* payment of the "adjusted compensation" Congress
had voted to give World War I veterans only in 1945. With bitter humor
they called themselves the Bonus Expeditionary Force, and camped out on
the Mall or in vacant government buildings. For the most part an orderly
bunch, many came with wives and children in tow. Nonetheless, President
Hoover's White House issued an order to clear them out of Washington.
Many left peacefully, but a riot by some remaining veterans on July 28 was
quelled by the D.C. police and a contingent of the U.S. Army with "machine guns, tanks, and tear gas, brandishing sabers and bayonets" and personally led by Chief of Staff General Douglas MacArthur and two of his
junior officers, George Patton and Dwight David Eisenhower. Many were
wounded and two veterans killed by the very army they had once served in
(Leuchtenburg 262–63; Allen, *Since* 83; Wecter 37).

While most of Harburg's lyric describes anyone fallen on hard times in
the '30s, the military images in the verse and the release identify the singer
as a down-and-out veteran, thus specifically referencing that disgraceful
event in Washington:

> When there was earth to plough or guns to bear
> I was always there—right there on the job
>
> . . . . . . . . . . . . . . . .
>
> Once in khaki suits,
> Gee, we looked swell,
> Full of that Yankee Doodle-de-dum.
> Half a million boots went sloggin' through Hell,
> I was the kid with the drum.
> (qtd. in Meltzer, 157–58)

The topicality and realistic depiction of joblessness in this early Harburg lyric already indicate what would be "Yip" 's progressive, liberal outlook throughout his long career.

Following the moderate success of their book show *Face the Music*, Moss Hart and Irving Berlin dropped all pretensions to plot and collaborated on the tuneful, mostly satiric, and eminently successful topical revue *As Thousands Cheer* (9/30/33; 400 performances). The show proclaimed its topicality through a newspaper format, each sketch or song preceded by a headline "with individual scenes depicting news events, the funnies, the lonelyhearts column, the society page, and other features" (Green 76). Hart's satire named names: the Hoovers vacating the White House "with the President giving his cabinet a Bronx cheer" (Bordman 484); evangelist Aimee Semple MacPherson trying to get Gandhi off his hunger strike; and John D. Rockefeller "going after his children with a carving knife after they have made him a present of Rockefeller Center on his ninety-fourth birthday" (Green 77). Especially funny, because its real-life source is so absurd, was a sketch of a Metropolitan Opera radio broadcast during which commercials keep interrupting the singing. In fact, the Met had just recently found sponsors for its Saturday afternoons on the air—incongruously, a cigarette company and a mouthwash (Allen, *Since* 269).

What *As Thousands Cheer* did *not* satirize was anything about the new president, Franklin Delano Roosevelt, his unprecedented number of executive orders to implement his New Deal goals for the nation's relief and recovery, or his convincing of Congress to enact swiftly legislation to set up and fund agencies to carry out his programs. Up and running in the few months before *As Thousands Cheer* opened were the Farm Credit Administration (FCA), Civilian Conservation Corps (CCC), Tennessee Valley Authority (TVA), Federal Emergency Relief Administration (FERA), Agricultural Adjustment Act (best known as "Triple A"), National Industrial Recovery Act (NRA, with its famous Blue Eagle symbol and "We Do Our Part" slogan), Public Works Administration (PWA; not to be confused with the later, more effective WPA), and others in FDR's alphabet soup of agencies (see Wecter 72–185 *passim*). Their conspicuous absence from the revue says that along with elected and appointed state and national politicians, journalists and radio commentators, America's satirists and humorists—most of whom were of a liberal stamp—were giving FDR his hundred-day New Deal Honeymoon and then some.

Irving Berlin was never a lyricist in the "socially conscious vein of E. Y. Harburg or Harold Rome" (Green 76). Still, if most of his songs didn't have the satiric point of Hart's sketches, Berlin could still rise to the occasion of social relevance when dramatic requirements demanded. Berlin's big num-

bers in *As Thousands Cheer* were of the splashy, sizzling variety typified by
"Heat Wave," introduced by Ethel Waters, or of the charming, sentimental
type exemplified by what became the perennial seasonal favorite, "Easter
Parade." But Waters—the highest-paid woman on Broadway, no small feat
for a black in 1933 (Woll 149)—also performed topical, though not satiric,
numbers. In "Harlem on My Mind" she impersonated Josephine Baker,
relishing her Parisian high life but still longing for her Harlem roots and
home. Waters sang "Supper Time" following the headline "UNKNOWN NE-
GRO LYNCHED BY FRENZIED MOB." She portrayed "the man's widow who
wonders aloud as she sets the table how she will be able to tell her children
that their father 'ain't comin' home no more' " (Green 77). Even before
the out-of-town tryout, some questioned the place of this song in a generally
lighthearted revue, but Berlin and producer Sam Harris insisted "Supper
Time" stay in, and it "became one of the most moving pieces ever sung in
the theater" (77). Waters later wrote, "If one song can tell the whole tragic
story of a race, 'Supper Time' was that song" (qtd. in Green 77). Between
Harburg and Gorney's "Brother Can You Spare a Dime" and Irving Berlin's
"Supper Time," two Broadway songs in just a little over twelve months
confronted some very real social ills of the Depression era, yet neither song
was satirical.

### The Failure of Mid-Decade Satire

Like *Let 'Em Eat Cake*, most satirical musicals in the middle years of the
1930s failed at the box office. These included first-class fare (though not in
a first-class production) like Bertolt Brecht and Kurt Weill's *The Threepenny
Opera* (4/13/33; twelve performances) and tasteless stuff like *Saluta!* (8/28/
34; thirty-nine performances), in which Milton Berle as the emcee of "a
sleazy New York night spot . . . is persuaded by his gangster cohorts to sail
to Italy and stage an opera in competition with the fascists' official productions" (Bordman 489).

Even shorter—thirty-two performances—was the run of *Parade* (5/20/35),
but it was also infinitely more important as the first overtly leftist satirical
revue. Scheduled for production by the Theatre Union, which was organized in 1932 to produce "militant, Marxist labor plays" (Goldstein, *Political*
39), *Parade* somehow ended up at the Theatre Guild, one of the most
respected yet least political producing organizations in New York. George
Sklar and Paul Peters's script and songs couldn't seem to shake the negatives. Whether because the authors viewed their satiric targets "more as
enemies than as humorous figures" (Smith 165–66), or because Guild actors

used to performing in classics and highly "literary" plays had forgotten how to "cultivate the antic mood successfully" (Brooks Atkinson, qtd. in Goldstein, *Political* 119), *Parade* got off on the wrong foot.

The revue's sketches and songs for the most part were hard-hitting body blows. The first scene set the tone for the evening, with "the police ignoring radio reports of violent crimes but rushing to break up a parade of poor people" (Bordman 493). One skit spoofed the "idea of the master race, in which under an American Hitler all citizens try to make themselves over as Indians," and another had a Depression-era college grad futilely seeking employment in a department store (Goldstein, *Political* 119). Inventive Jerome Moross composed the music, with interpolations by equally inventive Marc Blitzstein, Kay Swift, and others. But quality music alone couldn't save the revue. Eating a loss of about $100,000, "*Parade* was the Guild's last foray into radicalism" (120).

If the politically neutral Theatre Guild could produce the openly left-wing *Parade*, why shouldn't the left-leaning Group Theatre mount Paul Green and Kurt Weill's antiwar parable *Johnny Johnson* (11/19/36)? The Green/Weill show was as benign as *Parade* had been caustic, rising above specific ideologies in its seriocomic tale of a simple country stonecutter and true pacifist who enlists in the Great War, naively believing it will be the "war to end all wars." Johnny's view of war's origins is not the "Marxist view that its cause is the capitalist-imperialist desire to reap a profit from armaments" but rather "the humanitarian view that war is caused by government and military leaders so obsessed with the idea of national honor that they are indifferent to life itself" (Goldstein, *Political* 313). Given the ongoing pacifistic mood in the United States, *Johnny Johnson* should have stood a fair chance of success. Green presented its theme with much theatricality, and Weill's first American score was in a refreshingly personal idiom. But *Johnny Johnson* was still a disappointing sixty-eight performance flop. Its failure can't be blamed on any radical sentiments in the play, since it transcended all party lines, expressing the prevailing pacifistic, isolationist, and antiwar sentiments of the American public. More likely, as Goldstein suggests, *Johnny Johnson* was the first entirely stylized, non-realistic Group Theatre production in its acting and staging demands. Accordingly, even such outstanding Group regulars as Luther Adler, Morris Carnovsky, Elia Kazan, and Jules (later John) Garfield weren't sure of their footing. Further, the musical's roots in folk play, allegory, and parable may have been a bit much for audiences used to commercial Broadway musicals to grasp.

The successful musical satires of the early '30s, followed by this string of flops mid-decade, including his own *Let 'Em Eat Cake*, suggests that George S. Kaufman uttered a self-fulfilling prophecy in the famous quip

"Satire is what closes Saturday night." But satire would make a tremendous comeback in the final years of the decade.

### The Cradle Will Rock *and Public Support for the Arts*

If the Depression had anything like an upside vis-à-vis the performing arts, it was as a wake-up call for public funding. In the summer of 1935, more social legislation was signed into law than in any previous year in the country's history, including "the most liberal relief program ever undertaken by any government, the Works Progress Administration" (Wecter 96). Mostly, the WPA provided jobs constructing new roads, bridges, and public buildings like libraries, court houses, schools, and post offices — or renovating old ones — and also occasional massive projects like New York City's North Beach airport. The WPA also provided services for children so parents could work. By the beginning of 1941, the agency had served six hundred million school lunches and run nearly fifteen hundred nursery schools; many women not employable out of the home worked at sewing literally millions of pieces of clothing for children and adults in need. At the same time, the federal government acknowledged that, along with conventional blue- and white-collar workers, writers, musicians, artists, and theatre people had fallen on hard times and needed an assist from Washington. Hence, when just about a month old, the WPA authorized and funded the Federal Art, Federal Music, Federal Theatre, and Federal Writers Projects (the last not "Literature," given the mundane work it offered many writers). The goal was to put back to work *in their own fields* artistic, talented Americans.

In August 1935, Hallie Flanagan, the energetic and forward-thinking head of Vassar College's experimental theatre, became the National Director of the Federal Theatre Project with a seven million dollar budget to work with. Soon FTP "units" or "projects" were set up across the country, "supporting about twelve thousand five hundred actors through the nation at an average 'security wage' of eighty-three dollars monthly, better and steadier pay than most had ever received before" (Wecter 263). At first no admission fees were charged for any Federal Theatre events, a second "relief" feature of the program beyond employing theatre workers: free entertainment for a country much in need of it. Even when it became necessary to charge for some productions, the top ticket price of fifty cents even in New York still allowed the Federal Theatre to gross "at its peak . . . about a million dollars yearly in box-office returns," playing to "an estimated twenty to twenty-five million people, of whom a majority had never seen a play before." For bringing widespread, affordable, quality theatre to all segments of the American public during years of crisis, the Federal Theatre Project ranks as one of the greatest theatrical efforts of all time. And yet, the short-lived FTP marked the first and only time the U.S. government provided any funding for theatre prior to the founding of the National Endowment for the Arts (NEA) in 1965, a date that pathetically underscores the fact that the United States was dead last among the world's chief industrial nations to institute permanent and ongoing government funding of the arts.

While the WPA and the Federal Theatre did immeasurable good combating unemployment both generally and among theatre workers, those same New Deal agencies were responsible for complicating the lives of a young composer-lyricist named Marc Blitzstein and his cohorts. Thanks to the federal government, Blitzstein's left-wing jazz opera *The Cradle Will Rock* literally *made* history by being in the wrong place at the wrong time with the wrong producer. In New York during the '30s, numerous left-leaning revues, musicals, and plays were produced without incident by theatre groups in sympathy with or allied to the Communist Party, socialism, workers' movements, or trade and industrial unions (see Goldstein, *Political passim*). Such productions raised little ire among the press or the public. But a pro-union, rabidly antimanagement musical set in Steeltown, U.S.A., produced by a *government agency*, and funded with *federal money*, was a different matter.

*Cradle* opened during a time of terrific ferment in the steel industry. On March 1, 1937, John L. Lewis and the CIO successfully unionized Big Steel's United States Steel without so much as a strike. But that same spring Republic Steel's autocratic Tom M. Girdler and his recalcitrant combine of companies known as Little Steel were resisting unionization with a force that climaxed in violence. On Memorial Day at the Republic plant in South Chicago, strike-breaking police and Girdler's thugs wounded ninety and killed ten mostly unarmed strikers, shooting seven in the back as they fled (Allen, *Since* 291–93; Houseman 250). Such was the brutal, real-life melodrama against which Blitzstein's "proletarian opera" played its first historic performance in June 1937.

The Federal Theatre produced *Cradle* with funding from its parent agency, the WPA. The relationship between the WPA and *Cradle* mirrors that between governments and theatres down through time: whatever agency provides the money also has the say-so—or thinks it has. *Cradle* made history because it premiered despite the government's efforts to suppress it, thereby taking a strong stand for free speech on the American stage.

Like the kinds of theatre it's modeled on, *Cradle* is quite simple. Blitzstein wrote it with the broad strokes of a medieval morality play or one of Ben Jonson's satiric comedies, in which all is laid out in black and white, with few gray shadings at all. This is first evident in the cast of characters; nearly all have the generic names of morality figures or the type-characters in Jonsonian satire — Reverend Salvation, Editor Daily, Dr. Specialist, Harry Druggist, etc. In Steeltown, U.S.A., Mr. Mister owns not just the steel mill but the entire town and nearly everyone in it — except for young Larry Foreman. Although Foreman doesn't appear until scene 7 of the ten-scene show, the plot concerns his effort to unionize the mill, which he finally does, flatly rejecting Mr. Mister's attempts to bribe him.

Alongside this storyline is Blitzstein's "secondary theme of literal prostitution personified by the Moll, set against the background of prostitution of another kind" (*Marc* side 1). That "secondary theme" was in fact the real source of the opera. In 1935, Blitzstein showed Bertolt Brecht a revue sketch he wrote that included what would later become the prostitute's big song in *Cradle*, "The Nickel under the Foot." The German émigré playwright (and communist) told Blitzstein, "To literal prostitution you must add figurative prostitution — the sell-out of one's talent and dignity to the powers that be" — "the press, the church, the courts, the arts, the whole system" (qtd in Houseman 245–46; Callow 289). Blitzstein took Brecht's advice and, out of gratitude, dedicated *Cradle* to him. The amount of stage time given to this "figurative prostitution" argues that this theme is as central to the show as the struggle for unionization. The five scenes between Moll's arrest for soliciting in scene 1 and Larry Foreman's entrance late in the action are mostly devoted to flashbacks satirically depicting how the members of Mr. Mister's Cradle of Liberty Committee sold their souls to the antilabor steel magnate and his social-climbing wife. Blitzstein named Mr. Mister's ultra-right-wing toadies the Cradle of Liberty Committee to reference "the anti–New Deal American Liberty League, . . . established in 1934" (Goldstein, *Political* 189), but otherwise this politically explosive show is almost devoid of explicit topical references. Still, its satiric vignettes of America's elite prostituting itself to big business, was, like its pro-union stance, intensely provocative.

John Houseman richly recounts the circumstances surrounding *Cradle*'s first performance in his memoir *Run-Through*; other accounts offer additional detail. Blitzstein himself observed of the saga that "the story of *The Cradle*'s opening has taken on a somewhat legendary gloss and blur over the years and there are many embellished and apocryphal versions of it" (*Marc* side 1). Since this has been an oft-told tale, the narrative here focuses specifically on the government's attempt to suppress the show and how *Cradle*'s production team defied that mandate.

After writing the opera in five weeks of frenzied creative activity in 1936, Blitzstein auditioned it to such sympathetically liberal to left-wing theatre people as Herman Shumlin, Martin Gabel, and Harold Clurman. But *Cradle* was a political hot potato, since it dealt with unionizing steel just when Little Steel's resistance to unionization was making almost daily headlines. After all the others turned it down, the leftist Actors' Repertory Company agreed to produce it (*Marc* side 1).

Some time after that, Blitzstein played *Cradle* for the artistic director of Federal Theatre Project #891, a twenty-one-year-old named Orson Welles. Instantly taken by the piece, Welles said he wanted to direct it. Blitzstein agreed, thrilled that the theatre's reigning *wunderkind* wanted to stage his opera. Then, claiming lack of funds, Actors' Repertory dropped the project. Enter the managing producer of #891, "Jack" Houseman—also destined to be a formidable producer/director/actor, and only twenty-four himself at the time. Once Houseman heard *Cradle* he was ready to do it, though he knew that the endeavor "bore absolutely no relation to anything either of us had done before and . . . was guaranteed, in the circumstances, to land us both in the most serious possible trouble." Houseman immediately invited Federal Theatre National Director Hallie Flanagan to dinner at his apartment, where Blitzstein played and sang the show for her, testing the waters for the FTP's official blessing—and funding. Flanagan loved it: "It took no wizardry to see that this was not a play set to music, nor music illustrated by actors, but music + play equaling something new and better than either. This was in its percussive as well as its verbal beat Steel Town U S A: street corner, mission, lawn of Mr. Mister, drugstore, hotel lobby, faculty room, night court: America 1937. Would we do it on Federal Theatre? Jack Houseman would produce it and Orson Welles would direct it and I didn't see why they needed any scenery" (Flanagan 201).

Which, ultimately, they didn't. With a green light from Flanagan, Welles and Houseman cast the show and began a long, leisurely rehearsal period at the Maxine Elliott Theatre, with their company of sixty conforming to the allowable 10 percent quota of non-relief performers and the rest "reliefers." Sets and costumes were designed and built, Feder worked on his lighting design, and musical director Lehman Engel rehearsed his twenty-eight-piece orchestra five days a week, five hours a day. Such were the luxuries of Federal Theatre time and money. But in May everything began to hit the proverbial fan.

Because of *Cradle's* subject, "There were," wrote Hallie Flanagan, "rumors in Washington that it was dangerous" just when Little Steel was resisting all attempts to unionize (202). Worse yet were threats of Washington making major cuts in the WPA, including the various Arts Projects. The left-leaning *Cradle* and its producing company were bound to get caught in the crossfire.

On June 10, writes Flanagan, "we received the definite order to cut the New York project by 30 per cent, involving the dismissal of 1,701 workers" (202). Her allegiance more to the theatre projects than to her bureaucratic superiors, Flanagan brought to New York Lawrence Morris, an assistant director of the FTP's Washington office, to see a *Cradle* runthrough. He "pronounced it magnificent" (Flanagan 202), but to no avail. On June 12, all national FTP directors received a seemingly "routine memorandum prohibiting 'because of any impending cuts and reorganization, any new play, musical performance or art gallery to open before July 1st' "(Houseman 255). Just a year after Congress brought the Federal Theatre to a close, Hallie Flanagan wrote that that memorandum "was obviously censorship under a different guise" (202–203). The undisturbed openings of other federally sponsored music theatre productions more benign in nature—a *Carmen* at the Mosque Theatre in Newark on June 18, and a *Tales of Hoffman* at New York's Theatre of Music on June 22—suggest that the June 12 directive was not in fact general but indeed aimed specifically at *Cradle* (Gordon 141).

From this point forward the activity of *Cradle*'s production team begins to play like a theatrical conspiracy—which in a very real sense it was. The first preview performance had been scheduled for June 16th. Since "[t]here was no specific rule forbidding invited guests at rehearsals," Welles and Houseman invited an audience for the evening of June 14. The several hundred who attended that dress rehearsal would be the only audience ever to see the opera as fully staged and designed by Welles. The performance was technically shaky, but the audience left enthusiastic about the show itself.

Then things got worse. The WPA posted armed guards around the Maxine Elliott both to prevent public performances and to keep members of #891 from absconding with anything of use to remount *Cradle* somewhere else. Then the government padlocked the doors, officially "sealing" the theatre. The indignity of the padlocking was what drove Welles to take a strong stand: the show *would* go on—somewhere (see Leaming 135).

On June 15, the entire staff of #891 piled into Houseman's makeshift office in the bright pink powder room of the Maxine Elliott to strategize. Houseman and Welles got the good news that it was legal to play the show anywhere except on federal property. But the rest of the news was bad. Local 802 of the musician's union—an AFL affiliate with no sympathy for the CIO tactics promoted in *Cradle*—ruled that since the show was "operatic," if it also played a full-size Broadway house, the musicians must be paid Broadway scale and their number increased to conform to the size of an opera orchestra (Gordon 142; Houseman 258–59). Even if Welles and Houseman could raise the money, Engel couldn't rehearse new musicians into the difficult score on one day's notice. They now had no orchestra. The news from Actors Equity was equally discouraging: the Equity members of *Cradle* who had rehearsed the play and been paid by one management (the Federal Theatre) were enjoined from performing the play "on any stage" for a different management (now consisting of Houseman and Welles; Houseman 260).

The music problem was easily solved. Blitzstein had performed *Cradle* for so many backers' auditions he could play and sing the entire opera himself. Also, Equity inadvertently left a loophole for the cast to wriggle through; the union had enjoined them against performing "on any stage" but said nothing about playing from the auditorium. Coercing no one, Welles and Houseman *invited* the cast to show up wherever Blitzstein was performing *Cradle*, and to rise from their seats in the audience to play their parts. Some conservative cast members bowed out, as did others afraid of losing their relief-work pay as their only means of support. But by and large few defected from the ranks.

Still, two problems confounded Houseman and Welles: no theatre, and no piano. The latter was expeditiously solved. Around 5 P.M. on June 16, the company's gofer, Jean Rosenthal, "a pint-sized child just out of college" (*Marc* side 1) who would later become one of Broadway's great lighting designers, sallied forth with a ten dollar bill and Houseman's orders to find a piano and a truck. In record time the intrepid young woman phoned back to say she'd rented an upright and hired a truck. Now what? " 'Keep riding around,' I said, 'and call in every fifteen minutes for orders' " (Houseman 262). And so she did—for nearly two hours—until Houseman could tell her where to deliver the piano.

Finally, around 8:00 P.M., the broker in "distressed theatres" who was brought in to locate a performance space offered Houseman the cheap and available Venice Theatre at 58th Street and 7th Avenue. In moments he had his $100 rental, and the production team moved north in a convoy of taxicabs. With the new location confirmed, the crowd outside the Maxine Elliott started their nineteen-block trek, those on foot collecting others on the way. Curtain was extended to 9:00 P.M. to allow time for the exodus.

Meanwhile, Jean Rosenthal had her orders and, with the help of four firemen next door, heaved the upright onto the stage of the Venice, a stage whose tacky backdrop of a Neapolitan vista was a permanent reminder that the run-down theatre was used for Italian-American variety shows. Conspiratorially, Feder and his lighting assistant arrived with one spotlight, apparently smuggled from the Maxine Elliott, and began rigging it up on the front of the balcony to use as a follow spot. Lehman Engel showed up with the piano-vocal score concealed under his winter overcoat on that hot June night. Once Blitzstein got there, he ordered the back ripped off the piano for increased volume in the vast house.

The audience arrived in an excited, anticipatory mood, overflowing the Venice's 1,700-plus seats. Reporters and photographers stood in the aisles. There would be no reviews of *Cradle* that night — critics rarely attend previews. But there would be front-page headlines. As Feder was testing his spotlight, its beam fell on an Italian fascist flag draped from one of the boxes, anathema to the mostly liberal-to-left audience. One spectator tore it down amid sympathetic cheers and laughter. Soon thereafter, at 9:05, what was less a performance than an event began (Leaming 136).

Houseman and Welles made curtain speeches, Houseman emphasizing that what they were doing was "a gesture of artistic, not political, defiance." Finally Welles declaimed, "We have the honor to present — with the composer at the piano — *The Cradle Will Rock!*" (Houseman 267).

The curtain rose. There was Blitzstein in his shirtsleeves "at his eviscerated piano before a washed-out view of the Bay of Naples with Vesuvius smoking in the distance." Not knowing which of the cast had arrived, Blitzstein was ready to sing the whole opera alone. *Cradle* has no overture, just a few opening chords on the piano. Blitzstein set the first scene, "A Street Corner — Steeltown, U.S.A.," and started singing Moll's opening song. It was then that the performance became an "event" monumental in the annals of the theatre. In Houseman's inimitable words, for no one could better capture the moment,

to Marc's strained tenor another voice — a faint, wavering soprano — had been added. It was not clear at first where it came from, as the two voices continued together for a few lines —

> I ain't in Steeltown long
> I work two days a week;
> The other five my efforts ain't required.

Then, hearing the words taken out of his mouth, Marc paused, and at that moment the spotlight moved off the stage, past the proscenium arch into the house, and came to rest on the lower left box where a thin girl in a green dress with dyed red hair was standing, glassy-eyed, stiff with fear, only half audible at first in the huge theatre but gathering strength with every note:

> For two days out of seven
> Two dollar bills I'm given . . .

It [is] almost impossible, at this distance of time, to convey the throat-catching, sickeningly exciting quality of that moment or to describe the emotions of gratitude and love with which we saw and heard that slim green figure. Years later, Hiram

Sherman wrote to me: "If Olive Stanton had not risen on cue in the box, I doubt if the rest of us would have had the courage to stand up and carry on. But once that thin, incredibly clear voice came out, we all fell in line." On technical grounds alone, it must have taken almost superhuman courage for an inexperienced performer (whom we had cast in part only because we had already exceeded our non-relief quota) to stand up before two thousand people, in an ill-placed and terribly exposed location, and start a show with a difficult song to the accompaniment of a piano that was more than fifty feet away. Add to this that she was a relief worker, wholly dependent on her weekly WPA check, and that she held no political views whatsoever. (268–69)

Taking their cue from Olive Stanton, the other actors followed, even singing duets and ensembles from opposite sides of the auditorium, or between balcony and orchestra. When the actor cast as Reverend Salvation failed to show, Hiram Sherman, who seemed to have memorized the whole opera, played that part as well as his own of Junior Mister, and some small ones as well. Blitzstein himself sang six or eight minor roles. By all accounts, the camaraderie among the cast was electrifying.

After the reprise-finale of the title song, "there was a second's silence— then all hell broke loose" (Houseman 274). When I recounted this event in a lecture in 1999, I learned the audience didn't just applaud. A woman in her eighties informed me, "They didn't just cheer and clap; they made Blitzstein and the cast sing some of the songs over and over, and the crowd sang along. I know—I was there."

Between the late start, the ninety-minute show, an intermission stuck in for the occasion, and a closing speech by poet Archibald MacLeish, who rather redundantly told the audience they had just seen history being made, it took till midnight to clear the crowd from the Venice. Houseman had to come up with more rent money, "but it was well worth it."

That historic night had a number of repercussions. That evening moved Welles and Houseman to form what became their highly regarded Mercury Theatre later that year. That performance also bestowed special notoriety on the already controversial *Cradle*. Blitzstein's biographer Eric A. Gordon observes "that by refusing it a home, the Federal Theatre did the work the greatest favor possible. Whereas the play might have occupied the Maxine Elliott stage for a few weeks or even a few months and then died a natural death, now, overnight, it became an established masterpiece" (144). Most important, that first performance of *The Cradle Will Rock* stood up against the government's attempt to silence it, thereby demonstrating the free exercise of First Amendment rights in the performing arts. Never again did the federal government try to censor or repress any theatre piece for its political or social content. Nevertheless, the flap caused by *Cradle* contributed to Congress's termination of the Federal Theatre Project on June 30, 1939.

With front page stories generating enthusiasm for what the press called the "runaway opera," on June 17, Houseman rounded up enough backers for what he termed a "commercial" run at the Venice, still with the performers planted in the audience. With the cast's best interests at heart, he decided on a two-week run, "the maximum time allowed from Works Projects without loss of relief status" (Houseman 275). The company was enthusiastic, "including two who had defected the previous night." Equity Bond was posted, WPA forms filled out, and Marc Blitzstein, wearing so many hats, paid initiation fees to the Dramatists' Guild, the Musician's Union, and Actors Equity all on one day.

With just a day off to regroup, *Cradle* opened its so-called commercial run on June 18, with "no advance sale, no opening-night drama reviews, lots of publicity but no money to advertise." At first houses were small, but with strong word of mouth, leftover theatre parties shut out of the Maxine Elliott, and others who came out of "curiosity" or "Party loyalty," the show broke even by the end of the run (Houseman 275).

*Cradle*'s next run was at Welles and Houseman's Mercury Theatre, where it was performed on Sunday evenings. Again it was minimally mounted; along with Blitzstein at the piano, the actors' chairs were now on stage, giving rise to its nickname, the "oratorio version." It opened on December 5, 1937, and this time the critical press appeared. Virtually all of New York's most distinguished critics—some putting aside political biases—praised all aspects of the opera and its production. The same Brooks Atkinson of the *Times* who felt *Let 'Em Eat Cake*'s satire was too bitter praised *Cradle*'s "extraordinary versatility" and "enormous gusto." The *Post*'s often-reserved John Mason Brown fairly cheered, "*The Cradle Will Rock* is the most exciting propagandistic tour de force our stage has seen since *Waiting for Lefty* burst like a bombshell upon this town. The sincerity of the actors sweeps across the footlights carrying everything before it" (qtd. in Houseman 277).

Welles and Houseman's final mounting of *Cradle* was at the Windsor Theatre (on Broadway at last!), where it opened on January 3, 1938, for 108 performances. As composer and music critic Virgil Thomson described the audience:

It is roughly the leftist front: that is to say, the right-wing socialists, the communists, some Park Avenue, a good deal of Bronx, and all those intellectual or worker groups that the Federal Theater in general and the Living Newspaper in particular have welded into about the most formidable ticket buyers in the world. Union benefits, leftist group drives, the German refugees, the Southern share-croppers, aids to China and to democratic Spain, the New York working populace, well-paid, well-dressed, and well-fed, supports them all. (qtd. in Gordon 165)

Judging from Thompson's observation, *The Cradle Will Rock* may have had yet a further impact on the performing arts in America by bringing more working-class people into Broadway theatre, many for the very first time.

## I'd Rather Be Right

In the months after the first historic performance of *The Cradle Will Rock*, two more musicals produced by the Federal Theatre Project opened in New York—without incident, since both were as non-controversial as *Cradle* had been incendiary. Their greatest social service, since they ran during the crushing recession of 1937–38, lay in employing for a short time large numbers of work-relief theatre workers. *Swing It* (7/22/37) was a sixty-performance African American show with a thin book about "the down-at-heels crew and entertainers of a rickety Mississippi show boat in their effort to find a better lot in Harlem" (Bordman 504); it had a fairly strong score by Eubie Blake, who was working with a new lyricist, Milton Reddie. The premise allowed for numerous musical numbers, dance routines, and other "specialties," thus employing a large cast of black work-reliefers. The second FTP show that fall was a children's musical "extravaganza" (Flanagan 318) with a score by Lehman Engel and book and lyrics by Theresa Helburn, one of the prime movers of the Theatre Guild, adapted from Andrew Lang's "Prince Prigio" tales. The cast alone of *A Hero Is Born* (10/1/37) numbered nearly a hundred, all work-reliefers but for the allowable quota of "ten-percenters." The production's sizable orchestra and its profusion of sets, costumes, lighting, and special effects also gave work to a small army of musicians and technicians. As part of the FTP's national "Drama for Children" series, *Hero's* fifty performances in a full-size Broadway house was an impressive run for a children's show.

In November, two musicals opened that, like *Cradle*, made history. The first depicted the incumbent head of state as the star character in a full-length musical comedy. The second began as a left-leaning amateur satirical revue by and for a labor union's members and became the second-longest-running musical of the 1930s.

In the spring of 1937, George S. Kaufman and Moss Hart came up with the idea for a satirical show about the president, not a fictional president as in *Of Thee I Sing* but *the* president, Franklin Delano Roosevelt. There had been musical theatre precedents for musical theatre presidents, if only in revues, but for FDR to be the singing and dancing star of a book show — ultimately played by George M. Cohan — was quite a leap. This is especially so since FDR was just then emerging with a qualified victory from the most damaging personal crisis of his presidency. Kaufman and Hart took advantage of even that, making his embarrassing battle with the Supreme Court the focal point of the satire in *I'd Rather Be Right* (11/2/37).

At the time of his landslide victory over Kansas Governor Alf Landon in 1936, Roosevelt was at a height of popularity unrivaled by any previous president. In his inaugural address on January 20, 1937, FDR declared, "I see one-third of a nation ill-housed, ill-clad, ill-nourished" (Allen, *Since* 281). His mission to better the lives of U.S. citizens was continually blocked by the Supreme Court, which invalidated or watered down much of his progressive social legislation. Frustrated, Roosevelt tried to "pack" the Court with members favorable to New Deal policies. So unpopular was this attempt that FDR's popularity dropped precipitously by early summer 1937. But Roosevelt prevailed, albeit in a limited way. The Supreme Court began upholding more liberal legislation, perhaps fearing for their own jobs (see Allen, *Since* 297). Then, fortuitously, conservative Justice Van Devanter stepped down, allowing FDR to make his first Supreme Court appointment, which he did in the person of New Deal advocate Alabama Senator Hugo L. Black. Black's appointment tipped the scales to the liberal side.

Roosevelt's misguided attempt to pack the Court, the New Deal, and the Depression gave Kaufman and Hart plenty to satirize. What is striking — and most likely contributed to the show's 290-performance run — is that the explicit satire and political wisecracks are always good-humored. No matter how many jokes the authors made at Roosevelt's expense, they always portrayed him sympathetically.

The show has the thinnest of plots: a young man can't marry his girl because his boss's business has failed and he can't get a raise or promotion. His boss has told him he'll never have enough for a family to live on until the government balances the federal budget. (Indeed, marriages were down in the early years of the Depression by about 3 percent from 1929.) On the Fourth of July in Central Park, the young man dreams that FDR befriends the unhappy couple and promises to balance the budget so they can marry. In spite of the political humor, there is an undercurrent of melancholy; the young lovers and the president grow increasingly distressed at the long-lasting Depression. Toward the end of the show, Kaufman and Hart turn statistics into theatre. After FDR apologizes to Phil and Peggy for not balancing the budget yet, Phil says, "You know, it's funny, isn't it. All this business about the whole country, and balancing the budget. You wouldn't think it would touch Peggy and me, but I guess it does. And we want so little, Mr. Roosevelt. Just the right to work, and be married to each other—and—bring up our kids. We don't want much. If we could have just that. That isn't too much to ask, is it?" (Kaufman and Hart 119–20).

To which the President replies, "Phil, Peggy—you want my advice? Get married. Take your life and live it. You'll manage. People have done it before. You'll come through somehow. Listen—suppose I *don't* balance the budget? There'll be a baby born every minute, just the same. But I'll balance it! I'm not through trying—not by a darned sight!" (Kaufman and Hart 122). It's moments like this that put a warm, humanizing spin on the show's depiction of FDR.

*I'd Rather Be Right* resonates with topical political humor. Central is the running gag of FDR's running battle with the Supreme Court. As Roosevelt continues searching for schemes to balance the budget, the "Nine Old Men" pop up from the Central Park shrubs to squelch every piece of legislation FDR proposes, usually proclaiming in unison, "Ah, no! No, you don't! Oh, no!" and then they're gone again (Kaufman and Hart 35–36). At one point, after chastising FDR for calling them "Old fogies," the justices stay on stage long enough to do a song and dance routine with nine scantily clad chorus girls called "A Little Bit of Constitutional Fun" (62–63). The justices leave *with* the girls, provoking FDR to utter one of the show's most topical lines, "You know, if I'd suggested putting six new *girls* on the Bench, I'll bet they'd have said 'All right' " (63).

Lorenz Hart provided lyrics that matched the humor and satire of Kaufman and Hart's book. Except for the romantic ballad "Have You Met Miss Jones," Rodgers and Hart's songs did not become hits, but they kept the show's comedy going at an incredible clip. When the Cabinet (all of whose real names are used) enters, they sing that they look and act so homogeneous that they could be a Gilbert and Sullivan chorus. Then, like G&S soloists making an entrance, some of them sing little solos about who they are or what they do. Here's Postmaster-General Farley, notoriously free with patronage jobs:

> I keep my popularity forever hale and hearty
> By finding jobs for everyone in the Democratic Party.
> A job for every uncle and a job for every niece—
> I give a job for every vote, and how the votes increase!
> Some guys are such good voters they get twenty jobs apiece!
>    Three cheers for the land of F. D.!

Frances Perkins, secretary of labor, and sole female cabinet member:

All of these strikes keep a girl on her toes
I've barely got time to powder my nose.
I fight for the workmen and fight for the bosses,
And the more that I fight, the bigger their losses.
It would help the whole thing a great deal, I suppose,
If I gave it all up and just powdered my nose.

And Henry Morgenthau, secretary of the treasury:

> I'm quite a busy man right now—
> I'm Secretary Morgenthau
> You may have heard that I attend
> To what you call the money end.
> Since first this land of ours began,
> I am its top financial man.
> I have achieved, you must admit,
> The biggest goddam deficit!
> (Kaufman and Hart 23–24)

Not to be outdone in political tomfoolery, FDR lists what he'd like to tell the press "Off the Record" in act 2:

> My speeches on the radio have made me quite a hero,
> I only have to say "My Friends" and stocks go down to zero.
>     Don't print it; it's strictly off the record.
> The radio officials say that I'm the leading fellow—
> Jack Benny can be President and I'll go on for Jello.
>     Don't print it; it's strictly off the record.
> It's pleasant at the White House, but I'll tell you how I feel:
> The food is something terrible—just sauerkraut and veal;
> If Eleanor would stay at home, I'd get a decent meal—
>     But that's off the record.
>                                           (107)

Kaufman and Hart even took a whack at the Federal Theatre Project—once in each act. About midway through act 1, out of nowhere come a theatre director and a bevy of beautiful girls costumed like escapees from a Rudolf Friml operetta. They ask Phil, Peggy, and FDR if they can put on a show since they are "the Federal Theatre, Unit No. 864," and "Whenever we see three people together, we're supposed to give a show." The girls perform "Spring in Vienna," a pointless send-up of all such pointless, schmaltzy operetta numbers. The director tells FDR it cost $675,000 to produce, prompting the president to remark, "Six hundred and seventy-five thousand dollars. Well, you can't take it with you. . . . Of course, there's *one* way the budget could be balanced—just like that!" (57).

The second-act whack at the FTP is sillier yet. FDR's grandchildren can't ride the merry-go-round because the driver is staging a work stoppage. So Roosevelt arbitrates a labor dispute between the owner and driver of the Central Park carousel, two broadly caricatured stage-Italians. Wishing to abide by National Labor Relations Board regulations, FDR tells his secretary, "I want to see the Wagner Act." After repeated offstage calls for the Wagner Act, in bound two German acrobats, doing lifts and flips accompanied by the requisite grunts and whoops; they are, of course, Hans and Fritz Wagner—the Wagner Act, Federal Theatre Project No. 34268 (90). Preposterous and funny, yes; acerbic satire, no.

## Pins and Needles

Like *I'd Rather Be Right*, *Pins and Needles* (11/27/37) was a show topically tied to its time, but what a time it had—an amateur revue running 1,108 performances! In 1935, after failing to establish a multi-union "consortium for the sponsorship of a professional theater," David Dubinsky, president of the International Ladies' Garment Workers Union, persuaded ILGWU to found—and fund with $25,000—"an amateur theater for a city-wide audience" (Goldstein, *Political* 206). With Louis Schaffer in charge, the union leased the Princess Theatre—the same that housed Jerome Kern's pioneering musicals two decades earlier—renaming it The Labor Stage. They sponsored a new play contest and gave seven performances of the winner, a play about union activities among tobacco workers. Next they revived John Wexley's *Steel* for fifty evenings and toured it to steel-producing cities. Then came *Pins and Needles*.

The revue's songwriter was the mostly untried but definitely leftist Harold Rome. Rome had written some of the songs for a show at the Green Mansions resort in the Catskills, then later had the chance to play them for Louis Schaffer. At first Schaffer and other ILGWU members found the material "too lighthearted." But after what amounted to a number of backers' auditions and private performances for unionists, the union changed its mind and, although they couldn't know it yet, a smash hit was born (207). As the revue took shape, to Rome's songs were added dialogue skits by Arthur Arent, Marc Blitzstein, Emanuel Eisenberg, Charles Friedman, Daniel Gregory, and Rome himself, about as left-leaning a bunch of sketch writers as you'd dare get together without the room listing to one side (205). These were the only professionals involved; the performers were all members of ILGWU's locals: "cutters, pressers, dressmakers, embroiderers, and makers of white goods, knitgoods, and neckwear—and like their locals, they

were a racially integrated cast" (205–206). Theatre programs and the published piano-vocal score proclaimed union pride by printing each cast member's garment trade and Local number.

Initially, *Pins and Needles* was preaching to the choir. It was a collection
of satirical songs and sketches performed by union members largely *for*
union members, and for a limited run. "No advertisements were placed in
the major dailies, and in return no major critic attended the show's opening
night" (Bordman 506). There was no advance sale, and at first the show
played only on weekends, both in expectation of small houses and so as not
to interfere with the cast's regular jobs (Goldstein, *Political* 205; Bordman
506). But the show caught on, and as early as 1938 Schaffer moved it from
the 299-seat Labor Stage to the 849-seat Windsor Theatre, where *The Cradle
Will Rock* had had its Broadway run. To everyone's amazement, *Pins and
Needles* stayed at the Windsor until June 22, 1940 (Bordman 506; Goldstein,
*Political* 205).

This phenomenal success came not just from the subject matter and
quality of its songs and sketches but also from its balanced and reasonable
tone. The revue was a product of the "non-Communist Left" (Goldstein,
*Political* 205). There were of course Communists in ILGWU, as there were
in most trade and craft unions in the 1930s, but since David Dubinsky "was
an ardent New Dealer" and Louis Schaffer a socialist, "[t]he political messages of the lyrics and sketches were solidly those of the Popular Front,
decrying the fascist menace and recommending the solidarity of workers"
(207, 212). The show's most famous number, "Sing Me a Song of Social
Significance," exemplifies the tone of light satire. Sick of the old moon-
June-croon clichés in love songs, the singer wants to know that his/her
potential partner is up to date with what's going on in the world:

> Sing me of wars and sing me of breadlines,
> Tell me of front page news.
> Sing me of strikes and last minute headlines,
> Dress your observation with syncopation!
> Sing me a song of social significance,
> There's nothing else that will do—
> It must get hot with what is what
> Or I won't love you.
> (Rome, *Pins* 5–6)

In Malcolm Goldstein's analysis, "Rome brought off the trick of making
fun, not only of love songs, but of the overwrought seriousness of individuals
who have no time for them" (208), to which I would only add that Rome
was even ribbing those too-earnest leftist types who have to see *everything*,
even their own love lives, in terms of "social significance."

The revue's approach was forthright as well as balanced. Rome was ready to call a fascist a fascist when he saw one, and he saw three in a piece called "The Harmony Boys" from one of the show's revisions. With no holds barred, Rome took after these notorious Nazi sympathizers — "radio priest" Father Coughlin, Senator Bob Reynolds, and Fritz Kuhn, founder of the German-American Bund. Here are Coughlin and Kuhn:

FATHER COUGHLIN:
I'm the big noise from the little shrine
I shock my flock with words divine
Tho some folks wish that I would choke
Hitler, Goebbels and Goering think I'm okey-doke.

FRITZ KUHN:
I'm the biggest hund in the whole darn bund
Right now I don't feel too gezund.
Last night I acted indiscreet
I yelled "Heil Hitler" in Delancy Street.
(Rome, *New Pins*)

Father Coughlin and cohorts aside, one reason *Pins and Needles* had such longevity in the late 1930s was that most of its political barbs were gently padded. In addition, the show's strong pro-union and proletarian stance was increasingly acceptable to many people pinched by the Depression. Also, the skits and songs were very well written and delivered with energy and enthusiasm by the amateur cast. Finally, the revue continually kept abreast of the news by adding material or updating older songs and sketches; a person could return again and again during the three-year run and see virtually a new show every time. At several points in its run, *Pins and Needles* changed its name to reflect just that: *New Pins and Needles, Pins and Needles of 1938, Pins and Needles of 1939.*

One of the most telling of the later additions, "The Red Mikado," had fun with the rival productions of the Federal Theatre's all-black *The Swing Mikado* (3/1/39) and Mike Todd's commercially produced *The Hot Mikado* (3/23/39), also all black. More significantly, the sketch minced no words in excoriating one of the most publicly embarrassing slurs to African Americans in the decade. In April 1939, the Daughters of the American Revolution refused the gifted African American contralto Marian Anderson the use of Washington's Constitution Hall because she was black. Secretary of the Interior Harold Ickes intervened, arranging for her to perform from the steps of the Lincoln Memorial instead. Over seventy-five thousand people attended (Stillman 382). Harold Rome gleefully changed Gilbert and Sullivan's "Three Little Maids from School" into "Three Little D. A. R.'s" in order to satirize the D. A. R.

> Three little D. A. R.'s are we,
> Reactionary as we can be,
> Filled to the brim with bigotry,
>     Three little D. A. R.'s.
>
> Everything is a source of fun,
> We're all descended from Washington,
> We don't rent halls to Anderson,
>     Three little D. A. R.'s
>                             (Rome, *New Pins*)

Rome and his cohorts continued to add, subtract, and revise such timely and topical material almost until *Pins and Needles* closed in June 1940.

## The Curtain Falls on '30s Satire

In all, fifteen satiric book shows or revues opened in the 1930s, a figure never equaled or surpassed in a single decade. In fact, musical satire effectively died with the '30s, successfully resuscitated only rarely thereafter. Of the fifteen shows, five opened and closed during the run of *Pins and Needles*. To some degree all five shifted their satire from the U.S. economy to global issues, primarily fascism and dictatorships.

*Hooray for What* (12/1/37) began with the noblest intentions of socially minded lyricist E. Y. "Yip" Harburg. Distressed by affairs in Europe, Yip wanted to do a musical "about the need for preserving peace and the dangers of the armaments race" (Green 180). Howard Lindsay and Russel Crouse wrote the script and Harold Arlen composed the score for a show written for that zaniest of musical comedy zanies, Ed Wynn. But Wynn "had to dominate his shows. . . . Gone by the time the show reached New York was the taut, hard-driving book, [and] much of Agnes De Mille's anti-war ballet" (Bordman 507). All that was left of the anti-armaments stance was Wynn as a screwball scientist who invents "a gas to kill apple worms. When the world powers discover it kills humans with equal efficiency, they trip over one another trying to steal it" (507). Though the point had been blunted and Harburg's vision blurred, Wynn's clowning kept *Hooray for What* playing 200 times.

Max Gordon got Charles Friedman and Harold Rome of *Pins and Needles* to create some new revue material, confident he'd have a hit (Goldstein, *Kaufman* 304). He had them write a "topical, left-of-center series of comic blackouts and musical numbers"; he also brought in George S. Kaufman and Moss Hart both as play doctors and associate producers of *Sing Out the News* (9/24/38). All five men were left leaning but enough at odds with one another to create differences. Occasionally a guest at the White House, Gordon saw the revue as a way to support FDR's New Deal politics; with his strong leftist sentiments, Rome "felt that Kaufman and Hart lacked firm political convictions . . . firing off jokes at virtually everything left, right, and center"(304). With no unifying vision, *Sing Out the News* was more scattered and less focused than *Pins and Needles*.

Still, some material made its point; one song even became a hit. One humorous skit depicted Hollywood moguls stressing over how to film their epic *Marie Antoinette* without mentioning "Revolution," while in a serious skit a young boy tries to break up a fight between "a marching band of 'reds' and a marching band of bourgeoisie"—both groups beat him up, and a cop arrests the *boy* for inciting a riot (306). Rome's hit was "Franklin D. Roosevelt Jones," in which, thankful for what Roosevelt had done, a black couple names their son for FDR. *Sing Out the News* sang out just 105 times.

*Knickerbocker Holiday* (10/19/38), by distinguished playwright Maxwell Anderson and with music by equally distinguished composer Kurt Weill, was not the theatrical triumph later generations seem to remember it being; it played only 168 times. After his collaboration with Laurence Stallings on *What Price Glory*, a prose World War I comedy-drama, Anderson wrote almost nothing but verse plays, winning the Pulitzer Prize for his 1935 tragedy *Winterset*. Anderson's verse comfortably carries his plays' dramatic action, but this author of viable poetic drama never learned how to use songs in a play to help tell the story. Nearly all the songs in *Knickerbocker* are explanatory, not dramatic, reeling out points of the satire or just reiterating what was said in the dialogue, which Anderson wrote in prose, not in his more accustomed verse (see Jones, "Maxwell" 97–102 *passim*).

Anderson intended *Knickerbocker Holiday* as a send-up of both totalitarian dictatorships and aspects of the American political system. Although the show is weak as an attempt at a well-crafted musical, its political satire is strong. The story, such as it is, comes smack out of Gilbert and Sullivan's *Mikado* (see Jones, "Maxwell" 99). It opens on a bizarre holiday in Old Dutch New Amsterdam called "Hanging Day," coincidentally the day the new governor, Pieter Stuyvesant, is to arrive—all within a narrative frame of Washington Irving writing his *Knickerbocker's History of Old New York*. The Council of rotund, inept Dutchmen figure they better string up someone in honor of the holiday or *they'll* be strung up. They choose the town's fiercely independent ne'er-do-well Brom Broeck, who loves and is loved by

Tina, Councilman Tienhoven's daughter. But Tienhoven plans to marry her off to the much older Stuyvesant, occasioning the show's one memorable number, "September Song." All ends happily, thanks to Irving stepping in as a deus ex machina, convincing Stuyvesant it will stain posterity's image of him if he hangs Brom, whose independence and hatred of taking orders may qualify him as the first true "American."

It's not clear whether Anderson meant Stuyvesant as a composite of Europe's totalitarian dictators or FDR, who some feared was having dreams of autocratic grandeur himself (see Goldstein, *Political* 395). But Stuyvesant as Roosevelt does seem redundant, since the playwright already included a buffoonish Old Dutch Roosevelt ancestor in the Town Council. Anderson, as a man "against encroachments upon the freedom of the individual" (394), opposed totalitarianism but was equally wary of the New Deal's social programs. In the show he comes down on the side of democracy. Stuyvesant's one-man rule loses to the bumbling of the democratic Councilmen, the musical pitting Stuyvesant's view that "a government is a group of men organized to sell protection to the inhabitants of a limited area—at monopolistic prices" against Brom's that a democracy is "where you're governed by amateurs" (Anderson, *Knickerbocker* 40–41, 51). Brom's individualism wins because, in Anderson's vision, it is so "American": "a democracy has the immense advantage of being incompetent in villainy and clumsy in corruption . . . let's go back to the rotation of amateurs! Let's keep the government small and funny, and maybe it'll give us less discipline and more entertainment!" (88).

The next allegedly satirical musical had even "less discipline" than Anderson's flawed libretto but gave "more entertainment" to its audiences, playing 307 times. *Leave It to Me* (11/9/38) was the first show Samuel and Bella Spewack wrote with Cole Porter providing the music and lyrics; ten years later the three would do *Kiss Me, Kate* (12/30/48). The forgettable book for *Leave It to Me* was less than an excuse for some equally forgettable shotgun satire of international relations. A bathtub manufacturer's generosity to FDR's re-election campaign gets him appointed ambassador to the Soviet Union, an appointment he wishes never happened. Aided by a wheeling and dealing newspaper reporter, the reluctant ambassador does all he can to be recalled, but each scheme backfires, until he devises a global peace plan, whereupon he is whisked home immediately. Failing to take careful aim at specific, selected targets, the satirical buckshot in the Spewacks' book and Porter's lyrics mostly misses the mark. The musical's true historical interest is extrinsic, showing how political changes in the real world can materially alter a piece of theatre. Josef Stalin made his musical comedy debut in *Leave It to Me*, singing nothing but "*Nyet, nyet, nyet,*

*nyet*" (Richards 2: 36). Initially that was perfectly acceptable fun, since the U.S. was on reasonably good terms with the USSR. But on August 21, 1939, just when the show was to begin its national tour, Moscow signed its non-aggression pact with Berlin, and Stalin was immediately purged from the musical (Stillman 382; Bordman 513).

*Sing for Your Supper* (4/29/39), sponsored by the Federal Theatre Project, was the last of the socially aware musicals of the 1930s, opening just two months before Congress terminated the FTP and its funding on June 30. The revue's sketches mostly satirized the international scene, while the songs dealt with matters stateside and were generally upbeat and optimistic (Bordman 515). The two most memorable songs were wholly positive, yet one still got the show in trouble with Congress. "Papa's Got a Job!" was a song and dance celebration of what the number's title declares. "The Ballad of Uncle Sam," a virtual oratorio for soloist and chorus, catalogued "the composite make-up of the typical 'American'—his ethnic origins, his professions, his religions, and his unshakable faith in democracy"—and extolled "the richness and diversity of America in a hymn of hope for the future" (Goldstein 266; Bordman 515). More for composer Earl Robinson's openly leftist persuasions than the number's actual content, Congressman Martin Dies and his House Un-American Activities Committee ironically cited this patriotic paean, making *Sing for Your Supper* "the object of some of the most violent attacks before the Committee, and later on the floor of Congress" (Flanagan 366). The revue ran for only forty-four performances, but the irony continued into 1940. Retitled "The Ballad for Americans," the piece was vindicated twice. First, Paul Robeson, continually suspected of un-American activities, made a popular recording of it. Then—a slap in the face to Commie-hunting Dies—millions of radio listeners heard this anthem to American diversity broadcast as the theme of the 1940 *Republican National Convention* in Philadelphia (366).

After *Sing for Your Supper* the plethora of socially relevant, satirical musicals ended. For the next six years social consciousness all but disappeared from musical Broadway. This can perhaps be explained by creative exhaustion, by relief that the Depression's end was in sight, or by writers of musicals finally catching the mood of audiences who viewed international politics "as no laughing matter," as Morrie Ryskind observed as early as 1933. The press, movies, radio, popular song, and print and broadcast advertising kept the 1939–1945 war before the eyes and ears of America. But just as World War I had done, World War II knocked most topical satire and social relevance off the musical stage. Yet if ephemeral topicality all but vanished, about midway through America's involvement in the war a kind of musical emerged that embraced broader social themes and reshaped American musical theatre for the remainder of the twentieth century.

## ✳ 4 ✳

# World War II and the Rodgers and Hammerstein Years

### Wartime Prosperity

World War II ended the Great Depression and returned prosperity to the United States. In March 1940, seven months after Britain and France declared war on Germany, over eight million Americans were still out of work, but by 1944 most of the jobless of 1940 were working again, bringing unemployment to an all-time low of about 800,000. The wartime demand for every employable American created seventeen million new jobs in the military or in manufacturing (see Stillman 390; Lingeman 136; Blum 91; Wecter 120).

As in the past, men were the bulk of America's workforce during the war, at one time or another over thirteen million employed by the U.S. armed forces. Millions of others were still at work, or back at work, in stateside jobs, war related or not, although conscription and volunteer enlistment took its toll on certain "industries"—professional baseball, for one. Of approximately 5,700 professional ballplayers, over 4,000 went into the service. But the game went on, and fans, buoyed by new jobs and salaries, packed the ballparks in record numbers, as they did other leisure activities, musical theatre included (Lingeman 312).

Thanks to the defense-driven employment boom, unprecedented numbers of women went to work. Just over 100,000 served in the armed forces. On the homefront, by the fall of 1943 some seventeen million women were employed—about a third of the total work force. Of those, about five million worked in defense industries; the rest filled civilian jobs vacated by men in the service. By 1943, women's wages in factories had increased over 50 percent since 1941. While the country was years away from equal pay for equal work, women were paid well enough to spend some of it on themselves (Perrett 346, 343, 95).

Most working Americans made a living wage, and many had discretionary income. Men, women, even children had money "for luxuries if they were rich, for amenities long denied them if they were of moderate means,

for small conveniences, decent food, and some recreation if they were workers" (Blum 92). After the Depression, not just the wealthy rejoiced to have
disposable income. Jewelry sales rose 20 to 100 percent in different parts of
the country, with war workers, not the rich, spending most freely: " 'People
are crazy with money,' one Philadelphia jeweler said. 'They don't care what
they buy. They purchase things . . . just for the fun of spending' " (97).

*Advertising the War*

From fall 1939 through summer 1945, it was virtually impossible to pick up
a newspaper without seeing a banner headline or at least a front-page story
dealing with the war. Weekly magazines like *Time, Life, Look, Newsweek,*
and *The Saturday Evening Post* also covered the war and war-related homefront activities incessantly. First through the Office of Facts and Figures
(OFF), and later through the Office of War Information (OWI), the government issued pamphlets, leaflets, and the like to inform Americans about
the war and persuade them of their duty to support it by buying bonds,
enrolling in civil defense activities, or participating in scrap metal, paper,
rubber, and kitchen fats drives. To this day, I vividly recall an afternoon
when I was playing outside my suburban Chicago home not far from the
Great Lakes Naval Air Station when a low-flying formation of bombers
passed overhead, opened their bomb bay doors, and dropped countless
brightly colored handbills displaying the familiar Minute Man logo and the
caption "BUY WAR BONDS!" To a boy of three or four it was a sight both
thrilling and scary.

Such direct persuasion, as well as the government's promoting of the war
effort through other media, proved tremendously effective. Nearly every
bond issue was oversubscribed, raising astronomical figures for defense, and
by mid-1943 over twelve million Americans had volunteered for one or
another form of civil defense work, only about a million fewer than would
eventually serve in the armed forces (Lingeman 59). But perhaps the
greatest effect of such government and media efforts was to create among
virtually all Americans a sense of national unity stronger than ever before
in the country's history.

Even more than the print media, radio kept the war in front of the nation.
By 1944, NBC filled 20 percent of its air time with news, compared to 3.6
percent in 1939; CBS devoted a full 30 percent of its programming to war
news alone (223). And, too, radio had the capacity for almost instantaneous
reporting not enjoyed by print media. In addition to hard news and related
stories, radio's entertainment programming from soap operas and Westerns

to variety hours and quiz shows assailed America's ears with reminders of the war through stories, skits, songs, even jokes, as well as spot announcements from OFF and OWI for everything from bond drives to scrap drives, civil defense enrollments to USO contributions. Commercial advertising enlisted the war to sell things. Ad men made even the most unlikely products appeal to the consumer's sense of duty, guilt, or patriotism: "Don't be a public enemy! Be patriotic and smother sneezes with Kleenex to help keep colds from spreading to war workers—America needs every man—full time!" (qtd. in Lingeman 292). The most famous wartime ad slogan was that of Lucky Strike cigarettes. When American Tobacco changed the red bull's-eye's background color from forest green to white, they could proclaim patriotically, "Lucky Strike Green has gone to war!"—the green dye needed for defense manufacture (see Lingeman 231; Perrett 291).

Like radio and advertising, the American film industry kept the war before the public, with the direct encouragement of Washington. By mid-1942, the newly created Bureau of Motion Pictures, nominally a subsidiary of the OWI, had published a fat manual for Hollywood's guidance, especially encouraging "the casual insertion of a constructive 'war message' in a picture whenever possible" (183). The result of the government's directive and Hollywood's own initiative is staggering; 818 (or 53 percent) of the 1540 Hollywood films released between 1939 and September 30, 1945, were in some way "War Related." The highest number for a single year came in 1943, when 252 of 397, or 63 percent, of the movies released touched on the war (Shull 84).

Hollywood also churned out vast numbers of newsreels, shorts, animated cartoons, and documentaries related to the war, as well as 160 "Victory Films" between 1941 and 1945—informational and promotional films on everything from the latest military equipment to scrap metal drives. These were shown in commercial movie houses along with the regular features and short subjects (Doherty 308). Anyone who went to the movies (and roughly ninety million did each week) could not escape being reminded of the war (9).

### Tin Pan Alley Goes to War

Popular songwriters also responded to the war. Unlike Hollywood films, the total number of war-related songs has yet to be tabulated, but the figure must be astronomical. The on-line catalogue of World War II American sheet music in Brown University's John Hay Library lists 658 titles (plus foreign material as well), with another 150 to 200 still uncatalogued. And the numbers grow as more attics are scoured for such ephemera. These figures include only published war-related songs; there were likely more that were recorded but never printed, or just performed on the radio, in night clubs, in movies, or on USO tours. Many of the songs were fleetingly topical. Some were literally written, rehearsed, and performed overnight; "We'll Knock the Japs Right into the Laps of the Nazis" was introduced by Broadway's Bert Wheeler in a New York City nightspot the very night of the Pearl Harbor attack (Lingeman 211). Other songs like "I Don't Want to Walk without You" only obliquely glanced at the war, many of these reflecting the loneliness of the serviceman abroad or the girl back home. Because of their generality, many such songs went on to become perennial favorites of American popular song, notably Irving Berlin's "God Bless America," written well before Pearl Harbor and immortalized in Kate Smith's rendition, and Jerome Kern and Oscar Hammerstein's enduring "The Last Time I Saw Paris," a song occasioned by the fall of that city in 1940, its wistful melody and lyric evoking Paris before the Nazi occupation. But topical or general, innumerable war-related songs kept the war present to the music listening public.

The full, rich subject of wartime popular song is beyond the scope of this history, but it has some relevance, since a number of Broadway songwriters kept the war before the public through popular song rather than staged musicals. Given the far greater audience for popular songs, perhaps they felt that they could contribute more to homefront morale via the airwaves, phonograph records, and occasional songs in movies.

Once the United States entered the war, Broadway's Irving Berlin became one of the most prolific and patriotic writers of war-related popular songs. In 1941, he wrote the direct appeal "Any Bonds Today?" which gained wide popular currency. Throughout the war Berlin continued to write songs supporting government initiatives, both on his own and with Washington's encouragement (Lingeman 221). With the war years spawning committees, commissions, or bureaus for just about everybody, the Songwriters War Committee commissioned Berlin and others to write songs encouraging homefront participation in everything from victory gardens to civil defense, usually "with highly forgettable results" (221). Berlin's efforts include "Arms for the Love of America," "Angels of Mercy," "I Paid My Income Tax Today," and "There Are No Wings on a Fox Hole." Far more popular were two songs evoking the absent soldier's loneliness, both from his all-soldier revue *This Is the Army* (discussed later), "I Left My Heart at the Stage Door Canteen" and "I'm Getting Tired So I Can Sleep." Even more popular, then as now, was Berlin's "White Christmas," — its original movie context reflecting a GI's thoughts of home.

A young private first class was nearly as prolific as Irving Berlin in writing popular songs for the war effort. Before the war, Frank Loesser had barely gotten his feet wet on Broadway, supplying lyrics only for the ill-fated revue *The Illustrators' Show* (1/22/36). But Loesser would move on from his wartime and then Hollywood songwriting to become one of Broadway's most innovative composer/lyricists. His first major wartime song was the hit "Praise the Lord and Pass the Ammunition," supposedly based on the incident of a Navy chaplain taking up the duties of a fallen gunner at Pearl Harbor. Throughout the war Loesser both wrote on his own and supplied lyrics to other composer's melodies. In 1942, PFC Loesser worked with another Broadway-great-to-be, Jule Styne, to create the heart-tugging ballad of wartime absence and loneliness "I Don't Want to Walk without You." That same year three other Broadway songsmiths, Lew Brown, Charlie Tobias, and Sam H. Stept, wrote "Don't Sit under the Apple Tree," in which an absent soldier admonishes his girl not to sit there "With anyone else but me, / Till I come marching home." In 1943, Loesser teamed with Broadway veteran Arthur Schwartz to write a hilarious response in which the girl reassures the soldier that he has nothing fear since, with things as they are stateside, "They're Either Too Young or Too Old." Throughout the war a number of Loesser's songs focused specifically on the military, such as "What Do You Do in the Infantry?" in 1943 and "First Class Private Mary Brown" in 1944; these ranged through every mood from the comic to the nostalgic to the stirringly patriotic. Then in 1945 he reminded America of the grim reality of war in his memorable "Rodger Young," a tribute to a young man's sacrifice to save fellow soldiers pinned down by Japanese fire in the Solomon Islands. What makes this song so affecting is its narrative detachment and absence of sentimentality. Apparently no one thought it would become popular, since Burl Ives recorded it as the flip or "B" side of what became his major hit, "The Foggy, Foggy Dew" (Kinkle I: 413). And yet "Rodger Young" had a powerful impact on Americans at the time; for some of us it still does.

While yet to compose for Broadway, Jule Styne was honing his craft writing war-associated songs with various lyricists, mostly Sammy Cahn. In 1943, as the war dragged on and the loneliness of the girls back home was the subject of more and more songs, Styne and Cahn wrote "I'll Walk Alone (because to tell you the truth I am lonely)," which topped the Hit Parade eight times in 1944. Also in '43, Styne and Cahn wrote the more upbeat but prematurely anticipatory "Vict'ry Polka." And with the end of the war in sight in 1945, the two collaborated on what would become another standard, "It's Been a Long, Long Time."

Other Broadway songsmiths did their part as well. While they were few compared to the legions of strictly Tin Pan Alley types boosting the war effort, it is telling how many of their songs became classics, or at least major hits in their own day. Hailing the Army Air Corps in 1942, Harold Arlen and Johnny Mercer produced one of the biggest hits of the war, "Captains of the Clouds." Later, when a victorious end seemed ever more in sight, Mercer contributed the upbeat "G.I. Jive," writing his own swingtime music. Of course swing was the thing in the 1940s, and in late 1942 occasional Broadway writer Fats Waller's "Swing Out to Victory" linked the current music craze to the war effort. As did Waller's contribution to specific war-appeal jingles, the often hilarious "[Get Some] Cash for Your Trash," given new life in the 1978 Waller revue *Ain't Misbehavin'*.

Even George M. Cohan came out of songwriting retirement for the first time in more than a decade to cheer "For the Flag, for the Home, for the Family" late in 1941 or early 1942. This would be Cohan's final musical tribute to the U.S.A. he loved; on November 7, the flags would be at half staff for him.

Broadway's Jimmy McHugh and Harold Adamson penned the hit "Comin' in on a Wing and a Prayer" in 1943, but the most memorable songs with Broadway associations late in the war were a revival and a most unlikely import. Written for the fifteen-performance flop *Right This Way* (1/4/38), Sammy Fain and Irving Kahal's "I'll Be Seeing You" became the number-one hit of the summer of 1944, and was "spontaneously taken up as the anthem" of the liberation of Paris by the Allied Forces (Perrett 278). Then in 1944, sometime Broadway lyricist Mack David wrote the English-language words for the "American Version" of the *German* wartime song "Lili Marlene," an infectious ballad of a faithful woman awaiting her soldier's return. German or not, it took the country by storm—becoming one of the most loved and most sung songs of the entire war.

### Broadway and the War

The Broadway musical did not display much interest in the war and in fact during the war years developed very differently from the topical shows of the 1930s. Yet the war materially affected commercial theatre, including musical theatre. The number of plays and musicals continued its descent begun in the Depression, but the theatre experienced an enormous upturn in attendance and revenue. War prosperity partly accounts for this, but also, with the reduced number of shows to choose from, long-running hits ran longer and ticket prices were higher than ever, not just for Broadway but also for touring shows. The year 1941 set records for road receipts, and throughout the war years "the legitimate theatres in New York and on the road enjoyed unprecedented prosperity" (Lingeman 286).

The essential fact about musicals during the war years is that topicality all but disappeared—squelched, in Gerald Bordman's analysis, by the war's enormity: "The initial reaction was to change the emphasis of the librettos. Real war was the topic of the day, and real war was no joking matter. . . . For the most part the new offerings . . . carefully eschewed the political, economic, and social implications in the headlines" (515). But Bordman's explanation alone is incomplete, failing to account for the war's strong presence in the media of radio, movies, and popular song. In the world of entertainment (other than sporting events), about the only place Americans *could* turn without constant reminders of the war was the musical theatre.

There are two reasons Broadway mostly avoided the war. First, with New York both a major port of embarkation for troops heading overseas and a major shore leave destination point, the last thing soldiers and sailors wanted to see were plays and musicals about the war. Second, and equally important, Washington wasn't watching. Wartime Washington created committees to supervise or encourage nearly every segment of the American public to unite in the wartime effort, including agencies whose specific charge was to make sure Hollywood, radio broadcasters, songwriters, and the recording industry kept the war before the public. But there was no such commission shooting off comparable directives to Broadway producers. From the government's point of view, the Broadway audience was small in comparison with the audiences that could be reached by film, radio, and recordings. One ironic result of this was that in the very years musical theatre began to develop into an important medium for true artistic and cultural expression, musicals also became less fully representative of widespread popular culture, a role taken over by the truly mass media of radio, recordings, motion pictures, and, eventually, television.

Still, Broadway did its part for the war effort, but more off stage than on. By mid-July 1940, even before the first peacetime Selective Service Act, "Every musical show on Broadway featured the national anthem as a curtain-raiser or finale" (Perrett 33). And in grudging compliance with federal orders for "coastal dimouts," Broadway's marquees were dimmed for the duration. In addition, Broadway contributed time and talent supporting wartime fund raising and service causes. On December 15, 1941, just a week after Pearl Harbor, the *New Republic* ran an ad for a Victory rally at Madison Square Garden with tickets "ranging from 28 cents to $1.10" and attractions including "3 Choruses—3 Dramatic Tableaux" (Perrett 203). Broadway's biggest wartime fund raiser wasn't an event but a person. By the time of the war, Kate Smith was best known as a radio personality, but she had done her time on the musical stage, as in De Sylva, Brown, and Henderson's *Flying High*. Smith has been likened to World War I's super-personality Elsie Janis when it came to selling bonds. Smith undoubtedly still holds the all-time individual record, raising nearly forty million dollars over sixteen hours on the radio on September 21, 1943 (Perrett 299). Other stars of plays and musicals made curtain speeches in the theatres, pitching support of War Bonds, scrap drives, and, because it was most closely tied to the entertainment world, USO donations. Not money but servicemen's morale was raised through the volunteer work of Broadway's stars and lesser lights at the Stage Door Canteen on 44th Street, immortalized in song by Irving Berlin. Run by the American Theatre Wing and staffed solely by the theatre community, the Stage Door was a serviceman's center where soldiers and sailors could go for a cup of coffee, a meal, or dancing and "flirting with the pretty starlet hostesses." "On a given night there would be lines in the street outside the canteen, and 500 young men from at least six different nations inside" (Lingeman 46).

## Black Musical Theatre during the War

There were some striking and regrettable similarities between the status of blacks in the U.S. Army and the production of black musical theatre during the war. Like the segregated black military units commanded by white officers, most black-performed musicals were white-created and directed; in both, whites were in the position of power, with the blacks executing their ideas and orders. As in the 1930s, white writers, composers, and directors continued to reshape black characters and experiences in the whites' image of them, just as white platoon sergeants and higher-ups molded black recruits in the image of whatever they supposed a black soldier should be.

Not that there weren't some happy results. In fact, of the eight black-performed musicals from the fall of 1939 to the spring of 1945, the only ones with runs ranging from respectable to spectacular had white creative teams; one of these was a revival. Even with all-star personnel, others were anything but hits. *Swingin' the Dream* (11/29/39) tried to "swing" Shakespeare the way the *Swing* and *Hot Mikados* had successfully "swung" Gilbert and Sullivan. But even with Jimmy Van Heusen's score, Benny Goodman's sextet as the pit band, and a cast including Louis Armstrong as Bottom, Butterfly McQueen as Puck, and "Moms" Mabley as Quince, *Dream* turned into a thirteen-performance nightmare.

*Cabin in the Sky* (10/25/40) was a different story, though with its Russian-born composer Vernon Duke (né Vladimir Dukelsky), choreographer

George Balanchine (Gyorgi Balanchivadze), and set designer Boris Aronson, it appeared more like *Shtetl in the Sky*. In fact, when Duke was asked to write the score for Lynn Root's book—a fantasy about love and faith in the African American South—the composer initially balked, confessing he was not "sufficiently attuned to Negro folklore." Ultimately he and lyricist John Latouche wrote their "own kind of Negro songs instead" (Woll 194). A strong book, a score whose hit was "Taking a Chance on Love," and a distinguished black cast including Ethel Waters, Dooley Wilson, Todd Duncan, Rex Ingram, and dancer-choreographer Katherine Dunham let *Cabin in the Sky* run 156 performances and go on to become "the first black-performed Broadway musical to be filmed in Hollywood" (195).

Cheryl Crawford's revival of *Porgy and Bess* (1/21/42) did even better. Crawford tinkered with the fully scored opera by cutting some of the musical material and turning the recitative into spoken dialogue. The payoff of these changes, and of bringing Todd Duncan, Anne Brown, and J. Rosemond Johnson back in their original roles, was a 286-performance run (over twice as long as the 1935 original), with a successful national tour to follow.

The biggest hit among white-created shows for black casts also turned operatic recitative into dialogue for Broadway audiences, but this recitative was considerably older than Gershwin's. It was the work of Georges Bizet and his librettists, and the revisions were the work of Oscar Hammerstein, 2nd, transforming the perennially popular opera *Carmen* into what became the extraordinarily popular near-opera for Broadway *Carmen Jones* (12/4/43). With 503 performances and glowing reviews from many of the same critics who had crucified *Porgy and Bess* in 1935 (see Woll 188–89), the show was a hit with both the public and the press. Yet, in retrospect, much in Hammerstein's attempt to contemporize *Carmen* rendered it a curious and rather unsatisfying hybrid. The original Meilhac and Halévy libretto, based on Prosper Mérimée's story, remained essentially unchanged (no happy ending to placate Broadway tastes), as did virtually all of Bizet's score; those critics who expected this updated *Carmen* to swing were pleasantly surprised that it didn't. But settings, character names, and occupations were greatly altered, even making them relatively relevant to the current war. Instead of opening outside a cigarette factory in Seville, the action began "*Outside a parachute factory, near a Southern town*" (Hammerstein, *Carmen* x). Later scenes shifted to the South Side of Chicago and a baseball stadium not geographically specified. While Carmen herself (with the added surname Jones) remained pretty much intact, Don Jose became Corporal Joe, toreador Escamillo prizefighter Husky Miller, and Carmen's two sidekicks Mercedes and Franquita Myrt and Frankie. Hammerstein rendered the original

French lyrics and recitative-turned-dialogue into English, retaining *"with very few minor exceptions"* the same song order and the same general sense of each song ([vi]). Robert Russell Bennett, one of the American theatre's most intelligent, innovative, and brilliant arrangers and orchestrators, retained most of the Bizet orchestrations and musical arrangements but judiciously reduced and stylistically altered them to be more in keeping with Broadway expectations.

Hammerstein's considerable skill as a librettist and lyricist notwithstanding, his lyrics for *Carmen Jones* display what continued to be a singular weakness throughout his career, a perfectly dreadful ear for creating authentic dialect, whatever that dialect might be. This is obvious in his version of the familiar "Habanera," now titled "Dat's Love":

> You go for me an' I'm taboo
> But if yore hard to get I go for you,
> An' if I do, den you are through, boy,
> My baby, dat's de end of you.
> (Hammerstein, *Carmen* 14)

While most such clumsy renderings of vernacular speech and dialect simply flaw the overall artistic excellence of Hammerstein's collaborations with Richard Rodgers, in *Carmen Jones* they inadvertently tend to reduce the black characters to theatrical stereotypes, an irony given Hammerstein's progressive social thinking.

The last wartime white-written black musical was *Memphis Bound!* (5/24/45), its book by Albert Barker and Sally Benton with music and lyrics by Don Walker and Clay Warnick, with an assist from Gilbert and Sullivan. Black entertainers heading to Memphis on a riverboat run afoul of a sandbar. They perform *H. M. S. Pinafore* to finance floating their boat again, but despite a cast headed by seemingly inexhaustible sixty-seven-year-old Bill Robinson, the show sank after thirty-six performances (*Best Plays* 44–45 432; Bordman 547).

All three of the even partly black-created musicals to reach Broadway during the war were revues and only one a moderate success—*A Tropical Revue* (9/14/43), produced by white impresario Sol Hurok. Actually a dance concert, the show was conceived by gifted black choreographer and dancer Katherine Dunham and performed by her own exceptionally talented dance company. After an initial run of two months, Dunham's creation enjoyed a successful tour and an equally happy return engagement on Broadway the following season (Bordman 538). No one associated with *Harlem Cav-*

*alcade* (5/1/42) or *Blue Holiday* (5/21/45) could have been happy with their shows. Noble Sissle produced the first in collaboration with columnist and theatre-dabbler Ed Sullivan (later of TV fame). The revue is notable only because it was one of the few musicals to contain any war-topical material. "Tim Moore and Joe Byrd appeared as air raid wardens, but were stationed in a cemetery [the ancient 'blacks spooked in a graveyard' bit], and Flournoy Miller devoted his malaprop routines to trying to fill out a draft board questionnaire" (Woll 208). Critic John Mason Brown declared, "I had too much of an old thing" (qtd. in Woll 208), and so had audiences, after forty-nine performances. Briefer yet was the run of *Blue Holiday*, a black revue featuring Ethel Waters, the Katherine Dunham dancers, and the Hall Johnson Choir. Thanks to weak material, these fine performers were out of work after eight performances.

During the war, touring black shows were welcomed nearly everywhere, but in some cities black performers had to put up with segregated hotels and other public facilities. Black audiences, however, were not as welcome as the shows, at least not in the best seats in the house. As a case in point, the *Carmen Jones* tour encountered protests over segregated seating in St. Louis, Kansas City, Louisville, and elsewhere (Woll 189), a situation reflecting the wartime status of blacks on the civilian homefront as well as in the military.

### Latin Manhattan

The government's stepped-up pursuit of President Roosevelt's Good Neighbor Policy toward Latin America made its mark on Broadway musicals. South-of-the-Border fads and fancies began even before FDR named Nelson Rockefeller Coordinator of Cultural and Commercial Relations between American Republics for National Defense in July 1940. Anglos across the nation caught "Latin" fever for the culture, food, dress, and music of the Caribbean and Central and South America; Spanish language classes in and out of the military filled to capacity (Perrett 164). But mostly the exotic rhythms and fancy footwork of Latin American dances captured the nation as never before, particularly the rumba (or "rhumba") and conga. Herman Hupfeld's "When Yuba Plays the Rumba on the Tuba" in *The Third Little Show* (6/1/31) had parodied a previous rumba craze in the late '20s and early '30s, but that was nothing like what happened during the first few years of the war. "In nightclubs, dance halls and theaters the Latin American craze threatened to sweep everything before it," to the extent that the *New York*

*Times* remarked, "There were more and better rumba bands in Manhattan than Havana" (qtd. in Perrett 164). Broadway more than kept up the beat, including numbers by some of its more prominent songwriters.

In the revue *The Streets of Paris* (6/19/39), Carmen Miranda introduced "The South American Way"; from then on she more than any other performer came to epitomize Latin song and dance for Americans. Two months later, in *George White's Scandals of 1939–40* (8/28/39), Sammy Fain and Jack Yellen contributed "The Mexiconga." Another two months and Rodgers and Hart plugged not one but two Latin numbers into their college-campus romp *Too Many Girls* (10/18/39) — "All Dressed Up Spic and Spanish" and "She Could Shake the Maracas," performed by Diosa Costello and Desi Arnaz. Cole Porter got into the Latin act with "Katie Went to Haiti" in *DuBarry Was a Lady* (12/6/39), after which Irving Berlin jumped in with "Latins Know How" in *Louisiana Purchase* (5/28/40). Johnny Mercer and Hoagy Carmichael created Latin-swing fusion in "The Rhumba Jumps" for *Walk with Music* (6/4/40), while Jay Gorney added to the craze with "In Chi Chi Castenango" in *Meet the People* (12/25/40). But then, after Sammy Fain, Will Irwin, and Jack Yellen's "Thank You, South America," another Carmen Miranda number in *Sons o' Fun* (12/1/41), the Latin fad vanished from Broadway as suddenly as it began. But it continued on in Hollywood films, popular song, and ballroom dance. While Broadway can't take credit for starting the Latin dance craze, it certainly helped popularize it.

## War-Related Musicals and Revues

Like the musicals in the two previous decades, wartime Broadway shows can be pretty nearly divided into two camps: many diversionary, escapist entertainments and a handful of more topical ones. Most of the war years' long-running hits were book shows of the first variety (see appendix C), along with some revues. Such a revue was *The Streets of Paris* (6/19/39), in which one routine gently spoofed the appearance and timidity of British Prime Minister Neville "peace for our time" Chamberlain and his naive belief that signing the Munich Pact would appease Hitler by allowing him to annex the Czech Sudentenland. "Doin' the Chamberlain" was a dance number in which "Moustached, somber-suited chorus boys stepped out gingerly with their umbrellas" (Bordman 515).

The first book musical after Pearl Harbor was *Banjo Eyes* (12/25/41) starring Eddie Cantor, linked to the war by just a single song interpolated into Vernon Duke, John Latouche, and Harold Adamson's score. Cantor played a greeting card salesman who dreams racehorses give him tips on winners,

but only if he doesn't place a bet. Nothing topical—or plausible—about
that. Cantor insisted on adding Cliff Friend and Charlie Tobias's rousing
"We Did It Before (and we can do it again)," which he had introduced on
his radio show the Wednesday after Pearl Harbor. The flag-waver stayed in
for the show's 126 performances. Nearly all the war news was bad by February 1942, so the revue *Of V We Sing* (2/11/42) balanced satiric sketches on
subjects like unions, Mother's Day, and the Brooklyn Dodgers with patriotic
musical numbers like "You Can't Fool the People," "Red, Whites, and
Blues," and the title song (Bordman 528). *Of V We* sang only seventy-six
times.

The one and only Broadway show centrally devoted to the war was a
genuine hit. Timed to open on Independence Day 1942, Irving Berlin's *This
Is the Army* did for the military in World War II what his *Yip Yip Yaphank*
had done in World War I. *This Is the Army* had an all-soldier cast, including
the ex-soldier songwriter himself, billed as "Sgt. Irving Berlin (1917)" (Bordman 531). Like the 1918 soldier show, this revue presented songs and skits
about army life. Some of the soldier-performers had already made, or would
make, theatrical or musical names for themselves—Ezra Stone, Burl Ives,
Gary Merrill, Julie Oshins, and Joe Cook Jr.—just as some of Berlin's songs
went on to national radio and recording popularity, notably "I'm Getting
Tired So I Can Sleep," "I Left My Heart at the Stage Door Canteen," and,
the biggest hit of all, "This Is the Army, Mr. Jones." Berlin himself reprised
"Oh, How I Hate to Get Up in the Morning" from *Yip Yip Yaphank*. *New
Yorker* critic Wolcott Gibbs perhaps best explained the revue's success: "It
was a service show entirely executed by servicemen, and it told more,
through the medium of vaudeville, about the qualities that made it possible
for a non-military nation to raise an effective fighting force than any ten
plays celebrating desperate and rhetorical gallantries on the battlefield" (qtd.
in Lingeman 288). A pre-planned tour limited the show to playing 113 times,
but "every performance was sold out to the limit of standees" (Bordman
531). The revue was a philanthropic effort, raising (including sale of the
movie rights) an "impressive $10,000,000 for the Army Emergency Relief
Fund" (Lingeman 288).

Other than *This Is the Army* the musical stage was silent about the war
throughout the summer of 1942, and fall saw just very brief runs of the new
season's only two war-related shows. A flag-waving revue called *Let Freedom
Sing* opened on October 5 but closed after eight performances despite a
score by socially conscious composer-lyricist Harold Rome with interpolations by the equally relevant Marc Blitzstein. Rome's songs included "It's
Fun to Be Free," "I Did It for Defense," "Little Miss Victory Jones," and
"Johnny Is a Hoarder" (Bordman 532). But nothing Rome wrote seemed to

help. Judging from the success of his *Pins and Needles*, Broadway audiences apparently found unions infinitely more entertaining than wartime patriotism. The book show that followed, *Count Me In* (10/8/42) by Nancy Hamilton and future theatre critic Walter Kerr, ostensibly told of a man helping the war effort by selling phony maps to Japanese spies, but it was mostly an excuse for irrelevant specialties. Critic John Mason Brown told *Count Me In* "count me out," as did the public after sixty-one showings (532).

A *Ziegfeld Follies* in name only (4/1/43) was nothing *but* specialties, but the revue included a rare satiric look at the homefront during the war. Spoofing rationing, Milton Berle played "J. Pierswift Armour, a butcher flanked by tommy-gun toting bodyguards, who draws his war-scarce steaks from a safe deposit box" (536). The show's frivolous fluff let the *Follies* play 553 times despite almost uniformly hostile reviews. Not so lucky was *Jackpot* (1/13/44), a flop with music and lyrics by the more-than-competent Vernon Duke and Howard Dietz. It connected to the war only through a bond drive and a few characters in various branches of the service. *Jackpot* crapped out after sixty-nine performances. War associations in *Follow the Girls* (4/8/44) were equally flimsy, but the show ran forever. The flimsy book about a burlesque queen running a servicemen's canteen to help the war effort was a flimsy excuse for endless parades of showgirls in even flimsier attire. The "eye-filling chorus line and entertaining specialties" in this "glorified burlesque" kept *Follow the Girls* bumping and grinding 882 times (541), well beyond the end of the war. But from the Allied landing at Normandy on D-Day, June 6, 1944, until the Japanese surrender in 1945, no more war-related musicals appeared.

### The New Musical Realism: Pal Joey *and* Lady in the Dark

About a year before America entered the war, two musicals opened a month apart that were much more significant *as* musicals than the handful of ephemeral war-related shows. The importance of *Pal Joey* and *Lady in the Dark* was twofold. First, while neither show dealt with specific contemporary issues, both were significant in treating personal relationships or psychological problems with striking candor, authenticity, and realism. Second, the tone, mood, and sophisticated writing of both shows demonstrated that the musical could be taken seriously as theatre. While the war-related shows were transitory, the serious treatment of human affairs and the innovative artistry in *Pal Joey* and *Lady in the Dark* allowed these musicals to enjoy an enduring theatrical life.

John O'Hara's toughminded "Pal Joey" stories in the *New Yorker* were the source of his book for the musical that Gerald Bordman, mincing no words, calls "a cynical, snarling yet sentimentally lyrical examination of bought love . . . with a hollow, self-serving, two-timing little twerp as its hero and an equally self-serving, hard, past-her-prime matron as his vis-à-vis" (522). For the most part *Pal Joey* was an intentionally ugly, nasty musical. And Dick Rodgers and Larry Hart were just the composer and lyricist to match O'Hara's toughness in their witty, often abrasive, always realistic, and richly human music and lyrics.

In the musical, two-bit, opportunistic nightclub hoofer Joey Evans (Gene Kelly) uses married society dame Vera Simpson (Vivienne Segal) to get ahead, get her cash, and get his own club; she, in exchange, uses Joey for her sexual gratification, making Joey, in essence, a "kept man." Joey is also seeing Linda, a decent young woman he met in front of a pet shop. In its treatment of story and characters, *Pal Joey* made tremendous strides in what might be called musical theatre realism. By definition, of course, musical theatre can never be fully realistic, even within the conventions of theatrical realism for non-musical plays. In real life, people don't start singing as an extension of normal conversation. But, once *that* convention is accepted, musicals can achieve a considerable illusion of reality or authenticity. In *Pal Joey*, Rodgers, Hart, and O'Hara dared to depict fully fleshed-out, three-dimensional characters, not just the usual musical comedy types and stereotypes. They also avoided the contrived happy ending endemic to most musicals of the time. Instead, the resolution grows logically from the characters' psychological complexities. After both women dump Joey, he walks into the night—alone. Yet he has learned nothing; the show ends with the unregenerate creep trying to pick up yet another girl with "I Could Write a Book," the same song he used to seduce Linda at the top of act 1.

In addition to its believable characters and unsentimental story, *Pal Joey* furthered the musical's realism in other ways. Hart's lyrics were frank, often funny, and always character appropriate. For example, what became the very popular "Bewitched, Bothered, and Bewildered" (with much altered lyrics for radio and recordings) in the context of the show reflects Vera's vulnerability as well as her cynicism:

> When he talks, he is seeking
> Words to get off his chest.
> Horizontally speaking,
> He's at his very best.
>
> Vexed again,
> Perplexed again,

Thank God I can be oversexed again—
Bewitched, bothered and bewildered am I.
(Hart and Kimball 272)


Rodgers's score, too, contributed to the realism of this unconventional musical. Throughout *Pal Joey*, Rodgers wrote music precisely appropriate to characters and situations. For instance, for a newspaperwoman recounting her interview with pseudo-intellectual stripper Gypsy Rose Lee, Rodgers wrote the burlesque bump-and-grind number "Zip!" His deliberately cliché melodies and Hart's equally cliché lyrics for songs performed as nightclub acts, like "That Terrific Rainbow" and "The Flower Garden of My Heart," contrast with Joey, Vera, and Linda's sophisticated and personalized character-specific songs sung outside "performance" settings. In this way, lyric and musical styles demarcate the "real" world from the nightclub routines. In this same vein, Rodgers "dumbed down" his strictly instrumental dance music for the club sequences to replicate the tacky dance numbers performed in the cheap nightclubs of the day.

*Pal Joey*'s public outvoted the critics. It didn't help reviews that producer/director George Abbott risked opening a musical so honest and mature on Christmas night, when few were either in the mood or prepared for something like that, especially the first-night press who had to work on the holiday. But apparently Gene Kelly's "smiling warmth mitigated some of Joey's harshness," and, mixed reviews aside, the show played 374 times (Bordman 523). Clearly, some patrons of musicals were ready for more than the usual fare of fluff.

The distinguished trio of Moss Hart, Kurt Weill, and Ira Gershwin offered audiences another sophisticated theatre experience in the risky, experimental musical play about a career woman undergoing psychoanalysis, *Lady in the Dark* (1/23/41). This musical embodied the personal crusade of Moss Hart to depict and promote psychoanalysis. Prior to writing it, Hart had experienced a nervous breakdown and underwent a course of Freudian psychoanalysis in an effort to work through it. (In *Lady in the Dark*, the specific symptoms and manifestations of Liza Elliott's illness make it clear, in today's terminology, that she was suffering clinical depression.) While Freud's ideas had filtered down from psychologists to the general public by the 1920s, a generation later there were still countless skeptics. These were the people Hart wanted to reach. He judged his own course of analysis a complete success and so determined to write a play both demonstrating the process and proselytizing its worth. (In the final version of the musical, the character Maggie Grant depicted the progress from doubter to believer.) Hart originally intended to write a serious play for actress Katherine Cornell as a troubled fashion magazine editor who seeks psychiatric help but concluded, after discussing the project with theatrical friends and colleagues, that his pro-Freudian play would reach more people as a musical. Thus, Hart brought on board Kurt Weill to compose the score and Ira Gershwin (in retirement since George's death three years earlier) to write the lyrics (Green 200).

Hart also had a theatrical mission. Given the complexity of his subject, he sought to solve the ongoing problem of realism in musicals. His solution was ingenious, if only for this show. At first blush, *Lady in the Dark* looks like two different plays. Realistic scenes of straightforward, largely serious dialogue take place either in the office of Liza Elliott (Gertrude Lawrence), editor of (then-fictional) *Allure* magazine, or the office of her analyst Dr. Brooks (Donald Randolph). With one psychologically plausible exception, these scenes contain no singing. Interspersed between the dialogue scenes, but kept entirely separate from them, are lavish, often playful, expressionistically bizarre and phantasmagoric musical sequences, all exposing Liza's sleeping or waking dreams and nightmares.

"Brilliant" doesn't do justice to the concept. Real-life encounters play out in conversations between people; in dreams, anything can happen. Dreams constitute our inner reality just as mundane human intercourse does our conscious daily lives. Hart explained that the musical sequences, while disjunct from the dialogue scenes of Liza's "waking" life, were intended to be "part and parcel of the basic structure of the play. One cannot separate the play from the music, and vice versa. More than that, the music and lyrics carry the story forward dramatically and psychologically" (qtd. in Green 200).

What's particularly ingenious about *Lady in the Dark* is that the audience experiences Liza's psychoanalysis with her step by painful step, never knowing or understanding more than she does at any point in the process. The classic example of this playwriting strategy begins with the first fantasy sequence, "The Glamour Dream." From the audience's point of view, it is inexplicable that this severely dressed career woman suddenly should appear all in blue, elegantly coifed and drop-dead gorgeous. All the scenery and props are blue as well, as are Liza's chauffeur's uniform and the *"blue Picasso"* he puts in the back seat of her *"blue Duesenberg with the blue license plates"* before whisking her off for a night on the town, where she is pursued by seemingly every eligible bachelor in Manhattan (Hart 25). The audience is left wondering, "Blue? Why blue?"

They get the answer only when Liza does, during her psychological breakthrough late in act 2. It turns out that her parents not only thought Liza plain but said so in front of her. Her father called her his "little ugly duckling," backed up by her mother saying, "I'm afraid you're never going to be able to wear *blue* [italics supplied], my darling, and we must be careful how we do your hair, but we shall make the most of your good points, Liza, won't we?" (139). The meaning and significance of "The Glamour Dream" are instantly made manifest to both Liza and the audience. That same recollection of her parents also explains psychologically and makes plausible dramatically Liza's singing the one song occurring in a "real life" scene. Liza's parents didn't just disparage her appearance, they also made Liza sing in front of company. That mortifying childhood experience accounts for the few bars of a melody—the rest apparently blocked or repressed—stuck in Liza's head throughout the play. Only after Dr. Brooks succeeds in integrating her conscious thoughts with her unconscious can Liza, in the final scene, fully recall and sing the haunting "My Ship," the song her parents had made her childhood self perform.

In all respects but one, Hart and Gershwin delineate the course of Liza's psychoanalysis in painstakingly authentic detail—both through her sessions with Dr. Brooks and in the lyrics of the musical-fantasy sequences. The only false note is the brevity of Liza's course of analysis. The action of the play covers just about two weeks, although in fact psychoanalysis is a long, slow process. But Hart, Gershwin, and Weill crafted the book, lyrics, and score of *Lady in the Dark* with such consummate artistry that apparently no one noticed or cared, since audiences kept the show going for a split run of 467 performances, 162 following the opening and another 305 commencing September 2, after an eleven-week summer vacation. *Lady in the Dark* also had the distinction of being "not only . . . a consistent sellout during its lengthy engagement, but, reportedly, was the first in theatre history to play to standees at every performance" (Richards 2: 56).

### The Rodgers and Hammerstein Revolution

It has become something of a commonplace for critics and writers on musicals to refer to the "Rodgers and Hammerstein revolution." Yet this, like all revolutions, had its antecedents. Jerome Kern and Guy Bolton explored better ways to write musicals in their Princess Theatre Shows during World War I; in the 1920s, Kern and Hammerstein created an integrated musical play in *Show Boat*; and both *Pal Joey* and *Lady in the Dark* demonstrated how musicals could treat story and characters realistically. These were models for Rodgers and Hammerstein to build on.

Still, it is no exaggeration to call 1943 to 1959 "The Rodgers and Hammerstein Years." Six of their nine shows became hits, fairly dominating the Broadway musical stage for those sixteen years, and their musicals also influenced other librettists, lyricists, and composers by establishing both a model and a standard for a new kind of musical play. Further, Rodgers and Hammerstein demonstrated that musicals could be "idea-bearing," socially conscious, and socially responsible, yet still entertain audiences and make money.

Oklahoma!

Clouds thickened over Manhattan on the morning of March 31, 1943. By afternoon the snow was general all over Broadway. By six P.M. it was sleet—sloppy and slushy on the sidewalks, streets, and gutters of the Great White Way. Theatre marquees were darkened in grudging compliance with the wartime orders for coastal brownouts. Not a cheery prospect for theatregoers, especially first-nighters going to a new musical.

Nor had the day been bright for the staff of the show opening that night at the St. James Theatre. They faced the rare occurrence of an opening night that wasn't sold out. The reviews from New Haven weren't as bad as subsequent legend would have it, but they didn't presage a blockbuster either. Moreover, the producer was the Theatre Guild, with a string of sixteen previous consecutive flops. Small wonder the Guild made the almost unheard-of gesture of giving the cast "comps" for relatives and friends. To further paper the house, staff members went out into the snow to offer passing servicemen free seats.

Complicating matters, the musical itself was risky. The director hadn't staged a Broadway show since 1935; like the Guild, the lyricist/librettist was trailing a string of recent flops; and the choreographer was best known, if known at all, for choreographing a ballet by Aaron Copland. Only the composer could boast of some recent hits, but even he was nervous about this show. The cast of virtual unknowns dragging back into New York after the out-of-town tryouts resembled less a theatrical company than the walking wounded. Actor Howard Da Silva got laryngitis in New Haven, dancer Marc Platt seriously injured his foot in Boston (as would dancer Kate Friedlich on opening night), and, from New Haven to Boston, an outbreak of measles ravaged the company (see Wilk 195–216).

Nevertheless, the show went on, and *Oklahoma!* became a runaway hit, playing 2,248 times—a record run for a Broadway musical that remained unbroken for two decades, until *Fiddler on the Roof* surpassed it by about a thousand performances.

Opening night reviews were wildly enthusiastic:

Wonderful is the nearest adjective, for this excursion of the Guild combines a fresh and infectious gaiety, a charm of manner, beautiful acting, singing and dancing, and a score by Richard Rodgers that doesn't do any harm either, since it is one of his best. (Lewis Nichols, *New York Times*)

Jubilant and enchanting . . . a superb musical. (Howard Barnes, *New York Tribune*)

A beautiful and delightful show, fresh and imaginative, as enchanting to the eye as Richard Rodgers's music is to the ear. It has, at rough estimate, practically everything. (John Anderson, *Journal-American*)

Despite such lavish praise, critics were silent on exactly what made this new show so special. Only later generations of scholars, critics, and popular writers, armed with hindsight, really understood what *Oklahoma!* had done for the progress of the American musical. In his 1993 book written for the show's fiftieth anniversary, Max Wilk exaggerates the disappearance of earlier kinds of musicals with the advent of *Oklahoma!*, but his other remarks summarize the musical's subsequent impact fairly well:

After this night, with this one performance of *Oklahoma!*, the American musical theatre would never be the same. Farewell to those years of European-based operettas, to the Ziegfeld extravaganzas, to claptrap books designed for star performers, and to rowdy semiburlesque shows. By 11:20 P.M. on this night they were all history. This simple and winning story of America's growing up on the frontier, set to a wonderful score, with its honest characters and brilliant choreography all melded into a theatre piece, was something new. A successful vision, a prototype from which everything would now flow. (217)

In truth those semiburlesque musical comedies, claptrap star vehicles, extravagant revues, and operettas lingered on through the 1940s, even while Rodgers and Hammerstein continued to break new ground and other likeminded writers followed their lead.

Wilk's "all melded into a theatre piece" expresses well what characterized this new kind of musical. Oscar Hammerstein achieved in *Oklahoma!* what he had attempted with some success sixteen years earlier in *Show Boat* — the creation of the totally integrated musical. If opening night critics didn't see anything particularly groundbreaking or revolutionary, it was because everything in *Oklahoma!* looks so natural. In this simple boy-meets-girl story of the cowboy Curly thwarting the malevolent hired hand Jud Fry and winning the hand of the farm woman Laurey, Rodgers and Hammerstein's songs always grow naturally from the preceding dialogue. Some continue the dramatic action ("The Surrey with the Fringe on Top," for example); others provide character revelation (Jud's too-often-cut "Lonely Room" and Ado Annie's "I Cain't Say No"); while still others reveal the development of relationships between characters ("People Will Say We're in Love" and "All er Nothin'," to name two). Not one song in the show is superfluous or irrelevant to story or character! Reprises do not just pound potential hits into the audience's ears but drive the action forward while reminding the viewer of what came before. Curly and Laurey's first-act "People Will Say We're in Love" becomes the second act's "Let People Say We're in Love" when they can finally admit their mutual feelings. Choreographer Agnes De Mille not only conceived dances to reveal "the subconscious fears and desires of the leading characters" (Green 212), as in Laurey's psychologically accurate and terrifying dream ballet closing act 1, she also began to utilize dance in the dramatic action, as in "The Farmer and the Cowman" at the top of act 2. (De Mille and others like Jerome Robbins would carry the storytelling possibilities of dance much farther in subsequent musicals.) Lemuel Ayers's authentic yet stylized settings and Miles White's costumes evoked in their simplicity the Indian Territory just after the turn of the century without extraneous musical comedy glitz and glitter. Even the orchestrations of musical arranger Robert Russell Bennett captured the sounds of the American frontier. With *Oklahoma!* all production elements converged on the single goal of making an organic musical theatre piece capable of containing and expressing themes and ideas of real import.

The theme that first appears in *Oklahoma!* recurs in nearly all of Hammerstein's collaborations with Rodgers—the need for eradicating racial, ethnic, and cultural prejudices, promoting tolerance and acceptance of differences, and bringing about reconciliation, if possible. This social vision had its roots in Hammerstein's liberal social thinking since at least the 1930s. According to his son James, Hammerstein had helped organize the Anti-Nazi League in the '30s but withdrew his support when it was clear the league was becoming a communist front (Citron 182, 194). It's tempting to trace Hammerstein's social advocacy to his Jewish heritage, but his mother was a Scots Presbyterian, and Hammerstein identified himself hardly at all with his Jewish roots. Still, it's perhaps no surprise that Hammerstein, "who was violently anti-discrimination" (Citron 193), at first expressed his views cautiously, since during the war racial and ethnic discrimination was widespread.

Hammerstein greatly altered and expanded upon Lynn Riggs's *Green Grow the Lilacs*, his source for *Oklahoma!* He kept intact the play's single plot of Curly's courtship of Laurey and his defeat of the contemptible Jeeter (the musical's Jud), but everything else in *Oklahoma!* was Hammerstein's own invention, including the secondary plot of Will Parker wooing Ado Annie, with the peddler Ali Hakim as a reluctant rival suitor. (Hammerstein also transformed the original Ado Annie from a shy, awkward, and sexually naïve young woman into a comic man-trap.) Will doesn't appear in *Lilacs*, and the peddler only once—just as a peddler. As will be seen, Hammerstein's addition of the subplot reinforced his theme of prejudice, tolerance, and reconciliation—also not in Riggs's play.

While *Green Grow the Lilacs* is peopled with cattlemen and farmers in the Indian Territory just prior to its statehood as Oklahoma, Riggs never touched on the conflicts stemming from their divergent economic interests. It was very much a part of the American West that "[f]armers challenged the cattlemen, but contrary to western myth, their attempt to farm was not the source of most violence" (White 344). The animosity was mutual: "Cattlemen and cowboys disliked farmers on principle. . . . Barbed wire provided low-cost technology to separate the interests of cowman and agriculturalist. . . . Cattle ranchers sometimes resorted to violence to combat the threat of farmers and sheepmen" (Slatta 185–86). In *Oklahoma*! Hammerstein—who either knew his history or did his research—used the historical reality of the "range wars" to launch his advocacy for tolerance and reconciliation. His one explicit statement of this occurs in "The Farmer and the Cowman," the opening number of act 2. Most of the insults the farmers and cattlemen trade off during the square dance are good-natured ribbing; others, however, are in dead earnest:

> [CARNES]
> I'd like to say a word for the farmer.
> He come out west and made a lot of changes.
> WILL (*Scornfully; singing*)
> He come out west and built a lot of fences!
> CURLY
> And built 'em right acrost our cattle ranges!
> CORD ELAM (*A cowman; spoken*)
> Whyn't those dirtscratchers stay in
> Missouri where they belong?
> FARMER (*Spoken*)
> We got as much right here—
>                         (Rodgers, 6 *Plays* 52)

After which an all-out brawl ensues between the farmers and cowmen, "*the women striving vainly to keep peace by singing*"

> The farmer and the cowman should be friends,
> Oh, the farmer and the cowman should be friends.
> One man likes to push a plow,
> The other likes to chase a cow,
> But that's no reason why they cain't be friends.
>                         (51–52)

Their refrain is both a clear statement of differences between cattlemen and agriculturists and a plea for mutual understanding and reconciliation of

those differences. The melee calmed, Ike caps off the song by explicitly
stating Hammerstein's sentiments:

> And when this territory is a state
> And jines the Union jist like all the others,
> The farmer and the cowman and the merchant
> Must all behave theirsel's and act like brothers.
>                                        (54)

Jud, Laurey's farmhand, is evil incarnate, a drifter not productively tied
to the land as are the ranchers and farmers. To both groups a hired hand
was beneath contempt. Even in Hammerstein's sometimes idealistic world
of eradicating prejudice, some irreclaimable groups or individuals (similar
to Jacques and Malvolio in Shakespeare's romantic comedies) cannot be
brought within the finale's circle of reconciliation and must either be done
away with (as is Jud) or banished (see Frye 165).

The finale in both Riggs's play and Rodgers and Hammerstein's musical
symbolizes the reconciliation of differences. In both, cowman Curly's marriage to farm woman Laurey cuts through the barbed wire of animosity
between cattlemen and farmers. Hammerstein's own invented subplot dou-
bles this effect with Ado Annie Carnes, a farmer's daughter, wooed, won,
and, we assume, wed to another cowboy, Will Parker. These marital unions
of opposites signal old rivalries, prejudices, and animosities stripped away,
and the birth of a new, harmonious society (see Frye 163–64) — as does the
imminent *union* of the new state of Oklahoma with the United States of
America in the show's stirring title song.


## Carousel


Rodgers and Hammerstein's next great success, *Carousel* (4/19/45), was based
on Hungarian playwright Ferenc Molnar's *Liliom*. While he retained the
basic plot, Hammerstein added his prejudice/tolerance theme. By transfer-
ring the story from Budapest to New England — specifically Maine — and by
greatly altering Molnar's secondary plot, Hammerstein again infused social
advocacy into a story where none existed before. In the main plot, Billy
Bigelow (Molnar's Liliom), a roughneck, bullying carnival barker, marries
Julie, a devoted young girl who passively endures Billy's physical abuse,
openly confessed in her song "What's the Use of Wond'rin'." Out of work
and about to become a father (articulated in Hammerstein's brilliant lyric
for the introspective "Soliloquy"), Billy participates in a robbery, kills him-

self when it goes sour, and tries to redeem himself after death by returning to earth to commit one good act. The major changes relevant to *Carousel*'s tolerance theme involve a shift in two characters' ethnicity. In *Liliom*, Linzman—the prototype of *Carousel*'s mill owner Mr. Bascombe and target of the attempted robbery—is Jewish. Linzman is not the factory owner but holds a management position in the firm, perfectly plausible for late-nineteenth-century Budapest, but less than likely for a Jew in Maine at the time—hence a change purely for the sake of realism. More significantly, Hammerstein changed Molnar's Wolf Beifeld, a Jew, to become Enoch Snow in *Carousel*'s altered subplot. A Jewish fisherman in Maine during the 1870s and '80s is unlikely, but more to the point is that Snow's pivotal part in the prejudice/tolerance statement of the musical would not be possible if he were Jewish.

Hammerstein's advocacy of accepting "class" differences occurs only late in act 2, and then through dance and dialogue, never song. In Agnes De Mille's scene 4 ballet, the audience first meets Louise, Billy and Julie's daughter, after a time lapse of fifteen years since Billy's death earlier in the act. Also introduced are the six Snow children, accompanied by their father, now very prosperous, strolling along the beach. Their mother and Snow's wife, the former Carrie Pippiridge—still Julie's best friend from their mill-working days—is not in the scene. In *Liliom* Wolf Beifeld, the original Mr. Snow, also greatly improves his economic and social status, rising from porter, to steward, to proprietor of the Café Sorrento, but these rungs on the upward mobility ladder appear in only casual references in Molnar's dialogue. But when Hammerstein transformed Wolf into Enoch, he made him a walking exemplar of the Down East American Calvinist-Presbyterian capitalist archetype so brilliantly delineated in R. H. Tawney's classic *Religion and the Rise of Capitalism*. This alteration allowed Snow to espouse the kind of intolerance Hammerstein so despised. His entire verse of his first-act duet with Carrie, "When the Children Are Asleep," details his plans to move up from fisherman to fish entrepreneur:

> When I make enough money outa one little boat,
> I'll put all my money in another little boat.
> I'll make twic't as much outa two little boats,
> And the fust thing you know I'll hev four little boats!
> (Rodgers, *6 Plays* 125)

And so on, incrementally, until he has "a great big fleet of great big boats!" (125), to which Enoch adds a sardine cannery in the ensuing dialogue, proudly proclaiming, "I'm goin' to get rich on sardines. I mean *we're* goin' to get rich—you and me. I mean you and me—and—all of us." He then addresses Carrie as if she were a part of his capitalistic vision (which she is), viewing her primarily as a baby factory. By the middle of act 2, Snow has his cannery, six kids, and a prominent place in the community—a place from which he and his brood can and do look down on others. In heavily WASP Maine, a Jewish Snow and his kids could not plausibly look down on others, since the others would look down on them.

At the start of De Mille's ballet, Louise happily romps alone on the beach or with two "little ruffian boys" (Rodgers, *6 Plays* 168). When Enoch and the six Snow kids troop on and Louise invites them to play, to a child they categorically snub her; "one little horror" even returns after the rest have left to hurl verbal insults like "Your father was a thief." At the end of the ballet, children "dressed for a party" also reject Louise (169), making it clear she has been marginalized not just by Snow family prejudice but through more widespread class biases. Louise screams after them, "I hate you—I hate *all* of you!" (169; italics supplied).

In the ensuing dialogue scene, Mr. Snow tries to keep Enoch Jr. from talking to Louise (172). Even when Junior manages to, revealing his crush on her, he says he'll marry her only if he can "persuade Papa to let me marry beneath my station" (173). At which remark Louise throws a well-deserved fit. Whereas the ballet and dialogue scene dramatize class bias and its effect on the recipient, Hammerstein has not yet expressed the need to eradicate such attitudes and behavior, and the musical is almost over. This occurs only in one of the last lines of dialogue, when the Doctor says to Louise's graduating class, "The world belongs to you as much as to the next feller. Don't give it up! And try not to be skeered o' people not likin' you—jest you try likin' *them*" (179). (Hammerstein's Mainers talk just like his Oklahomans, another of his clumsy attempts at regional dialect.) The Doctor's sentiment, however, is veritably swamped by the reprise-finale of "You'll Never Walk Alone." As Stephen Citron observes, "Hammerstein the librettist seems to be telling us to embrace others, while Hammerstein the lyricist tells us in song that we must keep the faith" (175). Audiences embraced *and* kept the faith with *Carousel* 890 times.

## Allegro

When *Allegro* opened on October 10, 1947, Rodgers and Hammerstein had three shows running concurrently on Broadway, a feat achieved by few writers of musicals. *Allegro* was their first of just two shows for which Hammerstein wrote a completely original book, the only two, interestingly, that do not express his concern about prejudice and tolerance, although *Allegro* embodies social statements of another kind.

*Allegro* is the chronicle of a young man's life from birth in 1905 to 1940. In a rural Midwestern community, Joseph Taylor Jr., the son of a generous, compassionate country physician, grows from baby, to child, to high school kid who falls for the girl next door. He goes to college, goes to medical school, marries the next door girl, and begins practicing country medicine with his dad, but he is lured by a med school friend and the urgings of his social-climbing, material-minded bride to take a post at a prestigious Chicago hospital with a lucrative private practice as a "society doctor" attached. Eventually Joe gets fed up with treating phony ailments of phony people, and more than fed up when he learns his proffered appointment as the hospital's physician-in-chief came not from his own medical talents but from his wife's influence on the millionaire trustee she's sleeping with. Joe turns down the post, leaves his wife, and, followed by a wisecracking colleague and a nurse who barely conceals her love for him, heads home to help his father build a community hospital.

A simple story, but not simply told, which may be why by mid-'40s standards 315 performances marked *Allegro* as a comparative failure. Audiences were hard put to grasp the expressionistic devices Hammerstein used to tell a realistic tale: an on-stage Greek-type chorus speaks and thinks for Joe long before he first appears as a character played by an actor. From birth until college, Joe is just an invisible, imaginary spot wherever the chorus "thinking" for him or a character addressing him is looking. His grandmother and mother both die in act 1 but "come back" later to speak and sing as Joe's conscience and the pull of his roots, as in the heart-tugging "Come Home." Director/choreographer Agnes De Mille's dances reveal character psychology and personality, especially that of Joe's girl-then-wife Jenny. Scenes take place simultaneously in real life and in characters' thoughts, as in the college lecture sequence. By 1947, audiences should have been prepared by Thornton Wilder's 1938 *Our Town*, but they were apparently perplexed and put off by Jo Mielziner's minimalist settings (a bed for a bedroom, chairs for a classroom, etc.).

Whereas *Allegro* contains not a trace of Hammerstein's prejudice/tolerance theme, the libretto expresses the dangers (to oneself) of social climbing, materialism, and the postwar years' runaway consumer culture. Even more central is a personal concern of Hammerstein's that also resonates with larger societal implications. While working with composers like Sigmund Romberg and Jerome Kern, Hammerstein had considerable success, but nothing like the celebrity he achieved collaborating with Dick Rodgers. Like most celebrities, he was swamped with speaking engagements and invitations to join boards and committees and attend all manner of dinners and fundraisers; today it would be the TV talk show circuit. Hammerstein said of men like himself and Joe, "the first thing you know they are no longer writing or practicing medicine or law" (qtd. in Citron 181–82). According to Stephen Sondheim, who at seventeen was a production assistant on *Allegro*, "[Oscar] was so successful, he had so many responsibilities, that they cut into his artistic life. . . . He accepted these responsibilities because he felt they were worth attending to. But at the same time he found himself farther away from his profession. He transformed that into the story of a young doctor who comes to the big city at the behest of his upwardly mobile wife" (qtd. in Citron 182). Clearly fed up with the obligations of celebrity that kept him from what he should be doing—writing musicals—Hammerstein made *Allegro* "more about himself than about the red-blooded American, Dr. Joseph Taylor, Jr., he had chosen as protagonist and alter ego" (Citron 182). But the musical was also about any individual's fight to maintain integrity and values in the face of the distracting clutter lurking in contemporary American culture.

## South Pacific

In the 1,925-performance, Pulitzer Prize-winning *South Pacific* (4/7/49), issues of prejudice and tolerance for the first time became the actual drive-mechanism of character conflicts in both the primary and secondary plot of a Rodgers and Hammerstein musical. The show's source was James Michener's *Tales of the South Pacific*, a collection of nineteen short stories about the men and women of the U.S. armed forces in the Pacific Theatre during World War II. Ethnic and racial tensions were central to two of Michener's stories, which made them congenial to both Hammerstein and Rodgers as the core of the musical's two plotlines. Still, in order to more fully articulate his advocacy of accepting racial and ethnic differences, Hammerstein significantly altered both stories.

In January 1948, Joshua Logan—who went on to direct *South Pacific*—told Dick Rodgers to read the story "Fo' Dolla'" as a possible basis for a musical. "Fo' Dolla'" tells of the brief, intense love affair between U.S. Marine Corps Lieutenant Joseph Cable and Liat, the beautiful sixteen-year-old daughter of Bloody Mary, the Tonkinese souvenir seller. Dick read it, Oscar read it, and both saw its potential, but "[t]he more we talked about the plot, the more it dawned on us that onstage it would look like just another variation of *Madama Butterfly*" (Rodgers, *Stages* 259), something the writers of *Miss Saigon* obviously didn't worry much about. So they read on, finally lighting on "Our Heroine," the story of nurse Ensign Nellie Forbush and French planter Emile De Becque that both complemented and contrasted with the Cable-Liat tale while embodying the same essential issues in its character conflicts. Parts of other stories were brought in, chiefly to include such comic characters as Luther Billis, the company wheeler-dealer, but the heart of *South Pacific* would be "Our Heroine" for the main plot and "Fo' Dolla' " for the underplot.

Hammerstein's plotting of *South Pacific* was a departure for him, even though he took the device directly from Michener's stories. In *Oklahoma!* and *Carousel* an actual person (Jud and Jigger, respectively) largely serves as the antagonist to a happy outcome for the romantic couple, but in *South Pacific* the "blocking figure" isn't a person but the ingrained prejudice and racial bias within characters. Hammerstein thus shifted his abhorrence of intolerance from the incidental references in *Oklahoma!* and *Carousel* to its central position as the source of conflict in both plots of *South Pacific*.

The issues in the story of Nellie and Emile are the more straightforward and so more easily resolved, though at first it may seem perplexing that there are issues at all. Nellie is white, Emile is white; no problem. Emile is considerably older and French, Nellie younger and American—still no innate obstacle to romantic or marital happiness. But then, in the musical, Nellie learns that Emile had lived with a Polynesian woman and that the two mixed-race children on his plantation are his. In Michener's "Our Heroine," Nellie learns Emile has eight children ranging in age from twenty-three to seven—all daughters, inexplicably—and by not just one non-white woman, but a number of them who were Javanese, Tonkinese, and—the last straw for Nellie—Polynesian. In Michener's frank language, "Nellie Forbush, of Otolousa, Arkansas, could not speak. . . . Emile De Becque, not satisfied with Javanese and Tonkinese women, had also lived with a Polynesian. A nigger! To Nellie's tutored mind any person living or dead who was not white or yellow was a nigger" (111–12). Though not in the musical, this passage supplies the subtext for Nellie breaking off her marriage plans with De Becque. She can't escape being an American Southerner whose racial bias is directed specifically against blacks, with whom she equates Polynesians. Only at the end of the show when Emile returns from a dangerous reconnaissance mission does love triumph over bigotry, and the couple is reunited.

In the Nellie/De Becque story, the question of racial bias is fairly easily resolved, probably because both characters are white and Nellie's prejudice is more or less "once removed": Emile isn't the problem, just (in her eyes) the specific "race" of the woman he slept with. But Cable and Liat's story is a different matter. Michener only hinted at prejudice in "Fo' Dolla'," but Hammerstein uses this plot of *South Pacific* to expand upon his theme vigorously and eloquently, although his resolution raises some questions.

Michener goes to great lengths to identify Liat and Bloody Mary as Tonkinese — essentially Vietnamese in a later day, and so essentially Chinese in appearance (167; and see Rodgers, *South* 18). Planters on French-owned South Pacific islands brought many people from Tonkin, then a French dependency, to work on their estates. But the musical never makes very clear the ethnicity of Liat and Mary. The one direct reference to their being Tonkinese disappeared when Cable's song "My Girl Back Home" was cut from the show. Liat and Mary's race, nationality, or ethnicity in the musical was so unclear that Richard Rodgers persists in referring to Liat as Polynesian in his autobiography (*Stages* 261).

In the Michener story, Cable never speaks a racially biased word or thinks a bigoted thought, and not because he is inarticulate. Joe Cable is of Main Line Philadelphia stock, a product of prep school and Princeton University. When he decides he must break off his love affair with Liat, his words are brusque, direct, but not very explanatory: "I can't. . . . I love her, Mary, . . . but I can't marry her. . . . I can't. I can't take her home with me" (177–78), strongly implying, "I could never face my parents." Cable knows that his WASP family's intolerance would extend to Asians, not just to those island races Nellie classifies as "nigger." From this moment, the Liats of the story and the musical are very different people. Michener's Liat says, "I knew it could never be. . . . You love me. You will go away somewhere. I will marry somebody else" (180), which she does. Hammerstein's Liat is heartbroken but independent; according to Bloody Mary, she "won't marry no one but Lootellan Cable" (Rodgers, *South* 159), remaining very much alone at the end of the musical.

To accommodate expressing his own position on prejudice, Hammerstein altered Cable's character for the musical. As in the story, all Cable says openly to the Tonkinese mother and daughter is, "Mary, I can't . . . marry . . . Liat," but the stage direction "(*Forcing the words out*)" indicates that he'd really like to say something else (Rodgers, *South* 123). Whereas Michener's Nellie attributed her racist views to a "tutored mind" — a learned, not innate, bias — she sees things differently in *South Pacific*. Late in act 2, with Cable on stage to hear her, Nellie says to De Becque, "I can't help it. . . . There is no reason. This is emotional. This is something that is born in me" (Rodgers, *South* 135). After Nellie leaves, De Becque says to Cable, "I do not believe it is born in you. I do not believe it" (136). And Joe replies, "It's not born in you! It happens *after* you're born":

(CABLE *sings the following words, as if figuring this whole question out for the first time*)

> You've got to be taught to hate and fear,
> You've got to be taught from year to year,

It's got to be drummed in your dear little ear—
You've got to be carefully taught!
You've got to be taught to be afraid
Of people whose eyes are oddly made,
And people whose skin is a different shade—
You've got to be carefully taught.
You've got to be taught before it's too late,
Before you are six or seven or eight,
To hate all the people your relatives hate—
You've got to be carefully taught!
You've got to be carefully taught!
      (*Speaking, going close to* EMILE, *his voice filled with the
      emotion of discovery and firm in a new determination*)
. . . Yes, sir, if I get out of this thing alive, I'm not going back there!
I'm coming here. All I care about is right here. To Hell with the rest.
                               (Rodgers, *South* 136–37)

Richard Rodgers characterizes "Carefully Taught" as a song revealing Cable's epiphany about the irrationality of learned bigotry: "Oscar and I felt it was needed in a particular spot for a Princeton-educated young WASP who, despite his background and upbringing, had fallen in love with a Polynesian [sic] girl. It was perfectly in keeping with the character and situation that, having once lost his heart, he would express his feelings about the superficiality of racial barriers" (*Stages* 261). But Rodgers also says "Carefully Taught" "was not intended as a 'message' song," yet it stands out as the most explicit statement of Hammerstein's concern about learned biases in the entire Rodgers and Hammerstein canon.

What is problematic in the Cable/Liat plot is its ending. In Michener's story, the affair simply ends; Cable is shipped out to another base. Only in "A Cemetery at Hoga Point," the final story in *Tales of the South Pacific* and separated from "Fo' Dolla' " by eight others, is it mentioned in passing that Cable was killed on a beachhead some time after he broke off with Liat. But in the musical, soon after resolving to overcome his learned prejudices and return after the war to marry Liat, Cable is killed while on the reconnaissance mission with De Becque. While this has the effect of making Cable more of a romantic hero than the cad he seems to be in Michener, the musical's ending raises questions. Stephen Citron suggests that Hammerstein's motive for Cable's death may have been "to satisfy censors who might object to the liaison as fostering miscegenation" (193). More broadly, in 1949 it was one thing for a Broadway show to advocate in theory for interracial harmony and even relationships, but it would have been quite another to let the latter actually happen. Cable's death seems to be an attempt to placate potential ticket-buyers of the "I don't care if they live next door, but they're not going to marry my daughter" mindset, who otherwise might have stayed away in droves. How much Hammerstein dared and how soundly he dramatized his advocacy as integral to the musical is impressive, but it's also unfortunate that the integrity of his vision was compromised for the sake of commercial success.

## The King and I

With *The King and I* (3/29/51), Hammerstein further perfected his dramatic craftsmanship while continuing to promote tolerance and respect among peoples of different cultures. Specifically, the core of the musical is the ongoing conflict between the feisty Welsh school teacher Anna Leonowens and the rigid King of Siam. Whereas Cable and Nellie's prejudices create crises at just a few isolated moments in *South Pacific*, the cultural biases of Anna and the King are central to their personalities and inform every interaction between them. In no other musical did Hammerstein so skillfully embed his advocacy of tolerance in the plot and characters. The sophisticated playwriting, Rodgers's superb musical score, and Hammerstein's articulate lyrics harmonize to make *The King and I* the best integrated of their musicals. Add a cast starring Gertrude Lawrence and Yul Brynner, directed and choreographed by Jerome Robbins, and it's clear why it played 1,246 times.

Hammerstein's source was Margaret Landon's novel *Anna and the King of Siam*, based in turn on Anna Leonowens's two autobiographies of her years in what is now Thailand, *The English Governess at the Siamese Court* and *The Romance of the Harem*. Given the nature of his source, Hammerstein focused his prejudice/tolerance concern specifically on the lack of understanding and lack of sympathy between widely divergent countries and cultures. Throughout the musical, the cultural differences in the early 1860s between the West—specifically Britain (and by implication America)—and the East—specifically Siam—are at loggerheads. Discussing the terms of her teaching with the Kralahome, the King's minister, in the opening scene, Anna experiences her first East/West clash of values. Anna, who comes from a land where a contract is a contract, says, "The King has promised me twenty pounds a month and a house of my own." The Kralahome, who lives in a land where the absolute ruler's whims constitute the law, replies, "King do not always remember what he promise. If I tell him he break his promise, I will make anger in him. I think it is better I make anger in him about larger matters" (Rodgers, *King* 11).

Once Anna starts teaching, she and the King butt heads on every conceivable subject, from whether the children should be taught Western rather than Siamese geography to proper modes of etiquette and paying respect to royalty—not to mention Anna's perpetual complaints about the promise and the house. Yet Hammerstein gives each of them a private moment of sung thought, a comic/dramatic soliloquy in which each reflects, if only briefly, on whether his or her way is the only way. The King goes first, after his son Chulalongkorn challenges the time-honored Siamese view of astronomy with Anna's explanation of the earth's rotation. In "A Puzzlement," the King confesses

> There are times I almost think
> I am not sure of what I absolutely know.
> Very often find confusion
> In conclusion I concluded long ago.
> In my head are many facts
> That, as a student, I have studied to procure.
> In my head are many facts
> Of which I wish I was more certain I was sure!
> (Rodgers, *King* 33)

Later, alone in her room after a furious shouting match with the King over the promise of a house, Anna blows off a lot of steam venting everything she wished she had said to his face in "Shall I Tell You What I Think of You." Yet, if only fleetingly, she half admits British cultural norms may not be the only ones.

> I do not like polygamy
> Or even moderate bigamy
> (I realize
> That in your eyes
> That clearly makes a prig o' me)
> (Rodgers, *King* 55)

Of course the concept of priggishness would be entirely foreign to the King—but not to Anna. For one brief instant, she questions whether her inculcated Victorian prudery, not the reality of the King's multiple marriages, is the source of her distaste for his polygamy. So, bit by bit, barriers to cross-cultural understanding break down as Anna and the King come to accept that there are ways of doing things other than their own.

In Anna, Hammerstein created a strong female lead as a way of investigating attitudes toward women. This theme is dramatized through conflicts in the storyline rather than made a topic for discussion. The young woman Tuptim is delivered to the King as a "present" from the Prince of Burma, although she loves Lun Tha. The King insists that Anna is his "servant,"

not, as she insists, his employee. And throughout act 1, the King denies
Anna a private house, keeping her instead in the palace as one of his harem.
Only three times do conventional views of women's inferiority appear in
the dialogue. Early on Anna is speaking with Lady Thiang, the head wife,
in the presence of the other wives:

> ANNA
> Lady Thiang, why do you call me "sir"?
> THIANG
> Because you scientific. Not lowly, like woman.
> ANNA
> Do you think *all* women are more lowly than men?
> (THIANG *translates this to the wives, all of whom smile*
> *broadly and nod their heads, apparently quite happy*
> *with the idea of female inferiority.* ANNA'S *voice is in-*
> *dignant*)
> Well, I don't.
>
> (Rodgers, *King* 26)

As act 1 ends, the King agrees to give Anna her house, while praying to
Buddha, "Help also Mrs. Anna to keep awake for scientific sewing of dresses,
even though she be only a woman and a Christian, and therefore unworthy
of your interest" (Rodgers, *King* 77). Yet, at the finale, the dying King's
letter to Anna reveals he had something of a change of heart: "I think it
very strange that a woman shall have been the most earnest help of all"
(135).

In *The King and I* Hammerstein attempted to convey the necessity of
coming to terms with cultural differences of literally global dimensions, but
in the end he could not escape a Eurocentric bias himself. Throughout the
play Anna and her son Louis are appalled by such Siamese customs as men
clothed only from the waist down, or people showing respect for the King
by groveling on all fours with their heads touching the floor. Hammerstein
tries to balance this Western attitude toward the East in a very brief song
at the top of act 2, "Western People Funny." Lady Thiang and the wives
take the position that Westerners also look pretty peculiar to Asians. But
the number doesn't work; in fact it rather backfires, in light of what happens
during the play's finale:

> Western people funny,
> Of that there is no doubt.
> They feel so sentimental
> About the oriental,
> They always try to turn us
> Inside down and upside out!

. . . . . . . . . . . . .
They think they civilize us
Whenever they advise us
To learn to make the same mistake
That they are making too!
(82, 83)

Intrinsically, this is a rather splendid critique of the cultural intolerance that causes Westerners to exoticize non-Westerners and try to make them over. But Hammerstein undermines his critique at the end of the play. As the King lies dying, his son and heir makes one of his first proclamations showing respect to the King no longer by all-fours groveling but by Western bowing and curtseying. Here Hammerstein is as guilty of valuing Western mores (often equated in this play with feminine civilizing tendencies!) over Eastern ones. Anna and her values, it seems, triumph over a weakened and dying king. As with the mixed messages at the end of *Carousel* and the questions raised by Cable's death in *South Pacific*, the problem of ending a musical dramatically once again conflicts with and weakens Hammerstein's well-intentioned advocacy for the equal treatment of all human beings.

### Pipe Dream

Rodgers and Hammerstein's next collaboration was *Me and Juliet* (5/28/53), a dreary, workmanlike backstage musical about the love triangle of a female chorus singer, a nice-guy assistant stage manager, and an alcoholic, unstable stage electrician once the singer's boyfriend (Rodgers, *Stages* 281–83). The script was Hammerstein's last original book. Not only is his prejudice/tolerance theme absent, there is no apparent thematic core at all. With little going for it but a few nice songs like "Keep It Gay," "Marriage Type Love," and "No Other Love," audiences dismissed *Me and Juliet* after 358 performances.

With a run of only 246 performances, *Pipe Dream* (11/30/55) was even less commercially successful, but it intrinsically had a lot more going for it. With its roots in the eccentric but lovable denizens of Monterey, California's Cannery Row depicted in John Steinbeck's *Sweet Thursday*, *Pipe Dream* is a musical of considerable charm. It also contains a number of rather splendid songs that have received less attention than they deserved down through the years: "All At Once You Love Her," "The Next Time It Happens," and "Will You Marry Me?" to name but three. *Pipe Dream* is also a musical with an entirely new take on Hammerstein's tolerance theme. The down-and-out male residents of the Palace Flophouse, the working girls of the Bear Flag Café and their motherly madam Fauna, a drifter and part-time hustler named Suzy, and Doc, a marine biologist (who, unlikely as it may seem, winds up with Suzy), at first appear an odd assortment of humanity for a musical, but somehow the whole thing comes together. With these oddballs and outcasts for characters, Hammerstein makes a real pitch for what has come to be called the celebration of diversity. As Doc sings in the show's first song:

> It takes all kinds of people to make up a world,
> All kinds of people and things.
> They crawl on the earth,
> They swim in the sea,
> And they fly through the sky on wings.
> All kinds of people and things,
> And brother, I'll tell you my hunch:
> Whether you like them,
> Or whether you don't,
> You're stuck with the whole damn bunch!
>
> (Rodgers, *Pipe* 21)

While the theme of accepting every individual's "otherness" is implied throughout the show, Hammerstein specifically focuses on a different kind of acceptance altogether—acceptance of oneself. Suzy, this motif's focal point, has a terrible self-image. Fairly early on, Fauna tries to raise her self-esteem in the song "Suzy Is a Good Thing," and for a while Suzy believes it. But as time goes on she again finds it hard to see how anyone (including herself) can find her worthy of their love. When Suzy runs out of the second-act party mistakenly thinking Doc has rejected her, Hammerstein gives her the very telling lines, "He don't think I'm good enough for him. I see it in his eyes. He don't think I'm good enough—and I don't think so either!" (126). At the end, when Suzy finally accepts that Doc really loves her, she can finally accept herself as well.

## Flower Drum Song

Hammerstein based his next musical, *Flower Drum Song* (12/1/58; 600 performances), on C. Y. Lee's novel of the same name. Every character is either Chinese or Chinese-American, although more members of the original cast were Japanese, Korean, black, or Caucasian American than Chinese. In *Flower Drum Song*, Hammerstein dramatizes the need for tolerance and understanding across generations and between traditional versus modernized or assimilated lifestyles within one ethnic community. Most, though not all, of the younger characters are wholly assimilated Chinese-Americans, whereas the older generation by and large honors, reveres, and follows time-honored traditions. In this show Hammerstein expresses his view almost entirely through the dramatic action. Only "The Other Generation," first sung by the elder characters Wang San and Madam Liang and later reprised with different lyrics by young though fairly traditional Wang Ta and the Americanized Suzie, directly conveys how one generation doesn't understand the other. Hammerstein also continues *Pipe Dream*'s paean to diversity in one of his rare excursions into a satirical or topical lyric. In Madam Liang's "Chop Suey," that "Chinese" dish invented by Americans in which "Everything is in it—all mixed up" becomes the character's metaphor for why she likes her new country (Rodgers, *Flower* 61). Here Hammerstein sharply juxtaposes some clashing cultural icons of the 1950s to celebrate America's seemingly impossible but somehow functioning diversity:

> Living here is very much like Chop Suey:
> Hula Hoops and nuclear war,
> Doctor Salk and Zsa Zsa Gabor
> Harry Truman, Truman Capote and Dewey—
> Chop Suey!

He even references the raging school-integration issue of the day,

> Chop Suey,
> Chop Suey,
> Rough and tough and brittle and soft and gooey—
> Peking Duck and Mulligan Stew,
> Plymouth Rock and Little Rock, too.
> (Rodgers, *Flower* 61, 64)

Other than these songs, the show reveals the gaps between generations and between traditional and assimilated cultural norms through plot alone. A fairly traditional young man thinks he is in love with a wholly assimilated nightclub performer who definitely lives in the fast lane, while a fast-living Americanized man has been contracted to a *very* traditional "picture bride" newly arrived from China. Ultimately each winds up with the woman whose mode of living most nearly matches his own, so there is nothing here about reconciling conflicting cultures to create a new harmonious one, as in *Oklahoma!* Instead, the show simply dramatizes people from disparate generations and with different cultural values coming to understand and accept one another.

## The Sound of Music

No one but some close friends, family, and theatrical colleagues could have even guessed in 1959 that *The Sound of Music* (11/16/59; 1,433 performances) would be the last Rodgers and Hammerstein show — Hammerstein had terminal cancer and died at his home in Doylestown, Pennsylvania, on August 23, 1960, ending the extraordinary collaboration that virtually remade the American musical. Their final show was unique in that the libretto was not Hammerstein's, yet at the same time it proved a fitting finale to the team's sixteen-year partnership, in a sense bringing Hammerstein's thematic concerns full circle. Howard Lindsay and Russel Crouse (*Life with Father, Arsenic and Old Lace*, and the books for such musicals as *Anything Goes, Red, Hot and Blue*, and *Call Me Madam*) wrote the script, with Rodgers and Hammerstein brought in to supply the music and lyrics. Still, in terms of its thematic core, *The Sound of Music* is very much a Rodgers and Hammerstein musical.

The show was very loosely based on *The Trapp Family Singers* by Maria Augusta Trapp, and on a German film, *Die Trapp Familie* (Wilk, *Overture* 123). Set in 1938 Austria just before and after the German *Anschluss*, the story told of a postulant who becomes, first, governess to Captain Von Trapp's seven children and later his wife. Lindsay and Crouse's very skillful dialogue contains a gradual build-up of explicit references to Germany and the Third Reich (only nine such passages in the entire play), with the effect that the Nazi takeover of Austria shifts almost imperceptibly from being the musical's background to its foreground, forcing the staunchly anti-Nazi Von Trapp, his new wife, and children to flee for their lives at the finale. The show also pits Von Trapp's integrity ("I am an Austrian — I will not be heiled" [Rodgers, *Sound* 63]) against the purely pragmatic compromising of the captain's sometime fiancée Elsa and one-time friend Max, who with no qualms accepts the post of First Secretary of the Ministry of Education and Culture in the new Nazi regime. The high-principled Von Trapp, on the other hand, refuses a commission in the navy of the Third Reich at great risk to himself and his family (126–30).

*The Sound of Music* makes no mention of the Nazi persecution of Jews and other minorities, focusing entirely on the fear and hatred of the Nazis among characters who are all Austrian Catholics. And yet, an audience in the late '50s and early '60s could not escape being reminded of the larger human tragedy brought on by World War II and the Holocaust. When Rodgers and Hammerstein wrote *Oklahoma!*, the most graphic details of the deathcamps and Hitler's persecution of Jews, gypsies, and other minorities were not yet revealed. Still, it was then that Hammerstein first expressed on the musical stage his liberal and humanitarian interest in the eradication of prejudice and the need for acceptance and tolerance, however obliquely, in his analogy of "the farmer and the cowman." None of his shows before teaming with Rodgers had more than glanced at this issue (at most, Julie's story in *Show Boat*), one that, once begun, remained a virtual constant in the rest of his collaborations with Rodgers, until in their final show together Hammerstein confronted Nazism. However buried his connections to his Jewish roots, the revelation of Nazi atrocities may have brought to the surface Hammerstein's need to respond to intolerance and bigotry in the public forum of the musical theatre, a need that finally, sixteen years later, directly brought the Nazis in as villains in one of his most successful shows.

### The Rodgers and Hammerstein Legacy

The most significant, influential, and lasting contributions of the Rodgers and Hammerstein musicals — and, specifically, of Hammerstein the librettist — were threefold. First, the productions in their totality, meaning not just Dick and Oscar's music and words but the collaborative contributions of a distinguished series of directors, designers, and choreographers, went farther toward perfecting the integrated musical than any single show or group of shows before them. Both the overall form of their shows and the specific ways Hammerstein wove together dialogue, song, and dance became models for generations of other writers. Second is Hammerstein's clear and deliberate *intention* of having his musicals be meaningful and relevant, a salient characteristic of non-musical drama back to antiquity. Yet, wisely, Hammerstein never did what many years later Stephen Sondheim observed many young writers doing — "start[ing] with themes instead of stories and characters" (Rich 88). While Hammerstein's liberal thinking on prejudice and tolerance long predated his first show with Rodgers, he never let himself be social advocate first and storyteller second, no matter how important the ideas he wanted to convey. Instead — the third major contribution of the Rodgers and Hummerstein musicals — Hammerstein continued to find ever more sophisticated ways to express his ideas and beliefs through a show's story and characters, never sacrificing entertainment value to his social advocacy. During the Rodgers and Hammerstein years and beyond, Hammerstein's techniques for embedding serious issues in the story of a commercially viable musical became models for future librettists and lyricists.

## ✻ 5 ✻

# From Isolationism to Idealism
# in the Cold War Years

*TV, Rock and Roll, and Declining Broadway Audiences*

From the end of World War II through the early 1960s, great changes in American politics and society swept through the nation, although, ironically, most middle-Americans scarcely noticed. The prosperity that began during the war continued almost unabated through both the Truman and Eisenhower administrations—the heart of the postwar and cold war period. Social historians Douglas Miller and Marion Nowak find parallels between the 1950s and the 1920s in that both "postwar periods were relatively prosperous and highly conservative. . . . Fatherly Republican Eisenhower was only a more popular version of the Harding/Coolidge-type politician" (Miller 6).

This prosperity fostered the attitude of smug complacency among many middle-class Americans. But the prosperity also fostered a very prosperous musical theatre, not just in terms of revenue but in terms of the richness, variety, and generally high quality of the shows. These years produced a number of musicals rich in social meaning as well as diversionary shows of perhaps the highest quality ever written (see appendix D). It was, after all, the period of *Annie Get Your Gun, Kiss Me, Kate, Guys and Dolls, The Pajama Game, Damn Yankees, My Fair Lady,* and *The Music Man,* all of which played one thousand times or more. And yet, at the same time dramatic changes in the country's economy, media, and culture began having an immediate and irreversible impact on the musical stage that not even Broadway's higher ticket prices and longer runs of fewer shows could counteract.

In the postwar years, the cost of mounting all Broadway productions spiraled out of control even faster than the cost of a ticket, which doubled between 1944 and 1960 (Brockett 515). The number of new musicals shrank more than new plays, since, with few exceptions, producing a musical replete with many and lavish sets and costumes, large cast, orchestra, and technical crews is astronomically more costly than mounting a play. In the

cold war years there were fewer musicals on Broadway than any time
since—and including—the Great Depression. In 1951–52, only seven new
musicals opened, nine each in the seasons of '52–'53 and '53–'54; the number bounced up to twelve in the season following, but then crashed to an
abysmal low of five in 1955–56 (Bordman 580, 583, 586, 590, 596). Similar
figures would continue to the end of the century.

Skyrocketing ticket prices kept some former spectators away, but even
more than the rising cost of admission, television radically changed entertainment habits, keeping housebound countless Americans who once went
out at night. Moviegoing was similarly affected, registering a drop in weekly
attendance from 86 million in 1946 to around 36 million in 1950 (Miller
314). In 1946, there were fewer than seventeen thousand TV sets in use, but
by 1949 about a quarter of a million were being installed *each month*, mostly
in private dwellings. By 1953, two-thirds of U.S. homes had at least one, and
by 1957 there were 40 million televisions in use and 467 TV stations. One
regularly scheduled kind of TV programming in the 1950s—seen only rarely
since—drew many theatregoers away from Broadway. Series like *Studio
One*, *Playhouse 90*, and *Play of the Week* presented televised versions of
current and recent Broadway plays—sometimes even musicals—often live,
not on kinescope (videotape's precursor), and at virtually no cost to the
viewer. People didn't have to go to Broadway; Broadway was coming to
them.

While such sophisticated TV fare kept adults out of theatres, rock and
roll was changing the musical tastes of their children. Instead of listening
to show music or more conventional popular music, teens were turning to
rock and roll. This musical seduction of America's youth dates roughly from
1955, when Bill Haley and the Comets swooped down upon an unsuspecting public with "Rock Around the Clock" in the film *The Blackboard Jun-
gle*, setting off "the national merchandising of rock culture" (Leuchtenburg,
*Feast* 65). White recording artists made cover versions of rhythm and blues
numbers previously recorded by blacks for an almost exclusively African
American audience. Thanks to the likes of Georgia Gibbs, Pat Boone, the
Crew Cuts, Jerry Lee Lewis, and Elvis Presley, this "sanitized" black music
aimed to attract a listenership of teenaged white, mainstream, middle-class
Americans. And attract them it did, with the effect of further shrinking
present and future generations of musical theatre audiences (see Miller 291–
312). In 1978, Stephen Sondheim, addressing the rock phenomenon, spoke
to these changes:

I can't predict the future, but I do know that what's happened is, obviously, a split
between popular and theatrical music. It has widened over the last twenty years

because the notion of popular music, which has to do with relentlessness, electric amplification and a kind of insistence, is, I think, anti-theatrical; anti-dramatic, to be a little more accurate. I don't think that kind of music can ever define character, because it's essentially always the same, and it must be the same, because that's its quality. It's also a performer's medium; it's the singer, not the song. . . . Pop music has as strong a hold as ever, and it weakens the theater audience. I mean, so many young people miss in the musical theater what they can get on a record. How can I tell them that the musical theater is just a different way of looking at things? They haven't been exposed to it, so it seems wishy-washy and unsatisfying to them because it is not what they require from music. (Sondheim, "The Musical" 29)

As Sondheim sees it, if people haven't been exposed to musicals by the time they are teenagers, it's unlikely that they will develop a taste for them as adults. So, it's not just higher ticket prices that continue to drive the average age of audiences upward. Even early in the twenty-first century, many thirty and fortysomethings rarely attend musicals, not because of the cost but because they never developed an appreciation of them.

## The Political and Social Moods of Postwar America

If changes in the economy, culture, and entertainment habits most affected the production and attendance of musicals, the mixed moods of the American people most inspired a wide range of socially meaningful shows. In the postwar and cold war years there was a dichotomy within both the American government and the American people: on the one hand, increasingly liberal social thought and, ultimately, social change in domestic affairs (notably in the civil rights and race relations arena), and, on the other, conservative attitudes and policies regarding the international scene—especially the position of the U.S. vis-à-vis the U.S.S.R. In large part, the conservatism within America's swelling middle class was rooted in the fear of possible nuclear war and a communist threat to the nation. According to historians Miller and Nowak, "the last years of Truman's presidency proved a trying time—a period of suspicions, accusations, loyalty oaths, loathings, extreme American chauvinism" (13–14). This was the period when Truman issued Executive Order 9835 initiating loyalty reviews for government employees (1947); the Whitaker Chambers–Alger Hiss fiasco (1948) resulted in Hiss's five-year prison term for perjury; Joe McCarthy first gained national attention for alleging communist infiltration in the State Department (1950); and Julius and Ethel Rosenberg were arrested and tried as Soviet spies (1950: Miller 22, 13; Leuchtenburg 29–30). Americans' concern, even paranoia, over a clear and present danger *within* the United States underscored feelings of isolationism. Despite the success of our troops in World War II, the war itself seemed to foster xenophobic sentiment.

Brigadoon: *An Isolationist Utopia*

That conservatism in general and isolationism in particular were still abroad in the land was made manifest in 1946 when American voters elected the particularly conservative, notoriously obstructionist Eightieth Congress, which, among other things, "enacted a displaced persons measure discriminating against Catholics and Jews" (Leuchtenburg, *Feast* 15). Senator Robert A. Taft, standard-bearer of the Republican Party's conservative wing, expressed the isolationist tenor of the times when he said, "It would be ironical if this Congress which really has its heart set on straightening out domestic affairs would end up in being besieged by foreign problems" (qtd. in Goldman 57). The war made isolationists or xenophobes of Americans who never were before. Ernie Pyle, war correspondent par excellence, wrote of our troops abroad, "Our men . . . are impatient with the strange peoples and customs of the countries they now inhabit. They say that if they ever get home they never want to see another foreign country" (qtd. in Blum 65–66). For many in the postwar years, "[t]he business of America was America. It was to get on with this business without dependence on other nations and without interference from them" (Goldman 113–14). This was the atmosphere in which *Brigadoon* (3/13/47) opened and played 581 times.

Five years after the musical premiered, librettist Alan Jay Lerner, campaigning for Adlai Stevenson, publicly spoke out against Eisenhower's candidacy and Joe McCarthy's demagoguery (Citron 242). And yet *Brigadoon* contains strongly conservative and isolationist political sentiments. The later liberal Democrat Lerner once wrote that his father Joseph's "influence on me was indelible." Joseph Lerner, founder of the Lerner Shops, was "a dedicated Republican, as had been his father before him" (Lerner, *Street* 18). While Lerner notes that he and his father "parted company" in their politics, Joe's conservative influence on the young writer of *Brigadoon* seems apparent. Or, perhaps, like many Americans in the immediate postwar years, Lerner was simply weary of the price the United States had paid for its involvement in World War II. The only published indication of his politics in the 1940s suggests this: "Political and social satire, which by their very nature are critical, no longer suited the mood of the country that was rallying together to preserve a way of life that suddenly was seen clearly and deeply as precious as existence itself. If anything, people wanted to be reminded of who they were and the roots from which they had sprung; not what was wrong but what was right. Looking back to earlier times may be an escape, but it can also be a reaffirmation" (qtd. in Jablonski 16). In any event, *Brigadoon* depicts an isolationist utopia, and a pretty scary one at that.

Lerner clearly followed the model of Rodgers and Hammerstein's first two musicals, in which two couples are each challenged by an antagonist trying to come between them. And, as in Hammerstein's libretti, the social and political thinking in *Brigadoon* is inseparable from its story. Two New Yorkers, idealistic, romantic Tommy Albright and cynical, skeptical Jeff Douglas, get lost hunting in the Scottish Highlands and stumble upon an unmapped village called Brigadoon. When the Americans arrive, the townspeople are having a market fair and preparing for the wedding of Jean MacLaren and Charlie Dalrymple later that day. Tommy and Jeff stare at the people in traditional Scottish plaids and tartans of archaic design and the townsfolk stare back at what to them is the equally outlandish garb of the New Yorkers — each group reacting as if they were looking at beings from another planet, or at least from another century, which they are. Yet, cutting through the mutual bewilderment and suspicion, Tommy and Fiona, sister of the bride-to-be, are instantly taken with one another and before the day is over have fallen in love. Meanwhile, Meg Brockie, the acknowledged town hoyden, has aggressively fallen in lust with Jeff, who does not reciprocate her passion. Lerner goes Hammerstein's usual two-couple plots one better with three couples simultaneously facing barriers to their ultimate happiness: Jeff simply wants no part of Meg; Jean and Charlie must deal with the bride's rejected suitor Harry Beaton; and Tommy has to wrestle with a tinge of doubt Jeff has planted in his mind.

When Tommy comes upon a bible inscribed with Fiona's birthdate as October 10, 1722, and learns that "today" is May 24, 1746, he insists on learning the mystery of Brigadoon. Rather reluctantly, Fiona takes him and Jeff to the schoolteacher, Mr. Lundie, who tells them that "what happened in Brigadoon was a miracle. . . . Two hundred years ago the Highlands of Scotland were plagued with witches; wicked sorcerers who were takin' Scottish folk away from the teachin's of God an' puttin' the devil in their souls. . . . It dinna matter they were not *real* sorcerers, because ye an' I know there is no such thing. But their influence was very real indeed" (Richards 1: 192–93). Brigadoon's minister, Mr. Forsythe, "worried about the witches. . . . So he began to wonder if there wasn't somethin' he could do to protect the folk of his parish not only from them, but from all the evils that might come to Brigadoon from the outside world after he died" (193). The minister "asked God that night to make Brigadoon an' all the people in it vanish into the Highland mist. Vanish, but not for always. It would all return jus' as it was for one day every hundred years. The people would go on leadin' their customary lives; but each day when they awakened it would be a hundred years later. An' when we awoke the next day, it was a hundred years later. . . . Ye see, in this way Mr. Forsythe figured there would be no change in the lives of the people. They jus' wouldna be in any century long enough to be touched by it" (193). The one stipulation in "Mr. Forsythe's contract with God" was that if any townsperson leaves Brigadoon, "the enchantment is broken for all" (194). Mr. Forsythe also knew that miracles require a sacrifice, so he deliberately excluded himself from his prayer for Brigadoon by praying from a hill *beyond* Brigadoon, thereby offering his own mortality in exchange for the town's virtual immortality. Finally, when Tommy asks what each night's hundred-year sleep is like, Mr. Lundie replies that he thinks he hears voices: "they're voices filled with a fearful longin'; an' often they seem to be callin' me back. I've pondered it when I'm awake; an' I think—I have a feelin' I'm hearin' the outside world. There mus' be lots of folk out there who'd like a Brigadoon" (194).

Mr. Lundie's hermetically sealed society, virtually impervious to disrupting influences from the rest of world, is, in effect, a highly desirable isolationist utopia—one not just cherished by the townsfolk of Brigadoon but also actively wished for by people in "the outside world." *Brigadoon's* opening followed two world wars, a twelve-year depression, and the communist triumph in eastern Europe. Is it any wonder that the thought of a Brigadoon-like retreat brought comfort and solace to many Americans in 1947?

That the cold war was definitely on Lerner's mind when he wrote *Brigadoon* is apparent from an exchange of comic dialogue between Jeff and Meg:

> MEG:   (*Quickly*) What happened to the lass ye were engaged to?
> JEFF:   She fell in love with a Russian.
> MEG:   A Russian?
> JEFF:   Yes.
> MEG:   Russia is in Europe, isn't it?
> JEFF:   Yes, more and more.
> MEG:   (*Mystified*) Oh!
> JEFF:   It's not far from here. You just cross the Channel and turn left.
> (183–84)

Though irrelevant to the story, Jeff's last line suggests more than mere travel directions.

According to Mr. Lundie, Reverend Forsythe's sole motive for having his beloved town come to life one day every hundred years was to protect it from "all the evils" in the outside world forever. Brigadoon is a safe haven, but it's also eternally static, homogeneous, and conformist. Even more troubling is the minister's rider clause that the miracle will end if any townsperson tries to leave. Harry Beaton is hardly a radical but is sufficiently different from the other denizens of *Brigadoon* to make him something of a social pariah. He is distressed that the miracle has prevented him from attending the University of Edinburgh and thereby gain exposure to the outside world. Driven by this disappointment and by Jeannie's marriage to Charlie, he attempts to leave. Harry must be destroyed not because he is a malevolent figure but because he will break the magical pact. In an Orwellian way, the nonconformist must be sacrificed for the greater good.

Attempting to flee Brigadoon, Harry dies from a fall when Jeff trips him. Jeff the cynic feels nothing for his act; he's convinced the whole day has been a dream and Harry, therefore, is imaginary — like the rest of Brigadoon. This kind of skepticism plants enough doubt in the romantic Tommy's mind that he returns with Jeff to the States despite his feelings for Fiona. The penultimate scene of act 2 finds Tommy in a New York bar, discontented with all things American, including his fiancée. Phrases of conversation evoke brief reprises of five songs, sending flashbacks through Tommy's mind to the idyllic village and lovely Fiona. He recalls Mr. Lundie's remark that an outsider could come to live in Brigadoon "if he loves someone here — not jus' Brigadoon, mind ye — but someone in Brigadoon enough to want to give up everythin' an stay with that person" (Richards 1: 194). With that thought in mind, Tommy returns to Scotland to see if, just possibly . . . and sure enough, as Jeff and Tommy are about to give up and leave the spot where Brigadoon had been, a sleepy Mr. Lundie appears, takes Tommy's hand to lead him into the miraculous village, and speaks the musical's last lines: "Ya shouldna be too surprised, lad. I told ye when ye love someone deeply anythin' is possible. . . . Even miracles" (211).

*Brigadoon*'s romantic ending portrays an idealism that resonated in a number of musicals well into the 1960s. Unlike those later musicals, however, *Brigadoon*'s idealism is allied to retreating from the world, not changing or bettering it. Tommy is self absorbed; his return to Brigadoon is idealistic, personal wish-fulfillment. Yet he learned from the legend of Mr. Forsythe, whose personal sacrifice for his community made him a true idealist. Tommy accepts Mr. Lundie's words that sometimes to gain everything you want, you must give up all you have. And so he gives up the comforts (and the annoyances) of his known world to take the chance on returning to Fiona and Brigadoon. This strain of visionary idealism, part of the American national character, jibes with *Brigadoon*'s expression of the conservative isolationism prevalent in the postwar United States.

This reading of the political position expressed in *Brigadoon* is supported by facts surrounding the motion picture and later stage revivals. Professor Thomas Doherty, head of the Film Studies Program at Brandeis University, is convinced it was no coincidence Hollywood filmed its version of the musical in 1953 and released it in 1954, those archconservative years when Senator Joe McCarthy was at the height of his popularity with the American public (Leuchtenburg, *Feast* 34). Furthermore, while *Brigadoon* had been mounted by New York's City Center six times in the '50s and '60s for brief limited runs as part of its "popular priced" series of revivals, only on October 16, 1980, did *Brigadoon* open for its first commercial Broadway revival, staying for 133 performances. Like the date of the film, its opening date coincided with an equally conservative time among Americans, less than a month before Ronald Reagan was elected president. Then, in 1986, not too distant from Broadway, the New York City Opera at Lincoln Center revived *Brigadoon*, in the middle of what Haynes Johnson calls "the most conservative administration of the century" (14) — to which, one might add, one of the most isolationist as well, its tone set by the all-American chief executive dubbing the Soviet Union "the Evil Empire."

## Paint Your Wagon *and* Camelot

As *Brigadoon* displayed an isolationist vision regarding the international scene, four years later Alan Jay Lerner just as visibly expressed his self-proclaimed liberal views on domestic affairs in *Paint Your Wagon* (11/12/51). Like the recent *South Pacific* and *The King and I*, *Paint Your Wagon* expressed the need for inter-cultural understanding and the acceptance of inter-ethnic romantic relationships, though far less dramatically.

The tolerance theme, however, isn't central to the plot of *Paint Your Wagon*, since nothing is terribly central and there isn't much plot. Set in the boom and bust days of the California gold rush, the musical is less a story than a tapestry of life in the mining camps and towns. The saga mostly concerns prospector Ben Rumson, a crusty widower, and his illiterate teenaged daughter Jennifer. Rumson strikes it rich, builds a mining town he names for himself, *buys* a new wife from a Mormon who has an extra, and sends Jennifer East to be educated and turned into a lady. When the veins of gold dry up, Ben moves on, stays put in what was Rumsontown, or dies, in Lerner's various endings. The advocacy of inter-ethnic relationships enters through the love story of Jennifer and Julio Alveras, a Mexican prospector. The Anglo miners discriminate against Julio, but there is no opposition to the couple's romance, not even from Jennifer's father, where one might most expect it. To the contrary, Ben always comes to Julio's defense against the other prospectors, and when Jennifer returns from back East, Rumson gladly gives them his blessing.

To be theatrically effective, the prejudice/tolerance theme need not be central but at least should be dramatic. While *Paint Your Wagon* advocated inter-ethnic tolerance, without conflict the show lacked dramatic punch, effectively weakening the theme's potency. What the show mostly had going for it were some fine performances headed by James Barton's Rumson, Agnes De Mille's choreography, and Frederick Loewe's vibrant score, some of which so evokes the American West that during the folksinging craze of the later 1950s countless Americans thought "They Call the Wind Maria" was a folksong, not a show tune! *Paint Your Wagon* played 289 times before *its* vein ran out, losing much of its investment—a refrain to be heard increasingly on Broadway.

Lerner's progressive views in *Paint Your Wagon* and his protestations to being a Stevenson Democrat in the 1950s notwithstanding, *Brigadoon's* vision of a longed-for isolationist utopia subtly resurfaced in *Camelot* (12/3/60), beneath the facade of Arthurian legend. In fact, here the utopian references, while visible, seem almost Lerner's private, personal vision, not one the public would have necessarily perceived in the musical they attended 873 times. If *Brigadoon* advocated a hermetically sealed utopia as a retreat from the world's encroaching dangers and ugliness, *Camelot* laments a utopia failed, lost, or destroyed. King Arthur's magical realm, much like the Scottish town, is an idyllic closed society in which everything, even the weather, runs according to plan:

> The rain may never fall till after sundown.
> By eight the morning fog must disappear.
> In short, there's simply not
> A more congenial spot
> For happ'ly-ever-aftering than here
> In Camelot.
>
> (Lerner, *Camelot* 14)

Even with Arthur's lofty goals for it, his Round Table is no United Nations, since all the initial representatives are knights from Arthur's own realm. It is only and *specifically* when a foreign interloper, the French Lancelot du Lac, enters the scene that everything starts falling apart, including Arthur's marriage to Guinevere. This alone defines Camelot as an exclusively isolationist utopia; keep the foreigners out or there'll be trouble. Although Arthur dreams of a peaceful kingdom and of what would later be called disarmament, a stage direction reveals that he is disillusioned about such a possibility the very moment he utters it (Lerner, *Camelot* 66). Near play's end, formerly tranquil Camelot is in chaos; Arthur, caught in a snare of treachery cast by his wicked son Mordred, must choose between his own creation of civil law and love for his queen; and when Lancelot returns to rescue Guinevere from the stake, he does so by slaughtering his own Round Table compatriots. At the end, all Arthur has of what had been a present reality is now the all-but-vanished past of a failed utopia:

> Where once it never rained till after sundown;
> By eight a.m. the morning fog had flown . . .
> Don't let it be forgot
> That once there was a spot
> For one brief shining moment that was known
> As Camelot. . . .
>
> (ellipses in text; 114)

Precisely what utopian scheme Lerner is mourning along with Arthur is hard to say, unless perhaps his own wistful realization that even within the United States itself the tensions and complexities of the cold war world make a Brigadoon or a Camelot impossible. As a final note, the association of *Camelot* with the Kennedy dynasty came after the fact; the show was never intended to reflect JFK's years in office as a kind of Camelot. The musical was written and opened before he was even inaugurated. The association of its title with the Kennedy clan came about purely because of the young president's love of the show.

### The "Cold War Musicals"

The cold war unquestionably lay behind the altogether serious isolationist vision in *Brigadoon*, yet it also provided fodder for a mixed bag of other musicals, only two of which were serious. The remaining "cold war musicals" were flat-out musical comedies that used aspects of East-West tensions or America's fear of internal communism as their premise, their setting, or the object of their comedy. This comic treatment of such issues likely had the effect of diffusing their audiences' fears and concerns, at least temporarily. The very presence of shows comically treating the cold war during the Truman, Eisenhower, and Kennedy years argues that the producers willing to back them felt a lighthearted treatment of America's most pervasive source of anxiety would entertain audiences. Sometimes, they were right.

*Barefoot Boy with Cheek* (4/3/47) kicked off the cold war musicals. Max Shulman based his silly libretto and lyrics on his equally silly book; one

Sidney Lippman wrote the score. Set at the real University of Minnesota, the story featured unreal characters like Asa Hearthrug, Clothilde Pfefferkorn, and Yetta Samovar, "a campus 'pink' [out to] convert all of the University . . . (and especially Alpha Cholera Fraternity) to her political thinking" (Bordman 557). This silliness spoofed the postwar commie scare, but only 108 times.

Nothing silly, however, about the next cold war–inspired music theatre piece. *The Consul* (3/15/50), Gian-Carlo Menotti's opera for Broadway, depicted a woman's efforts to persuade officials in a nameless Iron Curtain country to grant exit visas for her persecuted family, an attempt so frustrating she finally commits suicide (573). Though set in a communist country and addressing the horrors of Stalinism, *The Consul* also spoke to audiences' fear of the Red Menace from within. This cheerless though well-crafted opera played 269 times in a mainstream Broadway house. In fact, the New York Drama Critics Circle voted it best musical for 1949–50 over both conventional musical comedies (*Miss Liberty* and *Gentlemen Prefer Blondes*) and worthy serious pieces (*Lost in the Stars* and *Regina*, Marc Blitzstein's operatic rendering of Lillian Hellman's *The Little Foxes*).

George S. Kaufman, Leueen MacGrath, and Abe Burrows wrote the book of *Silk Stockings* (2/24/55), and Cole Porter supplied the music and lyrics — his last effort, as it would turn out, for the musical stage. The story was another happy-ending variation on Romeo and Juliet, using the cold war as the unfriendly milieu in which a man and a woman from opposing sides prove love can leap over the Iron Curtain. Taken mostly intact from the 1939 Greta Garbo film *Ninotchka*, the musical updated the action to contemporary Paris, where American theatrical agent Steve Canfield tries to help a Russian composer defect to the West and falls in love with Ninotchka, a party-line Soviet operative whose mission is to bring the musician back to Moscow. Steve has nearly won Ninotchka when a Soviet delegation swoops down and whisks her back home. Steve follows and somehow both return to the West (and each other) before the final curtain (Bordman 593). In a lighthearted way, the show contrasted Eastern and Western Bloc mores and made America's popular notions of Soviet political methods the object of comedy (a bestselling Russian book is *Who's Still Who*). But *Silk Stockings* was in no way serious satire or commentary on international relations. As light, diversionary entertainment, it played 478 times.

About the silliest of the sillier cold war musicals, *Li'l Abner* (11/15/56; 693 performances) had the potential to deliver a lot more satire than it did, based as it was on Al Capp's long-running comic strip which was often as satiric as it was silly. Yet had the writers retained Capp's satiric point of view, the musical would have looked very different; Al Capp, like Harold

Gray of "Little Orphan Annie," was one of the few openly right-wing cre-
ators of American comic strips, whereas the musical's creators — Norman
Panama and Melvin Frank (book), Johnny Mercer (lyrics), and Gene de
Paul (music) — were centrist to left-leaning. As a result, the musical retained
Capp's fundamental funniness but dropped his politics. The story's focus is
Daisy Mae's perennial attempt to catch the title character in the annual
Sadie Hawkins' Day chase and marry him — which in the musical she finally
does. Most of Capp's Dogpatch characters appear, from Earthquake
McGoon and Appassionata von Climax to General Bullmoose and Marryin'
Sam. The cold war gets into all this strictly by the backdoor. The U.S.
government declares Dogpatch "the most useless piece of real estate in the
U.S.A. [and] decides to test an atom bomb there" (Bordman 601), requiring
the townsfolk to evacuate. Removing a statue of the town's founder, Jubi-
lation T. Cornpone, they unearth a plaque revealing that Abraham Lincoln
proclaimed Dogpatch a national shrine, and so the town is spared. Throughout, *Li'l Abner* is just plain fun, with just one glance at cold war prepar-
edness in the atomic testing incident.

The 1950s saw no more cold war musicals, but three opened during John
F. Kennedy's brief term as president. In *Mr. President* (10/20/62), Howard
Lindsay and Russel Crouse's book and Irving Berlin's score depicted fictional U.S. president Stephen Decatur Henderson breaching diplomatic
etiquette by landing in Moscow even though the Russians canceled their
invitation to him while he was in flight. "His humiliation costs him the
next election" (Bordman 628). Not satirical, the show seems mostly a cautionary tale about survival in international diplomacy. *Mr. President* stayed
in office for 265 performances.

*Tovarich* (3/18/63) also touched on Soviet-American relations in the cold
war years and ran one performance fewer than *Mr. President*. Based on
Jacques Deval and Robert E. Sherwood's hit play in the 1936–37 season,
the musicalization had a book by David Shaw, music by Anne Crosswell,
and lyrics by Lee Pockriss. A prince and his grand duchess wife, both Tsarist
loyalists, escape to the West with four billion francs of the Tsar's, awaiting
the day the Russian monarchy is restored — something only sentimental Ro-
manoff royalists could ever conceive of doing. As a cover, they work as butler
and maid for an American family in Paris, until Soviet operatives locate
them and abscond with the cash to Red Square. Happy with their employers
and the West, the couple is content to stay put (Bordman 629–30). The
closest *Tovarich* gets to any meaning is its backward look to a remembered
past as preferable to the troubled complexities of the cold war years.

The last and shortest lived of this trio of oddities was rather a send-up of one of JFK's pet projects, the Peace Corps. With book by Jack Weinstock and Willie Gilbert, music by Mary Rodgers (Richard's daughter, with the hit *Once upon a Mattress* behind her), and lyrics by Martin Charnin (later of *Annie* fame), *Hot Spot* (4/19/63) mixed the Peace Corps with the cold war and America's containment policies to check the spread of international communism. In the mythical country of D'Hum, Peace Corp member Sally Hopwinder (Judy Holliday) convinces the ruler "to proclaim a communist threat so that more American money will be forthcoming" (630). But even sparkly Holliday couldn't keep *Hot Spot* from fizzling out after forty-three performances.

The cold war did not "officially" end until the dissolution of the Soviet Union in 1991, but these were the last American musicals to treat the U.S.-Soviet standoff. Only one London import late in the cold war period brought the subject back to New York audiences. *Chess* (4/28/88) used the game as both the medium and the metaphor for East-West diplomacy and duplicity. *Chess* spins a somewhat murky tale of U.S.-Russian relations via a series of world championship matches between each country's chess master. The show had lyrics by Tim Rice, a score by Benny Andersson and Björn Ulvaeus of the Swedish rock group ABBA, and (for the New York version) a revised book by playwright Richard Nelson. *Chess* needed a new script for Broadway, since many U.S. tourists perceived the London production as anti-American. Even Broadway's *Chess* painted a pretty unsavory picture of both the Americans and the Russians. Neither chess master is a model citizen of his respective homeland. Freddie Trumper, the U.S. chess champion, is arrogant, conceited, obnoxious, petulant, and loud—everything his real-life prototype Bobby Fischer was reputed to be. The Russian master Anatoly is sexually irresponsible, charmless, and wholly neglectful of his wife. Apart from Florence Vassy, a Hungarian-born American who is first Freddie's, then Anatoly's, lover, the other characters are mostly assorted reporters and Soviet and American intelligence agents who execute the moves of both superpowers.

Despite its vivid chess metaphor for global politics and some strong musical numbers like "One Night in Bangkok," "Where I Want to Be," "Someone Else's Story," and "Heaven Help My Heart," Broadway checkmated *Chess* after just sixty-eight moves. The musical was partly done in by history. By the time the American version was written, Soviet Premier Gorbachev had begun to implement his policies of perestroika and glasnost, which the revised musical's dialogue acknowledges as harbingers of the softening of hardline maneuvers dramatized or discussed in the show (Rice, *Chess* 61). By its Broadway opening, then, much of the musical's punch was undermined by changed circumstances in the real world. The long-term effect was that shifts in international affairs rendered *Chess* virtually meaningless and irrelevant, except as an historical curiosity.

### Social Thought and Social Change in the Postwar and Cold War Years

If the feelings of many Americans during the Truman and Eisenhower years grew more conservative respecting international relations, sentiment on domestic issues became increasingly liberal. In 1945, the year *Carousel* opened, there were few signs of racial or ethnic "equality" beyond Jackie Robinson becoming the first black major league ballplayer and Bess Myerson the first Jewish Miss America (Leuchtenburg, *Feast* 9). But by early 1948, President Truman made some modest headway in the field of civil rights. He was the first president to appoint a black to a federal judgeship. His attorney general filed *amici curiae* briefs on behalf of the federal government supporting suits brought by the NAACP to end school segregation, "an undertaking that would bear fruit after Truman left office." But his most widely applauded action in the area of race relations was his 1948 executive order to desegregate the armed forces (Miller 183; Leuchtenburg, *Feast* 15–16, 20–21).

During the Eisenhower administration, on May 17, 1954, the Supreme Court unanimously found for the plaintiff in *Brown v. Board of Education*, in word if not yet in fact desegregating U.S. public schools based on Chief Justice Earl Warren's words, "in the field of public education the doctrine of 'separate but equal' has no place" (*Feast* 92).

A year and a half later, in Montgomery, Alabama, Mrs. Rosa Parks, a black seamstress tired after a day of work, refused to give a white man her seat on a city bus. This defiance of segregation ordinances led to Mrs. Parks's arrest and trial, spurring the massive, prolonged boycott of Montgomery buses organized by the young Reverend Martin Luther King Jr. He had just come there to assume his first pastorate but was now mounting his first act of civil disobedience in the cause of civil rights. It worked; "for months, buses rolled nearly empty through the streets of the Cradle of the Confederacy. . . . The long boycott ended in victory when on November 13, 1956, the Supreme Court unanimously affirmed a lower court ruling invalidating Alabama's segregation statutes" (97).

Less than a year later, the "moderate leadership" of Little Rock, Arkansas, was set to abide by a court order to admit nine black students to Central High School, but Governor Orval Faubus refused and ordered in the Arkansas National Guard to block their entry. Things remained at an impasse for several days until reluctantly, "[w]ith the prestige of his office at stake,"

President Eisenhower federalized the Arkansas National Guard and sent in a thousand paratroopers to escort the nine black children into school on September 18, 1957. While it drew national attention to segregated education, Ike's action did not curtail it in Little Rock, where Faubus simply shut down the city's high schools in 1958 and 1959. But a beginning had been made. Such was the social atmosphere within which the progressive-minded musicals from the 1940s through the early 1960s were produced (96).

### The Liberal Viewpoint in Musicals of the Postwar and Cold War Years: Bloomer Girl

Even before Harry Truman took those first steps toward civil rights for blacks, one musical advocated precisely that, among other things. *Bloomer Girl* (10/5/44) was *Oklahoma!*'s first legitimate heir. It not only embraced the Rodgers and Hammerstein model for an integrated musical but even went beyond Hammerstein's subtle presentation of theme in its very open social advocacy. Lyricist E. Y. Harburg, whose politics—like Harold Rome's —were left of center, wanted to do a musical set during the Civil War. He asked book writers Sig Herzig and Fred Saidy to put some more meat on Lilith and Dan James's play about the introduction of bloomers by "putting greater emphasis on the issues of women's rights and Negro rights. In that way, he felt, audiences of 1944 could accept the theme as pertaining to the struggle for freedom everywhere" (Green 180). The combination of the solid Harburg–Harold Arlen score, Agnes De Mille's imaginative dances (including her powerful Civil War Ballet), and a strong cast headed by Celeste Holm, David Brooks, and Dooley Wilson, kept audiences coming 654 times.

The story is slight, but its resonance during the war was strong. The book "recounted the rebellion of Evelina Applegate, daughter of a Cicero Falls, New York, hoopskirt manufacturer, ... [who] actively supports the campaign of her aunt Dolly [historically, Amelia] Bloomer ... to replace her father's profitable hoopskirts with the more comfortable garment that soon carried her aunt's name" (Bordman 543). Although also an outspoken abolitionist, Evelina agrees to marry a Southern slaveholder (probably with every intention of changing his ways). Harburg was likely attracted to how the nineteenth-century fashion rebellion of bloomers paralleled American women's slacks replacing skirts in the war years not just in defense plants but for everyday civilian wear. The image of "pants" standing for greater female rights and individuality is unmistakable in both the musical and the nation at that time. Further, through Dooley Wilson's character, the African

American Pompey, and his two songs, "The Eagle and Me" and "I Got a Song," *Bloomer Girl* "sang eloquently of the Negro's yearning for freedom" (Green 180).

Also in the mid-1940s, for the first time since Eubie Blake, Cecil Mack, and J. Milton Reddie's *Swing It* in 1937, at least one black was on the creative team of two very different musicals. *St. Louis Woman* (3/30/46) was a case of black book, white music and lyrics. Arna Bontemps adapted the script from his own novel in collaboration with Countee Cullen, Harold Arlen wrote the score, and Johnny Mercer the lyrics. While in rehearsal, members of the all-black cast balked at offensive stereotyping in the script and demanded rewrites (Woll 200). With only 113 performances, *St. Louis Woman* was not a success, but it introduced Pearl Bailey to the Broadway stage and Arlen's classic "Come Rain or Come Shine" to the world. Arlen found black music and sensibilities congenial to his mode of composition and later wrote scores for two more all- or nearly all-black musicals during the cold war years — *House of Flowers* (12/30/54; 165 performances) with book and lyrics by Truman Capote, and *Jamaica* (10/31/57) with book and lyrics by Fred Saidy and E. Y. Harburg. *Jamaica* ran 555 performances, giving long-term employment to its large, mostly black cast headed by Lena Horne, but neither show had any blacks on its creative team.

*Street Scene* (1/9/47), however, brought together three truly distinguished collaborators, including as lyricist poet Langston Hughes, one of literary America's most prominent blacks. Elmer Rice adapted the libretto for this Broadway opera from his 1929 play, and Kurt Weill, who by then had a solid musical reputation on two continents, composed the score. Like Rice's play, the opera depicted the virtually deterministic effects of tenement living in New York City, but despite Hughes's presence this was not in any sense a black musical. The entire cast was white, except for the tenement's live-in janitor, Willie, and his wife, transformed from a Swedish-American couple in Rice's play. (In 1929, it would have strained credibility for a black to be living in the same apartment house with whites, even as custodian, but by 1947 this was plausible.) It also gave credence to the presence of a blues number Willie sings, showcasing one of many musical styles in Weill's deliberately eclectic score, which reflected the polyethnic, polyglot character of the United States itself. As a rather grim opera for Broadway, *Street Scene* ran a modestly respectable 148 performances.

## Finian's Rainbow

The night after *Street Scene* opened, the always upbeat team of Fred Saidy and E. Y. Harburg, this time working with composer Burton Lane, offered

Broadway a show that was anything but grim — the buoyant, tuneful, magical, and pointedly satirical *Finian's Rainbow* (1/10/47). Most remembered for its romantic tale of Finian McLonergan and his daughter Sharon, and the shenanigans of Og the Leprechaun, the show produced no fewer than four hit songs — "Old Devil Moon," "Look to the Rainbow," "If This Isn't Love," and "How Are Things in Glocca Morra?" But when its authors published *Finian's Rainbow*, they subtitled it "A MUSICAL SATIRE BY E. Y. HARBURG & FRED SAIDY" (Harburg, title page), unambiguously declaring the librettist and lyricist's intention. *Finian's Rainbow* is unique in the postwar and early cold war years as the only topically satirical musical to make a success of it on Broadway, becoming a major hit with 725 performances.

Saidy and Harburg aimed their satiric attack at bigotry and intolerance. The butt of their razor-sharp but good-humored barbs is an unregenerate Southern bigot from the mythical state of Missitucky, U.S. Senator Billboard Rawkins. Contemporary audiences would have recognized his name as a direct send-up of Mississippi's notoriously outspoken racists on Capitol Hill, Senator Theodore Bilbo and Representative John Rankin. Plot is at a premium in *Finian's Rainbow* but without deleterious effect to the musical's charm or its consistently funny, never vituperative satire. In the thin storyline central to the satire, Senator Rawkins is determined to buy at a tax auction the one remaining parcel of Rainbow Valley that isn't his already ("Ain't satisfied to represent the state. Wants to own it outright" [Harburg 4]). Rainbow Valley is home to the musical's large population of black and white sharecroppers, who work and live in an idyllic state of racial harmony. Rawkins wants the property for both self-serving and political reasons, which for him are essentially one and the same. The changes made by the Tennessee Valley Authority terrify him; he doesn't want to see the same things happen to his ol' Missitucky home: "Cuts into his sleep, makes him see things at night. Electric power spillin' out of the river and pourin' over the valley. Shacks lightin' up, people learnin' to read and write, everybody makin' money. . . . First thing you know, poll tax gets paid off — Rawkins gets laid off" (23). By the end of the musical, the senator is not only thwarted but "converted" through efforts of the sharecroppers, Finian, Sharon, and her newfound boyfriend Woody Mahoney, a union organizer, of all things, though not much is made of this. Also thrown in for good measure is help from a Gospel quartet, a Leprechaun, and a magical pot of gold. More than the ending, it's the middle that drives home Saidy and Harburg's point about bigotry, specifically anti-black bigotry. Still, Rawkins's intolerance, like that of his real-life Washington counterparts, extends beyond blacks. Hearing of the newly arrived Irishman Finian, the senator typically exclaims, "An immigrant! Damn! My whole family's been havin' trouble with immigrants ever since we *came* to this country!" (50).

In this musical fantasy Rawkins discovers the consequences of racism by falling victim to a magic spell. Just when he is trying to throw everyone, black and white, off "his" property, Sharon is trying to explain racial discrimination to some sharecroppers' children. Unaware she is standing over the buried pot of gold (a necessary stance for wishes to come true), she says, "There's nothing wrong with being black—(*With mounting emotion against* RAWKINS) But there's something wrong with the world that he and his kind have made for Henry [a little black boy]. I wish he could know what that world is like. I wish to God he were black so—" (83). Instantly—darkness! thunder! lightning! When Rawkins recovers from being a "*trembling heap on the ground*," he is black indeed, a condition he has to (but does not learn to) live with until the end of the play. Till then he must live out Sharon's wish for him to experience life on the other side of the color bar.

Rawkins's exploits while black are hilarious. He is dragooned into joining the Passion Pilgrim Gospeleers, an improbable three-man black Gospel quartet whose number-four was seduced away by "a bouncin' Babylonian Jezebel from Biloxi, Mississippi" (115). Surprised that they can make a living doing what they do, Rawkins learns from the Second Gospeleer the realities of work if one is black: "You either tote that barge, lift that bale, shine that shoe—or sing. We sing" (116). Singing with these authentic blacks sounds fine to Rawkins, since his bigoted heart had just been softened a bit by one of Og's Leprechaunish spells. He happily jumps in for the missing baritone on "The Begat," arguably the show's funniest song, which purports to catalogue the entire human race starting with Adam and Eve. In one stanza Harburg unabashedly displays his always liberal stripe along with his idiosyncratic wit as a lyricist:

> When the Begat got to gettin' under par,
> They Begat the Daughters of the D.A.R.
> They Begat the Babbitts of the bourgeoisie
> Who Begat the mis-begotten G.O.P.
>
> (118)

thus tracing the conservative Eightieth Congress and Republican Party during Truman's administration back to the complacent middle class of the 1920s and from there to the Daughters of the American Revolution.

Being black opens Rawkins's eyes: "you can't get into a restaurant. You can't get on a street car. You can't buy yourself a cold beer on a hot day. . . . You can't even go into a church and pray. . . . The law says you can't." To which Og asks, "Is it a legal law?" And Rawkins replies, "Of course it's legal. I wrote it myself" (111). After Rawkins's further adventures, coupled with his former crony Sheriff Buzz Collins informing him he "got no rights in this state" (126), Og finally wishes the senator white again. But the lessons he learned remain: "I'm with the people. All part of my new platform— anti-poll tax, a dam in every valley, and a rainbow in every pot. And, incidentally, I'm runnin' for re-election next November" (139).

### *Race Relations and Idealism:* Lost in the Stars

In 1949, two more socially progressive musicals appeared on Broadway, Rodgers and Hammerstein's *South Pacific* (4/7/49) and Maxwell Anderson and Kurt Weill's *Lost in the Stars* (10/30/49). Both tackled prejudice and racial discrimination more seriously than any prior Broadway shows. Also, Anderson and Weill were the first writers of a musical to depict race relations specifically between blacks and whites, and Anderson made the motif of idealism and sacrifice integral to the play's theme of racial bias and its consequences.

*Lost in the Stars* was Anderson and Weill's adaptation of Alan Paton's poetic and potent 1947 novel *Cry, the Beloved Country*, set in South Africa. The exotic locale may have made the theme easier for American audiences to take, but Anderson and Weill clearly intended their dramatization of apartheid's effects as an analogy for the evils of segregation, "Jim Crow" laws, and other discrimination against blacks in the United States. Anderson's musical theatre adaptation was only a partial success; there are major flaws in its structure, character development, and the function of musical numbers. Since these problems are treated extensively elsewhere (see Matlaw 260–72 and Jones, "Maxwell" 102–09), they appear here only when relevant to the social issues in the musical.

Depicting the effect of apartheid on individuals both black and white in South Africa, the plot of both novel and musical are very much the same. Reverend Stephen Kumalo, a simple, not to say naive, black Anglican minister in a rural district, goes to Johannesburg to bring home his sister, Gertrude, and his son, Absalom. Once there, he discovers Gertrude is a prostitute who elects to stay in the city, leaving Stephen to care for her young son, Alex. Worse yet, Stephen learns that Absalom is accused of murder and involved with a young girl pregnant by him. Unable to find work to pay for schooling, Absalom fell in with some bad company, including the son of Stephen's brother, John, a somewhat powerful but corrupt political presence in the city's black community. Absalom's companions plan to rob Arthur Jarvis's house, chosen because Jarvis was a black rights, anti-apartheid advocate who showed his trust in blacks by never locking his door. Rather coincidentally, Arthur was also the son of white supremacist James Jarvis, whose lush plantation lies in the hills above the pitiful valley where Reverend Kumalo has his church. It goes without saying that the elder and younger Jarvis did not get along. At any rate, the robbery was planned for a time when Arthur would not be home, his cohorts convincing a reluctant Absalom to carry a pistol just to scare any servants in the house. As bad luck would have it, Arthur enters, Absalom panics and shoots, Arthur dies, and Absalom is tried for murder. Thanks to John Kumalo's crooked legal connections, Absalom's companions get off scot-free by successfully perjuring themselves, but he follows his father's agonized advice to tell the truth and for this is sentenced to death by hanging. The rest of the novel covers quite a long stretch of time, during which James Jarvis reads his son's writings for the first time and very, very slowly comes to understand Arthur's point of view. By the end of the book it is therefore plausible that James in good conscience provides material aid to Stephen Kumalo's community. Meanwhile, Stephen patiently and resignedly awaits the day Absalom will hang; in the novel's last few paragraphs Stephen is alone at the top of a hill, waiting for the sun to rise — and his son to die.

In the musical, the time after the trial is impossibly compressed: Stephen has a crisis of faith and almost resigns his pastorate when the promise of aid comes from Jarvis — much too fast to be credible. Kumalo's faith in both God and man is restored. Worst of all, the musical ends absolutely improbably. In the penultimate scene James Jarvis chastises his grandson Edward (Arthur's son) for playing with Stephen's nephew Alex; apparently he hasn't been reading, let alone been touched by, his son's writings. The only possible explanation for Jarvis's changed outlook — but much too quickly for plausibility — is part of a sermon he overhears Stephen delivering. The final scene, specified by Anderson as *"before daylight the next morning"* (Richards 2: 173), finds Stephen in his house, not on the hill, waiting for Absalom to be hanged. Enter James Jarvis — just the day before showing himself still a white supremacist — now walking into a black man's home; that alone strains credibility. Jarvis offers to aid Stephen's parishioners and to wait with him for the fatal sunrise. Then comes the most improbable moment of all, set forth in the stage direction that ends the play: *"The clock strikes four. STEPHEN sits and buries his head in his hands. JARVIS goes to him, puts an arm around him"* (175). For Jarvis so quickly to make compassionate contact with a black does not ring true. In this drastic departure from the novel Anderson sacrificed credibility for theatrical polemics. He obviously wanted his point to be clear that even if a codified system of racial discrimination like apartheid would take years to dismantle, the races could still come together on an individual basis.

In dramatizing Paton's narrative, Anderson made the idealism/sacrifice motif intersect with the prejudice/acceptance theme throughout. At the outset both Stephen Kumalo and James Jarvis are in some ways idealistic. Idealism isn't the exclusive property of left, right, or center politics and can be part of social, philosophical, or religious thinking and belief as well. All that is required for idealism is to wish the world was not as it is but as it should be. Reverend Kumalo begins as a passive, faith-driven idealist, believing that God's will will be done. In white supremacist Jarvis's ideal world, blacks would acknowledge their inferiority and accept the restrictions the ruling white minority imposes on them.

In the course of *Lost in the Stars*, albeit all too quickly, Jarvis and Stephen come to embrace a new kind of idealism altogether. Each man still has his own vision of the world as it should be but comes to recognize it will be transformed only if each individual helps create the new society. For both Jarvis and Stephen, the soul-wrenching catalyst that helps reshape their feelings and commitments was perhaps the greatest sacrifice either could envision—the virtually reciprocal deaths of each man's only son. In the musical's final moments it is Jarvis who articulates the need for sacrifice in order to achieve a greater good. Still sunk in a despair without God, an existence without hope, Stephen hears Jarvis say, "Not hopeless, Stephen, and not without meaning. For even out of the horror of this crime some things have come that are gain and not loss" (Richards 2: 175). Gradually these words instill in the minister a new sense of active idealism and hope for the future through human participation and cooperation. Making the prejudice/acceptance issue and the idealism/sacrifice motif work as one is perhaps the most effective aspect of Anderson's adaptation of Paton's novel, revealing that in *Lost in the Stars* he was a better proponent of progressive social philosophy than he was a dramatic craftsman.

For all its flaws, *Lost in the Stars* had its strengths as well, not the least of which was the powerfully sung portrayal of Stephen Kumalo by Todd Duncan—the original Porgy in the Gershwin opera—and Kurt Weill's exceptionally beautiful score, which regrettably, was his last. Weill died on April 3, 1950, during the musical's run. All things considered, for a relentlessly serious musical on an explosive and delicate subject, *Lost in the Stars* did well to play 273 times in 1949–50.

## Kwamina *and* No Strings

Aside from Rodgers and Hammerstein's shows and Lerner and Loewe's *Paint Your Wagon*, the musical stage in the 1950s was absolutely silent on race relations and the issue of prejudice and tolerance generally. Then, just over a year after Hammerstein's death in August 1960, two shows appeared five months apart whose stories and interracial advocacy could have come from the hand of Hammerstein himself. The one telling difference is that these musicals made history as the first to dramatize interracial love affairs specifically between blacks and whites. While both relationships ultimately dissolve, each is depicted without overt editorializing. It is possible that the writers of both shows perceived that, thanks to the progress made in civil rights, Northern urban white audiences would be more ready than in the past to accept such musicals — and such relationships.

The first, however, failed after thirty-two performances. *Kwamina* (10/23/61) had a book by Robert Alan Aurthur [sic] and music and lyrics by Richard Adler, his first solo outing since the untimely death of Jerry Ross, his young partner on *The Pajama Game* and *Damn Yankees*. In *Kwamina*, Eve, a white woman, has a love affair with the title character, a Western-trained black physician, in an unnamed West African country recently freed of colonial rule. Torn between traditional and modern outlooks, the country is not a congenial milieu for a relationship that, under the best circumstances, is fraught with difficulties. At the show's close Kwamina decides he must stay and serve the medical needs of his people, and he and Eve mutually agree it would be prudent to part company (Bordman 624). The show neither condemned nor condoned the openly portrayed interracial love affair except to express that the time and place of the musical's setting were not conducive to its survival.

The thematic thrust of *No Strings* (3/15/62) is almost identical: there's nothing in the world wrong with the love affair between white writer David and black model Barbara, it's just that there's no world they can live it in. The musical had a book by Samuel Taylor, and both words and music by Richard Rodgers, his first show since the passing of his long-time librettist, and his only public credit as a lyricist. If *Kwamina* was all but forgotten nearly before it opened, *No Strings* strung out a run of 580 performances, suggesting that black-white romantic involvements per se were not anathema to early 1960s audiences. Rodgers and Taylor go Hammerstein one better by depicting a romantic and sexual relationship between a black woman from Harlem and a white man from Maine. Yet Taylor's dialogue and Rodgers's lyrics contain nary a direct statement about color and its problems, let alone anything close to the condemnation of racism in "Carefully Taught." The one explicit reference to race appears not in the musical but in the authors' note to the published edition. Its sentiment is patently progressive, but its language respecting both race and gender is positively prehistoric by later standards: "The part of Barbara Woodruff in *No Strings* is designed to be played by an American colored girl in her early twenties. It is proposed that she also be beautiful, have style, and wear clothes well; be intelligent, witty, warmly human, and wise. The play itself never refers to her color" (Taylor viii).

In the original, high-fashion model Barbara was played by the gifted "colored girl" Diahann Carroll, who had all the specifications Rodgers and Taylor requested in their note. Richard Kiley played her lover, a burned-out writer. In the world of Paris fashion and jetsetters where these two live, the interracial romance is accepted. But eventually David feels he must return home to rekindle his creative spark. He wants to take Barbara back to Maine, but there she'd be as out of place as he is in France. The closest Barbara comes to mentioning race is when she refers to being born in New York City "Uptown. Way Uptown" (Taylor 29), which she expands upon in her chorus of "Maine":

> When the sun goes down
> The kids are up and out,
> East of the Hudson.
> There's a sidewalk symphony
> Of song and shout
> Up north of Central Park.
> (83–84)

For a young woman from Harlem ("I have nice memories of home. Some." [82]) to rise to financial success and celebrity in Paris, returning to lily-white rural Maine is impossible. While regretfully agreeing to disagree, Barbara quips that she could wear her Paris originals to the Saturday night dances in Maine, adding flatly, "But we won't go." To which, David says, "Of course we'll go!" Barbara retorts, "Once. To show we're not cowards" (118). And David summarizes: "Ah, what a damned foolish thing it is. . . . That your warm, lovely world should be so bad for me, and the world I'm going back to so impossible for you" (118). Almost without a word spoken and without judging the love affair itself, Taylor and Rodgers criticize social contexts that render such relationships impossible.

### The Musical, the Middle Class, and Suburbia

By the late 1940s, some social commentators remarked on how conservatism was manifesting itself as conformity and complacency, largely within the burgeoning middle class. In 1947, essayist Mary McCarthy wrote in *Commentary* that "passivity and not aggressiveness is the dominant trait of the

American character" (qtd. in Miller 221), and novelist Fannie Hurst observed that in 1946–47, after the energizing war years of Rosie the Riveter, "A sleeping sickness [was] spreading among the women of the land. . . . They are retrogressing into . . . that thing known as The Home" (qtd. in Goldman 47; his ellipses). By the 1950s, not only women but all of America seemed to be retreating into the confines of domesticity. This included America's intelligentsia, whom social historians Miller and Nowak describe as staid, respectable, conformist writers who "came to defend bourgeois values: stability, material possessions, propriety, social adjustment, family" (220–21). Miller and Nowak attribute this to the nation's fear of communism internationally and within U.S. borders. The response to these fears was a heightened emphasis on "Domesticity, religiosity, respectability, [and] security through compliance with the system" (7).

In such an atmosphere where "critical dissent . . . was suppressed and attacked when it appeared" (378–79), it was difficult to criticize society or offer alternative visions. Nevertheless, a few musicals — openly, in the forum of the popular stage — dared to rush in where intellectuals and journalists feared to tread. And some of these musicals thrived.

Among diversionary shows containing casual, isolated moments of such commentary is one of the period's longest-running, most felicitously written, almost seamlessly integrated, and just possibly best ever two-plus hours of pure fun in the history of the musical — Frank Loesser, Jo Swerling, and Abe Burrows's *Guys and Dolls* (11/24/50). Loesser, a composer/lyricist of acute perspicacity, twice poked fleeting yet pointed fun at two phenomena that would encroach ever more widely on the American landscape in the 1950s: that sprawling monster, suburbia, and its evil twin, conformity.

Of course, suburbs weren't a new thing in 1950; some, like the communities in Westchester County north of New York City, had old roots indeed, and Oak Park, west of Chicago, dated back a hundred years (Leuchtenburg, *Feast* 78). Even Wilmette on Chicago's North Shore, where I grew up, did not in the 1950s resemble what we think of today as planned suburban sprawl. The houses were *not* made out of ticky-tacky and did *not* all look just the same, though their inhabitants may have. What began after World War II and escalated rapidly in the mid-'50s would be the Levittowns and Park Forests of America, homogeneous (one wants to say homogenized) houses with people all acting alike in their "new, artificially created, one-class cluster" (78). Even by the end of the 1940s when Loesser and Company were writing *Guys and Dolls*, "Trim workers' suburbs were rising in testimony to the fact that almost half of organized labor was in or quite near the middle-income brackets of the country" (Goldman 48). Whether blue-or white-collar, by 1950 there were 37 million suburbanites; two decades later that figure had nearly doubled (75).

The first of Loesser's two jokes at the expense of suburbia and suburban conformity names not a nouveau development but one of the oldest established Westchester County suburbs of New York. Freewheeling gambler Sky Masterson assumes the sort of man Miss Sarah Brown of the Save-a-Soul Mission would go for would be the conventional, gray-flannel-suit commuter: "You have wished yourself a Scarsdale Gallahad / The breakfast-eating Brooks Brothers type!" (Loesser, *Guys* 19). Then, very late in the play, when Sarah and Miss Adelaide resolve to "Marry the Man Today"—Sky and Nathan Detroit, respectively—and reform them after marriage, the ladies admit they want husbands who conform to middle-class suburban conformity (speech headings omitted):

> Slowly introduce him to the better things
> Respectable, conservative and clean.
> Readers Digest!
> Guy Lombardo!
> Rogers Peet!
> Golf!
> Galoshes!
> Ovaltine!
>
> (66)

Eleven years later, Loesser returned to suburbia-bashing in an incidental sidebar to his satire of getting to the top in corporate America in the hugely successful *How To Succeed in Business without Really Trying* (10/14/61), with a run of 1,417 performances. Adapted by Abe Burrows, Jack Weinstock, and Willie Gilbert from Shepherd Mead's book with the same unwieldy title, the show follows a seemingly sweet Mr. Nice Guy up his calculated rise in the business world. At one point Loesser turns from big business to take satiric aim at the complacent conformity of suburbia as he had done twice in *Guys and Dolls*. Our corporate ladder-climber J. Pierpont Finch loves and is beloved of—nay, verily, just about worshipped by—Rosemary Pilkington, a secretary. In the opening moments of "Happy to Keep His Dinner Warm," Rosemary's reverie of her ideal married-life-to-be, she repeatedly intones "New Rochelle" like a mantra to invoke the return of a classical Arcadia, not life in a Westchester suburb. Her most telling lines in the brief number depict the expected role-relationship for suburban husbands and wives of the day:

> I'll be there waiting until his mind is clear,
> While he looks through me, right through me.
> Waiting to say: "Good evening, dear,
> I'm pregnant; What's new with you from downtown?"
>
> (Loesser, *How To* 18)

Without missing a beat, Rosemary segues from offhandedly making her pregnancy sound about as consequential as "We're having pot roast for dinner" to the important business of asking her corporate demigod and husband about just another day at the office.

Two other musicals of the 1950s, neither of them so mainstream as *Guys and Dolls*, made assaults—one oblique, the other frontal—on American middle-class materialism, hypocrisy, and "[b]land, vapid, self-satisfied, banal" suburbia (Leuchtenburg, *Feast* 113). Both pieces, eventually destined for New York, premiered during the first Festival of the Creative Arts at Brandeis University in the spring of 1952, the same spring the young university graduated its first class of students. Neither work was a musical in the conventional sense; one was an opera and the other called itself an opera though it had at least as much dialogue as music. Leonard Bernstein's one-act opera *Trouble in Tahiti* had its world premiere at Brandeis on June 12, 1952, and two evenings later a concert version of Marc Blitzstein's adaptation of Bertolt Brecht and Kurt Weill's *The Threepenny Opera* debuted, with Blitzstein narrating the story between musical numbers. Both pieces were conducted by thirty-three-year-old Brandeis Professor of Music Leonard Bernstein, whom the *Time Magazine* review persisted in calling "Lennie" throughout, and who, as one of the most successful "crossover" composers in America, had already written some major concert pieces as well as the score for the successful if fairly conventional musical *On the Town* (12/28/44).

There's a terrific irony about the stupendous success of *The Threepenny Opera* in New York, given the fact that its German author, Bertolt Brecht, was a communist who refocused the satire in John Gay's eighteenth-century English ballad-opera *The Beggars' Opera* from politics to a savage assault on the materialism and values—or lack thereof—of capitalists. Even in Blitzstein's relatively genteel adaptation of this musical tale of beggars and thieves, crooked cops and whores, *Threepenny* retained Brecht's thinly veiled but still leftist indictment of the avarice, hypocrisy, materialism, and complacency of the middle class—in large part the very people who paid to see the show 2,707 times.

*Threepenny* opened off-Broadway at the Theatre de Lys on March 10, 1954, for an advertised limited run, closing on May 30 after ninety-six performances. But with the *Times*'s Brooks Atkinson leading the pack, press and public alike let out a howl to bring back the show for an open-ended run. And that is how Blitzstein's most commercially successful work came to be. On September 20, 1955, *Threepenny* returned to the Theatre de Lys for an extraordinary 2,611 performances, though that may not seem exceptional for an off-Broadway house that sat at most a couple of hundred people. But in view of *when* that run took place, it's quite astonishing. By the fall of 1955, Ike had been ensconced in the White House for quite some time, consumerism was on the rise, and suburbia continued its seemingly unstoppable sprawl. The postwar boom had resulted in an increasingly large, smugly materialistic middle class. *Threepenny* called for singers to "step out of" a scene, walk downstage, and sing right to the house, because these songs of attack and indictment sung *to* the audience were really aimed *at* the audience as targets of the musical's satire:

> Your vices and your virtues are so dear to you,
> But learn the simple truth from this my song:
> Whatever you aspire, whatever you may do,
> First feed the face and then preach right and wrong.
> For even honest folk can act like sinners
> Unless they've had their customary dinners.
>                         (Marc Blitzstein translation)

Although *The Threepenny Opera* lampooned its own audiences, it ran for nearly nine years.

Just about a year after the original New York opening of *Threepenny*, Leonard Bernstein's mini-opera appeared as one-third of a triple bill called *All in One* (4/9/55); *Trouble in Tahiti* led off, Paul Draper's one-man dance concert followed, and the closer was Tennessee Williams's one-act *27 Wagons Full of Cotton*. With few exceptions, the reviews were great, but attendance was awful, and *All in One* packed it in after forty-seven performances. New York audiences may not have bought such an "anthology" evening of unrelated theatre, dance, and music pieces simply because they weren't used to such an event. Also, what perceptive critics found so sharp about *Tahiti* might have hit a nerve among ticket buyers, especially those from the suburbs.

What Bernstein had written was a scathingly ironic look at what lies beneath the seemingly happy, tranquil joys of suburban life. By the time of *Tahiti*'s New York debut in 1955, numerous middle-class theatregoers were leading lives like the show's couple, Sam and Dinah, "in the little white house in Elkins Park," Brookline, Highland Park, or the other suburbs Bernstein catalogues throughout the piece. As *Tahiti*'s composer and very incisive lyricist, Bernstein exposed the boredom, malaise, conformity, and anxiety compressed in neat suburban households. Indeed, William Leuchtenburg notes that commentators on the era "found hard evidence for an 'age of anxiety' in the burgeoning of psychoanalysis [depicted in *Tahiti*], the manifestations of mental illness, and the bull market in tranquilizers, often some form of meprobamate like 'Miltown' " (*Feast* 104).

The most acute reviewers of *Tahiti* saw precisely what Bernstein was up to. Others missed the boat entirely, trying to make the piece into a satire, which it patently is not, since both Sam and Dinah are delineated in meticulously psychological and realistic detail. *Tahiti* is ironic, not satiric, made so by the juxtaposition of Sam and Dinah's deeply distressed marriage with a smug and smiling doo-wop trio painting a sunny mural of suburban bliss:

> Mornin' sun
> Kisses the windows: kisses the walls
> Of the little white house;
> Kisses the door-knob: kisses the roof: . . .
> Of the little white house in Scarsdale.
>
> . . . . . . . . . . . . . . . .
> Suburbia! Suburbia!
> Our little spot, out of the hubbub,
> Less than an hour by train.
> Suburbia! Suburbia!
> Sweet in the spring:
> Healthful in winter:
> Saves us the bother of summers in Maine.
>
> . . . . . . . . . . . . . . . .
> Up-to-date kitchen: washing machine:
> Colorful bathrooms, and Life Magazine,
> And a little white house in Brookline!
>
> . . . . . . . . . . . . . . . .
> Six days of work; fun ev'ry Sunday:
> Golf with the neighbors next door.
> Suburbia! Suburbia!
> Vitamin B: Chlorophyll tooth paste
> Who could ask heaven for anything more?
> (Bernstein, *Tahiti* 2–5, 61–62, 66–67)

Such creature comforts of a consumer culture (and a young son whom both tend to ignore) are about all that bind Sam and Dinah together. Far from satire, *Tahiti*'s depiction of a withering marriage in the deceptively lush green of suburbia achieves deep pathos.

Critics who recognized the opera not as satire but as something more profound rightly connected it to the bleak side of suburban living. Walter Kerr wrote in the *New York Herald Tribune* that Dinah was "an unhappy matron in the waste land of suburbia" and that the show "tees off on a grim, caustic scratchy note calculated to send half of Westchester flying back to the big city brownstones. It is lugubrious not only about suburbia, but about trivia." Brooks Atkinson in the *Times* showed that he understood the tone of the piece, noting that "Mr. Bernstein's brooding opera . . . looks

under the immaculate surface of life in the suburbs. . . . The main sequences of the opera . . . make a serious attempt to explore the minds of a
young husband and a young wife whose lives have become empty . . . [re-
sulting in] a sober, thoughtful look into life that is sleek only on the surface"
(critics' excerpts from *NYTCR* 1955 325–28).

All that remains to be said about Bernstein's excursion into operatic social
commentary is a word about the title. Ostensibly, *Trouble in Tahiti* is just
the name of the "escapist Technicolor twaddle" (83) that Dinah sees in the
afternoon and then goes to see with Sam without telling him she's already
seen it, rather than endure another painful evening at home talking to one
another — or not. But metaphorically, imagistically, the title is much more
than that. In the popular imagination, Tahiti is almost mythically envi-
sioned as an island paradise, an escape from the pressures, tensions, and
anxieties of the workaday world. In the 1950s, that was the myth of suburbia
as well. The opera's title, then, exposes the "trouble" there can be, in fact
is, in the idyllic "Tahiti" of suburbia. The opera also embraced what observers later in the decade found lying beneath the surface of suburbia's
idyllic facade. Miller and Nowak cite a *New York Times* article from August
7, 1959, giving the results of a medical and psychiatric study done in En-
glewood, New Jersey, showing that suburban living "is giving people ulcers,
heart attacks and other 'tension related psychosomatic disorders' . . . everything from crab grass to high taxes played a role in emotional difficulties"
(qtd. in Miller 138). Small wonder these years got labeled "The Age of
Anxiety," appropriately also the title of one of Bernstein's major symphonic
works.

### *Critiques of Idealism in Late '50s and Early '60s Musicals:*
### *"There's a place for us," or Is There?* — Candide

The 1950s were the heyday of Leonard Bernstein's output for the musical
stage. Before *Trouble in Tahiti*'s brief New York run, *Wonderful Town* (2/
25/53) became the second commercial hit to his credit, which, like *On the
Town*, he wrote with lyricists Betty Comden and Adolph Green. Following
*Tahiti*, Bernstein figured large in two more socially aware musicals: *Candide*
(12/1/56), a musical masterpiece but a commercial failure, and *West Side
Story* (9/26/57), an artistic and commercial hit that quickly became a classic.
An impressive team of collaborators came together to shift Voltaire's *Candide* from the page to the stage. Lillian Hellman, America's premiere female
playwright, crafted the book. Three witty and literate poets in their own
right, Richard Wilbur, Dorothy Parker, and John Latouche, wrote the lyrics;

and Bernstein composed the music. The result was a frothy, glittery score with lyrics to match, often parodying styles of European operetta and comic opera, even of particular composers—a score many consider, with justification, one of Broadway's finest. But Bernstein and his lyricists' contributions were shackled to Hellman's leaden script, which turned Voltaire's rapier wit into a bludgeon. Thanks mostly to its ponderous book, *Candide* collapsed under its own weight after just seventy-three performances.

The story of Candide and his bride-to-be Cunegonde connects by analogy to the United States in the 1950s. The couple starts out in a state of self-satisfied insularity in their small German village, a condition not far removed from suburban America's complacent apathy in the Eisenhower years. But their travels from Westphalia halfway round the world and back make of them very different people by the end. Dr. Pangloss, their tutor, has instilled in Candide and Cunegonde his peculiarly narrow view that "All's for the best in this best of all possible worlds" (Hellman 8), which is an apt summary of ideological complacency. Pangloss's idealism does not involve actively trying to make the world better—or even retreating from it, as in *Brigadoon*; rather, his perspective is entirely passive—everything is just fine as it is. One does not act but accept. There's a bright and happy side to everything, to wit: "It's been a long and bloody war, but if men didn't fight they would never know the benefits of peace, and if they didn't know the benefits of peace they would never know the benefits of war. You see, it all works out for the best" (3).

Through their misadventures, Candide and Cunegonde learn very painfully that this is not the case. If people are to have any ideals at all, they must be grounded in reality. They need to admit and accept their limitations, weaknesses, and fallible humanity, and must also concede that this is *not* "the best of all possible worlds" but an imperfect and uncertain place. People must be ready to make the best of their lives and their world in their own small ways. Candide conveys this attitude in his final words, spoken not out of cynicism but from having learned the hard way to face life realistically—words that the gut-wrenching finale then exquisitely embellishes: "We will not think noble because we are not noble. We will not live in beautiful harmony because there is no such thing in this world, nor should there be. We promise only to do our best and live out our lives. Dear God, that's all we can promise in truth. Marry me, Cunegonde."

> I thought the world was sugar-cake,
> For so our master said;
> But now I'll teach my hands to bake
> Our loaf of daily bread.

. . . . . . . . . . . . . . .
Let dreamers dream what worlds they please;
Those Edens can't be found.
The sweetest flowers, the fairest trees
Are grown in solid ground.
We're neither pure nor wise nor good,
We'll do the best we know.
We'll build our house and chop our wood,
And make our garden grow.

(141–43)


## West Side Story

With his next musical and a very different set of collaborators, Leonard
Bernstein continued to explore matters of current social relevance and challenge the validity of certain kinds of idealism. As far back as 1949, director/
choreographer Jerome Robbins got it into his head to create a Romeo and
Juliet musical set in present-day New York City. His original concept was
for a show titled *East Side Story*, treating such a love affair between an
Italian-Catholic girl from Little Italy and an Orthodox Jewish boy from
Mulberry Street and set at Easter-Passover time (Zadan 14). It was Robbins's
intention "to tell a tragic story with a theme of some depth in terms of
musical comedy without being operatic" (Green 233). Given that goal, the
premise of *East Side Story* had a few strikes against it from the start. Going
back at least to *Abie's Irish Rose*, there is always something inherently comic
and/or sentimental about Jewish-Catholic (whether Irish or Italian matters
not) misalliances in theatre or film. But Robbins wanted something serious.
Accordingly, he brought in Arthur Laurents to do the libretto and Bernstein
to write the score (Green 233; Zadan 15). But because of their other commitments, they eventually shelved the project. Still, the idea of a modern
Romeo and Juliet wouldn't go away, percolating in each of the trio's brains
from time to time and bubbling to the surface again in 1954, when Bernstein
ran into Laurents at the Beverly Hills Hotel pool. The composer later recalled, "We were sitting there and reminiscing and ruefully saying what a
shame that that wonderful idea never worked out, . . . and while we were
talking, we noticed the *L. A. Times* had a headline of gang fights breaking
out. And this was Los Angeles with Mexicans fighting so-called Americans.
Arthur and I looked at one another and all I can say is that there are
moments which are right for certain things and that moment seemed to
have come" (qtd. in Zadan 15).

When they told Robbins the idea he became "wildly excited because here was suddenly the living, breathing reincarnation of the *Romeo* story, and it was topical" (Bernstein qtd. in Zadan 15). In the 1950s, the majority of America's youth "went steady, married young, had lots of children, lived the conforming life of 'togetherness,' " to the extent that in the aggregate they became known as "The Silent Generation" (Miller 15). These teenagers passively accepted the values of their middle-American parents, embracing security, domesticity, conformity, and sociability as positive goals to attain. But in those same years juvenile delinquency was a serious problem. According to Miller and Nowak, "By 1956, . . . well over one million kids 'came to the attention of the police annually' " (280). Also in the '50s, Puerto Ricans left the island in such numbers that there were more in New York City than San Juan (Leuchtenburg, *Feast* 70). Between Shakespeare, street gangs, and the influx of Puerto Ricans, the raw materials were in place for the making of *West Side Story*. But again Bernstein, Robbins, and Laurents were immersed in other projects—and they still didn't have a lyricist. Then one day Laurents brought a complete unknown to audition for Bernstein, one he'd heard at a party six months earlier singing some of his own tunes. Thus it was that a young television writer named Stephen Sondheim had his lyrics, though not yet his music, first heard on Broadway. But he worried that he was unsuited for the job: "I've never been that poor and I've never even *known* a Puerto Rican" (Zadan 11–12, 14; Green 233). Nor was Sondheim happy about co-authoring the lyrics with Bernstein. But once the show was in tryouts, Bernstein had his own name removed as co-lyricist, giving full lyric credit to Sondheim in a generous and apparently rare gesture of recognition of the young newcomer's work (Zadan 12, 25).

With all pieces of the creative puzzle in place and two years of hard, if sporadic work, *West Side Story* finally made its debut on September 26, 1957. And when it did, what New York saw was indeed Jerome Robbins's vision of Romeo and Juliet transported and updated to the less than friendly sidewalks of The City itself, where the Montagues and Capulets' feud became the turf war between two juvenile gangs—the "American" Jets and Puerto Rican Sharks; where a Verona balcony became a back-alley fire escape, and sagacious Friar Lawrence turned into fatherly Doc, the drug store owner. Yet the story of two young lovers trapped in a hostile environment remained pretty much intact, except for intentional alterations of the Shakespeare original by Laurents, Sondheim, and Bernstein.

The reviews were strong but not the uncritical raves three months later for Meredith Willson's *The Music Man* (12/19/57), which also walked away with nearly all the season's awards and played 1,375 performances. *West Side Story* garnered only the Tony awards for Best Choreographer (Robbins) and Best Scenic Design (Oliver Smith) and had an original run of 732 performances, with another 249 after a tour, making the total number 981. While no *Music Man*, that kind of run was impressive for just about any musical at the time, and especially for one as risky and innovative as *West Side Story*.

The collaborators made their story of the impossibility of love transcending hatred communicate three statements of immediate relevance, all linked to some degree. And they achieved this through the musical's dramatic action and an occasional line or two of lyrics or dialogue, with no overt "preaching." First and most obvious is *West Side Story*'s continuation of the prejudice/acceptance motif, vividly driven home by the negative example of the triple fatalities in the gang war between the Puerto Rican Sharks and the hyphenated-American (Polish-American, Irish-American, etc.) Jets in what was then the notoriously rough West Side neighborhood called Hell's Kitchen. The only false note in this tough and realistic story of gang rivalry and ethnic hatred is rung at the end of the musical, when members of both gangs, Puerto Rican and "American" alike, together lift Tony's lifeless body and bear it offstage. Visually this reads as instant reconciliation between the gangs through Tony's death, as unrealistic as it is hard to believe that Bernstein, Sondheim, and Laurents would allow themselves such a moment of implausible sentimentality. Also, if that moment was intended to depict true reconciliation, it would militate against the musical's overriding critique of naive idealism discussed below. The only plausible explanation for the ending is the gang members' shock over the deaths fostering a fragile and temporary truce — but that's hard to convey in a silent moment on stage.

Second, *West Side Story* was the first Broadway musical to seriously question the universality of the American Dream. The aspect of the Dream under scrutiny is the myth of the United States as the land of opportunity for *all*, where the streets are paved with gold. For the Jets, Sharks, and their girls, the streets are paved with — well, pavement. For gang members from dysfunctional homes, broken homes, poverty-level homes, or perhaps no homes at all, to "own" the street is to have it all, or as the Jets' leader Riff says, "We fought hard for this territory and it's ours. . . . I say this turf is small, *but it's all we got*" (Richards 1: 285). Nothing has ever been handed to these kids, as the streets of gold myth falsely promises; they've had to fight for everything they've got, every inch of the way. And while most of the Puerto Rican kids prefer living in America, they also know they pay a price to do so:

> *I like to be in America!*
> *O.K. by me in America!*

*Everything free in America*
*For a small fee in America!*
(Richards 1: 298)

The Dream's failure cuts both ways. The Puerto Ricans can't have their fair share since they're discriminated against for their color, language, and ethnicity, depicted in the musical through Lieutenant Schrank's insults. But the American boys blame the Puerto Ricans for also being cut out of the Dream: "Them PRs're the reason my old man's gone bust" (283). *West Side Story* was bold enough to say that for both disadvantaged white youth and Puerto Rican immigrants the American Dream was more of a nightmare.

Finally, Laurents's reworking of *Romeo and Juliet* became the vehicle for dramatizing the most singular of all the musical's themes — the negative effects of naive or excessive idealism. Laurents replaced Shakespeare's reliance on chance and circumstance with largely character-motivated actions that ultimately doom the young lovers. His most striking change was to turn Juliet — who, until her suicide, is relatively passive — into Maria, not only still alive at the end but, through misguided ideals, beliefs, and action, is central to causing the musical's catastrophic events. Because of this alteration, Maria's "journey" through the show follows the same pattern of all true tragic figures since the Greeks: making a "tragic mistake" (Gerald Else's breakthrough retranslation of Aristotle's *hamartia*, more usually thought of as "tragic flaw"; see esp. 37–38); experiencing a major reversal of fortune or circumstances because of that mistake; and, late in the action, coming to a moment of recognition wherein the character realizes he or she was ultimately to blame for the tragic events triggered by that initial mistake.

In *Romeo and Juliet* much of what happens is out of the hands of the characters. Right from the top the Chorus refers to Romeo and Juliet as "A pair of star-crossed lovers." Elizabethan cosmology signaled to the audience that their lives would be governed by "the stars," not by character choices and actions, Romeo's rash impetuosity excepted. Arthur Laurents replaced chance or coincidence with meticulous character motivation for every action and incident in *West Side Story*. When Tony goes to Doc's drugstore, where the Jets and Sharks are having their "war council," he tries to prevent an all-out rumble by having them agree to a fair fight between each gang's best man. Tony's action is clearly driven by his having fallen instantly in love with Maria, sister of the Shark's commander Bernardo, at the dance two hours earlier. (The precise time of each scene appeared in the program to underscore how not just Tony's but all these teenagers' testosterone overload hurls them headlong into disaster.) If things had stopped with Tony's compromise, tragedy might have been averted. But when Tony tells Maria about the fair one-on-one combat, she, so naively idealistic as to suppose that their love transcends ethnic hostilities and, just a month in the United States, still envisioning America as a land of perfect peace and harmony, says to him, "You must go and stop it. . . . *Any* fight is not good for us. . . . You must go and stop it" (Richards 1: 305). Out of his love for Maria, Tony agrees to this impossibility born of her excessively and naively idealistic vision of a totally peaceful and loving America. Sending Tony to stop *any* fighting is Maria's tragic mistake — a noble goal to be sure, but like all tragic mistakes it backfires in an ironic reversal from intention to result.

At the end of act 1 Tony's attempt to prevent any fight at all simply escalates the gangs' animosities. Bernardo kills Riff, so enraging Tony that he kills Bernardo with no thought that he's Maria's brother. After this point, Laurents substantially departs from *Romeo and Juliet*. For example, Romeo's death is caused by the contrived, coincidental plot point of Friar John getting quarantined and not delivering the note. So when Romeo returns to Verona, he *presumes* the sleeping Juliet is dead and poisons himself. She wakes up, sees her lover in fact dead, and stabs herself. That's all, folks; this is the stuff of melodrama, not tragedy.

As fine-tuned by Laurents in *West Side Story*, character, not coincidence, drives these actions, creating a far more plausible chain of events and investing them with meaning as well. Maria convinces Anita of how deeply she loves Tony in the "A Boy Like That / I Have a Love" musical scene. Convinced, Anita agrees to give Maria's message to Tony, who's hiding in the drugstore basement, that she will meet him there so they can run away together. At the store the Jets confront, taunt, and, in some of Robbins's most brutally realistic choreography, practically gang-rape Anita. Her hatred resurfaces, driving her to deliver a different and spiteful message of her own devising: "Tell the murderer Maria's *never* going to meet him! Tell him Chino found out and — and shot her!" (Richards 1: 326). This information drives Tony into despair and out into the streets, where he wildly and repeatedly yells for Maria's putative fiancée Chino to kill him too. Suddenly Tony sees Maria — still alive — but as he does Chino shoots Tony, mortally wounding him. Tony dies in Maria's arms but not before a brief exchange about finding love "Somewhere." Maria is left alive and alone, her thoughts turned more to rage than love and through that rage to a stunning moment of realization. Wildly waving the gun at the assembling Sharks and Jets, Maria screams (stage directions omitted) in the strategically placed final speech in the musical, "How many bullets are left, Chino? Enough for you? And you? All of you? WE ALL KILLED HIM; and my brother and Riff. I, too" (328).

Those last two little words may well be the most important in the musical. Maria's "I, too" verbalizes her sudden painful awareness that her excessive and naive idealism about how things *should* be in America drove her to send Tony to stop the rumble entirely, which in turn began the chain reaction that resulted in three deaths. Like many tragic figures before her, Maria does not die but must live, carrying with her those heavy thoughts of personal guilt and responsibility. And in terms of its themes, while *West Side Story* dramatizes the need for tolerance and eradicating prejudice, it also dramatizes through Maria's story how a naively idealistic belief that all such problems may be resolved in an instant isn't just unrealistic but potentially damaging and dangerous. While the action of *West Side Story* does not speak out against idealism, it suggests, like the finale of *Candide*, that if one's idealistic vision is to have any chance of succeeding, it must be grounded in a thorough understanding of life's practical realities.

## Idealism Pro and Con: Fiorello!

*Fiorello!* (11/23/59) is history. It's biography. It's politics. It's all these and more in a musical that compresses and romanticizes an early portion of New York mayor Fiorello H. LaGuardia's public life, not just to entertain but to remark on the American Dream and some varieties and consequences of idealism. Historically, *Fiorello!* was also a few other things. Along with *Gypsy* (5/12/59) in the same calendar year, *Fiorello!* proved for the first time that a mainstream musical without a love story as its central plot could become a hit. These two shows were also the first two Broadway hits whose stories were musical biographies of actual historical figures, no matter how romanticized or fictionalized. And finally, *Fiorello!* became the third musical to win the Pulitzer Prize for drama, also winning the Tony and New York Drama Critics Circle's awards for the season's best musical and running for 795 performances.

Since a key criterion for the Pulitzer in drama is that a play depicts aspects of the so-called "American experience," *Fiorello!* could have qualified through just the surface texture of its story. In shaping for the stage the early political career of a man who became an especially popular New York mayor (three terms from 1933 to 1945), authors George Abbott and Jerome Weidman and lyricist Sheldon Harnick structured LaGuardia's rise to prominence on the lines of the Horatio Alger rags-to-riches myth so central to the American Dream. The show opens before World War I with Fiorello as a poverty lawyer. He has an office in Greenwich Village and a support staff of Neil, his zealous young law clerk, Morris, his comically doleful office manager, and Marie, his willing, patient, and long-suffering (from her love for him) secretary. He also has a waiting room full of indigent immigrants needing help. The first song meticulously sets up Fiorello's integrity, crusading spirit, and altruism, first in Neil's serious, then in Morris's comic, descriptions:

> We're marching forward
> Incorruptible, he and I
> Battling with evil
> Fighting till we drop
> What a way to die!
> .   .   .   .   .   .   .   .
>
> That bench stays crowded
> It's a regular wailing wall
> Penniless and helpless
> Ignorant and scared
> He collects 'em all!
> .   .   .   .   .   .   .   .
>
> Here's one more client
> Who's another financial gem
> I've yet to see the meek
> Inheriting the earth
> But we inherit them!
> (Weidman and Abbott 9, 11, 18)

LaGuardia determines to get the Republican nomination for the Fourteenth Congressional District, which he does easily because no one else wants it, and then to achieve the seemingly impossible — win — in the face of Tammany Hall's hold on the Democrats there. Improbably, he does — not through the old-school methods of cronyism and promises of patronage but through personal charisma, addressing specific issues that matter to his prospective constituents, and, since this is a musical, addressing them in song with appeals to their ethnic pride and heritage. In the campaign sequence, Fiorello, an "Italian Jewish Episcopalian" (78), first sings in English in an "American" neighborhood about Tammany's tyranny. Moving to an Italian section, he sings in Italian and appeals to the Italian-Americans' desire for Trieste to be freed from Austrian domination. Finally, Fiorello winds up in a Jewish enclave, where a heckler yells, "I hear you're half Jewish. How come you never brag about your Jewish background?" To which LaGuardia retorts, "I figure if a man is only half Jewish it isn't enough to brag about" (55). He then sings another anti-Tammany attack, this time in Yiddish. The campaign sequence dramatizes Fiorello's political charisma and concern for ordinary people with ordinary problems, never considering that his unconventional political methods and causes could turn against him.

As the song moves between neighborhoods, Jerry Bock's music and Irwin Kostal's orchestrations change to reflect the ethnicity of each group La-Guardia is pitching: an American campaign song heavy with the brass of a Sousa march, an Italian tarantella replete with accordion accompaniment, and the obligatory wailing trumpet or cornet solo in an old-country-Jewish klezmer tune. In *Fiorello!* and most of his other shows with Sheldon Harnick, Bock's music conveys what I call "musical authenticity"; while not attempting pedantic accuracy, the music evokes the time period, locale, and ethnicity of a show's settings and characters. After decades of more or less "generic" theatre music, this was a major contribution to completing the integrated musical. In addition to lyrics, dialogue, and dance, now the music too helped set the mood, tell the story, and create the ambiance of the whole musical play—another step toward achieving the *Gesamtkunstwerk* ideal.

Once in Congress, LaGuardia actively supports the generally unpopular Draft Act, recognizing its necessity for the nation on the brink of World War I. To publicly demonstrate his belief, he enlists as a flier himself. As act 1 ends, Major Fiorello H. LaGuardia, flying ace, returns from the war, and Thea, a woman he met while crusading for better treatment of sweatshop workers, agrees to marry him.

Respecting the rags to riches motif, what happens in act 2 is simple enough. It is ten years later and Fiorello runs for mayor of New York against the incumbent, popular, and thoroughly corrupt James J. "Gentleman Jimmy" Walker, losing to Walker by over half a million votes. The action then shifts rapidly to 1933, when LaGuardia, after some soul-searching and struggles with friends and past political cronies, agrees to run against Walker again, this time on a Fusion ticket, and the rest is history after the second act curtain falls. The basic plot of *Fiorello!* thus dramatizes with crystalline clarity the qualities of self-reliance, determination, and resilience that mythically allow Americans to pull themselves up by the bootstraps and attain whatever they desire.

But there is more. The musical is a double-edged dissection of altruistic idealism, exposing its public good and its potential or actual private harm. Throughout the show, Fiorello fights for even unpopular causes he believes in, if those causes will bring the greatest good to the greatest number of people. Rejecting machine politics and cozying up to popular but corrupt politicians even in his own party, LaGuardia blows the whistle on the crooked finances of one Alderman Marconi, costing him much of the

Italian-American vote against Walker. In a word, Fiorello's incorruptibility and seemingly inexhaustible efforts to battle for the best interests of his city or country add up to a kind of practical idealism in which LaGuardia not only saw his world as it should be but actively set out to make it so.

And yet, he paid a high price for doing so. Determined to fight for sweeping social and political reform, the musical's Fiorello cannot see the trees for the forest. In looking at the big picture, LaGuardia often dismisses or ignores those people closest to him. The musical effectively dramatizes this by compressing time for two occurrences to happen simultaneously that historically took place some time apart. Fiorello is so caught up with attending an important political rally that he is unaware of how ill his wife Thea is. While he is at the rally, Thea dies; LaGuardia learns of her death only later that evening. Similarly, in his first run for Congress, Fiorello more or less sloughs off Ben Marino and his other allies who got him the nomination, and by his first run against Walker he has dismissed them from his political life entirely. While he doesn't dismiss his secretary, neither does he show appreciation for Marie's fifteen years of loyalty and hard work. Long after *Fiorello!* such behavior was given the name "career blindness" to describe people so devoted to work in the larger world that they are blind to the needs of family and friends close at hand. Abbott, Weidman, and Harnick recognized this pattern of behavior as early as 1959 and used it to show that even the most sincere idealism for bettering the world must be tempered with love and appreciation for those people closest to the idealist. Fiorello learns this at the end of the musical. When Ben and the boys ask him to throw his hat in the mayoral ring again, LaGuardia replies, only partly in jest, "And if I should decide to run again, I want all you politicians to know that my chief qualification for Mayor of this great city is my monumental ingratitude." Then, moments later, he fires Marie, so he can say, "I can't court a girl who's working for me. . . . Will you marry me? . . . Marie, I think you can learn to love me." To which she replies, making the point ever so gently, "Yes, I think I can. I've been practicing for fifteen years" (Weidman and Abbott 145–46).

### *The Seasons Change* — The Fantasticks

*The Fantasticks* brings together a number of themes in this chapter. It offers an implicit critique of naïve romantic idealism and, without stretching a point too much, perhaps even a commentary on the insularity of middle-America tucked away in their cozy, seemingly safe suburbias during the Eisenhower years. Its first act even embodies a very different take on the

Romeo and Juliet motif so central to *West Side Story*. The world's longest-running musical, Tom Jones and Harvey Schmidt's *The Fantasticks* opened off-Broadway at the tiny Sullivan Street Playhouse on May 3, 1960, continued there through the rest of the twentieth century, and closed on January 20, 2002, playing just short of forty-two years.

Without exaggeration, one could fill an entire book discussing the complexities and subtleties of *The Fantasticks*—its structure, meaning, point of view, use of myth and metaphor, and the craft of the writing itself. All that is pertinent here is that in act 1 the young lovers Matt and Luisa are embroiled in a comic, happily ever after rendition of the Romeo and Juliet story—one that has been deliberately contrived by their fathers to make them fall in love with one another. Matt and Luisa are naive romantic idealists. They are young, he about twenty, she sixteen; they are sheltered in their fathers' houses, particularly their gardens. They are innocent and, most of all, they are hopelessly, helplessly in love—with love. Act 1 ends with seeming happiness for all after the phony bandit El Gallo's phony abduction of Luisa, Matt's phony rescue (he thinks it's real, of course), and the end of the phony, pre-planned feud the fathers had concocted to bring their children together.

When act 2 opens, all of the principals discover that their happiness, perhaps even Matt and Luisa's love, is as phony as everything else: "Their moon was cardboard, fragile. / It was very apt to fray, / And what was last night scenic / May seem cynic by today" (T. Jones, *Fantasticks* 39). In the real as well as metaphoric sunlight, Matt and Luisa see each others' imperfections, the fathers begin to quarrel in earnest, the boy goes off to "see the world," the girl must stay behind. Both get hurt, but the pain causes them to mature. As in all genuine fairy tales—and *The Fantasticks* is a kind of a fairy tale, or at least is as timeless as one—in this process of maturation Matt and Luisa must sacrifice something very dear to themselves in order to learn and grow: their innocence, which includes their romantically idealistic view of the world and of each other. Still at her father's house, Luisa becomes infatuated with El Gallo, who emotionally seduces and abandons her to help open her eyes to reality; meanwhile, Matt's worldly adventures leave him battered physically and emotionally. Just before Matt's return, the omniscient Narrator (a.k.a. El Gallo) delivers the play's core statement—a metaphoric description of the birth, growth, death, and rebirth cycle of the "dying god motif" found in myth, religion, and seasonal change.

> There is a curious paradox
> That no one can explain.
> Who understands the secret
> Of the reaping of the grain?

> Who understands why Spring is born
> Out of Winter's laboring pain?
> Or why we all must die a bit
> Before we grow again.
> I do not know the answer.
> I merely know it's true.
> I hurt them for that reason
> And myself a little bit too.
>
> (*Fantasticks* 71)

As Matt limps home from his eye-opening misadventures, Luisa asks, "What in the world happened to you?" He replies simply and sincerely, "The world happened to me" (72). Only then are both, cognizant of life's harsh realities, ready to appreciate what they had before and to love each other for who they truly are.

The seasonal myth of growth, renewal, and regeneration was absolutely central to Tom Jones's thinking when he wrote *The Fantasticks*, as it would be for all his succeeding musicals (Jones interview). Whether the various implications of the myth projected in the show were equally conscious is difficult to say. But, conscious or not, all resonate with issues in the air during the decade preceding the musical's opening. Certainly, what the show critiqued as the insular innocence of Matt, Luisa, and their fathers had its real-life parallels, domestically, in the complacent and sheltered world of America's suburbia, and, globally, in the isolationist mood that continued to persist during the increasingly internationalist period of the cold war. So, too, *The Fantasticks* looked favorably, but not uncritically, at the concept of idealism, as had *Candide*, *West Side Story*, and *Fiorello!* All agreed that to be effective the idealist must have his or her eyes wide open and feet firmly planted in reality. Anticipating key concerns of the '60s and early '70s, *The Fantasticks* examines generational differences and the rebellion of youth. Taken together with its larger mythical motif, this richness of themes in a single show gave audience members something to ponder, and it helps explain—along with the richness of *The Fantasticks* as entertainment—the show's remarkable longevity.

# Black and Jewish Musicals since the 1960s

*The Drama Outside: Civil Rights Actions in the 1960s*

The social climate of the early 1960s fostered two diametrically opposed phenomena in the musical theatre: a decade-long decline in black musicals and the simultaneous emergence of musicals on Jewish themes. President Kennedy's personal charisma aside, the landscape of mainstream America in the early 1960s looked much the same as in the Eisenhower '50s. A suburban gray-flannel-suited commuter, his wife — whom *McCall's* magazine dubbed the source of the family's "togetherness," a key buzzword of the time — and two or three kids made up the representative American family.

Beneath this surface complacency, the Civil Rights movement escalated. Following the Montgomery bus boycott of 1955 and the Little Rock school desegregation standoff in 1957, the early 1960s witnessed an increase in mostly peaceful civil rights protests employing the tactic of passive resistance. In 1960, Congress passed the second Civil Rights Act (chiefly engineered through both houses by Texas Senator Lyndon Johnson). And in Greensboro, North Carolina, on February 1, 1960, a sit-in by blacks at a Woolworth lunch counter became the model for similar actions at other whites-only venues. In 1961 began the Freedom Rides of northern civil rights workers — black and white — into the South to work for black voter registration and black access to public accommodations on an equal basis with whites. That same year the Supreme Court supported Freedom Riders' rights in *Boynton v. Commonwealth of Virginia,* ruling that "restaurants in bus stations could not discriminate against interstate travelers," which of course the Freedom Riders were. In these same years, Kennedy appointed several blacks to high-level government posts, including Thurgood Marshall to the U.S. Circuit Court (Leuchtenburg, *Feast* 145).

But the struggle for civil rights could be brutal. Despite the Supreme Court's ruling, mob violence against Freedom Riders persisted in the South (145). In 1962, when James H. Meredith attempted to enroll in the University of Mississippi, in one night of violence two people were killed and 375 injured, nearly half of those federal marshals. On April 12, 1963, police commissioner "Bull" Connor greeted Martin Luther King Jr.'s huge Birmingham, Alabama, demonstration with attack dogs and electric cattle prods. The relative ineffectiveness of the Birmingham protest and the bombings of both King's brother's home and the movement's headquarters sparked riots by angry blacks.

Things really heated up by the mid '60s. In June 1963, Governor George Wallace almost single-handedly defied the federalized National Guard in his attempt to keep blacks from entering the University of Alabama. On August 28 that year, the huge civil rights march on Washington became most memorable for King's "I have a dream" speech. The following month, the bombing of a Birmingham church killed four black Sunday School children (148–50 *passim*). Then, to cap off his voting rights campaign for Selma, Alabama, Reverend King organized a march on Sunday, March 7, 1965, from Selma to the state capital of Montgomery. In an incident still infamous for its brutality, marchers trying to cross the Edmund Pettus Bridge were attacked by a contingent of Alabama State Troopers with tear gas and clubs. As the peaceful protesters retreated to Selma, they "met the furies of [Sheriff] Jim Clark's posse, urged on by their leader's command, 'Get those god-damned niggers.'" But, according to one historian, "Bloody Sunday, filmed for the evening news, appalled the North and created an instant constituency for a new voting law. King's tactics had worked to perfection" (Matusow 183).

### The Black Musical Bows Out — For Now

Prior to the 1960s, every decade of the century had seen at least a few commercially successful black-cast musicals on Broadway, whether written by blacks, whites, or mixed-race creative teams. But such entertainments virtually disappeared for the decade of the 1960s, only to return with renewed strength and vigor in the 1970s. At first glance it seems paradoxical that the African American musical nearly vanished during the days of the Civil Rights movement, a time when white America was increasingly aware of black America, and, as William Leuchtenburg and Allen Matusow both observed, increasingly sympathetic toward Reverend King's egalitarian mission. And yet, ironically perhaps, the Civil Rights movement was a principal *cause* for the disappearance of black musicals from Broadway in this period. Whether past black shows avoided racial stereotypes or played into them, they all depicted African Americans' differences from whites — their indigenous music, dance, humor, and folkways. Now, with America's blacks making demands to enter the nation's mainstream in education, employment, and non-segregated public accommodations, African Americans in the first half of the 1960s emphasized what blacks and whites had in common as human beings; a shared humanity was the basis for equal civil rights. Accordingly, musicals that emphasized black singularity were out of sync with the times. In addition, black writers in the 1960s may have felt that the issues blacks were fighting for were too serious to turn into musical theatre. That view would change in the early '70s.

Black shows by blacks throughout the 1960s were immediate flops. Langston Hughes turned his novel *Tambourines to Glory* into a musical (11/2/63) in which two sisters found a gospel church in Harlem, accompanied by traditional spirituals and additional songs by Jobe Huntley, but the public wasn't buying; it closed after twenty-four performances (Bordman 632). Traditional African American song supplied the musical component of two more black shows that didn't find a public. Even a cast including James Earl Jones and Cicely Tyson couldn't save *A Hand Is on the Gate* (9/21/66), "an assemblage of Negro poetry and folk song," from folding after twenty-one appearances, and *Trumpets of the Lord* (4/29/69), Vinnette Carroll's adaptation of James Weldon Johnson's *God's Trombones* as a series of hymns and sermons at a revival meeting, blew itself out after seven showings (650, 662). These shows' almost ethnomusicological replications of black life and music did not interest Broadway's largely white audiences, nor did their content have much relevance to contemporary blacks' struggle for equality.

Such musicals must have seemed quaint—or even offensive—to the talented black playwrights who emerged in the second half of the '60s, spearheading a vigorous renaissance in African American playwriting and production off-Broadway and elsewhere. By the mid-1960s, increasing numbers of blacks rejected the slow pace of integration as well as the tactic of civil disobedience for achieving their aims. In the summer of 1965, Watts was burning, in 1966, Chicago, in 1967, Newark and Detroit; and within minutes of the newsflash that Martin Luther King had been gunned down on April 4, 1968, "angry blacks were on the streets" from LA to DC, and by the end of the decade there were riots in over one hundred cities resulting in at least seventy-seven deaths (Leuchtenburg 154, 168; Marty 88). Black protest became much more militant, giving rise to black separatism, black nationalism, Black Power, Black Muslims, Black Panthers. Such anger—and racial pride—gave birth to a new breed of plays by black authors *for black audiences*. And as Allen Woll notes, "Black Broadway musicals, whether written by white or black authors, had always been designed for *white* audiences" (250; italics supplied). Hence, the very years that produced LeRoi Jones's (later Imamu Amiri Baraka's) *The Toilet* and *Dutchman* (1964) and *Slave Ship* (1969), Ed Bullins's *Clara's Old Man* (1965) and *The Electronic Nigger* (1968), Douglas Turner Ward's *Happy Ending* and *Day of Absence* (1965), and Lonne Elder III's *Ceremonies in Dark Old Men* (1965), failed to produce a viable black Broadway musical.

The one black-centered Broadway musical in the 1960s to address contemporary issues had experienced all-white writers, a racially mixed cast, and a so-so run of 293 performances. Given developments in the later '60s, its well-intentioned theme was rather out of touch. Written by Arthur Laurents, with music by Jule Styne and lyrics by Betty Comden and Adolph Green, *Hallelujah, Baby!* (4/26/67) traced American blacks' opportunities and status from the turn of the century to the Civil Rights period, mostly in the world of show business. This was fancifully depicted through the career of one Georgina, who appears in each decade but never seems to age. A tour de force for Leslie Uggams, the show gave her the chance to cut loose in some impressive musical numbers, but it also confirms Woll's assessment of black Broadway musicals. As a tuneful history lesson to bring whites up to speed about the Civil Rights movement, *Hallelujah, Baby!* gets an A for effort but failing marks for its incomprehension of the reality of black militancy in the later '60s.

## The Emergence of Jewish Musicals

Just when African American musicals were disappearing, Jewish-themed musicals flourished. From the opening night of *Milk and Honey* on October 10, 1961, through September 22, 1964, when *Fiddler on the Roof* premiered—less than three years—five such musicals opened on Broadway, four of them moderate to runaway hits.

Why the sudden emergence of Jewish-themed musicals? First of all, since the 1920s at least 90 percent of the book writers, lyricists, and composers of Broadway shows have been Jewish, many probably predisposed to write about Jews once such writing became acceptable. But the first two generations of Jewish writers of American musicals, mostly fresh off the boat or one generation removed from greenhorn parents, were more concerned with becoming Americans than displaying their Jewishness on Broadway and therefore wrote material appealing to mainstream, non-ethnic audiences. There was also a tacit assumption around Broadway that explicitly

Jewish musicals had no chance of commercial success. Hence, before World War II and for some time thereafter almost no Jewish characters and no specifically Jewish settings or themes appeared in musicals.

The immediate postwar environment was better, but not much better. Sheldon Harnick, lyricist of *Fiddler on the Roof*, the most successful of all Jewish musicals, says of his own generation of Jewish writers, "We had come through World War II and had a whole different attitude toward being Jewish than our parents. Before the war, even during it, my father would always tell me, 'Keep a low profile—fight for social justice, but keep a low profile' " (Harnick interview). But the time still wasn't ripe in the immediate postwar years. If Broadway had been uneasy about anti-Jewish sentiments earlier, that fear was exacerbated from the later 1940s to the mid-1950s by Truman's loyalty oath program, the McCarthy hearings, the Rosenbergs, and the HUAC blacklists. With the blacklists naming many Jewish personalities of Broadway as well as Hollywood, the last thing producers wanted to risk was an openly Jewish play or musical. And yet, in the decades after the war, most American Jews, firmly rooted as Americans, were more at ease expressing their ethnicity. And two postwar events underscored the American Jewish need to speak out: the horrific revelation of the Holocaust, and the founding of the State of Israel.

As the American public became more aware of the horrors of the Holocaust, public sympathy toward Jews both in America and worldwide increased. Further, after the war many American Jews moved from the inner cities to the hinterlands, where "the new Jewish suburbanites embraced the tolerant, cosmopolitan image of the suburbs" (Goren 295). The years between 1945 and the late 1950s saw the construction of some six hundred synagogues and temples, which "reflected their preeminent place in the suburban landscape as the accepted presence of a Jewish community" (295). On October 20, 1954, President Eisenhower himself was keynote speaker at a National Tercentenary Dinner at New York's Astor Hotel, launching the 300th anniversary of the first permanent Jewish settlement in America. There was extensive media coverage of the tercentenary, and celebratory events took place in no fewer than four hundred cities and towns. On November 17, the National Symphony played the commissioned *Ahavah Symphony* by David Diamond, along with concert works by Ernest Bloch and Leonard Bernstein (304). Feeling accepted as Americans, Jews could at last display pride in their ethnicity; indeed, they were encouraged to do so by the example of black civil rights activists (Fishman interview).

Hollywood, long the domain of Jewish studio moguls, had nonetheless steered clear of Jewish-themed movies, but that changed with *The Ten Commandments* in 1956. Released just eight years after the establishment of

Israel, the film was devoted to the Hebrews' flight from bondage to freedom, the receiving of the Torah, and their entrance into the Promised Land. Enormous numbers of Jewish viewers came to see the film, especially in major-market areas where it was shown, like other "big pictures," at a single theatre on a "two-a-day" reserved-seat basis. In Chicago, it played at my father's theatre, the McVicker's, where for several years its reserve-seat plan attracted unprecedented numbers of theatre parties from men's clubs, youth groups, and sisterhoods of Chicago-area temples and synagogues, Hadassah, B'nai B'rith, and other Jewish organizations. Protestant and Catholic group sales were also strong but not nearly so. Similarly, Leon Uris's *Exodus* became a best seller in 1958, and in 1960 the film version was a runaway hit, further bolstering positive (if romanticized) images of Jews. And on the New York stage in 1959 Paddy Chayefsky's warm, moving, yet hilarious *The Tenth Man* was a smash with critics and public alike. Set in a storefront Orthodox synagogue in Mineola, Long Island, the play depicts the attempted exorcism of a dybbuk from a young woman who in fact is schizophrenic. And shortly before *Milk and Honey* opened, the media coverage of Adolph Eichmann's arrest and trial exposed the Holocaust's atrocities more graphically than ever and further projected a positive image for American Jews (Sarna interview).

## Milk and Honey *and* Family Affair

The explosion of Jewish-themed Broadway musicals started with the foresight, risk-taking, and *chutzpah* of Broadway producer Gerard Oestreicher. With the number of new musicals declining since the 1950s (reaching a low of five in 1955–56), audiences were shrinking too, including the all-important Jewish sector. With Jews making up a significant segment of Broadway audiences, Oestreicher took a chance on a musical about American Jews in Israel. With a book by Don Appell and music and lyrics by Jerry Herman, *Milk and Honey* opened on October 10, 1961. Although the show lost money, its healthy run of 543 performances showed that Jewish musicals had a future on Broadway. With the first Jewish show a popular success, the next four constituted something of a bandwagon effect, with other producers eager to climb on board.

Though all five musicals touched on Jewish issues and themes, the differences among these shows far outweighed their similarities. The plot of *Milk and Honey* is conventional, almost generic, but its tone is unabashedly celebratory. The main story is a second-time-around love affair between two middle-aged Jewish Americans—Phil (Robert Weede), separated but not yet divorced, and widowed Ruth (Mimi Benzell). Phil meets Ruth while in

Israel visiting his daughter, Barbara, and son-in-law, David, a native-born Israeli, who live and work on a kibbutz. Ruth is visiting Israel as a tourist. Among her party of Jewish-American women is Clara Weiss, played by the former Yiddish theatre star Molly Picon. The show's dramatic tensions and complications remain either purely personal or intra-Jewish, not between Jews and non-Jews. Ruth hesitates about a relationship with a man who is still technically married, but in the end she decides that Phil is worth waiting for. Barbara is homesick for the United States but David won't give up the kibbutz for American middle-class conventionality "In my grey flannel suit, / In my new shiny car / In my split level house" (Herman, *Milk* 168). And Clara decides she's not betraying her deceased husband Hymie by agreeing to become the second Mrs. Sol Horowitz. Everything comes together plausibly and, for the most part, joyously, expressing both Israeli and Jewish-American pride in Israel—so much so that Herman's title song could almost serve as an unofficial Israeli national anthem. At the very least, it strongly appealed to American Zionism:

> This is the land of milk and honey.
> This is the land of sun and song and
> This is a world of good and plenty,
> Humble and proud and young and strong and
> This is the place where the hopes of the homeless
> And the dreams of the lost combine.
> This is the land that heaven blessed
> And this lovely land is mine.
>
> (64–65)

Although its cast was equally strong, A *Family Affair* (1/27/62) was far less successful than *Milk and Honey*. This musical farce with book and lyrics by James and William Goldman and music by John Kander was mainly a Broadway vehicle for stand-up comic Shelley Berman as the bride-to-be's guardian. The nice Jewish boy and girl who want to get married were *West Side Story*'s original Tony, Larry Kert, and *The Fantasticks*' original Luisa, Rita Gardner. The illustrious Morris Carnovsky and versatile Eileen Heckart played the boy's rather smothering parents. With such talent, the show should have had surefire audience appeal. But, as Bordman aptly puts it, the whole *Affair* was little more than "an extended Jewish joke" (625), with both families wrangling about when, where, and how the wedding should take place. The locale for all of this was Winnetka, Illinois, which couldn't have meant much to most Broadway audiences. I, however, appreciated the joke, since Winnetka is the upscale, heavily Jewish suburb next to Wilmette where I grew up on Chicago's North Shore—similar to many Westchester communities, which the writers may have avoided as a bit too close to home. But the characters were gratingly stereotypical, and the public broke off its engagement to *A Family Affair* after sixty-five showings.

## I Can Get It for You Wholesale

If *A Family Affair* failed in spite of name-recognition talent, with 300 performances *I Can Get It for You Wholesale* was a qualified success despite a lot going against it. Even before it opened, the show's producer David Merrick seemed doubtful that it would succeed. By 1962, Merrick was one of Broadway's shrewdest and most successful producers, and easily the greatest master of ballyhoo and hype since P. T. Barnum. But for *Wholesale* there was only perfunctory pre-opening advertising and press releases. Tickets for opening night were actually available that day, a rarity on Broadway, and certainly for a Merrick show. I grabbed one, as did several fellow theatre majors from Northwestern University visiting New York during spring break. As it happened, that evening of March 22, 1962, turned out to be more than an unheralded opening night; it became an event with a capital "E."

From our perch in the ethereal reaches of the Shubert Theatre's balcony, my friends and I had a clear if distant view of the stage and also of a good portion of the orchestra seats, many filled with luminaries of the American theatre. Conspicuous at the absolutely opposite ends of third or fourth row center were on the left, Leonard Bernstein, and on the right, Richard Rodgers. As this workmanlike—and, for its time, almost relentlessly dark—musical progressed, Rodgers politely but perfunctorily applauded each song, while Bernstein, arms folded across his chest, sat motionless in an attitude of "Okay, show me something"—until the middle of the second act. Then, in one of the show's few light moments, a secretary bemoans in song how her bosses and co-workers are on strictly formal terms with her while on a familiar first-name basis with each other. When the "Miss Marmelstein" number ended, Bernstein leapt to his feet and began clapping so wildly I feared for the person to his right. Following the maestro's cue, the entire audience rose to its feet for a prolonged ovation. What we had witnessed and what inspired Bernstein's enthusiasm was the Broadway debut of an unknown nineteen-year-old performer named Barbra Streisand. It was, as they say, worth the price of a ticket.

But generally speaking, theatregoers don't pay Broadway prices to watch a single performance of a single song in a musical's second act. Something else had to sustain *Wholesale*'s run of nearly a year. But what? There were no big stars. The leads were a mix of absolute or relative newcomers—

Streisand, Elliott Gould, Marilyn Cooper, and Ken Le Roy (*West Side Story*'s Bernardo) — with some stars of earlier days like Jack Kruschen, Harold Lang (the 1952 revival's *Pal Joey*), Sherree North, and, most prominent, Lillian Roth. None of these alone or in the aggregate would have been a surefire box-office draw. Even the writers, while prominent, were not at the time exactly household names. Jerome Weidman, co-author of *Fiorello!*, adapted *I Can Get It for You Wholesale* from his Depression-era novel of the same name. The music and lyrics were by Harold Rome, who had some fairly recent hits behind him (*Wish You Were Here, Fanny, Destry Rides Again*) but who was still no Richard Rodgers or Lerner and Loewe. About twenty-five years earlier, Rome had written the long-running pro-garment-union revue *Pins and Needles*. Now his *Wholesale* concerned corrupt, self-serving Garment District management.

Ironically, the show's strength may also have been its weakness. *Wholesale* was a thoroughly Jewish-centered musical, with a mostly Jewish cast as well. That alone may have appealed to some Jewish theatregoers. On the other hand, this was not a musical whose topic was Jewish mores, issues, or pride. *Wholesale* is a tough, ugly show set in the Depression. A callously aggressive young man named Harry Bogen (Gould) claws his way to the top of the garment industry. Victims of his self-serving rise to power include his kitchen-bound mother (Roth), his Bronx-bound sweetheart Ruthie (Cooper), and his very decent boss (Kruschen). By show's end, Bogen has slid into bankruptcy, having made enemies of everyone except his mother and Ruthie. *Wholesale* dramatized Harry's ruthless rise in the business world realistically. Just five months earlier, Frank Loesser & Co.'s *How To Succeed in Business without Really Trying* (10/14/61) treated J. Pierpont Finch's similar ascent up the corporate ladder with sweetness, humor, and very gentle satire. Audiences clearly preferred the comic approach; *How To Succeed* outran *Wholesale* by 1,116 performances. Still, something kept *Wholesale* going nearly a year.

The tone of *Wholesale* is tough, sardonic, cynical. The characters appear in an unflattering light; even "good" ones like Ruthie and Harry's mother are seen as naive and vulnerable. These are not flattering pictures of New York Jews in the Depression-era garment trade. Yet in the new climate of open, positive Jewish identity, Weidman and Rome clearly felt comfortable writing a show that de-romanticized its characters and gave them traits that could belong to any ethnic group. They just happened to be Jews navigating their way through the Jewish-dominated garment trade. For those who enjoyed *Wholesale*, this dispassionate portrayal of Jewish characters was a refreshing blast of reality. Those who stayed away weren't ready yet for such toughminded material in a musical.

## Funny Girl

The stuff of the next very successful Jewish-oriented show was biography. A genuine hit that played 1,348 times, *Funny Girl* (3/26/64) was in two respects something of a one-woman show, and therein lies much of its Jewishness. First, it was a musicalized biography of beloved Jewish comedienne Fanny Brice (née Fannie Borach)—whom many Broadway playgoers at the time would have remembered seeing on stage or, like myself, hearing as radio's "Baby Snooks." Second, it was a star vehicle for the very Jewish Barbra Streisand, who had achieved instant celebrity almost exactly two years earlier in *I Can Get It for You Wholesale.* Beyond that, explicit Jewish references in Isobel Lennart's story of Brice's rise to fame in the *Ziegfeld Follies* and her ill-fated love affair and marriage with gambler Nicky Arnstein are minimal, incidental, and mostly just for comic effect. These sporadic references appear in both Lennart's dialogue and Bob Merrill and Jule Styne's songs. The most extended is a musical joke in the midst of "Rat-Tat-Tat-Tat," a Ziegfeld production number saluting the doughboys of World War I. Brice appears in a comic specialty routine as "Private Schwartz from Rock-a-way," replete with stage-Yiddish dialect (Lennart 111–12). Otherwise, just a single reference to "chopped liver" and an occasional "Oy" or "Oy vey" comically punctuate Fanny's lyrics. Only one explicitly Jewish reference is genuinely funny because of the point it makes in its dramatic context. As she eyes with trepidation the red velvet chaise longue in a restaurant's private room where she and Nick are dining, the anxious and ingenuous Fanny sings, "What a beast to ruin such a pearl, / Would a convent take a Jewish girl?" (75). Other than these snippets, there's only the oblique observation in the "Henry Street" song that Fanny's Lower East Side neighborhood is heavily populated with C.P.A.'s, lawyers, and dentists, all traditionally, if stereotypically, Jewish professions (55–57). Still, an aura of Jewishness pervades the whole as the young Fanny moves away from her traditional Jewish roots toward cultural assimilation in the glittery world of show business.

## Fiddler on the Roof

These four Jewish musicals from the early 1960s marked the beginnings of a new Jewish consciousness in the United States. The fifth show, however, addressed issues of ongoing concern not to Jews alone but to Americans in general. *Fiddler on the Roof* (9/22/64) was so successful in crossing over to non-Jewish audiences that its 3,242 performances made it the first musical to break *Oklahoma!*'s longevity record.

*Fiddler on the Roof* treats three issues: the so-called "generation gap," prejudice and tolerance, and the survival of the Jewish community. These three themes are linked through the tale of Tevye and his daughters. In my courses on musical theatre, I not altogether facetiously remark that in certain essentials *King Lear* and *Fiddler on the Roof* are the same play: they're both about an old man whose daughters defy parental authority. How the plays differ in resolving that conflict defines their dramatic genre. Lear is tragic because he is rigidly unbending and, therefore, finally destroyed — inflexibility being a core feature of tragic figures. On the other hand (to use an apt phrase), Tevye learns to bend to most, though not all, of his daughters' challenges to his traditional Jewish beliefs, discovering in himself a flexibility that allows him to keep his children's love and still survive as a Jew in a changing world. Tevye's character is essentially comedic, and *Fiddler* is a comedy.

In the mid '60s, the subject of the struggle between generations was especially apropos. If earlier musicals dealt with it at all, they did so only casually and lightly, as in Rodgers and Hart's "Don't Tell Your Folks" from *Simple Simon* (2/18/30) or, more contemporaneously, Lee Adams and Charles Strouse's "Kids" in *Bye Bye Birdie* (4/14/60). *Fiddler*, however, made the generational conflict central to the plot and took it very seriously. Despite some lighter moments, such as Tevye concocting the cockamamie "dream" to help him squirm out of Tzeitel's marriage contract, the challenges to Papa by his three oldest girls raise serious questions about shifting family dynamics, and, through these, touch on issues of power, culture, and authority in a changing world. At the very time *Fiddler*'s Tzeitel, Hodel, and Chava were seeking to liberate themselves from convention by marrying whom they chose, America's youth were increasingly urging one another to "Question Authority" and "Never Trust Anyone over Thirty."

In adapting *Fiddler*'s book from Sholom Aleichem's stories, Joseph Stein exquisitely plotted the daughters' increasingly radical challenges to Tevye's parental authority. Tzeitel's challenge is least problematic. She and her beloved tailor Motel Kamzoil — a sweet guy, but dirt-poor and a bit of a schlemiel — ask Tevye's *permission* to marry, after Tzeitel was already promised to the butcher, Lazar Wolf. After an internal debate with himself, Tevye concedes, deciding his feelings for his daughter and hers for Motel are more important than the mere *customs* of matchmakers and marriage contracts.

Even before the socialist Perchik proposes to Hodel in modern Western fashion (Stein, *Fiddler* 75), this iconoclastic student radical causes a stir at Tzeitel's Orthodox wedding by asking Hodel to dance. (Men and women do not dance together in Orthodox tradition.) When Hodel willingly accepts, the rabbi himself admits, "it's not exactly forbidden" (67), and within moments Tevye gets Golde to dance and the rest of the wedding party follow suit. Later, Perchik and Hodel agree to marry without even asking Tevye's permission. They simply tell him they are engaged and ask only his *blessing*, thereby challenging both Jewish tradition and parental authority. Again Tevye's affection for Hodel and hers for Perchik win out over Tevye's distress at their "going over his head": "Love. It's a new style. On the other hand, our old ways were once new, weren't they? On the other hand, they decided without parents, without a matchmaker. On the other hand, did Adam and Eve have a matchmaker? Yes, they did. Then it seems these two have the same matchmaker" (79).

Thus far Tevye has been able to accommodate himself to the modern romantic notions and marital plans of his daughters, because neither has challenged beliefs central to Judaism. But when Tevye's third daughter, Chava, marries a non-Jewish Russian, the extent of her rebellion exceeds Tevye's tolerance, and he cuts her and her husband out of his life.

Rodgers and Hammerstein's musicals explored ramifications of prejudice and the importance of tolerance. *Fiddler*'s author Joseph Stein, lyricist Sheldon Harnick, and composer Jerry Bock raised infinitely more complex questions about these matters. Against the background of the tsarist regime's escalating persecution and evacuation of Russia's Jewish population, *Fiddler* depicts the complex webs of friendship and suspicion that bound Jews and non-Jews in a Russian shtetl in 1905. That peaceful if uneasy coexistence in Anatevka is displayed in "Tradition," when Tevye points out the village's Russian dignitaries crossing the stage: "His Honor the Constable, his Honor the Priest, and his Honor—many others. We don't bother them, and, so far, they don't bother us" (Stein, *Fiddler* 4–5). Relations between the Jewish and Russian villagers are still cordial. Russians heartily join with Jews to toast Tevye, Lazar Wolf, and Tzeitel's arranged marriage. Moments later, the Constable, apparently on close terms with Tevye, lets him know he's received orders for "a little unofficial demonstration" in Anatevka but adds, "Personally, I don't know why there has to be this trouble between people" (36), separating his own view of the Jewish community from the official position of the government he represents.

But Tevye can make no such separation. To him a Russian is a Russian, whether an officer of the repressive tsarist regime or simply a fellow villager who happens not to be a Jew. Well before Chava marries Fyedka, Tevye tries to warn her away from even befriending him: "Chava, I would be much happier if you would remain friends from a distance. You must not forget who you are and who that man is" (91). For Tevye the mere fact of

Fyedka's nationality is guilt by association with the Imperial Russian government. The Russian mistreatment of Jews made people like Tevye necessarily suspicious (and intolerant) of *all* gentile Russians, even decent men like Fyedka. *Fiddler* thus depicts how attitudes of intolerance and prejudice can cut both ways.

Yet when it comes to Chava *marrying* Fyedka, Tevye's objection is defensible in light of his unshakable Orthodox upbringing and beliefs. Here the issue isn't Fyedka's Russianness per se but his non-Jewishness. Tevye could bend for Tzeitel and Hodel, because all he was bending was custom. But this touches more than tradition. When Golde tells Tevye the village priest married Fyedka and Chava, Tevye replies straight from his Orthodox belief that a child married out of the faith is a child deceased: "Chava is dead to us! We will forget her." When Chava begs her father to accept her and her husband, for once Tevye stands firm in his internal debate: "Accept them? How can I accept them? Can I deny everything I believe in? On the other hand, can I deny my own child? On the other hand, how can I turn my back on my faith, on my people? If I try to bend that far, I will break. On the other hand . . . there is no other hand. No Chava. No—no—no!" (94–95).

During the Jews' forced evacuation from Anatevka in the musical's closing moments, Tevye seems to relax his stern view momentarily. Chava and Fyedka come to say goodbye and tell the family they are moving to Cracow because, in gentile Fyedka's words, "We cannot stay among people who can do such things to other people" (104). Tzeitel and Golde speak to Chava, while Tevye continues to pack silently. But then he turns to Tzeitel, *"prompting her under his breath as he turns to another box,"* and whispering, "God be with you!" which Tzeitel repeats to Chava, but the words are clearly Tevye's, an indirect expression of fatherly love if not acceptance or forgiveness. Chava's story links the musical's parent/child and prejudice/tolerance themes to its motif of the survival of the Jewish community, since every child who strays from the faith means not just one Jew less but potentially the loss of many more to be born to future generations.

*Fiddler* also examines what has allowed the Jewish people to survive so long, often under very adverse conditions. Tevye's initial explanation is simplistic, embodied in the single word that is the opening number's title—"Tradition." Like a fiddler playing on a rooftop, "Because of our traditions, we've kept our balance for many, many years" (1, 6). But through his dealings with his daughters, Tevye gradually comes to learn that survival in the modern world requires not just a belief in tradition. He finally sees that flexibility *plus* tradition has allowed the fiddler to balance on that roof for four-thousand-plus years.

During its extraordinary New York run and many national and international productions, *Fiddler* attracted countless Jews and non-Jews alike. Many of its non-Jewish viewers found *Fiddler's* Jewishness infectious. One very audible reason for this was Jerry Bock's score. As in *Fiorello!* Bock's technique of musical authenticity is evident throughout *Fiddler* in his evocative "Jewish" melodies for nearly every number. Not only that, but in "To Life" Bock used different musical styles and Jerome Robbins created ethnically different dances to characterize and distinguish between the Jews and the gentile Russians in the tavern scene. Further, while *Fiddler* depicted the hardships—and ultimate dispersal—of Anatevka's Jews, it warmly portrayed such religious rites and social rituals as the "Sabbath Prayer" and Tzeitel and Motel's marriage ceremony. The wedding, replete with *chupah* and the other trappings and observances of an Orthodox ceremony, conveyed strong theatrical images of Jewish solidarity and pride. When my non-Jewish fiancée and I saw the Chicago production starring Luther Adler, she remarked as we left the theatre, "This is the first time in my life I really wished I was Jewish." So charismatic was the show that in the late 1960s one gentile hippie acquaintance remarked that *Fiddler* hit him like "a Jewish happening." While *Fiddler* is the most *specifically* Jewish of the five Jewish musicals, it is not restrictively Jewish but touches a universal chord.

*Fiddler on the Roof* was the last major exclusively Jewish-themed musical. A few more would appear in the early 1970s and another much later in the century, but none was particularly successful, either commercially or critically. But from the late 1960s to the end of the century, Jewish themes arose in musicals that treated wider issues as well (*Cabaret, March of the Falsettos, Falsettoland, Grand Hotel, Ragtime, Parade*, etc.). Two conclusions can be drawn from these facts: that by the mid-1970s the taste for musicals purely on Jewish themes had declined, and that Jewish writers of musicals came to feel that the specifically Jewish-centered shows of the early '60s and '70s had served their purpose by putting Jewish issues before broad-based audiences, and that now it was time to link such issues to more general, non-ethnic concerns.

## The New Black Musical: Pride, Anger, and Broadway Success

After just three African American musicals opened—and quickly closed—during the entire 1960s, in the final month of the decade the black musical returned, regenerated and relevant. And with only an occasional hiatus thereafter, black shows continued to be a mainstay of both Broadway and off-Broadway theatre for the rest of the century. By the end of the 1960s, black writers, eschewing the separatist politics of black radical groups, began to take their cue from other minorities (hippies, Jews, the New Left), and — like them — began creating shows that would appeal to both black and white audiences. By the end of 1969, these new black shows started coming thick and fast — some of them genuine hits.

And some definitely not, including the first two attempts. Based on the play *Big Time Buck White*, the musical *Buck White* (12/2/69) had book, music, and lyrics by the talented Oscar Brown Jr. and starred the equally talented (though in a different arena) boxer Cassius Clay, a. k. a. Muhammad Ali. The show "described the turmoil that ensues when its militant Negro titular hero arrives to address the Beautiful Allelujah Days Society," but it "went down for the count of [sic] seven performances" (Bordman 666).

Ten nights later at Joe Papp's Public Theatre, Ron Steward and Neal Tate's *Sambo* (12/12/69) opened, billed as "a black opera with white spots" (Woll 255). *Sambo* portrayed alienated blacks in a white society through twisted fairy tale characters like Untogether Cinderella and Jack Horney (Bordman 670). Sambo himself was "variously a 'militant, drug addict, nationalist, spiritualist, entertainer, Son of Africa, child' " (Woll 255, quoting the *Village Voice*). The show played only thirty-seven times.

The racially mixed creative team that wrote *Purlie* (3/15/70) perfectly demonstrated the principle that if you've got something socially serious to say, one way to say it successfully is to soft-pedal the polemics, keep everything upbeat and hilarious, and couch it in a high-energy musical performed by an equally high-energy company. Headed by Cleavon Little and Melba Moore, *Purlie* played out a frontal attack on Southern redneck bigotry and a vindication of the human rights views of its title character, a "New-Fangled Preacher-Man." It was adapted from Ossie Davis's play *Purlie Victorious* by Davis himself, Philip Rose, and Peter Udell, with lyrics by Udell and music by Gary Geld — one black and three Jews, in that order. Davis was inspired to write his original non-musical comedy while stage managing the Broadway run of *The World of Sholom Aleichem*, hoping that his characters might become the African American "counterpart to Aleichem's Jewish characterizations" (Woll 256). The team that put together *Purlie* created some larger than life personalities who projected the show's progressive stance on human rights, none more so than the proactive man of the cloth, Purlie himself:

> AIN'T GONNA PROMISE NO CHARIOT RIDE,
> NO GLORIOUS LIFE ON THAT GREAT OTHER SIDE.
> I GOT A DIFF'RENT MESSAGE TO SPREAD.
> HOW 'BOUT SOME GLORY DAYS BEFORE WE ARE DEAD?
> (Davis 15)

In finding ways to bring blacks into Broadway audiences, *Purlie* was as proactive and dynamic as its title character. Philip Rose, the show's director and producer as well as co-author, hired as publicist Sylvester Leaks, the public relations director of the Bedford Stuyvesant Restoration Corporation, to generate group sales of African American theatre parties. Leaks, who had extensive contacts with church, fraternal, and social organizations, was so successful that his efforts not only helped *Purlie* extend its run to 688 performances but served as a model for other producers to increase black theatre attendance (Woll 257).

Unlike *Purlie*'s feel-good preaching, Melvin Van Peebles's *Ain't Supposed to Die a Natural Death* (10/20/71) took no prisoners, yet still surprised everyone by playing 325 times. Both white and black critics found what Van Peebles labeled his "Tunes from Blackness" a disturbing, unsettling experience, but they acknowledged the compelling artistry of Van Peebles's musical look at the grimmest aspects of black ghetto life (see NYTCR 1971 229–32; Woll 258–59). Venting pent-up feelings in song, the characters represented Harlem's underside: "the whore, the pimp, the corrupt black policeman, the beggar, the militant rifleman, the bag lady, and the homosexual queen" (Woll 258). Much of Van Peebles's success came from the honest authenticity of language, character, and situation. This integrity earmarks *Natural Death* as one of the new breed of black shows in the early '70s that addressed concerns of contemporary blacks without acknowledging the expectations of predominantly white audiences; "[i]nstead of writing shows for whites, authors of black musicals had to write for black viewers" (250). While that happened mostly off- and off-off-Broadway, Van Peebles proved a black show for primarily black spectators could have a life on Broadway as well. It did so in part by following *Purlie*'s lead in finding innovative ways to bring blacks into a Broadway theatre to fill seats left empty by the attrition of white viewers from an unflinching ghetto revue (see Woll 259–60).

*Don't Bother Me, I Can't Cope* (4/19/72) also depicted the difficulties of African American life but in a very different way. The tone of the revue prompted from critics adjectives like "friendly," "congenial," and "appealing," one critic actually calling the show a very upbeat "commercial for black dignity" (NYTCR 1972 304–306 *passim*). Its black creators, Vinnette Carroll, who conceived and directed *Don't Bother Me*, and Micki Grant, who wrote the words and music, set out to create a different kind of black theatre that could be appreciated by whites as well as blacks. In Ms. Grant's own words, "I believe there is room for all kinds of theatre; it doesn't have to be one or the other. There's room for angry black theatre and there's room for a show like ours, a show that has pride and dignity and music that is indigenous to our background. The show is *us*, and we hope we are

communicating to everyone. We are not doing the show to be *separate*"
(qtd. in Woll 261). Carroll and Grant succeeded in creating an "inclusive"
black revue; *Don't Bother Me* played an incredible 1,065 times. It also prefigured later black '70s musicals in giving anger a back seat to racial pride,
an approach that would characterize most African American shows for the
rest of the century. Even when Melvin Van Peebles returned to Broadway,
his earlier confrontational anger had mellowed into upbeat, off-the-wall humor in *Don't Play Us Cheap!* (5/16/72; 164 performances), a fantasy about
two bungling demi-devils who come to Harlem disguised as a rat and a
cockroach to break up a Saturday night party.

The last black musical of the early 1970s derived from a play that, almost
two decades before, proved seminal for future black drama. In 1959, Lorraine Hansberry paved the way not just for black playwrights to succeed on
mainstream Broadway but also for black *female* playwrights to attain success.
*A Raisin in the Sun* was then, and remains, one of the most richly compassionate and affirmative family dramas in the entire American (or even
English-language) repertory; in fact, it shares a number of plot points with
Clifford Odets's *Awake and Sing* and Sean O'Casey's *Juno and the Paycock*,
though it is much more life-affirming than either. In both the play and the
musical, a black family chases the American Dream, which after numerous
setbacks they finally achieve in the form of a home of their own. The
guiding spirit of the musical *Raisin* (10/18/73) was its producer, the late Ms.
Hansberry's former husband, Robert Nemiroff. The book was adapted by
him and Charlotte Zaltzberg, with lyrics and music by Robert Brittan and
Judd Woldin; all these white writers remained very faithful to Hansberry's
play. As producer, however, Nemiroff wisely put the musical's staging in
the very capable hands of black director/choreographer Donald McKayle.
The result of this interracial collaboration was a show that spoke both to
the black American experience and to the ideals and aspirations of all Americans regardless of color, so much so that *Raisin* played 847 times. After
*Raisin*, no more black musicals opened until January 1975, when *The Wiz*
began to "ease on down the road."

### Follow the Fiddler: The Broadway Wanderings
### of Jewish-American Musicals

About two years after *Fiddler on the Roof* opened and was an unmistakable
hit, a parade of Jewish musicals began to come and go on Broadway. These
shows are of more interest for their sociological implications than for their
content or merit. *Fiddler*'s popularity was due largely to its universal appeal

despite a very specifically Jewish story and issues. But after it opened, some producers apparently didn't grasp the connection between universality and popularity as they tried to ride the coattails of *Fiddler's* success with Jewish musicals that were anything *but* universal. These shows were too parochial even for the bulk of Jewish theatregoers, let alone anyone else, largely because most were performed, in whole or in part, in Yiddish and/or Hebrew. But they are of historical interest because writers wrote (or impresarios imported) these shows, and producers managed to raise money for their production, on the assumption that there was an audience for them.

First came *Let's Sing Yiddish* (11/9/66), a compilation of Yiddish folk songs and tales that ran for 107 performances. Next *Hello, Solly!* (4/4/67) appeared (I'm not making this up!), a Yiddish/English vaudeville, for just sixty-eight showings. After fourteen performances the producers withdrew *Sing Israel Sing* (5/11/67), an all-Yiddish book show about a kibbutz wedding, to translate it into English. It must have lost a lot in the translation, since the English version lasted just one week. An imported Israeli revue in Hebrew, Yiddish, and English rather pompously titled *The Grand Music Hall of Israel* (2/6/68) played sixty-four times before packing up to go home. Then *The Megillah of Itzik Manger* (10/9/68), an Israeli import in Yiddish and English, reset the story of Esther in a European shtetl seventy-eight times.

*The Grand Music Hall of Israel* returned as *The New Music Hall of Israel* (10/2/69), still in Hebrew, Yiddish, and English, and played four more performances than the first time. All in Yiddish except for a sometimes English-speaking narrator was the book musical *Light, Lively, and Yiddish* (10/27/70), running for eighty-eight performances, and, hard on its heels, *The President's Daughter* (11/3/70), a book show in Yiddish and English, for seventy-two showings.

Three Israeli imports showed up over the next couple of years. *To Live Another Summer, To Pass Another Winter* (10/21/71) was an all-Israeli revue performed entirely in English, no doubt helping to account for its 173 performances. Also in English, and with a similar run of 144 outings, was *Only Fools Are Sad* (11/22/71). Then the entertainment unit of the Israeli Army invaded Broadway with a Hebrew-language revue called *From Israel with Love* (10/2/72); it retreated after eight shows.

After October 1972, such narrowly focused Jewish-American shows disappeared for nearly ten years, to return only sporadically until their extinction in the mid-1990s. The most likely explanation for their diminishing returns, so to speak, is that producers looked at the generally abysmal track records of their predecessors and recognized that audiences for such shows, especially those in Yiddish, were literally dying out.

Two shows in the 1980s defied in different ways the general failure of

Jewish-American musicals by embracing a universality the other shows lacked. *Vagabond Stars* (5/29/82), a retrospective of Yiddish theatre songs and scenes *entirely in English*, had a book by Nahma Sandrow, lyrics by Alan Poul, and music—both new and adapted from Yiddish theatre originals—by Raphael Crystal. Like the other plays in the Jewish Repertory Theatre's six-play season, *Vagabond Stars* had a limited run of only twenty performances, but its all-English accessibility has let the show continue to live in the regions. Even more accessible was Sandrow and Crystal's next collaboration, this time with lyrics by Richard Enquist—an English adaptation of Avrom Goldfadn's Yiddish theatre piece *The Fanatic or the Two Kuni-Lemls*, now called simply *Kuni-Leml or the Mismatch*. Once again, the Jewish Repertory gave birth to this hilarious musical farce, which looks and sounds as if Gilbert and Sullivan could have written it if they were Jewish and lived a little farther east. Opening on June 9, 1984, *Kuni-Leml's* thirty performances at the Jewish Rep just whetted audience appetites for it, so on October 9 the show was moved to the Audrey Wood Theatre, where it played a strong off-Broadway run of 289 performances, winning the Outer Critics Circle Award for best off-Broadway musical of 1984–85, with Sandrow, Crystal, and Enquist taking the individual honors for best off-Broadway book, music, and lyrics.

From the mid-'80s to mid-'90s, bilingual shows came back for one last stand. A Yiddish-English revue redundantly titled *L'Chaim to Life* (11/5/86) was interesting for including some Yiddish-Latin numbers from the large Jewish community in Buenos Aires; the show's own lifespan was just forty-two outings. By comparison, *Those Were the Days* (11/7/90), another English-Yiddish revue, did all right by itself, playing 130 times. Openly trading on nostalgia, *Finkel's Follies* (12/15/91) is the most historically interesting of this subset of ethnic musicals. Long-time Yiddish-American actor, entertainer, and bandleader Fyvush Finkel conceived of the revue. The program forthrightly gave it the subtitle "An American Musical Vaudeville, sketches and songs reminiscent of the Yiddish vaudeville shows from the 1920s to mid-century" (*Best Plays* 91–92 344). Elliot Finkel and Phillip Namanworth's original musical numbers sought to capture the flavor of Yiddish musical theatre for those spectators old enough to recall it. *Finkel's Follies* also included (seemingly *in* Yiddish from their titles in the program) a generous sprinkling of the genuine article, including such classics of the repertoire as Goldfadn's "Rozinkes Mit Mandlen" (Raisins and Almonds) and Abe Schwartz's startling ballad of sweatshop protest "Di Greene Kuzeene" (My Greenhorn Cousin). Despite an extraordinary number of previews to get the show right, Finkel and friends lasted only sixty-five performances, corroborating the decline of Yiddish theatre and the Yiddish-speaking audience.

### The Mainstream Jewish Musical Returns — and Fades Away

While *Fiddler* continued playing until July 2, 1972, there were no new mainstream Jewish-centered musicals between its 1964 opening and 1970, when *The Rothschilds* appeared, ushering in another three-year spurt of general-audience Jewish shows on Broadway. In fact, with one lone exception over a decade later, these four shows were the last gasp for specifically Jewish-themed musicals in the century. The first two met with some success; the second two never should have happened.

In 1970, *Fiddler*'s Sheldon Harnick and Jerry Bock teamed up with author Sherman Yellen to adapt Frederic Morton's book into *The Rothschilds* (10/19/70). While they didn't come close to reaching *Fiddler*'s success, they did create an entertaining and moving musical account of a Jewish family's rise to fabulous wealth and power. From Mayer Rothschild's humble beginnings as a rare coin peddler in the Frankfurt ghetto to his five sons' virtually ruling Europe's banking life in the early nineteenth century, *The Rothschilds* depicts what it took for European Jews to make it in the face of covert and — often enough — overt anti-Semitism. *The Rothschilds* conveyed its theme purely theatrically, leaving audiences to draw whatever inferences they chose to about contemporary issues (see Green 303). The show overcame decidedly mixed reviews (see NYTCR 1970 181, 184–86) to survive for 507 performances.

Technically, Noah and his family pre-date the specifically Jewish personages later in the Old Testament, suggesting perhaps that composer Richard Rodgers, lyricist Martin Charnin, and author Peter Stone's Noah's ark musical *Two by Two* (11/10/70) is not a Jewish-themed show at all. But its source was Clifford Odets's *The Flowering Peach*, and Odets's depiction of Mr. and Mrs. Noah and their brood renders them just a more comic version of his Jewish Berger clan in the 1930s Bronx of *Awake and Sing*. In the musical, the family dynamic among Noah, his wife, and their three sons and daughters-in-law mostly plays like a Jewish-American family drama or, at some points, sitcom. And the show's primary theme of what it takes for survival is decidedly a Jewish one. According to *Two by Two*, it takes faith, fortitude, flexibility, ingenuity, tolerance, and — this being a Richard Rodgers musical, after all — a whole lot of love. Despite (or, some suggest, because of) Danny Kaye's cavorting as Noah, the ark sank after 351 performances.

Still, *Two by Two* was more seaworthy than *Ari* (1/15/71). Leon Uris's own rewrite of *Exodus* with music by the virtually unknown Walt Smith capsized after nineteen performances. Finally, *Molly* (11/1/73) unashamedly tried to capitalize on nostalgia. Based on Gertrude Berg's popular radio, then television, show "The Goldbergs," the musical starred Kaye Ballard as the archetypal Jewish mother, but she couldn't capture Mrs. Berg's charisma, and *Molly* folded after sixty-eight performances. This failure effectively ended Broadway's efforts to produce specifically Jewish-centered musicals, with one notable exception.

## Rags

In the mid-1980s, three men with excellent musical theatre credentials came together to write a completely original Jewish-centered musical. *Fiddler on the Roof's* author Joseph Stein wrote the book; Stephen Schwartz, composer/lyricist of such shows as *Godspell* and *Pippin,* contributed the lyrics; and Charles Strouse, composer of *Bye Bye Birdie* and *Annie,* among others, wrote the score. The result of what has continued to be their ongoing collaboration was *Rags* (8/21/86), a show that lasted only four performances on Broadway, but with major rewriting and reworking opened off-off-Broadway at the American Jewish Theatre on November 2, 1991, for fifty-nine performances. Subsequently, after still more revisions by Stein, Schwartz, and Strouse, *Rags* met with both critical and audience approval at such professional regional venues as Florida's Coconut Grove Playhouse in 1999 and New Jersey's Papermill Playhouse and Philadelphia's Walnut Street Theatre, both in 2000. Furthermore, Charlie Scatamacchia, the Manager of Professional Licensing at the Rodgers and Hammerstein Organization, confirms that since acquiring *Rags* in 1992 they licensed it for about 200 productions around the country through the end of 2000. Some were professional productions but most were community theatre, college, and other non-professional presentations. That its writers have continued to invest their time and talents to perfecting *Rags* for fifteen-plus years; that major regional professional companies have continued to invest their human and financial resources to produce it; and, most especially, that since 1992 there have been numerous non-professional productions across the United States indicates that *Rags* continues to speak to diverse and widespread audiences.

While the book for *Rags* is entirely of his own invention, Joseph Stein admits it came in part from constantly "being badgered to do a follow-up on *Fiddler*" (Stein interview). While *Rags* doesn't literally follow Tevye's family to Ellis Island and beyond, it does present a kaleidoscopic and unsentimental view of what Jewish immigrants faced and what kinds of lives they made for themselves in America just after the turn of the century.

The setting of *Rags* is historical—New York's Lower East Side, circa

1910. Its primary story is that of Rebecca Hershkowitz, an Eastern European woman whose husband Nathan came to New York six years earlier. When *Rags* opens, Rebecca has emigrated with her son, David, wanting to begin a new life in the United States with her husband. When Nathan fails to meet her at Ellis Island, she gets through immigration by a ruse of Bella's, a young woman Rebecca met on the crossing. Bella's father Avram dupes the officials by posing as Rebecca's uncle. Later he finds her lodgings on Suffolk Street on the Lower East Side. Soon she is working at Bronstein's Sweatshop, where her American Jewish employer exploits both Jewish and non-Jewish immigrant workers. Here Rebecca meets Saul, a less recent immigrant and now a union organizer. They form a strong friendship and, in some versions of *Rags*, fall in love too. But mostly Saul raises Rebecca's social consciousness; by the end of the show (1993 version), she's involved in leading a worker's protest.

Rebecca's estranged husband finally shows up, but vigorously denying his Jewish heritage. No longer Nathan Hershkowitz, he is now Nat Harris, an aspiring politician in tight with Tammany Hall, cozying up to politico Big Tim Sullivan in an effort to become ward boss of the heavily Jewish Fourth Ward. In the Boston tryout of *Rags* Harris/Hershkowitz went so far as to virtually offer Rebecca to Sullivan as a trophy in exchange for the political prize; but this ugly yet powerful moment was toned down or excised altogether in later revisions. In attempting to exploit his own family, the original Nathan "was nastier, more negative, and less rounded a character" than in the later rewrites (Stein interview). Still, throughout each version of *Rags*, Nathan remains unpleasant enough that Rebecca leaves him by her own choosing and is on her way to a more satisfying relationship with Saul as the final curtain falls.

Stein intentionally wrote the stories of its four principal male characters to dramatize the options open to Jewish immigrants to make it (or not) in America (Stein interview). At the most extreme is "Nat Harris," totally denying his heritage in order to get in with the powers that be and become a "real American." Then there's Ben, in love with Bella, whom her father calls "a Jewish boy without a hat" (I-3-13). Yes, Ben is a secular Jew and therefore anathema to Avram, but he is still a Jew and he never denies his cultural identity. Ben is a self-starting, incipient entrepreneur who goes from peddling a newfangled thing called a gramophone on street corners to finally moving to Philadelphia, opening his own phonograph store with money borrowed from his boss. In this, Ben personifies the positive spirit of immigrant-Yankee-Jewish ingenuity and free enterprise. Saul, the union man, expresses freely his liberal-left politics and works for social betterment. As for Avram, he starts life in the United States as a Lower East Side peddler with a pushcart and ends up . . . a Lower East Side peddler with a pushcart. He is the inflexibly traditional immigrant Jew too terrified by American society to change. Stein says he meant Avram to personify the man whose parochial behavior and convictions limit him to "remaining an Old World Jew" (Stein interview). The problems and options faced by the characters in *Rags* can be applied to all immigrants, which may help account for the show's continuing viability nationwide.

## *Black Comes Back—and Stays for Keeps*

When black shows returned to Broadway in 1975 after a three-year absence, their writers—both black and white—looked as if they had taken the time off to rethink their approach. With few exceptions these musicals abandoned protest in favor of pride in black heritage, culture, and music regardless of their creators' color. Most, though not all, of this new breed of revues and book musicals took a sharp turn toward feel-good entertainment and an equally sharp one away from strong statements of social significance.

As a happy deconstruction of *The Wizard of Oz* to a Motown beat, *The Wiz* (1/5/75) with its 1,672 performances was a hit of blockbuster proportions that inspired other entertainments in the same upbeat vein. The show had a large, all-black cast and the mostly black creative team of composer-lyricist Charlie Smalls, book writer William F. Brown (the lone white), choreographer George Faison, and that man-about-theatre Geoffrey Holder both directing and designing the costumes. More than any other show at the time, *The Wiz* proved black musicals could still (or once again) be popular on Broadway.

To Allen Woll, the new-style black show, starting with *The Wiz*, was retreating from "the 'problem' shows of the early 1970s" and advancing in a different direction altogether (265). Instead of addressing issues like racism, segregation, and discrimination, as did the early '70s black musicals, the new black shows stressed black culture, black history, and black heritage, especially musical heritage. Pride and joy replaced anger and confrontation. And the creators of these shows dug deep for their inspiration and material; "Historical figures and eras that had been neglected or ignored now became the source for post-Bicentennial black musicals . . ." (266).

Woll's remark is an especially accurate description of the proliferation of black revues, even more than black book shows. These revues looked back at the music of a particular black composer, the career of black entertainers, or the musical or dance styles of various periods. In this respect, these shows are similar to the "retro revues" of the '80s and '90s discussed in chapter 9, revues that deliberately capitalized on America's mass nostalgia at the time. But the black revues are different: the impetus for them came mostly from a desire to express black pride and heritage, not trade on potential audiences' nostalgia. Indeed, the content of many of the black revues would have been unfamiliar to or beyond the historical memory of most white *and* black viewers, and, hence, not much of a trigger for nostalgic feelings at all.

Still, Woll does not consider the fact that many retro revues of black music were conceived not by blacks out of racial pride but by whites who most likely had positive feelings about black culture but who also sought commercial success through the draw of black music and dance from earlier periods. Motivations aside, the result was a renaissance of black musicals surpassing even the decades between the two world wars.

The next black musical to appear after *The Wiz* expressed pride in black heritage *and* in America's musical heritage irrespective of color. Its limited engagement was proof that its motive was not to be a long-term commercial moneymaker. Its origins were with the forward-looking Houston Grand Opera, and with Guther Schuller, one of this country's great conductors, composers, arrangers, and advocates of music by and for Americans. In this case, Schuller reconstructed the lost orchestrations for the Houston Grand Opera's mounting of *Treemonisha* (10/21/75), the black-cast ragtime opera its composer, Scott Joplin, didn't live to see through production. Now it finally came to life in all its musical, scenic, and choreographic splendor for sixty-four performances. Then, just one night later, a solo performer (with accompaniment) also dug deep into black musical heritage, when Linda Hopkins sang the songs and told the gutwrenching story of Bessie Smith in *Me and Bessie* (10/22/75), and she kept doing so 453 times—a labor of love turned long-running triumph.

On the other hand, some black shows were strictly commercial ventures, such as two all-black revivals of previously white musicals. *Hello, Dolly!* (11/6/75) with Pearl Bailey in the title role had a disappointing run of fifty-one performances. Maybe Broadway had just "Dollyed" itself out by 1975. The second attempt in this dubious subgenre of allegedly moneymaking gimmicks was an all-black *Guys and Dolls* (7/22/76), directed and choreographed by the gifted Billy Wilson. Even though none of the cast had the immediate name recognition of Ms. Bailey, it fared much better than *Dolly*, playing 287 times.

*Bubbling Brown Sugar* (3/2/76) was the first of many black retro revues, and it was a hit. It was also devised by African American artists. Rosetta LeNoire conceived and directed the show; Loften Mitchell wrote the book. Songwriters for "black entertainment on Broadway and in Harlem from the turn of the century through the 1940s" wrote the songs, since the show was an "historical tour" through the times of "Bert Williams, Billie Holiday, Duke Ellington and others from the heyday of Harlem night life" (Woll 266). Clearly people wanted to hear these songs, since they kept coming to hear them 766 times. When Mitchell came under fire from other blacks for retreating from the social relevance of the earlier 1970s into escapist entertainment, he countered, "I would hope that this play would cause a rethinking in terms of the black community. I would hope that it would have some kind of contagious effect, a chain reaction that would make folks say, 'look a here, we ain't all that poor. We may be broke, but we're not poor' " (qtd. in Woll 267). It is probably no coincidence that this very positive backward look at black American popular culture opened when America was celebrating its Bicentennial, and it was definitely no accident that the next black-cast show was deliberately timed to be part of that celebration.

On September 25, 1976, the Houston Grand Opera returned to Manhattan with another event of major proportions. It was a kind of belated gift to New York (by some forty-one years), just as earlier that year the production in Houston had been the company's on-time contribution to the nation's Bicentennial—the first virtually complete mounting of *Porgy and Bess*. For the first time (including its 1935 premiere), New York heard George Gershwin's score almost intact and in order; the extended opening, for example, was restored, and "The Buzzard Song" put back in its proper place (Bordman 689). The opera was given an exceptional staging, as dramatically riveting as it was thrillingly sung, in settings fully capturing the milieu of the piece (as I saw when it toured to Boston). As with earlier productions, this *Porgy and Bess* provided a rare and needed opportunity for black opera singers. Houston stayed in New York for 122 performances and mounted a national tour.

*Your Arms Too Short to Box with God* (12/22/76) proved its popularity not only in its initial run of 439 performances, but by returning in revival for several months in 1980 and again in 1982. "Revival" is especially apt here, for what the black team of Vinnette Carroll, Micki Grant, and Alex Bradford created was the Gospel according to St. Matthew retold through gospel singing at a black Pentecostal revival meeting. The show was pumped up with high-octane energy that engendered a whole lot of infectious foot stomping and hand clapping on stage and in the house (it was impossible not to join in, as I discovered).

For all the talent behind it and all the visual splendor of its ultimate presentation, I have to conclude from seeing the unfortunate results for myself that the next black-cast musical must finally be considered misguided. The idea was to uproot Robert Wright and George Forrest's lush and lovely 1953 *Kismet* from its exotic twelfth-century setting of Arabian Nights Baghdad and transplant it to the equally exotic setting of the new show's title, fourteenth-century *Timbuktu* (3/1/78). The masterminds of this geographical, cultural, and racial metamorphosis were *Kismet*'s white author Luther Davis and the multitalented black Geoffrey Holder, who had been responsible for much of the success of *The Wiz*. While Davis tinkered with the book some for its new setting and racially different characters, equally Caucasian Wright and Forrest's lyrics, arguably some of the most elegant verse in an American musical, remained unaltered. Occasional music based on African drumming and dance rhythms was added for some of *Timbuktu*'s impressive choreographic sequences, but Russian composer Alexandr Borodin's music, which Wright and Forrest had used in the 1953 original, remained unchanged. The result was a cacophonous clash of cultures that made the whole affair look and sound a bit silly. The British *Black Mikado* had successfully transformed Sir Arthur Sullivan's score into contemporary jazz, soul, reggae, calypso, gospel, and other black musical idioms. Had this production done something similar, though in a more serious vein — to, say, "Africanize" the richly Middle Eastern strains of Borodin's music — perhaps the result would have been more aesthetically consistent. But while Tony Straiges's sets and Holder's costumes were gorgeous to behold, even the talents of Eartha Kitt, Melba Moore, and Gilbert Price couldn't overcome the show's problems for more than 221 performances.

In 1978, two black revues opened on Broadway that both celebrated the African American musical heritage and cashed in on black and white audience appreciation of that music for commercial success. Both *Ain't Misbehavin* (5/9/78), the revue of songs Fats Waller wrote or made famous, and *Eubie!* (9/20/78), celebrating the music of Eubie Blake, were conceived and directed by Caucasians, the former by Richard Maltby Jr. (with an assist in the conception by Murray Horwitz), the latter by Julianne Boyd. Both Maltby and Boyd, however, had the theatrical savvy to bring black talent on board their creative teams, in addition to the all-black casts of the shows. Maltby signed on Arthur Faria to choreograph and Luther Henderson to orchestrate *Ain't Misbehavin'*, while Boyd brought in two black choreographers, Billy Wilson for general dance and musical staging, and Henry Le Tang, arguably the guru of American tap choreography, for the tap dance sequences. *Ain't Misbehavin'* seemingly wouldn't quit, with a run of 1,604 performances. While *Eubie!* didn't come close to that, it still played 439 times.

At the end of the 1970s, two black book shows were obvious attempts to capitalize on the success of *The Wiz* by adapting other children's classics into fanciful black theatrical contexts, and both were disastrous failures. *But Never Jam Today* (7/21/79) sported a book by the gifted Vinnette Carroll and Bob Larimer, music by Larimer and Bert Keyes, and lyrics by Larimer solo. But after just eight performances this musicalization of Lewis Carroll's Alice books popped back down the rabbit hole. Peter Udell and Philip Rose, a couple of white guys who liked to write shows for black performers, tried to follow their hit *Purlie* with *Comin' Uptown* (12/20/79). They didn't succeed. Udell and Rose wrote the book, Garry Sherman the music, and Udell the lyrics, but not even Gregory Hines as their slumlord Scrooge kept this Harlem-revisionist rendering of Dickens's A *Christmas Carol* from joining the Ghost of Failures Past after forty-five performances.

Between the openings of these two Broadway flops, a little black heritage revue opened off-Broadway and just wouldn't go away till it toted up 1,372 performances. In recreating black New Orleans vaudeville of the 1920s, New Orleans import *One Mo' Time* (10/22/79) entertained modern audiences by celebrating black entertainment of the distant past, not by trying to create nostalgic feelings for that past.

*Black Broadway* (5/4/80), on the other hand, was literally nostalgia and pride in black heritage all at once, not just because of the songs but because of who sang them. Along with such current black talent as Nell Carter, Honi Coles, Gregory Hines, and Bobby Short singing numbers from the early days of black musicals, this concert revue brought back some stars of those shows to recreate their own shining moments: John W. Bubbles, the original Sportin' Life in *Porgy and Bess*, sang "It Ain't Necessarily So," now from his wheelchair; Edith Wilson recreated her 1921 debut at Town Hall in *Put and Take*; Elizabeth Welch brought back the "Charleston" she had originated in *Runnin' Wild*; and Adelaide Hall flew in from London to perform once again her hit with Bill Robinson in *Blackbirds of 1928*, "I Can't Give You Anything but Love" (Woll 272). As nostalgia *and* black pride, this show was the genuine article. Even with a limited engagement of twenty-five performances, *Black Broadway* — by focusing on the roots and genesis of black American music — became a model for many more African American revues in the '80s and '90s.

One hit black retro almost never got to New York, nearly expiring in its Washington tryout for lack of effective theatricality but then expertly and swiftly resuscitated at the eleventh hour by a seemingly unlikely theatrical paramedic. Although it was the creation of black choreographer Donald McKayle, at its inception the Duke Ellington retrospective *Sophisticated Ladies* (3/1/81) was not specifically a dance-centered revue. It was lugging around a book (rewritten over time by several hands) linking an enormous quantity of musical numbers, which were also part of the problem. The show "had to adapt orchestral and choral music as well as popular song for the stage," which, according to "unanimous pans in Washington," McKayle and Co. had failed to do (Woll 272). Enter, of all people, Michael Smuin, co-director of the San Francisco Ballet, whose objective distance solved the show's problems. Smuin threw out the cumbersome book, found ways to harmonize the disparate dancing styles of Broadway's Gregory Hines and Alvin Ailey's Judith Jameson, and worked closely with McKayle and tap choreography genius Henry Le Tang to hone and refocus their contributions already in place in the revue. In short, finding no implicit theatricality in Ellington's music, Smuin made dance the theatrically visual center of the show that tied everything together. Thanks to him, *Sophisticated Ladies* didn't have to sneak out of Washington after dark, and in New York it hit the ground dancing 767 times.

After these retros celebrating black music and culture that were created wholly or in part by African Americans, some black-oriented book shows by all white writers arrived on Broadway in the early 1980s. *Dreamgirls* (12/20/81) contained African American themes, was played by a huge, almost entirely black cast, yet once again was the product of an all-white creative team. It had a book and lyrics by Tom Eyen, music by Henry Krieger, and, most notably, striking staging and choreography by Michael Bennett. The musical celebrated that brand of black music called Motown at the same time that it depicted the cutthroat world of the Motown music industry in the '60s and '70s. This, as the plot of *Dreamgirls* amply illustrated, was a world where not only whites exploited blacks but black producers and promoters exploited black singers until they were exhausted, only to cast them aside for new talent. Still, for audiences struck by its visual and musical aspects, the show was mostly pure entertainment for 1,521 performances plus a national tour, affording long-run employment for numerous African American singer-dancers.

*The Tap Dance Kid* (12/21/83) was a mostly black musical with music by *Dreamgirls'* composer Henry Krieger and book and lyrics by Charles Blackwell and Robert Lorick. Its popular appeal came, largely and deservedly, from the dance sequences (mostly tap, naturally) that kept it on the boards for 669 performances. But the show was more than dance; using a simple story and rather more complex characters, it made some points about stereotyping, and not just racial stereotyping. The title character is a gifted preteen African American boy who has the chance to become a professional tap dancer at that young age. He and his slightly older, overweight, and very studious sister are the children of a yuppified black attorney and his similarly professional wife. Having achieved a place in the legal profession, the father objects to his son's aspirations on the grounds of racial stereotyping and virtual backsliding; he barely lets the kid eat watermelon. But even as the lawyer-father is too touchy about his son becoming a stereotype, he exposes a bias of his own. A single line of dialogue so powerfully drove home this point that the audience audibly gasped the night I saw the show. Once when his bright but chubby daughter had her nose in one of daddy's law books, the father said to her words to the effect of "Why do you have to be studying all the time? Can't you just grow up to be thin and pretty like your mother?" At the very time the attorney was trying to keep his son from becoming a "darky entertainer" stereotype, he revealed his own stereotypical view of what women should be.

Without flash, glitz, or glitter, the tiniest off-Broadway show proved black could still be beautiful, even if the show's content was unfamiliar to all but the most theatrically savvy spectators. Vincent D. Smith's *Williams and Walker* (3/9/86) brought the two pioneering black entertainers Bert Williams and George Walker fictionally back together in Williams's dressing room on the monumental night of June 10, 1910, when, as a headliner in Ziegfeld's *Follies of 1910*, Williams became the first black to cross the color bar in an otherwise all-white Broadway revue. (Historically, Walker had left their duo act in February 1909 after exhibiting signs of a degenerative disease that progressed until his death in 1911.) Pioneering was at the heart of Williams and Walker's careers both as a team and individually (see chapter 1). They were among the first to create and star in all-black musicals intended for a primarily white Broadway audience, also taking some real risks with the tone and content of their productions. While the centerpiece of Smith's creation was songs and sketches written or made famous by this remarkable black team, the little two-man show also contained its share of social history and commentary. For one thing, it reminded modern audiences that, to the end of his career, Bert Williams always "blacked up" in minstrel tradition. The press greeted *Williams and Walker* with near unanimous raves, but it ran only seventy-seven times at the American Place Theatre, most likely because of that venue's tight, repertory-like scheduling.

Long after the days when protest musicals—successful or not—proliferated both on and off-Broadway (see chapter 7), a very special kind of black protest show showed up in New York and became a total triumph. *Serafina!* (10/25/87) was a South African musical originally produced at Johannesburg's famed and controversial Market Theatre. In it, a company of black South African students (real ones!) from the Morris Isaacson High School put on a show praising the efforts of rebel leader Nelson Mandela of the African National Congress. Written by Mbongeni Ngema—much of it not even in English—with music by him and Hugh Masakela, *Serafina!*'s blend of high-powered social statements and young, energetic performers was enough for American audiences to welcome this foreign entry to Broadway 597 times after an initial eighty-one appearances at Lincoln Center.

*Black and Blue* (1/26/89) showed that large-scale black heritage revues could still make it big. This "Celebration of American jazz and blues" (*Best Plays 88–89* 402) featured black music and dance in the context of the black American experience. It had an enormous cast but few with any real star drawing-power save for singer Linda Hopkins and the rising young dancing talent Savion Glover. *Black and Blue* was created by Claudio Segovia and Hector Orezzoli, the two Argentinians earlier responsible for *Tango Argentino* (10/9/85), a revue of authentic tango dancing that came to Broadway via Buenos Aires and Paris. Conceived in Paris, *Black and Blue* authentically replicated the moods and modes of black music and dance and lasted for 824 performances — four times longer than *Tango*.

Another import, this one from London, celebrated the music of black bandleader, saxophonist, and tunesmith Louis Jordan (1908–1975). The revue's musical and physical verve kept Clarke Peters's *Five Guys Named Moe* (4/8/92) populated for 445 showings. In this retro of tunes Jordan made or made famous, five high-energy guys (all named Moe, of course) sang, danced, and instrumentally blared out Jordan's special brand of pop.

*Jelly's Last Jam* (4/26/92) was a book musical celebrating the music of an earlier black American while exploring the denial of one's racial and ethnic heritage, the rejection of persons of that same background, or the use of them for one's own ends. The title character was jazz innovator Jelly Roll Morton, and the denial issue was inseparable from black playwright/director George C. Wolfe and white lyricist Susan Birkenhead's telling of his story. New Orleans–born Ferdinand Joseph La Menthe adopted his stepfather's last name, Morton, when his biological parents broke up. His ancestry was Creole, which posed an ambiguity Jelly Roll took advantage of when denying his lineage. In the parlance of the Gulf Coast, a Creole is either "a white person descended from the early French and sometimes Spanish settlers" or, quite differently, "a person of mixed French and Negro or Spanish and Negro descent" (*Webster's Third* 534). Young, very light-skinned Ferdinand must have known his mother and father "were apparently descended from free colored Creole families long settled in Louisiana" (Leonard 541), but he refused to accept that ancestry. Even before becoming a celebrated jazzman, "Growing up in the polyglot culture of New Orleans, Ferdinand acquired a deep sense of Creole exclusiveness and an antipathy toward darker-skinned Negroes" (541). Accordingly, throughout his life Morton chose the purely European definition of his lineage rather than admitting his mixed-racial descent. As he vividly tells a reporter in the musical, "N'awlins born n' bred. But ya see what most folks don't understand is that my ancestors came directly from the shores of France. No coon stock in this Creole" (Wolfe 54).

Inauthenticity and its consequences inform most of Wolfe's imaginative musical biography of the gifted though self-denying and arrogant Jelly Roll, who in 1902 had the audacity to declare he "invented jazz"—a declaration the musical uses to good effect (Leonard 542). The show paints Jelly as a kind of racial/ethnic thief, denying his roots yet stealing the features of the black music with which he grew up to create his own brand of jazz. In a word, Jelly Roll purloined the substance while rejecting the source. At the very start, the Chimney Man, the show's otherworldly guide, judge, and raconteur, describes Jelly as "he who drinks from the vine of syncopation / But denies the black soil from which / this rhythm was born" (Wolfe 4).

Wolfe's treatment of Jelly's rise and fall dramatizes how his denial of racial heritage "was to influence his personal relationships and his evaluation of fellow musicians" (Leonard 541). For example, late in the show he is just about at the bottom, needs all the help he can get, and still has the gall to say to his former friend and partner, "Jack the Bear," "Jack, when are you gonna learn the only thing a nigga can do for me is scrub my steps n' shine my shoes" (Wolfe 91). The musical brings to mind the Faust legend, the Chimney Man playing a more heavenly Mephistopheles to Jelly Roll's Faust. Only at the eleventh hour, in a song called "Creole Boy," does Morton recant his past rejection of his heritage: "I WAS WRONG / . . . INSIDE EVERY NOTE OF HIS / IS WHAT HE CAME FROM . . . WHO HE IS" (97). Jelly's contrition lets him enter the halls of glory in death with the likes of Armstrong, Ellington, and Basie. Wolfe's challenging story and unconventional staging, plus a score of mostly Morton's own music with some additions by Luther Henderson, kept *Jelly's* on a roll 569 times.

The off-Broadway *Faith Journey* (7/21/94) was a tribute to the Christian social activism of Martin Luther King Jr., without the Reverend King ever appearing as a character. It had a book by Clarence Cuthberston, music by George Broderick, and lyrics by the two of them. Between them they created a musical play that in the words of *Best Plays of 1994–1995* attempted to portray "Evangelical influences on social progress in the era of Martin Luther King," with King's life during the crucial years of 1955 to 1964 as background. Given its perhaps rather narrow audience appeal as a musical essay on ethical and socially active Christianity, *Faith Journey* achieved a modest run of 193 performances.

Four years almost to the day after *Jelly's Last Jam* opened, George C. Wolfe came back for an even bigger triumph that would also prove to be the last black Broadway musical in the twentieth century. In November 1984 Savion Glover had just turned eleven when he took over the title role in *The Tap Dance Kid*—the boy whose father thinks tapping is demeaning to their race. In an almost ironic triumph of talent, artistry, and racial pride over such a view of tap, in 1996—and still only twenty-two years of age—Glover fulfilled "the kid's" dream by becoming just about the hottest dancing star on Broadway as both featured dancer and choreographer of *Bring in 'Da Noise Bring in 'Da Funk* (4/25/96), Wolfe's inventive history of African Americans *portrayed largely through tap*. Supporting the dancing was the music of Daryl Waters, Zane Mark, and Ann Duquesnay, who also sang the numbers, some narrative by Reg E. Gaines enacted by Jeffrey Wright to give the proceedings some verbal continuity and clarity, and the decidedly non-verbal but explosively effective pots-and-pans percussion of street drummers Jared Crawford and Raymond King. But mostly the show was dance, dance, dance, and yet more spectacular, high-energy dance by Glover and his four tapping compatriots, as they unfolded the odyssey of American blacks from the slave ships to the Civil Rights movement and beyond. Most often it was dance that dramatized, dance that made a statement. Dance showed how plantation slaves conspired to keep dance rhythms alive after 1739, when the use of drums became a criminal offense. In the "Uncle Huck-a-Buck" routine, dance humorously, satirically, and mercilessly took out after Shirley Temple's frequent film tap partner, Bill "Bojangles" Robinson, and other blacks who also did the Uncle Tom number to keep Hollywood whites happy (*NYTCR* 1996 223). Again as in *Jelly's Last Jam*, Wolfe had no problem publicly going after those of his own racial heritage who, in his estimation, sold out. And obviously neither Wolfe nor Glover saw tap dancing as negatively stereotypical of that heritage. Instead, tap's varied and virtuosic displays in *Bring in 'Da Noise* became an emblem of racial pride and a source of entertainment 1,130 times.

Two more black heritage revues appeared before the century was over, but neither on Broadway. The main ingredients of the first were not just musical nostalgia but humor and irony, perhaps even satire, rare things in retro revues of any kind. Starting with its pseudo-academic title, *A Brief History of White Music* (11/19/96) was a revue whose tongue was firmly planted in cheek. It had a cast of three with a band the same size and played off-Broadway at The Village Gate; its intermissionless performances crammed in over two dozen songs from bebop to the Beatles. The show's slightly snide appeal was ingenious. All the songs had their inspiration if not actual roots in the black genres of soul, rhythm and blues, and the like, but all had been written and originally performed by whites from the late days of swing to the heyday of rock and roll—the revue ending with half a dozen Beatles hits. The trio of African Americans performing the songs infused them with the authentic black hipness their vanilla pudding/white-bread creators and singers never quite pulled off. While the show paid tribute to whites trying to write and perform essentially black music it also was "gently ribbing white pop music of the 1940s to 1970s" (*Best Plays* 96–97 275). This unique combination of white pop and black humor sparked a run of 308 performances.

The twentieth century's last black musical was a whole lot more than what its title announced. From "Odun De" to "Let the Good Times Roll," *It Ain't Nothin' but the Blues* (4/26/99) featured not just blues but music ranging from indigenous African songs and chants to the compositions of black writers for Tin Pan Alley — much of it up-tempo, feel-good song, and not a bit bluesy at all. In this musical chronology, projections of scenes and images from black American history placed the songs in their proper societal contexts. And it worked — 276 times at Lincoln Center's Vivian Beaumont Theatre. As of this writing, no new black book shows or revues have opened in the early years of the twenty-first century. But with their consistently strong showing since the late 1970s, it seems likely that they will continue to be an appealing as well as meaningful voice both off- and on Broadway.

# ✱ 7 ✱

# Issue-Driven Musicals of the Turbulent Years

## *The Seeds of the Sixties*

By the late twentieth century, "The Sixties" no longer demarcated 1960 through 1969 but instead came to refer to a period in U.S. history marked by social and political unrest. For our purposes, The Sixties ran roughly from 1964 to 1972, but the seeds of rebellion among the young had been planted earlier. According to Miller and Nowak, it began in '50s suburbia, where "alienation was common. It is not surprising that middle-class suburban kids of the fifties formed the counterculture of the sixties" (137).

The counterculture got its bearings in the early 1960s. Students for a Democratic Society (SDS) sprang from an older socialist group in 1960. Tom Hayden drafted the *Port Huron Statement* (the manifesto of the New Left) and presented it to the 1962 SDS convention. The scope of the *Port Huron Statement* and, hence, the New Left's agenda, was very broad, but at its core lay a cry for "moral politics, reflecting an ethical rather than historical perspective," and for "participatory democracy" (Morgan 94, 95). But it was still early days in the forming of '60s radicalism, and both the manifesto and New Left remained virtually unknown except to a few campus radicals (Matusow 311, 312).

Other signs of unrest endemic to the later '60s were equally invisible to most Americans in the early '60s. Urban black riots didn't gain much national attention until Watts in 1965, and while hippies (not to be confused with the more politicized New Left) had been around for some time, the world's first Human Be-In at San Francisco's Golden Gate Park on January 14, 1967, introduced them to the American public (Matusow 275).

U.S. representation in Vietnam comprised only 11,000 "military and technical personnel" at the end of 1962. The "war in Vietnam" was several years off; well into 1964, the only protest came from relatively few "pacifist, religious, civil rights, and disarmament groups, . . . [with only] sprinklings of opposition evident on university campuses" (Marty 29). The fate of E. Y.

"Yip" Harburg's *The Happiest Girl in the World* (4/3/61) suggests most other Americans weren't paying much attention yet to our presence in Vietnam. *Happiest Girl* was a loose, fanciful, and very funny rendering of that most ancient of anti-war comedies, *Lysistrata*. Harburg and his co-librettists Fred Saidy and Henry Myers fiddled a lot with the play but still transferred to the musical Aristophanes' core premise entirely intact: *Happiest Girl*, like *Lysistrata*, is an anti-war play, albeit a comic one in which the women of Athens go on a sex strike until their men stop fighting. Harburg chose the music of long-deceased French composer Jacques Offenbach for his musical, since Offenbach's music sounds as risqué as Aristophanes' play and many of Yip's own often racy lyrics. Given the nation's general inattention to the incipient war in Vietnam, *Happiest Girl* was premature, playing only ninety-six times.

## Social Protest and Social Change in the Later '60s

On October 1, 1964, Mario Savio's Free Speech Movement accused the University of California, Berkeley, of violating First Amendment rights by denying students access to a space previously allowed for fundraising and political gatherings. Disturbances at Berkeley flared intermittently through January 1965, inspiring campus demonstrations nationwide. On March 24, 1965, University of Michigan students and faculty jointly sponsored the first "teach-in" to discuss war-related issues. Soon, about fifty other colleges and universities were holding similar discussions, including daylong "moratoriums" in which teachers and students focused on matters of war and peace in lieu of regular classes (Marty 29). On April 17, 1965, the first national protest against the war in Vietnam drew some 15,000 people to the Washington Monument. In the next few years, the numbers at such protests would grow to six figures, sometimes more.

Meanwhile, the Women's Movement was gathering steam. In 1963, feminists helped steer through Congress the Equal Pay Act assuring that "women must receive pay equal to that of men when they perform comparable work—the first federal legislation in American history to prohibit discrimination based on sex" (Marty 17). With that as a precedent, the Civil Rights Act of 1964 "forbade discrimination in employment on the basis of sex" (Leuchtenburg, *Feast* 194). In this same period, and especially after Watts in 1965, riots among urban blacks escalated in number, casualties, and destructiveness.

All these groups — college students, women, blacks — got some help from a seemingly surprising source, President Lyndon B. Johnson, who "determined to outdo Roosevelt as a liberal law giver" (Leuchtenburg, *Feast* 136). Egged on by the tireless efforts of LBJ, the Eighty-Ninth Congress passed the Higher Education Facilities Act to fund construction of college buildings and graduate centers, mass transit appropriations, the cornerstone legislation of Johnson's pet "war on poverty" program, and, as a "memorial to Kennedy, civil rights legislation" (139, 136). LBJ-inspired social legislation continued with the Civil Rights Act of 1964 and the Economic Opportunity Act of 1964, which instituted Head Start, the Job Corps, VISTA, and the Neighborhood Youth Corps. Poverty was the target of the Public Works and Economic Development Act and the Appalachian Regional Development Act. Enacted in 1965 were Medicare for the elderly and Medicaid for the indigent, the Elementary and Secondary Education Act providing grants for low-income school children, and, later that year, the Higher Education Act giving similar assistance to college students. These were followed by the Voting Rights Act, the Housing and Urban Development (HUD) Act of 1965, and more (194, 138, 139, 152; Marty 46). This progressive legislation all had been spurred on by the visionary idealism and activism of the president. If this had been his only legacy, unblemished by his 1965 order for bombing raids in North Vietnam and the protests that order engendered, posterity's estimation of LBJ purely as a leader working for domestic social change might have been very different indeed.

## Issue-Driven Musicals in the '60s and '70s: A Definition

An "issue-driven musical" is not just one whose authors began with a theme, issue, or polemical point of view instead of with a story and characters. "Issue-driven" also describes any musical in which a social or political agenda shares center stage with plot and is absolutely inseparable from the story (or, in a revue, its songs and sketches). If things were quiet in the early 1960s, by the time *Man of La Mancha* opened in 1965 the discontent of America's youth and (mostly urban) blacks was much more visible to mainstream America. From the New Left to the hippies, Freedom Riders to urban rioters, Women's Rights advocates to Vietnam protesters, the nation was both energized and challenged by voices of dissent seeking to change government, public institutions, and social reality. Throughout this period, several important issue-driven musicals elaborated upon those troubled and exciting times.

## Man of La Mancha

Two years to the day separated the assassination of John F. Kennedy on November 22, 1963, and the opening of *Man of La Mancha* on November 22, 1965. That the musical spoke to the visionary idealism of both JFK and his successor, LBJ, is purely a coincidence, since Dale Wasserman wrote the non-musical play *I, Don Quixote* in 1959. Virtually all of the musical's dialogue came from that play, with only such cuts as necessary "to make room for the songs" by Joe Darion and Mitch Leigh (Wasserman interview). While Wasserman maintains that he did not deliberately remake the show to reflect the "improve the world" activism of the mid-'60s, he does admit, "If I shaped it that way, it came out of a genuine feeling" (Wasserman interview). In writing both the play and the musical, Wasserman was more intrigued by the life of the lonely idealist Miguel de Cervantes than by his fictional alter ego, the lone knight Don Quixote de la Mancha. This fascination with both the author and his "mad knight" in part accounts for the two stories in the show running parallel: Cervantes in prison awaiting trial by the Inquisition, and the tale of Don Quixote and Sancho Panza as enacted by Cervantes and the other prisoners.

Wasserman's interest in the man as well as his book also helps account for why a few academically minded critics excoriated *La Mancha* as unfaithful to *Don Quixote*. Absent, they argued, was not only much of the satire but also the dark, brooding, even pessimistic tone of the novel's second part. But this was never Wasserman's intention. He confesses that when he first read *Don Quixote* in 1959, his interest was more in Cervantes than Quixote: "What sort of man was this—soldier, playwright, actor, tax-collector and frequent jailbird—who could suffer unceasing failure and yet in his declining years produce the staggering testament which is *Don Quixote?* To catch him at the nadir of his career, to persuade him toward self-revelation which might imply something of significance concerning the human spirit—*there*, perhaps, was a play worth writing" (Wasserman vii). If, then, *Man of La Mancha* expresses the courage to imagine and work for a better world, that was no misreading of *Don Quixote* by Wasserman but rather a thoughtful interpretation of the life of its author. The cavils of some critics aside, this very human tale told in an innovatively staged musical gave theatrical life to *Man of La Mancha* 2,328 times.

Wasserman's Don Quixote is a man who finds more solace in make-believe than reality yet at the same time crusades for impossible causes. Through Quixote, the play brings together the counterculture's visionary desire for escape (sometimes through drugs) and the increasingly militant

New Left's visionary agenda for change. The counterculture "attracted idealistic rebels and rebellious idealists, . . . [who had] a paradoxical desire to
change society while also escaping from it. . . . [They] saw things they
thought were wrong with society and created new communities as a way to
change them . . ." (Marty 70, 71, 125). Together, Wasserman's Cervantes and
Don Quixote come across as theatrical personae of these visions of escape
and social transformation.

Wasserman proclaims the musical's advocacy of illusion as "the most
meaningful function of [man's] imagination" (ix). His "illusion" is positive,
even though of late the word has taken on a pejorative connotation nearly
synonymous with the negative "delusion." But Wasserman is not espousing
belief based on false hopes; rather, he sees the need for such visionary
idealism. Guiding his project, he says, was a quotation from Unamuno:
"Only he who attempts the absurd is capable of achieving the impossible"
(ix).

While the musical is realistic enough to point out some of idealism's
pitfalls, *La Mancha* advocates strongly on its behalf from the moment Cervantes and his manservant are thrust into a dungeon full of cutthroats,
prostitutes, and highwaymen. These convicts routinely conduct not-so-mock
trials of new prisoners, aiming for a guilty verdict to justify pilfering their
possessions. The "senior" inmate known as the Governor puts Cervantes
through this ritual, with the Duke, a cynical, rock-bound realist, as prose-
cutor. It comes out that the Inquisition will try Cervantes in his capacity as
a tax collector for acting on his idealistic belief that the "law says treat
everyone equally" and so making "an assessment against the monastery of
La Merced." Or, as his pithy sidekick puts it, "He foreclosed on a church"
(9). That's enough for the Duke to summarize the case against Cervantes:
"I charge you with being an idealist, a bad poet, and an honest man. How
plead you?" To which Cervantes replies, "An idealist? Well, I have never
had the courage to believe in nothing" (9, 10), and he then offers as his
defense the story of Alonso Quijana, country squire, a.k.a. Don Quixote de
la Mancha, knight errant. Soon he is acting out his mad knight's adventures
with the aid of the other inmates, willingly or not.

Don Quixote's "illusion" is not so much that of an alternative reality
(though he does see and do battle with a giant where only a windmill
stands); his is an active, present-tense idealism, the "illusion" of the idealist
who believes he can "sally forth into the world to right all wrongs" (11). As
the play-within-the-play progresses, Cervantes assigns to the cynical Duke
the role of Dr. Carrasco, an unimaginative man of science with a private
agenda for bringing the lunatic "knight" to his senses — Carrasco is engaged
to Quijana's niece, and the old man's escapades as Quixote are a public

embarrassment. Wasserman defines the two men's different takes on the world in very few words. Carrasco: "There are no giants. No kings under enchantment. No chivalry. No knights. . . . These are *facts*." Quixote: "Facts are the enemy of truth" (40, 41). To the Don, like all idealistic thinkers before and since, there is a moral and spiritual reality more true than any factual reality. Then later, in the "real world" of the dungeon, the Duke and Cervantes, as themselves, not fictional characters, thrash this out: "A man must come to terms with life as it is!" To which Cervantes replies, "maddest of all, [is] to see life as it is and not as it should be" (60–61). No passive dreamer, Quixote actively pursues his idealistic goals; he is, as the show's most famous song declares, "willing to march into hell for a heavenly cause!" (49). According to Wasserman, the song touched a chord: "Student protest groups picked it up as a kind of anthem. From time to time on the evening news you'd see them at a protest, demonstration (even a riot), spontaneously bursting into 'The Impossible Dream' " (Wasserman interview).

Expressing *La Mancha*'s balanced view of idealism, the Padre takes a centrist stance somewhere between the extremes of the Duke/Carrasco's cynicism and Cervantes/Quixote's unshakable belief. In "To Each His Dulcinea," the Padre's lyrics express Wasserman's own view in the preface that a person needs something to believe in yet must also remain grounded in reality so as not to lose touch with it entirely.

Along with ennobling effects, the visionary outlook of idealism can have negative and damaging ones as well. The interior play focuses on Quixote's adventures at an unsavory inn, among its inhabitants the prostitute Aldonza. But where there's an inn, Quixote sees a castle; where there's a whore, he sees the virginal lady Dulcinea, whom he worships from afar in true chivalric fashion. Her more earthy philosophy is, "Cross my palm with a coin and I'll willingly show you the rest" (66). Initially, Quixote's descriptions of a better life actually demoralize Aldonza: "You have shown me the sky, but what good is the sky / To a creature who'll never do better than crawl?" (67). Yet, very slowly, Aldonza comes to embrace the Don's vision of trying to "reach the unreachable star" (49). For Dale Wasserman, that solitary transformation makes Don Quixote a successful idealist: "I believe that if an idealist makes but one convert—like Quixote with Aldonza—he will have done much" (Wasserman interview).

Aldonza's transformation dramatizes the reciprocal and redemptive effects of idealism. With his spiritual stuffing knocked out of him by Carrasco disguised as the Knight of the Mirrors, Alonso Quijana lies in bed dying. Aldonza, at last grasping the Don's notion of a higher reality, forces her way into his room and slowly re-instills in him his vision of her as Dulcinea, his mission of the Quest, and ultimately his idealistic Impossible Dream.

Thanks to what he had given her, she is able to give back, "allowing him to die in a state of transcendence," his belief system intact (Wasserman interview).

Similarly, from the moment Cervantes enters the prison he is portrayed as a coward in the face of both the Inquisition and the more immediate threats of the prisoners. Through his own act of telling the tale of the idealistic Quixote, Cervantes gains new courage to face the Inquisitors when he is led off at the end. (Historically, Cervantes did not burn: he was excommunicated.) The prisoners too, joining one by one the reprise of "The Impossible Dream," express renewed courage to face whatever lies ahead for each of them—all, that is, save one. Albert Marre's brilliant stroke of staging (not in any published stage directions) kept the still unconvinced Duke silent, arms folded, standing at the edge of the action as he watched Cervantes exit. No matter how redemptive visionary idealism may be, to think everyone can be won over to it would be naive. Had the Duke joined the song, the finale would have resonated with false, forced sentimentalism; keeping him out makes the ending more plausible and realistic. Still, if according to Wasserman the measure of an idealist's success is making "but one convert," his stage Cervantes must be given high marks for converting all *but one* of the prisoners.

## Cabaret

For every Don Quixote in contemporary America, there were numerous people determined to maintain the status quo. Nowhere was this more apparent than in resistance to the Civil Rights movement. In the South, white supremacist groups, aided or ignored by state and local authorities, roadblocked civil rights efforts in education, public access, and voting rights. The often brutal and violent opposition to civil rights activists both black and white impelled director Harold Prince to transform some stories of life in Berlin around 1930 into a cautionary tale for the United States in the 1960s. Those stories were Christopher Isherwood's *The Berlin Stories*, and together with the play based on them, John van Druten's *I Am a Camera*, they comprise the sources for *Cabaret* (11/20/66).

Hal Prince, a politically minded director, confessed that "It was only after we'd come by a reason for telling the story parallel to contemporary problems in our country, that the project interested me" (qtd. in Ilson 137). Prince and his collaborators—author Joe Masteroff, composer John Kander, and lyricist Fred Ebb—came to see their sources as "a parable of the 1950s told in Berlin, 1924 [sic]. To us, at least, it was a play about civil rights, the problem of blacks in America, about how it can happen here. . . . What attracted the authors and me was the parallel between the spiritual bank-ruptcy of Germany in the 1920s and our country in the 1960s" (Prince 68, 125). Initially, Prince was tempted to draw his parallels *too* vividly: "I went so far in one draft of the show to end it with film of the march on Selma and the Little Rock riots, but that was a godawful idea, and I came to my senses" (126). Essentially *Cabaret* is the story of two love affairs — one be-tween Cliff Bradshaw, an American writer, and Sally Bowles, an English nightclub singer, the other between two older people, Herr Schultz, a Jewish-German fruit dealer, and Fraulein Schneider, a non-Jewish German boarding house owner. Without ever leaving Germany, and largely through the two love stories, *Cabaret* powerfully drives home its parallels between the Nazi agenda and racism in the contemporary United States. This mu-sical wake-up call to Americans about "how it can happen here" illustrates well how an issue-driven musical can still be successful for its entertainment value thanks to a co-equal merger of story and theme.

As "a parable," *Cabaret*'s method is to express itself through analogies, parallels, and metaphors, not direct statement. The most explicit allusion was Joe Masteroff's changing the club where Sally Bowles sings from Ish-erwood's The Lady Windermere to the Kit Kat Klub. As Masteroff tells it, it was entirely unintentional that the club's initials were those of the Ku Klux Klan: "It never occurred to me. But then, who knows, it might have been unconscious" (Masteroff interview). He realized what he'd done only after spectators remarked on the chilling effect of the seeming coincidence.

The parallels to '60s America are numerous but subtle. After Prince scrapped the film-clip idea, set designer Boris Aronson came up with a huge tilted mirror reflecting the audience that "cast an additional, uneasy meta-phor over the evening" (Prince 133). When audiences entered the theatre they saw . . . themselves, hugely, somewhat grotesquely, reflected in that gi-ant mirror. When the mirror returned at the end, they were to left stare at themselves again. The message was both "It can happen here" and it *will* happen here unless we keep our eyes open, or, as Cliff says in the show, "if you're not against all this, you're for it — or you might as well be" (Mas-teroff, *Cabaret* 1967: 95).

Alongside *Cabaret*'s plot depicting two unhappy love affairs, the show exposes the racism inherent in fascism, as well as its propaganda techniques. Throughout the musical, the grotesque deterioration of the androgynous, almost unearthly Emcee of the Kit Kat Klub is emblematic of the crumbling Weimar Republic and its descent into decadence and then Nazism in the 1930s. Near the top of act 2, the creepy Emcee performs the cabaret number

"If You Could See Her through My Eyes" with a dancing gorilla — *"really rather attractive — as gorillas go"* — extolling her talents and charms. Like nearly all of the Emcee's numbers, this one ironically and sardonically references events in the "real life" scenes, in this case Fraulein Schneider's second thoughts about marrying the Jewish Herr Schultz. The song's final lines are "But if you could see her through my eyes, / She wouldn't look Jewish at all!" (92, 93). According to composer John Kander, "The song was to end that way, to have you laughing and then catch your breath, to make you the audience realize how easily you could fall into a trap of prejudice" (qtd. in Ilson 148). But it backfired. Many viewers were offended, including large, potentially lucrative Jewish theatre parties. As Kander explains, "Jewish members of the audience, my family included, all insisted that the song was really saying that Jews looked like gorillas" (148). Lyricist Fred Ebb had to change the last line to refer to an earlier song: "She isn't a meeskite [ugly person] at all!" (Masteroff, *Cabaret* 1967: 93).

"Tomorrow Belongs To Me," with its unforgettably beautiful melody, was used similarly but much more successfully. It is first sung by the Kit Kat Klub waiters, *"handsome, well-scrubbed, idealistic,"* standing impassively on a spiral staircase — the song envisioning an idyllic, idealized future. During Schneider and Schultz's engagement party ending act 1, the reprise of the number is begun by the prostitute Fraulein Kost, then by Herr Ernst, who for the first time displays his swastika armband; other neighbors join in, clearly in sympathy with the sentiments for the "Fatherland." With the reprise strategically placed at the end of the act, spectators leave for intermission humming the infectiously haunting tune until they stop dead (as *I* did) with the horrific realization, "My God, I'm humming a Nazi anthem." By directly working on the audience, *Cabaret* showed how easy it is to succumb to propaganda.

The attitudes of the four main characters in the "real world" of *Cabaret* range from awareness of the Nazi threat to utter denial. Cliff Bradshaw, the American, is most aware. He follows the news, observes the degenerating signs of the times, even reads *Mein Kampf* to get some grasp of Hitler's mind and the precepts of Nazism. Cliff is also enjoying vibrant yet decadent Berlin and his love affair with Sally. Only when he is beaten senseless by a couple of Nazi thugs does Cliff open his eyes. His awakening is shown in a metaphor that neatly connects the two acts of *Cabaret*. In act 1, totally caught up with Sally, Cliff sings "Why Should I Wake Up?" describing the lovely dream he's in. But by act 2, he is wide awake, and, counterpointing his first-act song, he fairly screams at his metaphorically sleepwalking lover, "Sally — wake up! The party in Berlin is *over!* It was lots of fun, but it's over.

And what is Berlin doing *now?* Vomiting in the street" (Masteroff, *Cabaret*
1967: 100). Cliff may awaken in act 2, but though he can see, he is unable
to act, except to return to the United States, which he does—alone.

Like Cliff's, Fraulein Schneider's eyes are open, but what she sees makes
her choose pragmatic, emotionally empty survival over a loving relationship.
About sixty, she is still "Fraulein" (never has been "Frau"), when Herr
Schultz, in his fifties, proposes to her; the promise of marital happiness
seems very real to both. But when pro-Nazi, anti-Semitic sentiments surface
among their neighbors, Schneider makes the practical choice. Fearing she
will lose her boarding house if she marries a Jew, she breaks off the engagement, remaining alone.

Sally Bowles is an ostrich—period. This young English wannabe singer
whose talent lies somewhere between slim and none has a philosophy of
life best summed up as "whoopee!" Or, as she puts it, "Life is a cabaret,
old chum" (105). She has no interest in politics and can't begin to fathom
what the Nazi takeover of Germany has to do with her. She has no sense
of responsibility or connection to anything that doesn't nurture her narcissistic hedonism; without consulting Cliff, she trades her fur coat for the
abortion of their child. When Cliff returns to the States, Sally returns to
singing in the now thoroughly decadent Kit Kat Klub, as clueless at play's
end as she was at the start.

Finally, there is Herr Schultz—pathetic, benighted Schultz, representative of countless German Jews at the time who could not foresee the danger
they were in (Masteroff interview). Schultz's blindness is that of ignorance
and denial, not, like Sally's, of avoidance. Upon leaving Schneider's boarding house, this sweet Jewish man speaks the play's most heartbreaking lines,
"[I]t will pass—I promise you! ... I *know* I am right! Because I understand
the Germans. ... After all, what am I? A German" (108). Through these
four characters in the "real life" action, *Cabaret* vividly dramatizes the importance of maintaining social and political awareness.

*Cabaret* presented its cautionary message through historical analogies
and parallels, some as covert as the innuendos of propaganda and hate
mongering that the show was trying to expose and counter. At the same
time, the musical was eminently entertaining, starting with its strong book
and lyrics and John Kander's score, which authentically captured the musical styles and decadence of 1930s Germany. It also featured the electrifying
performances of Joel Gray's Emcee, Lotte Lenya's Schneider, and Jack Gil-
ford's Schultz (Joe Masteroff himself admits that Cliff and Sally were less
strongly written and never quite came off as played by Bert Convy and Jill
Haworth). The result of subtly conveyed message in powerhouse entertainment was 1,165 performances.

Conversely, a few shows in the later '6os really clobbered the audience with relevance and found their potential customers shying away from the blows. These musicals were in the vanguard of the (dubious) "in-your face" issue-oriented shows that proliferated in the early '70s, shows in which entertainment value generally took a distant back seat to hammering the issues home. Two such failed efforts appeared even as *Cabaret* continued to run. *Now Is the Time for All Good Men* (9/26/67) had a book and lyrics by Gretchen Cryer and music by Nancy Ford, two women who would go on to far better things. It lasted only 112 performances at the small off-Broadway Theatre De Lys. The show's theme was the "mushrooming protest against the Vietnam War" (Bordman 655), based on the actual experience of Cryer's brother, "who had served two years in prison as a conscientious objector." The plot concerned "a pacifist English instructor [who] gets into trouble in a small Indiana town by teaching Thoreau's concept of civil disobedience" (Green 357). When the community learns he had been jailed as an army deserter, he loses his job, his girlfriend, and nearly his life before being run out of town.

The reference point for *Red, White, and Maddox* (1/16/69) was Lester Maddox, who wielded an ax handle to keep blacks out of his Georgia restaurant prior to later becoming that state's governor. Although the show had had a successful run in Atlanta, neither Maddox's notoriety nor the musical's questionable quality were enough to sustain it beyond forty-one showings in Manhattan. Written by newcomers Don Tucker and Jay Broad, with music and lyrics by Tucker, the show took Ax-man and his bigotry "on to the presidency of the United States and allowed him to virtually destroy the nation" (Bordman 661–62). The show hammered at the same frightening effects of white supremacy that *Cabaret* had communicated through subtle analogy and clever parallels.


### Celebration

Tom Jones and Harvey Schmidt's *Celebration* (1/22/69; 109 performances) was more cryptic than polemical. Jones took upon himself the task of creating a myth that *Celebration* dramatized but never explicitly elucidated. According to Jones, *Celebration* (in spirit like *The Fantasticks*) was about birth, growth, death, and regeneration. He was inspired to write it after reading of an ancient Sumerian ritual battle between Summer and Winter—Summer emblematic of youth, growth, and fertility, Winter of age, decay, and death. Indeed, *Celebration* reenacts that battle in its closing moments. Mostly, however, the story is that of an innocent boy named

Orphan who has been displaced from his beloved garden by the aging, materialistic Edgar Allen Rich. In his efforts to regain the garden, Orphan is aided by Potemkin, the musical's cynical narrator, and Angel, a not-so-angelic rock-diva whom Orphan has fallen for. Although Rich is defeated in the end, he manages to destroy the garden (Eden?). Orphan and Angel are at last united and exit together into the world while the ensemble reprises the very upbeat title song. But the world they enter has lost its innocence. As Potemkin states in his final narration,

> In this time of cold and darkness —
> In this terrifying night —
> In this seemingly endless Winter,
> Let us pray that they'll be all right.
> (T. Jones, *Celebration* II–47)

Jonathan Goldberg, a gifted Boston-area musical director, remarks with as much wit as acumen that "*Celebration* is *The Fantasticks* for jaded grown-ups." He's absolutely right. In both musicals the central myth is that of maturation through pain, experience, and loss of innocence. *The Fantasticks'* idyllic setting can support its wholly happy ending, but in the ever-darkening world of *Celebration* — and of the late 1960s — only severely qualified happy endings are possible. The musical's timelessness is in its myth.

What grounds that myth in the late '60s are "the cultural figures of the time" upon which Tom Jones based the characters. Some later audiences have perceived (and objected to) the show as "ageist," and Jones acknowledges that in the period of "never trust anyone over thirty," such an outlook "was in the general mind" not as an attack on age per se but upon what age had come to stand for. For Jones, Rich represents the false values of the older generation; Orphan the young flower child; Angel the groupie; and Potemkin the cynical, possibly drugged-out, drop-out (T. Jones interview). This group of late 60s archetypes expressed the range of views one would expect. The sardonic Potemkin's outlook, because conflicted, most fully embraces the dark world of the play. His "Not My Problem" pairs cynical detachment with a yearning for meaning:

> GOD IS DEAD
> THAT'S WHAT THEY SAID.
> DONE IN BY DARWIN, MARX AND FREUD
> FREE ARE WE
> FROM DEITY.
> OF COURSE IT SORT OF LEAVES A LITTLE VOID.
> (T. Jones, *Celebration* II–16)

A world that makes Potemkin cynical about the human race and seems to prove that youth's idealism becomes the materialism of age — this is the dark, cold world Orphan and Angel must learn to live in at the end. While redemption and regeneration are central to all of Tom Jones's musicals, the sunny hopefulness of *The Fantasticks* gave way in *Celebration* to a world in which it's much harder to be redeemed and regenerated, the show's tone reflecting the troubled, uncertain late '6os.

## 1776

In sharp contrast to the cryptic myth and dark mood enshrouding *Celebration*, the hit musical *1776* (3/16/69), like *Cabaret*, said what it had to say through historical analogy. Composer/lyricist Sherman Edwards was literally a one-show man, but what a show! Prior to *1776*, Edwards had been a history teacher and song writer/musician with Benny Goodman, Tommy Dorsey, and Louis Armstrong (Richards 1: 593); after *1776* he would never again be heard from on Broadway. At that time even his librettist Peter Stone had done more writing for TV and film than for the stage, his only two musicals the barely remembered *Kean* (11/21/61) and *Skyscraper* (11/13/65).

Of all Broadway musicals, *1776* most nearly but not quite literally replicates history (there is no evidence that the men of the Continental Congress periodically broke into song). In the published text, the historical note by the authors describes Edwards and Stone's extensive research. Edwards had worked on his brainchild for ten years before it came to Broadway fruition, while Stone, new to the project, quickly and enthusiastically became immersed in it. Their joint research unearthed personal characteristics and idiosyncrasies, interpersonal tensions, and even sartorial details of the men debating "independency" during that hot, sticky June and July of 1776. Why such painstaking research for a musical that wasn't an academic exercise and certainly doesn't play like one? Says Stone, "1776 was conceived as entertainment. But if it is indeed entertaining, it is, I believe, more than the songs and the jokes and the theatricality that make it so — it is the surprise of discovering that our Founding Fathers were men of flesh and blood and not cardboard" (*Best Plays 68–69* 306). The play illuminates the men, their relationships, their politics, and, in the case of John Adams and Tom Jefferson, their agonizing absence from their wives. At the same time it's a dramatic, absorbing, and often hilarious musical play about drafting the Declaration of Independence.

Why would a show celebrating the birth of the nation play at all during the height of protests against "the system," let alone 1,217 times? That it opened when it did is purely coincidental. For years Sherman Edwards had no luck trying to interest producers in his offbeat product until finally Stuart Ostrow was ready to take the gamble with the proviso that Stone be brought in to rewrite the book (Richards 1:591). The subsequent timetable of re-writes, casting, and rehearsals delayed the show until early 1969, so it was never intended as a feel-good antidote to the troubled times. But, judging from the musical's success, a healthy dose of patriotism was just what the doctor ordered. On the other hand, the founding fathers were radicals. Granted, perukes, buckle shoes, and knee breeches look a bit more formal than tie-dyed shirts, torn jeans, and sandals, but still the signers of the Dec-laration of Independence *were* revolutionaries. Writing of the play, Stone makes it clear he chose to include *both* an appeal to patriotism and an emphasis on the revolutionary character of what happened that sweltering summer in Philadelphia. In so doing, Stone made 1776 corroborate between past and present, or, in his words, "[T]he events of July 4, 1776, mean more to us during these troubled times than most of us could ever imagine. . . . What of the similarities between those times and these (states rights *versus* federal rights; property rights *versus* human rights; privileged rights *versus* civil rights) and the differences (if any)?" (*Best Plays* 68–69 306; Stone, 1776 172).

## Hair

If the substance of 1776 made it a show for all seasons, *Hair*'s content and vocabulary, encapsulating the look, sound, and feel of the late 1960s, tied the musical more to its moment in history than perhaps any other in the annals of the Broadway stage. And yet *Hair*'s form, musical style, and legal battles had a profound influence on the musical theatre — and other theatre as well — for decades to come. If *Hair* seems out of place chronologically with the preceding shows, that's because it is — both as the apotheosis of issue-driven late 1960s musicals and as the one show anticipating what was to come in the '70s. While the language and content of *Hair* may be "dated" and tied to its time, its spirit is not. Because of its still-popular musical score and its simultaneous celebration of both group rebellion and individualism, *Hair* continues to have an enormous and dedicated following among the young.

*Hair*, "The American Tribal Love-Rock Musical," had book and lyrics by Gerome Ragni and James Rado and music by Galt MacDermot. It was developed at the New York Shakespeare Festival's Public Theatre, thanks to risk-taker Joseph Papp, and it opened there on October 29, 1967. During a sojourn through other interim venues, *Hair* changed from its shorter, more conventionally plotted original version into the virtually plotless full-length musical that exploded onto the Broadway scene on April 29, 1968, produced by Michael Butler. Many were confused, perplexed, even offended; others saw *Hair* as proclaiming a revolution in American life, just as it would in fact transform and expand the shape, perhaps even the definition, of the musical. Bordman, usually fairly low-key in his remarks, goes so far as to say, "In every respect—commercial, historic, esthetic—it was far and away the most important musical offering of the season, possibly of the era" (658). In its content, tone, and point of view, *Hair* was a fully fleshed-out theatrical depiction of the hippie counterculture and the New Left during the late 1960s.

From the start, the show was associated with youth. Its writers were three young men, its original cast young, mostly unknown performers, and its content the depiction of the alternative lifestyles and outlooks of a significant segment of America's young people. But *Hair*'s intended audience was typical Broadway theatregoers. In the prefatory material to the published text (which, by the way, bears little resemblance to the version of *Hair* that played on Broadway and beyond), the authors make explicit that their target audience was America's still-entrenched mainstream middle class, and the musical's intention—beyond entertaining—was to educate that audience about the counterculture and, even more, to gain their sympathy for it:

The Kids are a tribe. At the same time, for the purpose of HAIR, they know they are on a stage in a theater, performing for an audience, demonstrating their way of life, in a sense, telling a story, in order to persuade those who watch of their intentions, to perhaps gain greater understanding, support, and tolerance, and thus perhaps expand their horizons of active participation toward a better, saner, peace-full, love-full world. They are trying to turn on the audience. (Ragni and Rado 1969, ix)

Not just the preface but the show itself proselytizes. After the Tribe performs the title song, the totally tolerant, middle-aged "Margaret Mead" character proclaims to the audience, "I wish every mother and father in this theater would go home and make a speech to their teenagers and say: [']Kids, be free, no guilt, be whoever you are, do whatever you want to do, just as long as you don't hurt anyone.' Right?" (Ragni and Rado 1995, 40). After which she sings "My Conviction," defending the gaudy plumage of hippie youth.

Of course, by 1968 theatre audiences were aware of the counterculture's sentiments on an array of topics. As briefly noted earlier, America's first real awareness of hippies came from the Golden Gate Park Be-In on January 14, 1967. On hand were counterculture gurus Allen Ginsburg, Gary Snyder, and Timothy Leary. Twenty thousand young people listened to Quicksilver

Messenger Service, Jefferson Airplane, and the Grateful Dead play acid rock. *Time*'s cover story for July 7, 1967, featured the hippies in their "Summer of Love." The magazine capped a hypothetical hippie creed with, "Blow the mind of every straight person you can reach. Turn them on, if not to drugs, then to beauty, love, honesty, fun" (qtd. in Marty 125). *Hair* put that mythical creed into practice. The Be-In was also a place of reconciliation: "Political activists from Berkeley mingled with dropouts from Haight-Ashbury, ending their feud and initiating a 'new epoch' in the history of man" (Matusow 275). Perhaps more than any other event, that one signaled a blurring of the lines between the "tuned-out" hippies and the activist New Left.

The burning of draft cards in *Hair* (ambivalent Claude burns his library card!) also smacks resoundingly of the New Left's political engagement. On April 15, 1967, six months prior to the off-Broadway opening of *Hair*, SDS unveiled its new stance of what it called "From Protest to Resistance" at an antiwar rally on Central Park's Sheep Meadow that drew some half million sympathizers. Sixty people organized by SDS leaders from Cornell publicly violated federal law by burning their draft cards. In spontaneous sympathy, about a hundred of the onlookers burned theirs too (Matusow 325). Then, just before *Hair*'s Broadway opening, Mark Rudd and friends — protesting the university's association with defense projects, among other things — noisily and effectively brought Columbia University to a standstill by taking over the president's office and five university buildings and holding a dean hostage (Leuchtenburg, *Feast* 176; Matusow 332–35). Despite such outward and visible signs of discontent, much of the older generation was still "bewildered by the ragamuffin army of disheveled, unkempt 'potheads' who dropped out of school and drifted from pad to pad with no visible ambition or direction." And, on the other side, "the discontented young felt alienated from the conformity of their 'uptight' parents" (Leuchtenburg, *Feast* 183). *Hair*'s writers set out to educate with the goals of understanding, comprehension, sympathy for, and, ultimately, conversion to the counterculture's values.

Once audiences got past their shock at the show's graphically "obscene" language, simulated sex, and brief nudity, the values they saw in *Hair* were, in the main, socially responsible ones (save for the open acceptance of drugs and what spectators probably called promiscuity or "free love"). One charge popularly leveled at *Hair* is that it is unpatriotic. But in fact, *Hair*, like *1776*, separates its criticisms from its affirmations. There is nothing in the songs, script, or staging that indicates the kids are un- or anti-American, collectively or individually. Rather, they are saddened by much of what America has become — material values replacing moral values, for example — and they plead for a return to those values beneficial both to society at large and to the dignity of each individual. Scarcely a major public issue goes unremarked either in one of *Hair's* numerous songs or in the dialogue: pollution and the environment in "Air"; poverty in "Ain't Got No"; civil rights and race relations in "Colored Spade," "I'm Black," "Dead End," "Black Boys," "White Boys," and "Abie Babie"; peace and anti-Vietnam protest in the long second-act sequence collectively called "The War"; and patriotism itself in "Don't Put It Down." Hostile critics of the show saw flag burning, but it simply wasn't there. "Don't Put It Down" expressly, if quirkily, shows how the Tribe is "CRAZY FOR THE RED BLUE AND WHITE" and, accordingly, the U.S. of A. Far from burning the flag, toward the end of the song, the Tribe's leader Berger, Woof, and Steve fold it with as much military precision, ceremony, and respect as the Color Guard at Arlington National Cemetery (Ragni and Rado 1995, 50).

*Hair* painted a rich — mostly authentic — portrait of hippie life, the life of communal living and communal sex, of pot smoking and acid trips, of acid rock and Eastern ritual. In addition to alienation and radical behavior, dress, and ideals, *Hair* exposed another quality intrinsic to hippie culture: innocence. The true flower child was a charmingly ingenuous creature. In *Hair*, Crissy, seemingly the youngest of the Tribe, most embodies these qualities. When she sings "Frank Mills," with an innocence approaching naiveté, her infatuation with a Hell's Angels biker who betrayed her is both whimsical and heartbreaking. Though desolate, she can still implore the audience

> I WOULD GRATEFULLY APPRECIATE IT
> IF YOU SEE HIM TELL HIM
> I'M IN THE PARK WITH MY GIRLFRIEND
> AND PLEASE
> TELL HIM ANGELA AND I
> DON'T WANT THE TWO DOLLARS BACK . . .
> JUST HIM
>
> (Ragni and Rado 1995, 53)

It can never be known just how many people *Hair* brought to a better understanding of the counterculture or sympathy with its outlook, but the show ran 1,844 performances, well into the 1970s.

## Hair *Goes to Court*

Laden with a potentially explosive cargo of full-frontal nudity, simulated sex, the putative desecration of the American flag, and language some deemed obscene, it's a miracle *Hair* encountered nary a censorious speed bump while on Broadway. But once touring companies hit the road, *Hair* kept running into roadblocks of "community standards" till it got mired in a legal pothole of legendary banned-in-Boston proportions.

The Boston production of *Hair* should have opened at the Wilbur Theatre on February 20, 1970. It did not. The City of Boston still had an official censor paid to keep an eye on live theatre and movies. Prior to *Hair's* arrival and never having seen the show, the censor "had *heard* of Hair's impending opening and raised the concern that such a controversial show would not only be an affront to the Boston community, but could possibly lead to other notorious shows . . . opening in Boston" (J. Johnson [emphasis added]). Louise Day Hicks, running against incumbent Garrett Byrne for Suffolk County District Attorney, made the censor's condemnation of *Hair* "a point on which to challenge the District Attorney" (J. Johnson). This forced Byrne to do battle with *Hair*, racing with Hicks to see who could be more holier-than-thou.

Once *Hair* was in previews, one look was enough for Garrett Byrne to declare "the show desecrated the American flag and contained scenes full of 'lewd and lascivious acts' " (J. Johnson). Thus armed, the D.A. tried to close the show on criminal (not civil) charges of obscenity and public displays of nudity and lewd behavior, based on sections 16 and 32 of Chapter 272 of the Massachusetts General Laws (313 F. Supp. 760–61).

Anticipating these actions, producer Michael Butler and the owners of the Wilbur Theatre engaged a legal defense team of impressive credentials. Heading it was Gerald A. Berlin, whose extensive First Amendment experience included serving as Attorney General for the American Civil Liberties Union. Berlin brought in two trial lawyers: Harold Katz, who had served on the mayor's council, and Henry P. Monaghan, constitutional law professor at Boston University; initially on board, but only briefly, was recent Harvard Law School graduate Alan M. Dershowitz (Berlin interview).

This being a case of First Amendment freedoms, Berlin based his strategy on the "doctrine of abstention," whereby lawyers must "exhaust all options at the state level before they could appeal to the Supreme Court" (J. Johnson; Berlin interview). Berlin took the "rarely sought" path of seeking a *civil* injunction against *criminal* charges and prosecution. But it paid off—once he determined where to seek injunctive relief. Normally that would be a single judge in the Massachusetts Superior Court, but "since Judge Swift had formerly been counsel to the Archdiocese of Boston, this hardly seemed a good place to go" (Berlin interview). So Berlin's team leapfrogged over the unfriendly Superior Court, to seek "injunctive and declaratory relief from a single Justice of the Massachusetts Supreme Judicial Court" (313 F.

Supp. 760). That one justice granted a temporary restraining order, but only pending the opinion of the full Supreme Judicial Court once all seven justices had seen *Hair* for themselves.

The full court's decision came on April 9, 1970. When each justice saw *Hair*, he was appalled by "members of the cast in the nude facing the audience," a "nude male performer . . . bathed on stage," and "clowning intended to simulate sexual intercourse or deviation." But the court concluded that *Hair* "constitutes, however, in some degree, an obscure form of protest protected under the First Amendment. Viewed apart from the specific incidents mentioned above, it is not lewd and lascivious, . . . The incidents . . . are separable from, and wholly unnecessary to, whatever theme this noisy, disorganized performance may have [judges as theatre critics!]." The Supreme Judicial Court was ready to grant injunctive relief from criminal prosecution only if *Hair* agreed "(a) to have each member of the cast clothed to a reasonable extent at all times, and (b) to eliminate completely all simulation of sexual intercourse or deviation" (357 Mass 771).

Rather than make such changes or risk criminal prosecution for not doing so, the *Hair* company opted instead to close the show while continuing to fight the ruling higher up. Had they complied, Butler and the rest would have yielded to what amounted to court-ordered censorship. Their voluntary act of closure took an unequivocal stand against allowing any censorship from any source to encroach on the American theatre.

Meanwhile, *Hair's* lawyers had one more court to go in Boston — Federal District Court. On April 13, Berlin filed for injunctive relief on behalf of the plaintiffs, heard in time by a three-judge panel of Judge Coffin of the Circuit Court and Judges Bownes and Garrity of the District Court — the same W. Arthur Garrity who a few years later gained notoriety as Boston's "Busing Judge." In Berlin's estimation, it was Henry Monaghan's oral argument based on the doctrine of abstention that turned around the initially hostile bench and led them to a two to one decision on May 6 in favor of *Hair's* appeal. "Of course, true to form, it was Garrity who dissented" (J. Johnson; Berlin interview).

The language was strong in the report of the court's holding supporting freedom of expression. Stronger yet were the words of Judge Coffin's opinion for the majority. Coffin stressed "the proposition that live theater productions, like movies, are within the ambit of protection of the First Amendment. . . . [T]he stage has been a traditional and important medium for the presentation and expression of ideas" (313 F. Supp. 761–62). Coffin and Bownes found that laws applicable to *public* lewdness and nudity that may be imposed on "an unsuspecting or unwilling person" do not apply to paid performances since audiences are willing spectators who may be presumed to be at least casually aware of a show's content: "We cannot escape the conclusion that to apply the standards of the street and marketplace to the world behind the footlights would be to sanction a censorship dragnet of unconstitutional proportions. . . . [If plays had] to convince a court that there was a 'reasonable excuse' for every scene which might be questioned, the chilling effect on theater generally would be of ice age proportions" (313 F. Supp. 765).

Berlin's tactics had virtually forced D.A. Byrne to exercise his final option by taking to the Supreme Court of the United States his appeal for a stay of the injunctive relief awarded *Hair*. On May 22, 1970, the Supreme Court heard the arguments for both sides of *Byrne v. P.B.I.C., Inc.*, and handed the district attorney a swift, stunning, and virtually silent defeat. The entirety of the ruling as reported in 398 U.S. 916 reads: "Application for stay denied by an equally divided court." There was no majority opinion because there was no majority. The vote was tied because Justice Blackmun, new to the court, abstained, having not been present for the arguments. The split-court decision overturned the memorandum of the seven Massachusetts Supreme Court Justices and upheld the two to one ruling of the lower federal three-judge panel that granted *Hair* injunctive relief against criminal prosecution. Judge Coffin's opinion thus stood as the last judicial word in support of First Amendment protection for theatrical expression. Once the Supreme Court decision was known, *Hair* re-opened at the Wilbur and became one of the most successful, longest-running productions in the annals of Boston theatre.

But all was not well — yet. As touring productions proliferated, some were so-called "bus and truck" companies playing short engagements in smaller metropolitan areas and then heading back to the road again. Most venues where *Hair*'s road companies played were under private management, but occasionally they were city-owned theatres and auditoriums. In some of these cases *Hair* "had encountered . . . resistance and had successfully sought injunctions ordering local officials to permit use of municipal facilities" (420 U.S. 548, n.1). In Mobile, West Palm Beach, Oklahoma City, Atlanta, and Charlotte, the musical swiftly won the court cases and went on to play its scheduled engagements. Then came Chattanooga, Tennessee, and trouble even though *Hair* had previously played Nashville and Memphis with no opposition or litigation.

On October 29, 1971, the producers applied to use a privately owned theatre, under long-term lease to the city, for a six-day run of *Hair* starting November 23. The board of directors controlling municipally owned facilities in Chattanooga refused, concluding solely from "outside reports" "that the production would not be 'in the best interests of the community.'"

"None of them had seen the play or read the script, but they understood from those reports that the musical, as produced elsewhere, involved nudity and obscenity on stage" (420 U.S. 546, 548). The District Court denied the producers' motion for a preliminary injunction against the board's decision. The producers then tried to seek a permanent injunction allowing use of the Chattanooga Memorial Auditorium, also under the aegis of that same board of directors. Once the board finally filed a response, the same District Court "concluded that the production contained obscene conduct not entitled to First Amendment protection and denied injunctive relief" to the *Hair* company (420 U.S. 546). The Court of Appeals affirmed the District Court's ruling, so it was off to the Supreme Court again on October 17, 1974. Henry Monaghan once more presented the oral argument on behalf of *Hair* and again won a stellar victory. By the time the Supreme Court ruled on the case, it was March 18, 1975 (420 U.S. 546). But the decision was well worth waiting for.

Harry Blackmun, who abstained from the Boston decision, wrote the opinion for the six to three majority in the Chattanooga case. Blackmun's opinion notes that *Hair*'s producers urged reversal of the lower courts' decisions on three grounds: "(1) respondent's action constituted an unlawful prior restraint, (2) the courts below applied an incorrect standard for the determination of the issue of obscenity *vel non*, and (3) the record does not support a finding that 'Hair' is obscene" (420 U.S. 552). The Court never had to deal with those sticky obscenity issues; it did "not reach the latter two contentions, for we agree with the first. . . . Accordingly, on this narrow ground, we reverse" (420 U.S. 552). In other words, the ruling in *Hair*'s favor was based solely on the unconstitutionality of "prior restraint"—that is, censorship before the fact by denying of the use of a public facility based only on prior information or hearsay, not on examination or observation of the actual theatrical production.

Beyond the six to three victory and Blackmun's opinion on prior restraint, the most liberating part of the Chattanooga decision for America's theatrical community had to be the eminent Justice William O. Douglas's brief but powerful opinion defending free speech in the theatre. He begins by quoting himself in an earlier opinion:

"I do not believe any form of censorship—no matter how speedy or prolonged it may be—is permissible" [380 U.S. 51 (1965)]. . . . A municipal theater is no less a forum for the expression of ideas than is a public park, or a sidewalk; the forms of expression adopted in such a forum may be more expensive and more structured . . . but they are surely no less entitled to the shelter of the First Amendment. As soon as municipal officials are permitted to pick and choose, as they are in all existing socialist regimes, between those productions which are "clean and healthful and culturally uplifting" in content and those which are not [his paraphrase of the purpose statement of Chattanooga's Memorial Auditorium when dedicated in 1924], the path is cleared for a regime of censorship under which full voice can be given only to those views which meet with the approval of the powers that be. (420 U.S. 563)

And though the full Court had no need to address *Hair*'s possibly objectionable content, Douglas faced the question head-on:

There was much testimony in the District Court concerning the pungent social and political commentary which the musical "Hair" levels against various sacred cows of our society: the Vietnam war, the draft, and the puritanical conventions of the Establishment. This commentary is undoubtedly offensive to some, but its contribution to social consciousness and intellectual ferment is a positive one. In this respect, the musical's often ribald humor and trenchant social satire may someday merit comparison to the most highly regarded works of Aristophanes, a fellow debunker of established tastes and received wisdom, yet one whose offerings would doubtless meet with a similarly cold reception at the hands of Establishment censors. (420 U.S. 564)

And so it was that anti-Establishment *Hair* scored two Supreme Court victories for the American theatre, one criminal, the other civil: protection against criminal prosecution for nudity and simulated sex on stage, and protection against prior censorship shutting a theatrical production out of a proposed venue. *Hair*'s legal victories had far-reaching significance for the future of American theatre: the protections it established made possible the production of such important plays as *Equus*, *The Elephant Man*, *Otherwise Engaged*, and *Curse of the Starving Class*.

### Protest, Divisiveness, and Diversity

In the spring of 1970, when *Hair* began fighting censorship in the nation's halls of justice, actions of young Americans against the Vietnam War accelerated. On streets and college campuses, protests and demonstrations escalated not just in number but in violence. There were still peaceful protests, but during that spring radicals destroyed campus facilities connected to the "military-industrial complex," and students and minorities demonstrated or rioted. Even after May 4, when at Kent State University members of the National Guard shot thirteen students, killing four, campus protests and violence continued unabated. I taught then at the University of Kansas in Lawrence; just days after the Kent State debacle, race riots broke out in town, on campus the Student Union was bombed, and the

Lawrence police shot and killed a passerby stopping to watch a demonstration. Such events exacerbated the sharp divides in American society.

Broadly speaking, the '6os polarized American society. On one side was the Establishment—the largely conservative (and suburban) white middle and upper-middle classes, bolstered by the largely conservative, also white, working- or blue-collar class. Opposite was the anti-Establishment, including the counterculture (hippies, street freaks, etc.), student radicals and other intelligentsia of the New Left, and ethnic and racial minorities— Native Americans, Hispanics, and, primarily, African Americans. By and large, it was an us-them polarization. But in the late '6os, further splintering paved the way for the shattered '7os. William Leuchtenburg has observed that starting around 1967 "Black nationalists, radicals, and other advocates of social change found increasingly that they had essentially different perceptions from many in the counter culture" (*Feast* 197). The Students' Afro-American Society attacked as "social misfits" gays at Columbia University demanding a lounge of their own. Key events of the early 1970s deepened these schisms: Arthur Bremer's shooting of George Wallace on May 14, 1972; the prolonged Watergate scandal, the break-in first reported on June 17, 1972; Nixon's landslide victory over George McGovern in November 1972; the Supreme Court's seven to two decision legalizing abortion in *Roe v. Wade*, January 23, 1973; and the Paris cease-fire agreement ending American involvement in Vietnam on January 27, 1973; along with the upsurge in the Women's and Civil Rights movements and the attendant backlash against it.

In particular, two widely heralded events early in 1973 were also widely divisive. *Roe v. Wade* removed almost all barriers to legal abortions but also further factionalized a country already polarized on the pro-choice/pro-life issue. And while America felt collective relief that the Paris agreement effectively ended U.S. involvement in Vietnam, the cease-fire brought home the remaining American troops, not as heroes but as emblems of a war we had lost—many returning jobless, homeless, and worse.

## "In-Your-Face" and Otherwise: Issue-Driven Musicals in the '70s

Musicals on Broadway and off echoed the anger and schisms in America. Unlike the late '6os issue-driven shows that put entertainment before message or at least made them coequal, a wave of in-your-face message-first musicals began by the early 1970s. The immediate audience response was something of a collective "Enough already!" But producers persisted, though most such shows were monumental flops.

A tiny revue called *Salvation* (9/24/69) at the tiny off-Broadway Jan Hus Playhouse found an audience for 239 performances. With book, music, and lyrics by Peter Link and C. C. Courtney, the show spoofed "the religious and moral extremes of the day" (Bordman 670). Conversely, the anti-war *Blood Red Roses* (3/22/70), set during the Crimean War, died a hideous death the very night it opened. According to the program, "Like World War I and America's Vietnam adventure, the Crimean War was a triumph of futility and brutality" (qtd. by Barnes, *NYTCR* 1970 332). So was the show, apparently. Nearly all the critics pointed out that most Americans knew nothing about the Crimean War, making it a lousy theatrical metaphor for Vietnam. Reviewers wondered why librettist John Lewin and composer Michael Valenti didn't just write about Vietnam in the first place. Martin Gottfried went so far to suggest that if this represented the *quality* of anti-war shows being produced, "Pacifism in the theatre must be temporarily outlawed for its own sake" (*NYTCR* 1970 334, 333).

*Mod Donna* (4/24/70), mounted at Joe Papp's Public Theatre, was the first professionally produced musical to deal with wife-swapping, while a chorus commented "on the women's liberation movement and sexual exploitation" (Bordman 670). The show was also one of the rare New York musicals on or off-Broadway by an all-female creative team — book and lyrics by Myrna Lamb, music by Susan Hulsman Bingham. The two couples and chorus in the preachy "women's issues" *Mod Donna* packed up and went home after forty-eight showings, whereas about seven years later a musical that treated wife-swapping humorously, if perhaps too frivolously, kept romping through 872 performances. But at least *I Love My Wife* (4/17/77) had seasoned professionals in book and lyric writer Michael Stewart and composer Cy Coleman, both of whom understood the simple fact that a Broadway stage is not a lecture hall.

*Picketing a Musical*: Lovely Ladies, Kind Gentlemen

While numerous musicals at this time directly dealt with issues, one show provoked a protest. On the night of December 28, 1970, I had to cross a picket line (with some guilty embarrassment) to get to the opening of *Lovely Ladies, Kind Gentlemen* at the Majestic Theatre (12/28/70), a less than stellar adaptation of John Patrick's *The Teahouse of the August Moon*. Adapted by Patrick himself with music and lyrics by Stan Freeman and Franklin Underwood, the show closed after sixteen performances. But as an event it stirred some controversy and increased the public's awareness of the need to hire ethnic performers for ethnic roles in the theatre. The pickets comprised about thirty members and supporters of the Oriental Actors of America. In San Francisco and Los Angeles that organization had previously demonstrated against stereotyping and negative portrayals of Asians in theatre and film, but it had never before challenged hiring practices (see "Too Many Okinawans"). Specifically, the protesters charged that while *Lovely Ladies, Kind Gentlemen* "has a cast of 45 actors, 12 of whom are Asian-Americans . . . the play calls for 37 Asian roles. The group also charged that 'not one Oriental was given the courtesy of an audition for the part of Sakini, the principal character, played by Kenneth Nelson.' " That the protest may have done some good is suggested by the production of John Weidman and Stephen Sondheim's *Pacific Overtures* about five years later, in which every member of the cast was Asian or Asian-American.

### *Multicultural Healing:* Two Gentlemen of Verona

On the plus side for ethnic casting, there were no protests, just near-universal cheers and a run of 627 performances, for a multi-ethnic, off-the-wall rock musical that even retained some resemblance to its Shakespearean source. *Two Gentlemen of Verona* (12/1/71) underwent a trendy makeover by John Guare and Mel Shapiro. Guare wrote the lyrics, Shapiro directed, *Hair*'s Galt MacDermot composed the score, and Joe Papp's New York Shakespeare Festival produced the show. Much of *Two Gentlemen*'s appeal lay in the way Guare and Shapiro conceived it. The published text gives few hints of how the roles were distributed ethnically, or that they were assigned this way purely for the fun of it, not to make a statement. All the script is explicit about is that when Julia gets really worked up, she slips into speaking or singing in Spanish; and, late in the play, there is a funny little stage direction describing a secondary character's entrance: "EGLA-MOUR *is heard: a thrilling baritone voice . . . He wears an army uniform. He carries the magic dove on his shoulder. He is Chinese*" (Richards, *Rock* 150). In terms of plot this is apropos of nothing; the actor playing Eglamour simply was—Chinese. Martin Gottfried in *Women's Wear Daily* provides a good breakdown of the show's ethnicities: "Valentine and Sylvia were black and her father, the Duke of Milan, was a big, bad, black daddy; Proteus and Julia were both Puerto Rican; Launce, the manservant, was Jewish, and Eglamour, Sylvia's fiance, was Chinese. This was not just a matter of casting—the lines were spoken in dialect and the contrast between the accents and the story-characters-language was wildly funny" (*NYTCR* 1971 172).

Like Shakespeare's own, this *Two Gentlemen* allegedly took place in a stage version of Verona and Milan, but the set no more resembled those cities than, say, Paducah, Kentucky. Guare and Shapiro provide one of the few hints of what they're really up to in the set description: "The three-level-high set, all crosswalks and staircases, is painted pink, yellow, orange, and if it looks like the fire escapes and construction in the tenements of a modern city, all the better" (Richards, *Rock* 76). The setting was to suggest urban America, and, most specifically, New York City. Before Broadway, *Two Gentlemen* had played the previous summer at the Delacorte Theatre in Central Park, the city's skyline framing the action. Writing of the move from outdoors to indoors, *Newsweek*'s Jack Kroll linked the show's diverse cast with its allusive setting of The City:

> ... under a chunk of open sky the scared New York of the '70s achieved a rare moment of glowing amity as John Guare and Mel Shapiro's adaptation used Shakespeare's very first comedy to reintroduce the fragmented city to its own piebald, polyglot dramatis personae. ... [I]t was brilliantly appropriate for Shakespeare's characters to be metamorphosed into blacks, Jews, Puerto Ricans, Chinese, and even some un-funky Anglos. In the precincts of Shubert Alley some of the summer glow has been lost; the spirit symbolized by the breakout of Frisbees, Yo-Yos, soap bubbles, and skip ropes at the finale was sweeter in the besieged Arcadia of Central Park. (*NYTCR* 1971 173)

Translating this image into audience response, my friend and colleague John Emigh, professor of theatre at Brown University, encapsulated the "very buoyant experience" of seeing the show as "a celebration of New York's diversity" and further categorized it, despite its absence of overt political content, as a political musical since it said "we," all of us, all races and ethnicities, "can do anything" (Emigh interview).

   *Two Gentlemen* became a model for much musical theatre casting in the remainder of the 1970s and beyond. Some socially relevant and other hit shows of the '70s displayed *Two Gentlemen*'s kind of casting diversity: *Godspell, Jesus Christ Superstar, Pippin, The Magic Show, A Chorus Line, Dancin', Runaways,* and *Working.*

### The Failure of Early '70s Issue-Driven Musicals

The first half of the 1970s was swamped with issue-driven musicals that failed to find an audience. With more and more Americans skeptical about the Vietnam War, the time seemed ripe to revive Paul Green and Kurt Weill's 1936 pro-peace, anti-war parable *Johnny Johnson* (11/11/71). Yet even with the increasingly unpopular war, *Johnny Johnson* died again the night it opened.

Eve Merriam had a shaky start on one of the few all-female teams writing for the musical theatre. With composer Helen Miller, she turned *The Inner City Mother Goose*, her book of versified social commentary, into the revue *Inner City* (12/14/71). The forty-some songs sang of how—with the muggers and molesters, druggies and protesters, rotten housing, rotten schools, rotten buses, subways, sidewalks, streets—it's really rotten to live in Manhattan. A cast of nine directed by Tom O'Horgan (whose stagings of *Hair, Jesus Christ Superstar*, and the non-musical *Lenny* were still going strong) kept this *kvetching* set to music alive ninety-seven times. But within a few years Ms. Merriam would be back with a major hit of major social relevance. Ms. Miller, whose music Martin Gottfried damned as "nearly atrocious" (NYTCR 1971 147), was never heard from again.

The fact that 1972 was an election year was relevant only to the first of four socially relevant flops to open that year in New York. Incumbent Richard M. Nixon was reelected with 45.9 million (521 electoral) votes to George McGovern's 28.4 million (17 electoral). On May 15, Nixon's only serious challenger, Alabama Governor George Wallace, was paralyzed in Arthur Bremer's assassination attempt and so abandoned his campaign. In March, during the primaries, Broadway briefly witnessed *The Selling of the President* (3/22/72), Jack O'Brien and Stuart Hample's fictionalized musical recasting of Joe McGinniss's book on Nixon's first campaign, with lyrics by O'Brien and music by Bob James. Set in the near future of 1976, the show satirized a presidential campaign packaged by ad-men, pollsters, and TV executives, and peddled through hype, the media, and what a later day would call spin-doctors. What seemed like a splendid idea for the time never realized its potential on stage, conceding defeat after five performances.

*Different Times* (4/30/72), with book, lyrics, music, and direction all by Michael Brown, traced a Boston family's life from 1905 to 1970. Brown's pastiche music sought to capture each decade's style, and the thin plot glanced at issues like women's rights, two world wars, anti-Semitism, youth protest, and the counterculture, without lingering long enough on any to offer a clear-cut point of view. This twenty-four-performance flop inspired one critic to recognize that ideas should be part of the infrastructure of a musical; Leonard Harris of WCBS TV2 ended his piece with, "But ideas are the lifeblood of a musical. And 'Different Times' suffers from tired blood" (NYTCR 1972 288).

By 1972, Americans had been reading Rachel Carson's *Silent Spring* for ten years and Paul Ehrlich's *The Population Bomb* for four, and an estimated twenty million people took part in the first Earth Day on April 22, 1970, in major cities, fifteen hundred colleges, and ten-thousand-plus elementary and secondary schools (Marty 142). Did New Yorkers really need the pro-environment musical *Mother Earth* (10/19/72) from California to alert them to ecological awareness and activism? Leonard Harris summed up the revue's superfluity: "This musical is on the side of the angels. Against pollution and overpopulation; for redwoods and endangered species. Can you imagine anyone making a musical that's in favor of pollution?" (*NYTCR* 1972 215). Critics uniformly praised the young cast but loathed Ron Thronson's "simpleminded" sketches and lyrics, though Toni Shearer's music was "better than average" (*NYTCR* 1972 214, 215). But music alone can't save a would-be relevant revue; *Mother Earth* was consigned to the toxic show dump after twelve showings.

Harburg and Saidy's sly and subtle reworking of Aristophanes' anti-war *Lysistrata* failed in 1961, when most of the United States was barely aware of Vietnam. By 1972, anti-war sentiments were strong and protests in full swing; perhaps another musicalized *Lysistrata* — called *Lysistrata* (11/13/72) — would have a chance. Not so. Even with Melina (*Never on Sunday*) Mercouri in the title role, it closed the week it opened. *Lysistrata*'s Peter Link was a talented composer, as his incidental music for the delirious A. J. Antoon *Much Ado About Nothing* set in Teddy Roosevelt's America amply shows. But judging from the reviews, *Lysistrata*'s adapter-lyricist-director Michael Cacoyannis was about as sly and subtle as a Sherman tank. While the time seemed right for a sharp, funny musical update of Aristophanes, Cacoyannis and Link couldn't deliver it.

## Social Relevance in the Later '70s

By the mid-1970s, the number of message musicals and rabble-rousing revues significantly diminished. What happened? Well, for one thing, Americans were getting tired of all the tumult. For another, audiences were accordingly getting sick of pointed, in-your-face, "meaningful" shows. But most of all, Watergate happened, followed not long after by the first ever resignation by a United States president. The real-life political drama helped knock all social comment, earnest or frivolous, off the musical stage. The public focused on the theatrics playing out in the White House, on Capitol Hill, at the Supreme Court, and in the media. Who needed to go to the theatre? It was in our living rooms on an almost daily basis. And, seeing that enough was enough, New York producers wisely steered clear of political, socially charged shows for the duration.

The mid- to late '70s saw only three socially relevant musicals. The first was *The Lieutenant* (3/9/75), a sung-through rock musical about the trial of a thinly disguised Lt. William J. Calley who, in real life, had been charged with ordering the slaughter of the My Lai villagers in Vietnam. Gene Curty, Nitra Scharfman, and Chuck Strand perpetrated this tasteless horror alleg- edly to put forth the argument that "American militarism, not the officer, must shoulder the real blame" (Bordman 684). Then why did they wait seven years after My Lai to speak out? By then the country just wanted to forget Vietnam and everything about it—including *The Lieutenant*, which closed after nine performances.

## The Club

Two issue-driven musicals by women became off-Broadway hits in the later 1970s. Eve Merriam's ingeniously conceived and executed *The Club* opened on October 14, 1976, for 674 performances, followed by Gretchen Cryer and Nancy Ford's personal yet accessible *I'm Getting My Act Together and Taking It on the Road* (5/16/78), which played an astounding 1,165 times. For *The Club* Merriam collected popular songs from 1894 to 1905 that depict women "teasingly and scornfully as sex objects, playthings and gold- diggers" (NYTCR 1976 122). Performing the numbers (and some equally sexist banter) were four members of an exclusive gentlemen's club, their black waiter, their white pageboy/bellboy (looking like he stepped out of the old Phillip Morris ads), and a lone piano player. But the performers were women in drag—not broadly caricaturing men, as male drag queens often do women, but instead carefully reproducing "the angle of a leg, the set of a mouth, the grip of a cigaret" (NYTCR 1976 123). Merriam's dissec- tion of sexism was so subtle that it took one of the few female critics, Sylviane Gold of the *Post*, to pinpoint the effect of this gender-bent ren- dering of the old, old songs: "performed by men, it would be little more than a vaguely mocking look at some of the sillier sentiments harbored in turn-of-the-century music-hall songs. But it's being performed by women impersonating men, and that relatively slight dislocation turns the 'musical diversion' into a refracting lens for the condescension and bigotry that in- form those good old songs and by implication, our culture" (NYTCR 1976 123).

## I'm Getting My Act Together and Taking It on the Road

Gretchen Cryer's up-front honesty in *I'm Getting My Act Together and Taking It on the Road* made it easy for audiences to buy into her views on the nature of relationships and the status of women—in the workplace and out. The "plot" or premise of Cryer and Ford's little musical is simple. Heather, a thirty-nine-year-old daytime soap actress and occasional pop singer and songwriter, is trying out her new act for her manager in an effort to make a comeback as a live club performer. This context allows her to air the new songs and sketches in her act, as well as her feminist views. There's also a lot of sharp, intelligent banter among her, her manager, and others at the rehearsal, chiefly members of her act. For all her feminist earnestness, Cryer had great good humor to name the act "Heather Jones and the Liberated Men's Band Plus Two," the "two" being a pair of "girls" who mostly provide doo-wop back-ups to Heather's vocals. That sort of humor had much to do with the show's success. In a word, what made the musical work is that while it was unabashedly feminist, it was also a whole lot of fun. Nor was its viewpoint on women a narrow one. There's a wonderful exchange, for example, during which Heather and one of the "girls" wonder where all of the men have gone since women have become strong and independent—not the way men seem to want them. There's Cryer's humor again, and a healthy dose of reality. Cryer also reminds the audience that there are other kinds of men, women, and relationships out there and that they all need understanding. She vividly dramatizes this through Heather's manager, a sweet (if conventional) guy having to cope with a younger, childlike, sometimes dependent, sometimes unfaithful, and ultimately suicidal wife.

Stanley Green observes that what made the Cryer-Ford collaboration unique was that they "always brought an intensely individual voice to all of their works. They have never been, nor are they ever likely to be, creators who can adapt themselves to concepts other than their own; their songs and librettos have all shown marked originality in both subject matter and viewpoint, as they have consistently reflected the collaborators' mutual attitudes and deep concerns" (357). *I'm Getting My Act Together* was packed with feminist ideas, but Cryer and Ford's sincere personal investment in their material made watching the show not like listening to a lecture, but talking with a friend.

### Rendezvous with History

Around the time the in-your-face message-musicals were dying out from lack of audience interest, three musicals appeared that are historically and socially significant because their fate directly or indirectly intersected with the mood and tenor of the times, making the timing of their openings account at least in part for their failure or success. One show was an artistic triumph but a popular and financial failure, one a total disappointment in every way, and the third a runaway hit of blockbuster proportions.

## *Musicals Meet the Bicentennial:* Pacific Overtures *and* 1600 Pennsylvania Avenue

It is arguable that the short Broadway life of Stephen Sondheim and John Weidman's *Pacific Overtures* (1/11/76) was partly a case of a show fortuitously intersecting with a real-life occasion, an unfortunate rendezvous with history, or, more bluntly, bad timing. *Pacific Overtures* is not a conventional Broadway musical. Its subject is the reopening of Japan to the West after more than two hundred years of isolation. Commodore Matthew Calbraith Perry's 1853 diplomatic and trade mission on behalf of President Filmore and the United States of America led the way. He was followed by other Western powers—specifically, admirals from Britain, Holland, Russia, and France in the musical. The show goes on to depict the deterioration of traditional Japanese values and customs in the face of nineteenth-century Western encroachment. The finale, called "Next," jumps to the contemporary twentieth century. The entire company, now in Western dress, proclaims the equality, even superiority, of Japanese industry, commerce, and technology to that of the United States despite the temporary inconvenience of World War II and the bombings of Hiroshima and Nagasaki:

> Never mind a small disaster!
> Who's the stronger, who's the faster?
> Let the pupil show the master
> Next!
> (Sondheim, *Pacific* 137)

Not the stuff of your average boy-meets-girl musical, nor was it written, scored, or staged like one. Sondheim's score employed the modalities and cadences of Japanese music, his lyrics the rhythms and spare, allusive diction and imagery of Japanese verse. Much of Hal Prince's staging and Patricia Birch's choreography derived from the traditional Japanese theatre forms of Kabuki and Bunraku (puppet theatre). And Boris Aronson's critically acclaimed settings composed mostly of sliding screens were equally based on the models of Japanese art and theatre, as was his stylization of Perry's gunboat, a threatening "black dragon" unfolding like so many ominous fans as it approached the harbor. Among all American musicals, *Pacific Overtures* was, quite literally, unique. The critics were pretty evenly divided in liking the show or not, but nearly all remarked on it being a challenging, daring intellectual exercise, particularly in the commercial theatre; and all universally agreed that it was beautiful to behold. But *Pacific Overtures* couldn't attract audiences long enough to make its money back, closing after 193 performances and losing its entire $650,000 investment.

Speculation about why *Pacific Overtures* failed has been lively and varied. Martin Gottfried, for one, takes the direct approach: "Perhaps it was as simple as a Kabuki musical being just too esoteric for the average theatregoer" (123). And Fran Soeder, who directed the off-Broadway revival in 1984, remarked of the Broadway staging, "There were theories that the size of the original production overwhelmed the material" (qtd. in Zadan 226). Yet another cause of the show's early demise may have been the aforementioned bad timing. With its all-Asian cast performing in the styles of traditional Japanese theatre, the musical did not present an impartial view, let alone an American view, of the opening of Japan. Instead, the show was, if you will, a "Japanese-eye view" of those events and their repercussions for traditional Japanese culture. Accordingly, *Pacific Overtures* could be viewed as having not only a pro-Japanese but an anti-American bias. The stage directions reveal the terrifying, unearthly "foreignness" of the Americans to Japanese so long isolated from contact with the west. The U.S. sailors, *"extravagantly stylized like fairy-tale ogres, stand at attention. Behind them, equally bizarre and scary, stand* TWO OFFICERS." The Reciter describes them as "Barbarians with hooked noses like mountain imps. Giants with wild, coarse hair and faces gray as the dead. Americans! Look how they glare." Of Commodore Perry, the Reciter says, "Surely he is the King of the Demons come to strike us blind and to devour our children" (Sondheim, *Pacific* 35). Similar touches abound, including the Americans speaking in a childish, condescending pidgin English to the Japanese.

Audiences may have been uneasy with these negative depictions of Americans, particularly in 1976. According to historian Myron A. Marty, "Few occasions have drawn ordinary Americans into common celebrations as fully and joyfully as did the marking of the Bicentennial" (241). It was one of the rare times in the 1970s when most Americans came together in feeling positive about the U.S.A. Almost as if courting further disaster, in addition to the show's potentially anti-American bias the already loaded finale contained the line "Fifty-seven percent of the Bicentennial souvenirs sold in Washington, D.C. in 1975 were made in Japan" (136) — a statistic audiences probably didn't want to hear moments before they left the theatre. According to Stephen Sondheim, the opening of *Pacific Overtures* in 1976 was "entirely a coincidence" (Sondheim letter). Nor can it be conclusively proved that America's celebratory mood negatively impacted on attendance.

But the likelihood is strong, since the show's tone ran counter to the upbeat view of America promoted that year.

On the other hand, another musical seemingly tailor-made for an opening during the Bicentennial suffered a more humiliating defeat than *Pacific Overtures*. *1600 Pennsylvania Avenue* (5/4/76) passed into musical theatre oblivion after just seven performances without even an original cast recording to remember it by. The show chronicled the American presidency from Washington to Teddy Roosevelt, with Ken Howard as all the presidents (having already played pre-presidential Tom Jefferson in 1776), Patricia Routledge as all the first ladies, and, observing all the Oval Office doings, Gilbert Price as a seemingly eternal black White House butler who offered an African American's slant on the country's goings-on. But historically germane or not, the show just wasn't very good; 1600's closing in less than a week signaled the fading powers of its collaborators, two hitherto gigantic figures of the musical theatre, Alan Jay Lerner and Leonard Bernstein. This would be Bernstein's last foray onto Broadway. Lerner would go on to try again, and yet again, each time with dismal results.

## Annie: *An Antidote for Malaise*

In 1971, *Annie*'s creator and lyricist Martin Charnin began to look for a project to counteract what he saw as the prevailing mood of the early 1970s: "It was a cynical, depressing time, Vietnam and Nixon and riots; there was a feeling that everything was hopeless. The optimist in me was looking for a project to get rid of this virus, to help cure this infection of the times. I had no interest in perpetuating cynicism as some of the darker musicals do" (Charnin interview). In this mood Charnin happened upon Harold Gray's old comic strip *Little Orphan Annie*, secured the rights, found congenial collaborators in Thomas Meehan for the book and Charles Strouse for the music, and the rest is enormously successful history. Charnin recounts that *Annie* took just a year to write, but another six to find producers and backers and mount the Broadway production (with himself directing) on April 21, 1977. Once tucked into the Alvin Theatre, the show settled in comfortably for 2,377 performances. Charnin's reasons for writing the show may in no small measure have been similar to the reasons for America's taking *Annie* to heart: "*Annie* was written as a response to a very terrible time in what was going on in this country. It was written as a direct emotional metaphorical response to Nixon, to Vietnam, to the results and disappointments of the '60s, to the terrible sense of what Jimmy Carter ultimately called the malaise that existed in the country; and what she, Annie, represented simply was this organic truth of spunk, spirit, and optimism created, ironically, in 1925 by a cartoonist who was as Republican as he could be" ("Musical Theatre"). Charnin was precise when he said *emotional* response, since *Annie* did not try to address directly or by analogy any current '70s political or social issues. Nor was the appeal to nostalgia. *Annie* was set in a somewhat romanticized version of the Depression-era 1930s, a time few could get nostalgic about even in the show's sanitized portrayal. Charnin didn't intend *Annie* to resonate with specific meaning; it was to convey a particular mood to late-1970s audiences—a mood grounded in *Annie*'s unshakable faith that however bad things look, the sun *will* come out "Tomorrow."

The success of the major issue-driven musicals of the later '60s—*Man of La Mancha, Cabaret, Hair,* 1776—can be attributed to the fact that, different as they were, each was well crafted, theatrically viable, and, above all, entertaining—the presentation of issues skillfully woven into the fabric of the whole. The failure of all but a few in-your-face message-musicals in the '70s was precisely because the polemics were too abrasive and the shows offered little in the way of entertainment. Compared with the miniscule runs of most message-musicals, the longevity of the wholly feel-good *Annie* at first seems a good barometer of the kinds of shows 1970s audiences wanted to see—shows with a conventional narrative storyline and some hummable tunes. But audiences also hugely populated a new kind of musical, one almost exclusively a product of that decade. These shows asked audiences to look into themselves, which was precisely what the new "Me Generation" wanted to do.

# ✳ 8 ✳

# Fragmented Society, Fragmented Musicals

### The "Me" Mentality

Although the public stayed away from heavyhanded message-musicals, they enthusiastically attended shows that were purely or primarily entertaining, and the 1970s had plenty to offer in that department. *Applause, Sugar, A Little Night Music,* and *Chicago* had runs in the high hundreds of performances. *The Magic Show, The Wiz, Shenandoah, Dancin', Ain't Misbehavin', The Best Little Whorehouse in Texas,* and *They're Playing Our Song* logged a thousand, fifteen hundred, and, in a few cases, close to two thousand performances—some shows running into the 1980s (see Appendix F). Of all such musicals, *Grease* (2/14/72) broke the long run record with 3,388 performances. But sharing New York's stages with these well-attended diversionary shows was the "fragmented musical." This is my term for musicals that forego traditionally linear narrative plots in favor of a seemingly random structure of disjunct and isolated (i.e., fragmented) scenes and musical numbers. These scenes and musical sequences are linked only by theme (not by plot or story), and they focus on individual characters (pre)occupied with personal introspection. The success of such musicals signaled a change in American culture.

For many Americans the 1970s were difficult times. The strides made in civil rights and women's rights and the U.S. exodus from Vietnam notwithstanding, Watergate, Nixon's resignation, several recessions, the "energy crisis," and, late in the decade, the Iranian hostage crisis challenged many Americans' trust in the government and their belief that it could solve problems on a global scale. Americans began to turn their attention from the public to the private. According to '70s historian David Frum, "Between 1972 and 1980, the proportion of Americans who said they followed public affairs 'hardly at all' or 'only now and then' jumped from 27 to 38 percent, while the proportion who paid attention to public affairs 'most of the time' dropped from 36 to 26 percent" (284). Frum says that cynicism was pervasive in 1970s America: "Never—not even during the Depression—had American pride and self-confidence plunged deeper" (64, 289). Shaken from the '60s and depressed by the '70s, many Americans turned inward, exploring their own feelings and psyches. Introspection was such a national obsession that "new journalist" Tom Wolfe declared the unofficial motto of the '70s to be "Let's talk about me!" (qtd. in Frum 99). Self-absorption and self-analysis found theatrical expression in the fragmented musicals.

## The Fragmented Musical

Fragmented musicals did not convey a sense of community; instead, they dramatized the splintered, inward-turning tendencies of the "Me Generation." These shows' literally and *intentionally* fragmented form and content emphasize the shows' inward-turning perspective. Fragmented musicals catered to audience narcissism, since introspective people enjoy watching themselves. The seven longest-running of them together played over fourteen thousand times—a good index of their popularity.

Fragmented musicals comprise a large block of a genre often referred to in musical theatre discourse as the "non-plot musical" or the "concept musical." The latter term, however, is problematic because of its non-descriptive quality. One would like to think that every musical worth mounting arose from its writers' and director's concept. By definition, a theatrical concept is whatever gives unity, clarity, and vision to a production. This can range from the most philosophical sense of Richard Wagner's *Gesamtkunstwerk* to the deliberate theatrical integration of performative elements in musicals starting with *Oklahoma!* Or it can be something as specific as a choice of locale and design for the production of a single play or musical, as in the many so-called "modern dress" productions of Shakespeare and other classics. Each of these things constitutes a concept, with the effect that the notion of "concept musical" is too broad to be of much value.

Just when "concept" and "musical" were first linked is forever lost in the mist of theatrical myth, but the *concept* of "concept musical" goes back at least to Martin Gottfried's review of *Zorbá*, directed by Harold Prince, in *Women's Wear Daily*, November 18, 1968: "Conception is the big word here—it is what is coming to replace the idea of a 'book' . . . there is even less room than in the usual musical [for story] because Prince's concept . . . apparently won out on every question about cutting" (NYTCR 1968 175). Gottfried continues to discuss "concept" and "conception" throughout the review. Over ten years later, in a piece on Hal Prince for *Cue Magazine* (9 November 1979), Gottfried consolidated his thoughts into a definition of "concept musical" as one that "is based on a stage idea, not a story, but a look, a tone—what the show will be like as a stage animal. The music, the dances, the story, the sets and the style of the performance are all dictated by that production concept. . . . [T]his conceptual approach to musicals is theatrical and pictorial rather than intellectual" (qtd. in Huber 12–13). By that definition, all the *Ziegfeld Follies* were concept musicals, which is preposterous. And if the concept musical is "theatrical and pictorial rather than intellectual," why are Stephen Sondheim's most cerebral shows, such as *Pacific Overtures* and *Sunday in the Park with George*, often called concept musicals?

Many critics came to view Hal Prince as "the guru of the 'concept musical'" (Bordman 664), but Prince rejected the term: "The whole label that was put on our shows, the whole notion of the 'concept' musical, was one that I really resent. I never wished it on myself. It caused a backlash and animosity towards the shows and us. I think for a lot of people it was like waving the red goddamn flag. And I kept hearing, 'We're sick of the goddamn concept musical.' And I kept thinking, 'Leave me alone . . . I never called it that.' It's called a 'unified' show, an 'integrated' show" (qtd. in Zadan 363).

What must have prompted the theatre world to evolve the fuzzy term "concept musical" for the musicals here called "fragmented" is that they looked different from conventionally plotted shows and so seemed to need a new name. But "fragmented musical" much more accurately describes the form, content, ideas, and even social milieu that defined the genre. With very few exceptions, fragmented musicals thrived only from 1968 to 1978, reflecting in form and substance what was happening in American society.

The polarized United States of the late 1960s became the fragmented United States of the '70s. The broad-based left coalition unraveled. Formerly united radical student groups began to splinter, and blacks and other minorities increasingly went their own ways. The counterculture, previously held together by protest against the war in Vietnam, began to fade as U.S. troops left Southeast Asia. Many hippies "retreated, some to rural communes in New Mexico or Vermont, most all the way back to the straight world" (Matusow 306). And the New Left, according to Leuchtenburg, lost many adherents, "because they felt exhausted and disillusioned after a period of hyperactivity" (*Feast* 230).

The counterculture collapsed also because it had attained many of its goals: "The sixties were years of causes—civil rights, the anti-Vietnam protest, the beginnings of the women's movement. . . . It was a 'can-do' decade, infused with the belief that if enough people joined together and pushed hard enough, they could turn the country's thinking and feeling around"

(Jones, "Musicals" 17). And they did. By the early 1970s, not only was the Vietnam War winding down but the anti-war position had become more fashionable than the pro-war stance among the American public; the Civil Rights and Women's movements had made great strides; and more Americans were even coming to understand the need for responsible behavior toward the environment. The members of the causes, the protests, the communes realized "We've won!" or, at the very least, "We're winning." Without causes and protests to bind them together, groups began to disband, cutting individuals adrift from their former communal anchors.

America suffered a mood swing from public, political engagement to personal concerns. As Myron A. Marty notes, "By the 1970s, even those sympathetic with the radicals' goals charged them with being infatuated with 'finding themselves,' leading to a 'culture of narcissism' " (23). Allen Matusow observed the same in mainstream America when in the early '70s "social discipline was eroding so rapidly that fashion condemned the whole of middle-class culture as 'the culture of narcissism' " (306). Thus the Me Generation evolved from what had begun as healthy, perhaps necessary introspection; but among many, this inward-turning became a kind of hedonistic narcissism. Fragmented musicals spoke directly to this self-absorption by depicting characters either asking "Who am I?" or, alternatively, proclaiming their self-worth. In both the self-questioning and self-proclaiming, it's the feelings of the individual *as* an individual that matter.

Because of this focus on introspection, a key feature of fragmented musicals is the centrality of character, not story—hence the term "non-plot musicals," which emerged to describe them. A number of these shows literally have no plot or story in any traditional sense. In others, a shred of plot or story exists but does not constitute the primary interest of the play as it does in most conventionally constructed musicals. But neither are these shows revues. Some of them, like some revues, focus on a theme (marriage, dancing, work), but what differentiates the fragmented musical from the revue is *character*. The revue format of separate songs, dance numbers, and dialogue sketches is performed by performers who remain performers. Most fragmented musicals are peopled with named characters who have distinct personalities, backgrounds, attitudes, aspirations, and agendas, all revealed through their individual processes of self-questioning and/or self-declaration.

The way these processes are organized is the final defining element of the fragmented musical. The usual linear progression of incidents logically and dramatically strung together as a coherent story is replaced by what may appear to the viewer as a series of seemingly (and sometimes in fact) haphazardly ordered songs, dance numbers, monologues, dialogue scenes, and visual images and effects, each of which exists to convey an aspect of the musical's central theme. Hence, the actual structure or form of these musicals not only appears fragmented but *is* fragmented by design, accurately mirroring the fragmented American society of the 1970s and the anxieties of inward-turning individuals.

Irony and paradox are key elements of some fragmented musicals, and there is also an overarching irony about form and substance in this musical genre. In a word, by depicting fragmented individuals within the shows' fragmented structures, these musicals became some of the most *integrated* musicals ever created. Their form, subject matter, songs, dances, visual presentation, and so forth work together to convey a single theme or idea. In this respect, the fragmented musical is a theatrical realization of the architectural dictum "Form follows function." Everything—including its seemingly random, fragmented structure—centrally conveys the musical's meaning or point of view.

Of the eleven fragmented musicals from 1968 to 1978, seven became long-running hits, while another had a vigorous life regionally, though not in New York. Their popularity affirms the retreat of audiences from the political to the personal, and the idea that it was "in their feelings that the Americans of the 1970s put their trust" (Frum 115).

## Hair—*The Prototype*

Ironically, *Hair*, a show in praise of all things communal, was the first fragmented musical. Within its communal context, *Hair* nevertheless depicted some individuals cut adrift and turning inward, since even in the communes of the '60s, private introspection did occur. The absence of a conventional plot in *Hair* prompted some bewildered and negative critical responses to the Broadway opening, such as Richard Watts Jr.'s "The 'book' if it may be called that . . ." and John J. O'Connor's "The original, rather harmless plot has been practically erased." But Clive Barnes was more perceptive: "Now the authors of the dowdy book—and brilliant lyrics—have done a very brave thing. They have in effect done away with it altogether. 'Hair' is now a musical with a theme, not with a story" (*NYTCR* 1968 288, 289). Because of *Hair*'s plotlessness, the order of most of the songs could be scrambled with no perceptible harm, since they follow no dramatic, logical, or emotional progression—an essential characteristic of nearly all fragmented musicals.

Beyond its non-linear form, *Hair* became the unwitting prototype for fragmented musicals whose thematic core was personal isolation and the introspection it engenders. Claude's transit through *Hair* exemplifies its introspective, fragmented character. At the top of the show in "Manchester, England" Claude sings, "NOW THAT I'VE DROPPED OUT / WHY IS LIFE DREARY DREARY" (Ragni and Rado 1995, 13), the number underscoring the counterculture's failure to provide his life with meaning. Later, when he is drafted to fight in Vietnam, neither his best friend Berger nor the entire Tribe can help Claude choose whether to go or to defect, prompting him to look into himself and sing,

> WHERE DO I GO
> FOLLOW MY HEARTBEAT
> WHERE DO I GO
> FOLLOW MY HAND
>
> WHERE WILL THEY LEAD ME
> AND WILL I EVER
> DISCOVER WHY
> I LIVE AND DIE
> (Ragni and Rado 1969, 118)

Just as Claude embodies the self-questioning impulse central to most characters in the ensuing fragmented musicals, Sheila expresses the personal self-proclamation often characteristic of the genre. The putative girlfriend of the Tribe's leader Berger, Sheila is portrayed as a sensitive New Left activist. Midway through act 1, Sheila brings Berger the gift of a yellow silk shirt. Berger, possibly on drugs, launches into an unprovoked verbal and physical attack on Sheila, ripping up the shirt and throwing it in her face (44–45). This abuse occasions Sheila's magnificent "Easy to Be Hard:"

> HOW CAN PEOPLE HAVE NO FEELINGS?
> HOW CAN THEY IGNORE THEIR FRIENDS
> EASY TO BE PROUD
> EASY TO SAY NO
> ESPECIALLY PEOPLE WHO CARE ABOUT STRANGERS
> WHO CARE ABOUT EVIL AND SOCIAL INJUSTICE
> DO YOU ONLY CARE ABOUT THE BLEEDING CROWD
> HOW ABOUT A NEEDING FRIEND
> I NEED A FRIEND
> (1995, 45–46)

While Sheila expresses sadness that a man concerned about "social injustice" could treat a person close to him so shabbily, most centrally she is proclaiming her value as an individual by saying, "Look at me, please; pay attention; I'm me, I'm worth something," even though much of her song is phrased as questions. Between Claude's self-questioning, Sheila's assertion of self-worth, and the very form of *Hair* as a whole, the ingredients were in place for the content, theme, and structure of all fragmented musicals to follow.

## Company

In all probability, *Hair* was a fragmented musical by accident, but Stephen Sondheim and George Furth's *Company* (4/26/70) was decidedly one by design. As a conscious effort, *Company* virtually pioneered exploring fragmented characters through fragmented musicals, even perfecting the form. Indeed, not only was *Company* a hit that played 705 times, it also remains the archetypal exemplar of the genre.

*Company* is a fragmented musical exclusively of the self-questioning kind, since it is driven by the single question posed continually by its central character, Robert: "Should I or shouldn't I get married?" For the whole show the audience watches this thirty-five-year-old New York bachelor watch his closest friends (five married couples), and the three young women he dates. At the end, the answer to his question remains ambiguous.

George Furth's dialogue scenes resemble little one-acts portraying different sorts of marriages, each scene almost able to stand alone and in any order, each disjunct from the others. There is no logical, or even possible, dramatic progression. This framework was a challenge for director Harold Prince: "*Company* was the first musical I had done without conventional plot or subplot structure" (Prince 149); and one for Sondheim as well: "A lot of the controversy about *Company* was that up until *Company* most musicals, if not all musicals, had plots. In fact, up until *Company*, I thought that musicals had to have very strong plots. One of the things that fascinated me about the challenge of the show was to see if a musical could be done without one" (qtd. in Zadan 124). Sondheim and his collaborators discovered that theatrical elements other than plot could provide the unifying structure for a theme-based musical when those elements furthered the play's core idea.

The key structuring device was Robert's surprise birthday party, a different variation of it opening and closing each act of the show. These "four" parties confused some viewers or led them to think that they were watching four sequential parties over the course of four years, the remaining scenes thereby presumed to follow a traditionally chronological progression. But *Company*'s creators had something else in mind:

We constructed a framework of gatherings for Robert's thirty-fifth birthday, each appearing to be the same, but dynamically different from the others. Pinteresque in feeling, the first was giddy, somewhat hysterical; the second (at the end of Act I), an abbreviated version of the first; the third, hostile and staccato; and the final one at the end of the show, warm, loving, mature. Since Robert never arrives for the final celebration, there was some question whether they represented one birthday or a succession of them. I am certain they were one. (Prince 149)

Stephen Sondheim expands upon Prince's view: "We always intended the birthdays in *Company* to be one surreal party. The play really takes place in the mind of the protagonist in a moment in time when he returns to his apartment on his birthday. Incidentally, this is why the characters don't know each other and are dressed for different occasions (e.g., Amy in her bridal costume)" (Sondheim letter). The birthday party is thus a perfect structure-plus-metaphor for containing the theme of *Company*. It's one party; the guests are Robert's married friends (but not friends of each other, according to Sondheim—more fragmentation); Bobby stands outside his apartment door dreading the annual "surprise." As he debates entering the apartment, he recollects scenes of himself with his married friends and girlfriends. The dialogue scenes and musical numbers enact these random, nonsequential thoughts. And the entire play taking place in Robert's head with no base of an external social "reality" further emphasizes the introspection and isolation that were the stuff of the Me Decade. Fragmented form and content mutually harmonize in *Company*.

The placement and functions of Sondheim's songs in *Company* at first seem peculiar compared to songs in integrated musicals; here people generally don't sing to, or with, each other in a scene. In two isolated exceptions, Amy and Paul in "Getting Married Today" more or less sing past each other in the same room, and in "Barcelona" Robert and April have a dialogue in song during their hilariously disastrous morning after. With both couples at cross-purposes, these numbers further highlight their dislocation and disconnection. No other songs take place within a scene as in "normal" integrated musicals. As Sondheim explained, "We had our songs interrupt the story and be sung mostly by people outside the scene commenting on the action taking place" (qtd. in Zadan 117). Such moments include "The Little Things You Do Together," Joanne's running commentary during the Harry and Sarah scene, and Robert's three girlfriends ganging up on him (in his head) in "You Could Drive a Person Crazy" while he's with Jenny and David. Dislocating most of the songs from the scenes reinforces the show's feeling of fragmentation and separation. Marta's "Another Hundred People" so brilliantly expresses that mood that it virtually becomes *Company*'s central metaphor for the terrible feelings of anonymity and loneliness that New York's faceless throngs engender.

All the musical and theatrical elements of *Company* coalesce to reveal Bobby's mental and emotional fragmentation. He can't deal with the idea of living with seemingly irreconcilable opposites, whether in his psyche or his apartment. In this regard, Harry and the other husbands' "Sorry, Grateful" is the thematic centerpiece of the show. An article by Gerald Berkowitz titled "The Metaphor of Paradox in Sondheim's *Company*" takes off from "Sorry, Grateful" to point out elements of contradiction and paradox—here called fragmentation—in all the musical numbers: "Contradiction is part of the basic method of the play, as well as its message; virtually every musical number is built on internal contradictions—within the lyrics, between lyrics and music, between the song and the dramatic situation, between the song and the convention in which it is written, or between the singer's intention and what actually comes out. This unbroken pattern in *Company*'s musical half makes paradox and contradiction the controlling metaphor of the play" (Berkowitz 95). Further, "The play does not resolve these contradictions, but demands that they be accepted without being resolved. The only way to cope with life—the only way to live it—is to embrace it with all its paradoxes."

This is something the husbands comprehend, but bachelor Robert never quite gets it. Professionals in the fields of psychiatry and psychology have long understood that totally conflicting contents can and do exist harmoniously in the unconscious mind. Sondheim understood this too, since it is the premise of "Sorry, Grateful" and, indeed, of the entire musical. In reply to Bobby's "Harry? You ever sorry you got married?" Harry explains,

> You're always sorry,
> You're always grateful,
> You're always wondering what might have been.
> Then she walks in.
> And still you're sorry,
> And still you're grateful,
> And still you wonder and still you doubt,
> And she goes out.
>
> . . . . . . . .
> You're sorry-grateful,
> Regretful-happy.
> Why look for answers where none occur?
> You always are what you always were,
> Which has nothing to do with,
> All to do with her.
>
> (Sondheim, *Company* 35–36)

Each pair of lines presents a set of unresolved and unresolvable opposites (quite literally, paradoxes) that Harry and the other husbands accept as a necessary condition of married life. Putting aside the fact that there's no actual chronology in *Company*, in the real time of the musical on stage it's quite early when Robert hears this litany of the husbands' irreconcilable yet accepted contradictions, as well as the very explicit "Why look for answers where none occur?"—the key line to understanding the entire musical.

By play's end, however, all Robert concludes for himself is "alone is alone, not alive" (116), in a song that comes down on the side of commitment, if not marriage. But Sondheim never felt right about "Being Alive" replacing a much more ambivalent number: "I feel that the end of the show was a cop-out. When Bobby suddenly realizes that he shouldn't be alone at the end of the scene, it's too small a moment and you don't believe it" (qtd. in Zadan 125). Hal Prince also felt the song didn't conform to the rest of the show: "I am afraid it imposed a happy ending on a play which should have remained ambiguous" (Prince 156). Neither Prince nor Sondheim has stated why "Being Alive" replaced the earlier song, but one might speculate that this was perhaps *Company*'s one small concession to conventional audience expectations of something like a happy ending in an otherwise perfectly conceived, written, and staged *integrated* fragmented musical.

## The Me Nobody Knows

*The Me Nobody Knows* (12/18/70, following an off-Broadway run), universally praised for its candidness and honesty, employed a cast of children and teenagers to convey its social message. Stephen M. Joseph, a teacher, had edited a book of prose and verse by children mostly from the neighborhoods of Harlem and Bedford-Stuyvesant. With Robert H. Livingston and Herb Schapiro, he turned these writings into a libretto; Will Holt wrote the lyrics, with some additional ones by Schapiro, and Gary William Friedman composed the score. The result looked into the minds, hearts, and souls of ghetto kids—black, Hispanic, poor white—in each case revealing the genuine "Me" the title proclaimed.

*The Me Nobody Knows* transcended revue because of its complex, introspective characters (whose presence was the through-line of the show) and its thematic coherence. Part of the musical's charm and honesty was that the script and lyrics allowed each young character to speak in a voice very much like the actor's own, with no authorial agenda or message imposed on the source material. With only occasional editing, the monologues came verbatim from the verse and prose in Joseph's collection; even Holt and Schapiro mostly just shaped the lyrics from the children's writings, tightening them up or adding necessary rhythm and rhyme while retaining the personal essence of the originals. What emerged was not a cavalcade of complaint but the touching self-assertion of children with difficult lives. Nor do the characters ever ask the audience for anything like sympathy — understanding, maybe, but not pity. If *Company* was the first fragmented musical to focus exclusively on self-questioning, *The Me Nobody Knows* was the only one entirely of self-affirmation. The characters ask the audience to view them as special and unique human beings, not as generic blacks, Hispanics, or poor whites. The songs and monologues honestly convey "This is Me." That "Me" might be the child of a single parent or a single teenaged parent herself, a kid working to escape poverty, or a thirteen-year-old heroin addict. But each "I" is an authentic voice saying attention must be paid.

Will Holt's often funny yet heart-wrenching lyrics for the first act finale, "If I Had a Million," illustrate this well. The ghetto kids speculate on what they'd do with that kind of money. Absent is any altruism, except a philanthropy that actually reveals one kid's stinginess: "I'd give some part of somethin' to everyone / A nickel to UNICEF, a penny to you," or another's streetwise idea of charity: "I'd go up the street where they're linin' up for welfare / And buy everybody some stoney pony wine" (Holt 15). The kids express everything from tightwad selfishness to outrageous spending sprees. One young entrepreneur would buy a toll bridge to double his million; then "buy a cashmere coat / Save the rest for college" (20). Holt's lyrics expose these street kids' innocence about vast sums of money. One girl's vision is at once tough and touching, when she sings, "I'd take my brother down to the store / And buy him a shirt so he wouldn't take mine"; another explains the kind of smarts it takes to survive in the ghetto:

> If I
> If I had a million
> Million dollars—wouldn't tell a soul
> I wouldn't say nothin' about it to no one
> As soon as they hear it your money gets stole.
> (15)

Reviewer Clive Barnes understood that the fragmented musical was the right vehicle to convey these narratives: "There is no story, of course — rather it is a picture of a place and a time. . . . There is no story, but there are dozens of stories. . . . The stories have a validity, a feel of truth to them. . . . And they are given by the cast with just the right unblinking honesty" (qtd.

in Holt 2). Like *Company*, *The Me Nobody Knows* feels integrated even while depicting fragmented young lives in a metropolis that fosters human fragmentation. The show's honest tone ties everything together—the honesty stemming not just from the source material and adaptation but from the fact that some of its young actors were from these poor neighborhoods. The special magnetism of *The Me Nobody Knows* drew in audiences 794 times, 208 off-Broadway and 586 in the show's Broadway run.

## Follies

When the lights came up on Stephen Sondheim and James Goldman's *Follies* (4/4/71), Boris Aronson's setting of *"the shell, the remnants, all that's left of what was once a famous theatre"* was an immediate visual metaphor for the splintered human lives that would soon fill the space; *"The stage itself is vast. The brick wall at the back is only partly there, vast chunks of the proscenium are missing"* (Sondheim, *Follies* 3). This is the backdrop for the reunion of "The Weismann Girls," now women ranging roughly from forty-nine to eighty, who in their youth were the glamorous centerpieces of Dmitri Weismann's annual *Follies*. These former Follies girls, along with their husbands or escorts, have been brought together one last time by the seemingly ageless but clearly eightysomething Weismann himself, still *"acerbic, vital, energetic"* and a little bit lecherous (7). The reunion's ruined setting underscores the characters' recollections and also suggests the devastation of their present lives. While *Follies* in great part is a musical about past mistakes—what Goldman characterized as *"the immediacy of the past and . . . regret for what's been lost and wasted"* (30)—it also concerns making sense of that past in order to salvage the present and future. This is the musical's affirmative side, which too many viewers and critics have missed.

The soul-searching that is the lifeblood of fragmented musicals is at work in *Follies'* key songs. The four central characters—Benjamin Stone, his wife Phyllis, Sally Durant Plummer, and her husband Buddy—are the only ones who engage in intense introspection. Of the twelve songs these four sing either individually or in various combinations, nine are wholly or in part sung thought, interior monologues, soliloquies set to music. Early in the show, wealthy, prominent, unhappy, and confused Benjamin Stone sings "The Road You Didn't Take," which embodies the fragmented content and method of the whole show as well as defining its tone. Ben is singing to Sally (whom he may have loved but did not marry), but Sondheim's lyrics depict a man thinking out loud, really singing to himself. Sounding like an angst-driven Robert Frost, Ben sings,

> The road you didn't take
> Hardly comes to mind,
> Does it?
> The door you didn't try,
> Where could it have led?
> The choice you didn't make
> Never was defined,
> Was it?
> (Sondheim, *Follies* 37–38)

Those telltale little tags, "Does it?" and "Was it?" and others throughout the song, are the giveaways that disturbing doubts and questions linger to plague the mature Ben. Similarly, Sally sings "In Buddy's Eyes" more for her own sake than to Ben, and just prior to Phyllis seemingly directing "Could I Leave You" to her husband, the stage direction says she sings it *"as if thinking out loud"* (73). Other numbers by the four, though personal in their content and processes of self-examination, are done as "performance pieces" in the Follies-like "Loveland" sequence close to the end of the show, as if Ben and Buddy had also been in the *Follies*. The effect is one of total dislocation; a huge gulf yawns between the glitzy show biz *style* of these numbers and the profoundly personal investment each singer has in the *substance* of his or her song. This sequence includes Buddy's "The-God-Why-Don't-You-Love-Me-Blues," Sally's "Losing My Mind," Phyllis's "The Story of Lucy and Jessie," and Ben's "Live, Laugh, Love," in which, originally, he suffered a breakdown during his performance (later changed for a London production).

In their thoughts the central quartet of characters interact with young performers playing their younger selves, almost always, as in their solos, raising doubts and regrets about both their past and present lives. If all this seems a bit depressing, *Follies* also expresses a very positive point of view. Granted, the only characters an audience gets to know well—extremely well—are the four principals; others just pass through the party with a line or two of chat or step forward to perform a musical number smack out of nowhere, as one might do at a reunion or cast party. These are the songs the secondary characters sang in the *Follies* way back when. These numbers are lighter than the main characters' musical introspection but still significant. The happily lightweight "Listen to the Rain on the Roof" takes on meaning because it's sung and danced by Emily and Theodore Whitman, *"a tiny, bright, papery couple in their seventies"* (31), who met at a *Follies* audition God-knows-when and have been together ever since. Their upbeat routine is their self-declaration of "We're still married and still in love. Our choices worked the first time." Hattie's "Broadway Baby" depicts the persistence needed to make it in the business, and Carlotta's tour-de-force "I'm Still Here" is a classic, and often hilarious, ode to survival.

Sondheim's pastiche music and lyrics looked back to the great songwriters for extravagant revues in Broadway's earlier years, just as the entire musical's self-exploration looked inward for the show's characters as well as contemporary audiences. It was a difficult, challenging, yet exceptionally tuneful show for most spectators, with the result that *Follies* played 521 times—not bad in terms of longevity—but that wasn't enough; the enormously costly show lost its entire $800,000 investment (Zadan 181).

## Godspell

No problem with expenses or making its money back for the next fragmented show. To look at *Godspell* (5/17/71), the biggest up-front production costs appear to have been for gallons of clown-white make-up, a chainlink fence, and a basketful of costumes straight from Goodwill or the Salvation Army. Its original cast of ten unknown performers, most likely working for Equity off-Broadway minimum scale, weren't exactly going to break the bank either. After three months at the Cherry Lane Theatre, the show that looks like "St. Matthew Meets Marcel Marceau" trekked to the other end of town (but still off-Broadway) and the Upper West Side's Promenade Theatre for a five-year haul. There it logged 2,124 performances before moving once more, this time to Broadway for a final 527. The total 2,651 showings miraculously defied *Godspell's* general crucifixion by the critical press.

With a book by John-Michael Tebelak and lyrics and music by Stephen Schwartz, the musical featured a Jesus in a Superman tee-shirt and nine other equally adorable multi-racial urchins acting out parables, playing assorted apostles, and interacting with the unsuspecting audience. The entire proceedings (too cute for words in most critics' eyes) purported to be a joyous, childlike, musical retelling of the Gospel according to St. Matthew. The fact of the matter is, however, that *Godspell* consists mostly not of the biblical narrative but of a random assortment of clowned, camped, and otherwise energetically enacted parables mostly from the Book of Luke, not from Matthew at all. (Audiences looking for a narrative retelling of the Book of Matthew had to wait until October 1971, when *Jesus Christ Superstar* opened.) Essentially, all Matthew provides *Godspell* is a frame—the baptizing of Jesus by John the Baptist at the top of act 1, and then, starting late in act 2, the last supper, Judas's betrayal of Christ, and the Crucifixion. In between these few events, the focus is on Jesus' teachings and the joy of following Him, the show consisting mostly of a glut of parables trotted out (in good fragmented musical fashion) in no apparent order; switch them around and no one would notice. The urchins act out the parables in a performance mode somewhere between enthusiastic improvisation and drama therapy for manic-depressives. Interspersed are mostly upbeat, feel-good, spiritually rewarding songs (also in no apparent order), written and performed in a variety of styles from gospel to folk, pop, rock, and one truly impressive vaudeville routine for Jesus and Judas, "All for the Best." *Godspell*'s form is surely that of a fragmented musical, though at first its content seems to resemble neither the self-questioning nor self-affirming introspection characteristic of all other examples of the genre. And yet *Godspell*'s Jesus does ask his followers to look into themselves, whether to find the germ of the good they think they lack or to realize they are no better than anyone else. In this sense there is a fair bit of "soul-searching" of the frag-mented musical kind going on, perhaps helping to account for the show's enormous popularity throughout most of the soul-searching '70s.

Not all fragmented musicals were hits, not even those whose marriage of substance and form more resembled the genre than *Godspell*. Two such ill-fated shows opened three days apart in 1972: *Dude* (10/9/72) and *Hurry, Harry* (10/12/72). Each title character was in search of himself. *Dude* was written and composed by Gerome Ragni and Galt MacDermot—two-thirds of the team whose *Hair* originated the fragmented musical—and directed by Tom O'Horgan, who had staged that theatrical breakthrough. But they couldn't recreate their earlier success. *Dude*, a thoroughly incoherent frag-mented show, was something of a space-age, allegorical morality play during which the New Age Everyman Dude crawled through every cranny of the cosmos in search of meaning. But *Dude* slipped into a black hole after sixteen performances. *Hurry, Harry*, by five musical theatre unknowns, played just twice. The show took Harry (fully Harrison Fairchild IV) on a fragmented journey of self-discovery, but unlike Dude, he didn't leave the planet. After explaining that Harry is engaged to a young woman named Muffy Weathersford, Douglas Watt of the *Daily News* summed up this inanity: "He postpones their marriage until he can find his true self, which takes all of two acts. . . . Harry, between visits to his analyst, Dr. Krauss, tries film and stage producing, joining a Greek fishing community, religion, and a couple of other things, including a visit to Africa" (*NYTCR* 1972 220).

## Pippin

Substitute pursuing war, hedonism, revolution, politics, the arts, and the church for psychoanalysis and Greek fishing communities and you have the path trod by the title character of *Pippin* (10/23/72), yet another fragmented musical about a young man's journey to find his "Corner of the Sky." Written by Roger O. Hirson with music and lyrics by Stephen Schwartz, *Pippin* played 1,944 performances, demonstrating the high entertainment value (if lack of clarity) in Pippin's quest, as staged and choreographed by Bob Fosse. The opening, "Magic To Do," with its fog, blacklight, and Fosse's idiosyncratic dance moves, told the audience that they were about to watch a play within a play. Next, Pippin (son of the historical Charlemagne, fictionalized beyond recognition) tells his university tutors that what he's looking for "can't be found in books" and then tells everyone, audience included, that "I've got to be where my spirit can run free / Got to find my corner of the sky" (Hirson 5–7). "Corner of the Sky" gained wide popularity among young people well into the 1980s, as much for its introspection as its melody.

Home from college, Pippin tells Dad, the Holy Roman Emperor, that whatever he does he wants to do "as well as I possibly can. Otherwise, my life won't have any meaning at all" (16). From this point forward, the show's vignettes depict Pippin's generally botched and futile attempts to find himself. Save for the long "Hearth" vignette that is the penultimate section of the show, the others could be performed in almost any order; in fragmented musical fashion, there is no necessary dramatic or psychological progression among them. Pippin tries and rejects military heroism, hedonistic sensuality (at his grandmother's urging!), and a revolutionary coup to overthrow his father. Then he tries to rule himself but makes a mess of that, too. The Leading Player informs the audience that offstage Pippin had also vetoed art ("you got to be dead to find out if you were any good") and religion ("The church isn't saving souls, it's investing in real estate" [54]).

Pippin rejects these callings because they aren't, as his song says, "Extraordinary" enough for him, in his eyes an extraordinary person. That's where Pippin's thinking went haywire from the start. Thinking an "extraordinary" being like himself should be destined for more than domestic happiness, in the "Hearth" episode Pippin finds it hard to settle down with the young widow Catherine, an "everyday, customary, kind of woman," her young son, and his ailing pet duck (57). Yet in the last scene Pippin declines a final chance for a truly exceptional act since it turns out to involve self-immolation. For rejecting the pyrotechnics, the Leading Player strips all the glitz and glamour from the set and from Pippin's life. Pippin finally accepts a more modest life with Catherine—also coming to accept that he's not so extraordinary after all (82). The musical suggests that Pippin did not sell out or compromise his self-image, but like Candide comes to a more realistic view of how to live a meaningful life. Hirson's book remains pretty fuzzy on some points but seems to conclude that, after all the searching, Happiness Is living with a young widow, her son, and a dead duck. Not exactly universal words to live by. Fortunately, Fosse's mounting of the original production wallpapered over most such ideational cracks.

## A Chorus Line

It's a good thing the next fragmented musical required no such cosmetic surgery, since if it had any wrinkles, there was no place to hide them. On its bare stage there was no smoke and darn few mirrors, just a white stripe on the floor behind which, at the start, twenty-four young dancers stood, their bare faces, their bare souls, their bare lives exposed to each other and to the audience as they vied to be employed, albeit anonymously, in *A Chorus Line* (7/25/75). Since 1968, *Hair, Company, The Me Nobody Knows, Follies, Godspell*, and *Pippin* had demonstrated that a musical doesn't need a plot, least of all a typical boy-meets-girl plot, to be popular with audiences. But on September 29, 1983, *A Chorus Line*'s unprecedented 3,389th performance broke all Broadway records, demonstrating that America's musical-theatregoers had come to totally embrace the non-plot, concept, or fragmented musical. And not just embrace it—they virtually hugged the show to death. *A Chorus Line*'s final tally of 6,137 performances made it the only fragmented musical to survive the 1980s, closing on April 28, 1990.

Conceived by choreographer/director Michael Bennett, *A Chorus Line* was a reality-based musical, its source taped interviews with actual "gypsies," as Broadway dancers call themselves. Then it went through a lengthy workshop process courtesy of Joseph Papp, at whose Public Theatre it premiered on April 15, 1975. Each step of the workshopping process led toward the final scripted musical by James Kirkwood and Nicholas Dante, with music by Marvin Hamlisch and lyrics by Edward Kleban. And everything was under the watchful eye and ever-revising hand of Bennett.

Since it was grounded in conversations revealing real dancers' different backgrounds, experiences, and feelings, it's only natural that *A Chorus Line* evolved as a fragmented musical depicting both self-doubt and self-proclamation, sometimes in a single character. If self-questioning is more prevalent, that's because such personal examination is endemic to the breed. No matter how self-assured they might otherwise be, when faced with an audition many singers, actors, and dancers question not just their talent and skill but their very self-worth. The opening number gets to the core of this identity issue when Paul sings, "WHO AM I ANYWAY? / AM I MY RESUME? / THAT IS A PICTURE OF A PERSON I DON'T KNOW" (Hamlisch 22).

For just under two intermissionless hours, director/choreographer Zach's audition combines dance combinations with interviews that get deep inside these gypsies. An audience gets to know them very well; some of the dancers even get to know themselves better than before.

Edward Kleban brought to the characters' introspective lyrics a psychological depth almost approaching Sondheim's. In "At the Ballet" three "girls" from dysfunctional families totally expose their psychological reasons for starting to dance. Kleban's lyric has them reveal tremendous emotional pain through very a few words, words that deceptively seem just descriptive: "EVERYTHING WAS BEAUTIFUL AT THE BALLET, / RAISE YOUR ARMS, AND SOMEONE'S ALWAYS THERE" (49). So, too, in "Nothing" Diana Morales lets herself be wholly known at the end of her narrative of Mr. Karp, the acting teacher who nearly destroyed her self-confidence and career:

> Six months later I learned that Karp had died.
> And I dug right down to the bottom of my soul . . .
> And cried,
> 'Cause I felt . . . nothing.
>
> (67)

Like Morales, the other dancers weren't destroyed despite the psychological trauma, personal hardships, or family troubles life had in store; they all survived to dance — and audition — another day. If A Chorus Line is about any one thing, it's about resilience.

A few of these resilient dancers proclaim their self-worth and abilities without an apparent shred of self-doubt or insecurity. One of them is Mike, who sings "I Can Do That," and another, thanks to the miracle of silicone, is Val who performs "Dance: Ten; Looks: Three" (commonly known as "Tits and Ass"). In her big dance solo "The Music and the Mirror," Cassie, too, asserts this sort of self-confidence, the song's lyric proclaiming her a virtual exhibitionist who needs a job and an audience in order to be what she fundamentally is — a dancer. It's only Cassie's dialogue that exposes the ups and downs of her roller-coaster career and the self-questioning attendant upon such changes of theatrical fortune.

This mixture of confidence and doubt, assertion and questioning obtains for most of the rest as they vie for a spot in Zach's chorus line. Which brings up the matter of plot. Compared to all fragmented musicals before and after, A Chorus Line has something of a linear plot, which is simply this: which eight dancers will Zach finally choose? From that it can be argued that there is some dramatic tension, suspense, and resolution of the kind found in well-made-play kinds of plots. But was this "plot" the soul of the show's audience appeal? Can anyone, except a few dyed-in-the-wool

*Chorus Line* junkies (similar to *Hair's* more countless groupies) actually *name* all eight dancers Zach selects? It's doubtful. Plot isn't where the fascination lies. It's in the inner drama of the show's human personalities, as is true of all fragmented musicals. Barring the thin thread of plot and the story of the Zach/Cassie relationship, which plays as both contrived and coincidental, *A Chorus Line's* substance and form are those of a well-crafted fragmented musical.

## Runaways

Nearly three years after *A Chorus Line* debuted, the final two fragmented musicals of the decade opened one night after the other. Like *A Chorus Line*, *Runaways* (5/13/78) was developed at Joe Papp's Public Theatre, in this case from the personal accounts of runaway teens and pre-teens. Elizabeth Swados conceived the production, wrote the book and lyrics, composed the score, and directed the show. For two acts a company of twenty-eight multi-racial, multi-ethnic young people portrayed the fragmented lives of runaway kids, belting out Swados's songs and monologues (including a number in untranslated Spanish) in the seemingly random format of a fragmented musical. For 267 performances, the kids let the audience know who they were, where they came from, and what life on the streets was like, but mostly why they ran away. But I can state from personal experience—no, eavesdropping is more like it—what *Runaways'* trouble was. On opening night, as I made my way through the packed lobby at intermission, I repeatedly heard words to the effect of "This is *so* heavy-handed" and, above all, "My God, is this didactic!" However honestly Swados had recorded the runaways' remarks, she apparently shaped and edited their thoughts into a finger-pointing agenda, hence the multiple "didactic" and "heavy-handed" comments at the act-break. In the show's simplistic and reductive thinking, the cause of the entire runaway problem boiled down simply to—parents. Nine of the twenty-one songs and speeches in act 1 alone, or nearly half, blame dysfunctional families, single-parent households, divorce, and other parent-driven problems for the kids' current status as junkies, criminals, or teenage prostitutes. Right from opening night, audiences were put off by *Runaways'* one-dimensional approach to a very complex problem.

## Working

*Working* (5/14/78) was as honest as *Runaways* was dishonestly skewed. And yet, this musical portrait of America at work taken from Studs Terkel's monumental collection of interviews lasted only twenty-five performances, despite previous success at Chicago's Goodman Theatre, where *Working* had been developed. The show was the brainchild of *Godspell* and *Pippin* composer/lyricist Stephen Schwartz. But this time Schwartz didn't work with just one collaborator. *Working* is truly a musical written by a committee. Schwartz shaped the show and pared down the monologues from the often-rambling oral testimony in Terkel's book, while songwriters Craig Carnelia, Micki Grant, Mary Rodgers, Susan Birkenhead, James Taylor, and Schwartz himself created a varied collection of musical numbers.

Although he gave no particular label to what he and his cohorts had done, Schwartz recognized that they had not written either of the two kinds of musicals most familiar to Broadway: "WORKING is not a 'book musical', of course in that there is no narrative thread carrying the action forward. But neither is it a revue, with the separate scenes occurring haphazardly and interchangeably" (Schwartz, p. c). It was, though namelessly, a fragmented musical. In talking or singing about their work, some of the characters, like "Lovin' Al" the parking lot attendant and "The Mason," take self-affirming personal pride in their jobs. Most self-proclaiming of all is the professional waitress. For her "It's an Art" to wait tables; whenever anyone asks her why she's "just" a waitress, she retorts, "Why? Don't you think you deserve to be served by me!" (II-3). For other workers, the drudgery of their tasks makes them turn inward in virtual self-questioning agony, such as the woman who is "Just a Housewife" and the group who are "Cleanin' Women" "WITHOUT FACES / COMIN' AND GOIN' ON A FIRST NAME BASIS" (II-17). Perhaps more anguished than any other is the young assemblyline worker in James Taylor's graphic and powerful "Millwork," whose routine of unfulfilling, soul-killing tedium has made her old and despairing before her time:

MILLWORK AIN'T EASY
MILLWORK AIN'T HARD
MILLWORK AIN'T NOTHIN' BUT
A GODDAMN AWFUL BORING JOB
. . . . . . . . . . . . . . .
IT'S MY LIFE HAS BEEN WASTED
AND I HAVE BEEN A FOOL
TO LET THIS MANUFACTURE'
USE MY BODY FOR A TOOL
I GET TO RIDE HOME IN THE EVENINGS
STARING AT MY HANDS
SWEARING BY MY SORROW
THAT A YOUNG GIRL OUGHT TO STAND A BETTER CHANCE
. . . . . . . . . . . . . . . . . . . . . . . .
AND IT'S ME AND MY MACHINE

FOR THE REST OF THE MORNING
FOR THE REST OF THE AFTERNOON GONE . . .
AND THE REST OF MY LIFE . . .
(Schwartz I-33–34)

The common denominator to all of the introspection in *Working* is its absolute authenticity, with no authorial agenda or editorializing. In the Director's Script Schwartz even requests the following note be included in theatre programs "where it is highly visible and likely to be read": "The characters in WORKING are non-fictional characters. Their names have been changed, but their words have not. Even in the case of song lyrics, the writers have tried to remain as faithful as possible to the character's original words" (p. e).

There is a common denominator to the characters in *Working* too. With the exception of an editor, c.e.o., and teacher, none of the others is even remotely a professional. They are steelworkers and newsboys, firemen and housewives and migrant farm workers, prostitutes and factory workers and meter readers and supermarket checkers, the kinds of people, some would argue, that make the country run on a daily basis, but also the kind that too many "professional" Americans never really "see" or, if they see, scarcely notice. This working-class anonymity is part of *Working*'s power but also, perhaps, part of the reason it failed on Broadway. The majority of people who attend Broadway shows are middle-Americans who have little real contact with the people the show portrays.

Conversely, *Working*'s "grassroots" or populist appeal helped account for its phenomenal popularity beyond Broadway. The musical has continued to have an ongoing life in professional regional theatre and in college, high school, community, and other non-professional theatres all across the United States. Statistical support bears this out. Music Theatre International leases performance rights to *Working* for all theatres, from regional Equity companies to community theatres. Although MTI was unable to locate the numbers for 1978 through 1989, in just the period from 1990 through August 31, 2000, MTI gave permissions for 351 separate American productions of *Working*, an average of just over thirty-five regional productions a year (Faircloth interview). From that figure it can be extrapolated that the number would have been at least as high, if not higher, during the show's first twelve years with MTI which were closer to its Chicago and New York appearances. Such a record of regional performances validates how this "working-class" fragmented musical continues to speak to production companies and audiences across the United States. Further attesting to the show's continuing viability, a revised, updated version of *Working* debuted at New Haven's Long Wharf Theatre in 1999.

*The Fragmented Musical's Legacy*

*Hair* opened on Broadway on April 29, 1968, *Working* on May 14, 1978, framing the ten-year period of fragmented musicals; there would be but two more before the end of the century. Other than those shows whose long runs continued into the 1980s, the phenomenon of the fragmented musical ended as abruptly as it had begun. Traditionally linear, plot-driven shows did not disappear during the period of the fragmented musicals, and as the 1970s came to a close more and more book shows of conventional form opened. At the same time there began wave after wave of revivals and a resurgence of revues, most appealing to the widespread nostalgia that began in the '70s and became even more pronounced in the '80s and '90s (see chapter 9). Still, the fragmented musical made an indelible contribution to the book shows of future decades. Interest in character psychology and the technique of sung thought goes back at least to Oscar Hammerstein's pioneering text for "Soliloquy" in *Carousel*, but even during the flush years of the integrated musical, story always took precedence over the inner lives of characters. No longer would this be the case. Fragmented musicals demonstrated how theatrically riveting for audiences the inner workings of the psyche can be, and as musicals entered the 1980s shows with even the strongest plots would also explore in song the characters' psychological lives.

Sondheim followed his fragmented *Company* and *Follies* with a musical adaptation of Ingmar Bergman's *Smiles of a Summer Night*, a film with a fairly linear plot. The ultimate Hugh Wheeler/Stephen Sondheim product, *A Little Night Music* (2/25/73), was fairly linear as well. Even with all its unconventional devices, like the quintet, it is still a story-oriented musical with a beginning, middle, and end. Yet, for all that, a full seven of the show's sixteen musical numbers (and, arguably, parts of others) are instances of reflexive sung thought; it is a show as entertaining for what is going on within the characters as between them. The same technique can be seen in the even more strongly linear *Sweeney Todd* in 1979, thematically discussed below. Granted, *Sweeney* had audiences on the edge of their proverbial seats on its strength as the musical "Thriller" it called itself. But the psychologically savvy Sondheim also gave audiences ample opportunity to look into the complex recesses of Sweeney's psyche in such moments as his act 1 "Epiphany" and his act 2 version of "Johanna." Johanna's own "Green Finch and Linnet Bird" is a metaphoric revelation of the young woman's neurosis which the Victorian world labeled "hysteria." If Sondheim gets inside Mrs. Lovett's head at all, it is to reveal that there isn't much difference between her inside and outside; her thoughts, accordingly, are appropriately transparent in "The Worst Pies in London." And though the number was cut, Judge Turpin's "Johanna" is a chilling exploration of psychological pathology.

As he moved into the 1980s and beyond, Sondheim continued to explore character psychology in his words and music for such shows as *Sunday in the Park with George, Into the Woods, Assassins,* and *Passion.* And in the last two decades of the twentieth century a growing number of other lyricists and composers, including William Finn and Maury Yeston, incorporated the introspective interest and methods of fragmented musicals into otherwise linear shows, demonstrable evidence that the fragmented musical had left its mark as a permanent legacy to the American musical stage.

### Personal Alienation in the Musicals of Sondheim and Others

Central to all fragmented musicals from *Hair* to *Working* was the theme of alienation from society; from there it found its way into some traditionally plot-driven musicals and one revue. Around 1990, *Washington Post* journalist and historian Haynes Johnson concluded that "American life grows increasingly fragmented and divisive" (468). More people than ever felt cut adrift from family or society; some were even losing touch with themselves. While varieties of alienation occur in many late-century musicals, the motif was absolutely central to three shows by Sondheim and three others by various writers.

### Sweeney Todd

With 557 performances, Stephen Sondheim and Hugh Wheeler's *Sweeney Todd: The Demon Barber of Fleet Street* (3/1/79) was at least on the edge of popular, if not financial, success. The musical's subtitle "A Musical Thriller" may have been enough of a red herring to throw people off the scent that *Sweeney Todd* was much more than that. At bottom *Sweeney* is profound social commentary—an indictment of not just the inequities of classism in Victorian England but of contemporary American culture as well. *Sweeney* suggests that the United States today is as over-industrialized and depersonalized as Charles Dickens's London, with the result that many people, like Sweeney, feel disempowered and without access to "the system" so that the only choices left are despair or desperate action.

Contemporary similarities were conveyed indirectly and metaphorically in *Sweeney's* thrilling, macabre, and often very funny story. *Sweeney's* plotline metaphor comes from the conventions of an older theatrical form, Elizabethan revenge tragedy, an observation first made to me by my then wife Sandra Pirie Carson moments after we left the second press performance on March 2, 1979. Its thematic metaphor for social dynamics has roots in Brecht's dog-eat-dog view of society in *The Threepenny Opera*, objectified in *Sweeney* to include literal cannibalism. And the visual metaphor in the original production was Eugene Lee's gargantuan set built largely from the rusted-out skeleton and grimy glass skylight of an abandoned iron foundry, a set too huge to be confined by the already huge stage of the Uris Theatre, the skylight jutting out over the first several rows of the audience (our seats were *under* it). The set dwarfed the actors, making them appear tiny, insignificant cogs in a callous techno-establishment society. Of these metaphors, the theatrical-structural one is the most potent, both because it is the most familiar and because it drives the action of *Sweeney* throughout, that action vividly dramatizing the theme of alienation and its consequences.

The premise of revenge tragedy (most familiar in *Hamlet*) is the dilemma of a person alienated from yet trapped within a hostile, often dangerous society. Revenge in such plays is given sanction (if at all) only because the hero, in order to redress a grievous wrong to family and/or self (Hamlet Sr.'s murder; Todd's wife's rape and apparent suicide), has no recourse to the law to redress the wrong because a representative of the law and establishment (King Claudius, Judge Turpin) perpetrated the crime he must avenge. Hence the protagonist must step outside the law and assume the role of private avenger, a risky business at best. In broad outline, from that premise the genre established a series of conventions of plot and character: the hero returning from afar (Hamlet from Wittenburg; Todd from Australia), the hero disguising himself, the hero missing one opportunity to effect his revenge, the hero slipping into madness real or pretended, a widening circle of killings and revenge, the death of the avenger, etc. All these and the rest appear with dramatic clarity as plot points in the musical, though only a few occur in *Sweeney Todd*'s immediate source, a play of the same name by British actor Christopher Bond (for details of revenge conventions in *Sweeney Todd* see Jones, "From Melodrama").

That *Sweeney*'s use of revenge conventions had its desired effect is clear from audience reactions to Todd. No turning away from him in fear and loathing as from an unregenerate serial killer in a Hollywood slasher. No laughing at him, except where appropriate, as a comically deranged murderer in a parody melodrama. To the contrary, the audience I was in was so moved by how deeply Todd had been wronged that when the vile Judge Turpin slipped from his grasp in act 1, audible boos, hisses, and groans broke out from a presumably sophisticated press-night audience. When Todd finally did in Turpin in act 2, the audience applauded and cheered. Then, when he discovered his zeal for revenge led him to unwittingly kill his beloved wife, Lucy (presumed dead), in whose name he was seeking vengeance, that same audience emitted audible if choked-back sobs. These turned to outright weeping when Len Cariou's Sweeney, knowing he must die for overreaching his revenge, raised his neck to receive the razor's edge from the demented Tobias. These were not reactions to the hero-villain of a "thriller" but to a truly tragic figure.

As an objective correlative to Bertolt Brecht's "What keeps a man alive? He lives on others. / He likes to taste them first, then eat them whole if he can" (Marc Blitzstein's translation), *Sweeney Todd* turned metaphoric cannibalism to actual cannibalism with Mrs. Lovett's human fillings for her meat pies. Something so grisly could work only if treated comically, as it was in act 2's opening "God, That's Good!" and the lilting, show-stopping waltz "A Little Priest" with which Todd and Mrs. Lovett close act 1. For all of this song's black humor and infectious melody, "A Little Priest" also seriously and forthrightly articulated the show's focal social commentary (ellipses for omitted lines not indicated):

> For what's the sound of the world out there?
> Those crunching noises pervading the air?
> It's man devouring man, my dear,
> And who are we
> To deny it in here?
>
> . . . . . . . .
> The history of the world, my love—
> —is those below serving those up above.
> How gratifying for once to know—
> —that those above will serve those down below!
>
> . . . . . . . . . . . . . . . . . . . .
> The history of the world, my sweet—
> —is who gets eaten and who gets to eat.
>
> (Sondheim, *Sweeney* 105, 108, 110)

## Nine

Suggested by Federico Fellini's film 8½ and adapted from the Italian by Mario Fratti, *Nine* (5/9/82) had music and lyrics by Maury Yeston and a book by Arthur Kopit. *Nine* is unique as the only musical of the twentieth century that confronts male mid-life crisis. With a cast of one man, twenty-two women, and four little boys (one of whom is Guido's nine-year-old self), *Nine* depicts fortyish film-maker Guido Contini at an impasse in his life, his career, and his creativity, which the shadowy Our Lady of the Spa explains are all pretty much the same: in a domino effect, when Guido's personal life begins to fall apart, the other facets of his life follow suit. For most of the show Guido is floundering, unable to find himself no matter where he looks. Throughout this unconventional musical he's torn between what seems to be genuine love for his wife, out-and-out lust for Carla, and some combination of these feelings for Claudia, whom he claims to worship as his muse and inspiration. As if this weren't enough, Guido is constantly trying to meet the demands of the other women in his life, from his mother to producers and press agents. He expresses his dilemma as well as anyone (a dilemma that seems to be only marginally resolved with the embrace of his wife at the final curtain):

> I WOULD LIKE TO BE EVERYWHERE AT ONCE.
> I KNOW THAT'S A CONTRADICTION IN TERMS,
> AND IT'S A PROBLEM, ESPECIALLY WHEN
> MY BODY'S CLEARING FORTY AS MY MIND IS NEARING TEN:
> (Kopit 13)

With Raul Julia as the abstracted auteur and a bevy of gifted, gorgeous women like Karen Akers, Shelly Burch, Liliane Montevecchi, and Anita Morris all under Tommy Tune's stylish direction, *Nine* kept people showing up 739 times to watch Guido almost terminally screw up his life in the very act of trying to sort it out—just like in the real world.

## Sunday in the Park with George

Stephen Sondheim and James Lapine's Pulitzer Prize-winning *Sunday in the Park with George* (5/2/84) dramatized in each act and through two different characters a rather rarefied form of isolation and alienation—the insularity of the artist-genius, a condition sometimes self-imposed and frequently perceived by the artist as necessary for the creation of art. *Sunday's* two stories depict a fictionalized portion of the life of the historical French pointillist painter Georges Seurat, and his entirely fictional American great-grandson (both called "George" in the musical). Yet the show is as much about art theory as the lives of the artists. The dialogue, lyrics, and action take up such issues as pure aesthetics and what makes art art, what the artist has to do—and sacrifice—to achieve it, and the relationship of the artist to his calling, his public, his critics, and, most essentially, to his life and himself.

Each George estranges himself from personal and professional relationships. Professionally, act 1's fictionalized Seurat distances himself from influential if conventional artists and critics as represented by the character Jules. In his personal life, George alienates his pregnant mistress — playfully named "Dot" by Sondheim and Lapine. She leaves him for Louis, a baker, when she realizes that because of his consuming absorption in artistic creation George can't give her or the child-to-be the attention they need. The second-act American George, already divorced, watches some of his associates in creating works of techno-art leave him for other pursuits, just as influential members of the art community begin to distance themselves from him because of the repetitiveness and growing commercialism of his creations. Some artists — not George alone — deem isolation from both personal relationships and the professional world necessary. This is most fully articulated in act 1 by Jules's wife, Yvonne: "Oh, I suppose Jules cares — but there are times when he just does not know Louise [their daughter] and I are there. George always seems so oblivious to everyone." And George himself says, "I am not hiding behind my canvas — I am living in it," "I am what I do," and "Louis will be a loving and attentive father. I cannot because I cannot look up from my pad" (Sondheim, *Sunday* 102, 107, 108, 117). Ironically, the solitary artist's perceived need for self-imposed insularity is portrayed in a consummate example of artistic collaboration in the musical theatre.

*Sunday in the Park* is one of those rare music theatre pieces whose artistry is its message. The show is arguably the twentieth century's apotheosis of Richard Wagner's vision and goal of the *Gesamtkunstwerk*, the theatrical work in which nothing exists purely for itself without connection to the whole. The contributions of *Sunday's* collaborators indeed harmonize to communicate a single drama and a single expression of the musical's intellectual and emotional content. A simple illustration: the first act fictionalizes the time in Georges Seurat's life when he was completing his acknowledged masterpiece, *Sunday Afternoon on the Island of La Grande Jatte*. As developer of the theory and practice of pointillism, Seurat devised a painting technique of applying to the canvas countless dots of pure color in close proximity for the eye of the beholder to mix and mingle into yet more variegated hues. This painting principle, organic to the show's subject matter, was not just the metaphor but the cue for the entire creative team crafting the musical. Not only were Tony Straiges's settings painted with Seurat's pointillistic technique, but the costume fabrics designed by Patricia Zipprodt and Ann Hould-Ward were handpainted with tiny dots of color to make them harmonize with the sets. In numbers like "Color and Light" Sondheim used quick staccato passages — the musical equivalent of pointil-

listic dots—while his lyrics consisted of clipped, often disassociated mono-
syllables. While painting, but occasionally glancing at Dot, George sings to
himself,

> Blue blue blue blue
> Blue still sitting
> Red that perfume
> Blue all night
> Blue-green the window shut
> Dut dut dut
> Dot Dot sitting
> Dot Dot waiting
> Dot Dot getting fat fat fat
> (51)

Such a non-linear lyric forces hearers to try making logical sense of it on
their own, just as the optic nerve of Seurat's spectator ultimately helps
complete the painter's color schemes.

This device, in the quest to achieve the perfect *Gesamtkunstwerk*, leads
to Lapine and Sondheim's most brilliant accomplishment in *Sunday*. When
they opted to write a show about art, they could have chosen just about any
artist from Michelangelo to Grandma Moses. But Seurat seems to have
been more than a happy accident. His pointillistic technique demands the
collaboration of the painting's viewer, observing it from just the right distance, to complete the work of art. Regarding the musical, Lapine said, "A
lot of people who come to Broadway come not to work. They come to
forget. And that's not what *Sunday* is about. If you just sit back and watch,
you're probably going to get bored. You really have to listen. And you have
to think. Not a lot, but you can't let it wash over you like certain other
shows" (qtd. in Zadan 314).

Sondheim and Lapine seem to have chosen Seurat specifically as an
artist whose approach to art mirrored their own. As Seurat forced viewers
to collaborate with the painting in order to fully appreciate it, Sondheim
and Lapine wrote a musical in which the audience had to similarly collaborate—to meet the show halfway. Put simply, just as Seurat had done with
easel art, Sondheim and Lapine plugged in the last piece of the more than
century-old *Gesamtkunstwerk* puzzle by making the *audience* itself the ultimate collaborator in creating the unified Master Art Work in the theatre.
And while plenty of people *were* bored enough or baffled enough to walk
out on *Sunday in the Park* (I watched a good number leave when I saw the
show well into its run), there were many more who cheered or, indeed,
wept openly at the sheer beauty of the first-act finale, when Seurat's painting

comes together in a living tableau. Enough sympathetic viewers were ready to work with the musical in the way Lapine describes 604 times.

*Sunday* dramatized solo artists' self-perception that insularity is needed to create, despite its deleterious effect of alienating them from both personal and professional associations. But at one point near the top of act 2, Sondheim and Lapine express how the need *to interact* with certain segments of contemporary American culture is equally damaging, since it takes the artist away from what his special gifts empower him to do in the first place — create art. In what looks like veiled commentary on cutbacks in the National Endowment for the Arts and other sources of both public and private arts funding in the United States, Lapine and Sondheim show how the pragmatic necessities of staying alive, producing one's art, and having it displayed increasingly compromise both the artist and the works. "Putting It Together" pointedly depicts how art is forced to intersect with contemporary social and political realities. In this number, young George is at a cocktail reception following the abortive unveiling of Chromolume #7, and he immediately makes it known that he'd rather be anywhere but there. But what young George needs to put together his artworks *are* there — the people who represent funding, displaying, publicizing, and the like — so he'd better be there too. With the artist needing to pay for his materials as well as eat, the artwork thus becomes an increasingly commercialized "product." After assaying what influential people are at the party, George determines, "It's time to get to work," meaning "working the room," as the expression goes (159). His song progressively heaps up all the ancillary but necessary components to making art, concluding near the end

> All it takes is time and perseverance,
> With a little luck along the way,
> Putting in a personal appearance,
> Gathering supporters and adherents . . .
>
> Lining up a prominent commission —
> And an exhibition in addition —
> Here a little dab of politician —
> There a little touch of publication —
> Till you have a balanced composition —
> Everything depends on preparation —
> Even if you do have the suspicion
> That it's taking all your concentration —
>                          (164–77 *passim*)

Aware that such self-promotion is draining his creative energies, young George travels to Paris in an attempt to refresh himself. There the apparition of Dot appears to him on the island of La Grande Jatte. Through Dot, George finds the inspiration to experiment again and have the courage and resolve to "Move On":

> Anything you do,
> Let it come from you.
> Then it will be new.
> Give us more to see . . .
> (198)

One final irony of genuine social interest involves the intersection of *Sunday* with the world of corporate advertising. The show itself eloquently espouses individual artistic creativity (sometimes no matter how high the price) while condemning the crass commercialization of one's art by merely reproducing for gain what worked and/or sold in the past. It is therefore either hilarious or frightening (or both) that the Xerox Corporation — seemingly with no appreciation for irony — for a long time used "Putting It To-gether" as its advertising jingle in commercials flakking products whose sole function is to clone copy after exact copy of reproductions of originals.

### 3 Guys Naked from the Waist Down

Just in terms of story, 3 *Guys Naked from the Waist Down* (2/5/85) drama-tized the title guys trying to make it as stand-up comics. In this offbeat show with book and lyrics by Jerry Colker and music by Michael Rupert, two of the guys do achieve careers for themselves, while the third, a troubled soul from the start, takes his own life. The expression of alienation lies not just in Kenny's suicide but in two songs, "The American Dream" and "I Don't Believe in Heroes," both historical overviews of the past several decades that concern the sources of rootlessness in the 1980s. The first song's lyrics and dialogue-breaks humorously trace how the American Dream changed def-initions decade by decade. In the 1950s, "when greasy-haired men said they were 'Boss,' pony-tailed women said they were virgins and everybody was lying," everyone's dream was "to make a lot of money." During the peace-and-love phase of the '60s, "we all had a dream: to give away a lot of money to just about everybody." The disco-happy, narcissistic '70s enjoined us to "SEE YOURSELF AS SOMEONE EVERYBODY ADMIRES / AH AH HAVE SOME FUN / AND LOOK OUT FOR NUMBER ONE," the same decade in which "we all had a dream: to invest a lot of money in a tropical island and have a French horny midget that says, 'Boss, Boss, de plane! de plane!' " These dreams prefaced those icons of the 1980s, the New Religious Right and the Wall Street rip-off artists. From which, the three guys conclude, they and the country need a new American Dream (Colker 54–56). Kenny later articulates his disillusionment and personal dislocation just before his suicide, lamenting, "I Don't Believe in Heroes Anymore." As a little kid he had Robin Hood and Sir Galahad and other idealized storybook figures to look up to; and then

WHEN I WAS A BOY OF TEN
J. F. K. HAD SHOWN THE WAY
TO PUSH THE RUSSIANS BACK FROM FIRING RANGE
AND IN MY TEENS A MAN CALLED "CHE"
SPREAD WORD OF MARX AND MAO TO SAY
THE WORLD MUST CHANGE

but

I SAT BEFORE MY T. V. SET
AND WATCHED MY HEROES DIE
I READ THE RAGS AND PAPERS
SHOWING THAT MY HEROES LIED
WITH EARLY DEATH THEIR ONLY WREATH
TO PASS THROUGH HEAVEN'S DOOR
I SEE THEIR CONTRADICTIONS
AND I DON'T BELIEVE IN HEROES ANYMORE
(87–88)

In the final stanza Kenny laments a world too complex, chaotic, and impersonal to sustain individual heroism, so that, without strong role models, many people feel isolated and alienated. *3 Guys Naked* vividly expressed the cultural alienation of the 1980s for 160 performances.

## Personals

*Personals* (11/14/85) utilized the conceit of writing, reading, and responding to personal ads to disclose the difficulties of meeting a life-long mate—or sometimes just a friend—in the 1980s. The revue began at Brandeis University, with sketches and lyrics by David Crane, Marta Kauffman, and Seth Friedman, and music by William Dreskin and Joel Phillip Friedman. *Personals* was a national student playwriting winner in the American College Theatre Festival and accordingly was presented at Washington's Kennedy Center. From there it was refined and rewritten for an off-Broadway production, and composers Stephen Schwartz, Alan Menken, and Michael Skloff came on board the creative team. *Personals* played at the Minetta Lane Theatre 265 times, during which its cast of six most often comically bared the souls of America's "relationally challenged" — the lonely, the neurotic, the insecure, the desperate, so desperate they'd go to any length to find a mate — well, almost any length: "Mother, I am not going to Rose Siegel's funeral just to meet her son. That's it!" (Crane 21). For all its fun and its quirky characters, *Personals'* songs and sketches are psychologically sound. "A Night Alone" comically depicts Sam, a New York bachelor, putting a brave face on a dateless weekend night. But soon he's pressing his buzzer just to talk to the doorman, who hasn't time to chat,

> SO I PACE AND I POKE
> AND I SMOKE HALF A PACK
> AS I PICK THE DEAD LEAVES
> FROM MY FICUS THAT'S DYING OF ROOT ROT.
>                               (27–28)

Subsequent channel-surfing and searching for dust bunnies are interrupted when Claire, a new neighbor in search of a blender for a party she's having, invites Sam to come (*"There is an immediate attraction"*). He lamely declines when he realizes Claire has a date: "No thanks, I've got lots of things I've got to do tonight. Really. I have to do . . . things" (30). Contrasting with Sam's comic number, "Michael" is a flat-out unfunny expression of real, raw, totally vulnerable, desperate loneliness. Kim, a woman close to the edge or possibly over it, sings what she'd *like* to say on the phone to the man she regrets having divorced. The song is powerful because it allows Kim to be "wholly known," in Arthur Miller's phrase. Kim's revelation of her desperate loneliness climaxes very simply with the words

> WELL, I'M LONELY.
> GUESS YOU KNEW THAT.
> AND I LOVE YOU.
> REALLY REALLY.
>
> . . . . . . . . .
> MICHAEL, MARRY ME.
> MICHAEL, MARRY ME AGAIN.
>                               (65–66)

Through its serio-comic depictions of both the wackos and normal folks who place and answer personal ads, *Personals* incisively painted portraits of individual psychologies that came together as an equally accurate sociological mural of alienation and fragmentation among singles in late-twentieth-century America.

## Assassins

The alienation Stephen Sondheim and John Weidman's *Assassins* (1/27/91) depicts is of the same order as that in *Sweeney Todd*—the sense of societal dislocation that drives people to commit desperate acts. But here it is infinitely more frightening than in *Sweeney* since those acts were historical realities—the attempted or actual assassinations of American presidents. *Assassins* was a show whose very existence courted controversy—even among those who didn't see it. André Bishop, then artistic director of Playwrights Horizons, where the show was produced, observed, "Some people said, their eyebrows raised to the heavens, 'Oh, you can't do a show about those killers. It's a taboo subject in America.' Others felt, before they saw the show or because they didn't see the show, that it glorified assassination; others were overwhelmed" (Bishop, Preface x). Controversy translated into dichotomy: almost uniformly negative reviews, countered by "the enthusiasm of audiences and . . . the long lines of people waiting for ticket cancellations every night" (Preface vii) until *Assassins'* run was aborted after just twenty-five performances, with no Broadway engagement to follow. Just what was this show that incensed some while others embraced it rapturously?

Groping for words to describe the show's format or genre, Bishop refers to "the revue/vaudeville/musical comedy scheme" of *Assassins*. But what in fact Sondheim and Weidman did was to resuscitate the form and methods of that dominant mode of 1970s shows, the fragmented (commonly known as "concept") musical, as an appropriate framework in which nine of the eleven successful or would-be assassins of American presidents could explain why they did it. While the show's ninety or so intermissionless minutes are filled with historical characters and events, or imagined extrapolations from historical events, unlike most conventional book musicals *Assassins* is not linear, as might be expected of an historically based musical. But neither is it a revue, with songs and sketches performed in any order as performance pieces alone. *Assassins* is peopled front to back with flesh-and-blood personages out of history, people with real names, real biographies, and real psychologies, baring their real souls about what drove them to their very real acts of not-so-quiet desperation. After its bizarrely riveting first scene at a carnival shooting gallery, *Assassins* begins in a tobacco barn with John Wilkes Booth, the earliest of the assassins, in flight after mortally wounding Lincoln. But from there the show does not proceed chronologically to end with John Hinckley's 1981 attempt on Ronald Reagan's life. Instead, the musical depicts scenes of the assassins in a seemingly random but theatrically effective order, including imaginative moments that bring figures from different time periods together. Just prior to the finale is the terrifying scene in the Dallas Book Depository. Led by Booth as their spiritual mentor (as he is throughout the play), apparitions of all of the assassins past and future appear to Lee Harvey Oswald, pleading with him to shoot JFK (not himself, as he had planned) in order to validate their own realized or attempted acts of presidential murder (speech heads omitted; ellipses in text):

> Through you and your act we are revived and given meaning . . .
> Our lives, our acts, are given meaning . . .
> Our frustrations fall away . . .
> Our fondest dreams come true . . .
> Today we are reborn, through you . . .
> We need you, Lee.
> Without you, we're just footnotes in a history book.
>                                   (Sondheim, *Assassins* 100)

Booth says, "this—right here, right now—this is the real conspiracy" (97), the conspiracy of America's desperate and marginalized taking drastic steps to get noticed. Most thoughtful writers on the subject have agreed that this is what *Assassins* is really about.

Sondheim's approach to composing most of the nine or so musical numbers is right in line with the show's overall approach of "fragmented history." By *Assassins*, Sondheim was no stranger to the effectiveness of pastiche numbers, songs written to replicate those of another time, place, or even specific composer and lyricist. *Follies* is full of these, but in no other Sondheim score do pastiche numbers dominate to the extent they do in *Assassins*. Each historically associated scene employs music appropriate to it. John Wilkes Booth and the Balladeer, the show's running narrator/commentator, perform what sounds mostly like a traditional American folksong in "The Ballad of Booth." The crowd babbling to the press about "How I Saved Roosevelt" do so to the patriotic strains of some actual and pseudo-Sousa marches, counterpointed by a kind of demented Italian tarantella sung by would-be FDR assassin Giuseppe Zangara, still angry even in the electric chair. "The Ballad of Czolgosz"—would-be anarchist and McKinley's assassin—the Balladeer sings to a tune right out of the last days of minstrel shows or early vaudeville, totally right for the scene's 1901 setting. The improbable duet "Unworthy of Your Love" finds Lynette "Squeaky" Fromme and John Hinckley, the would-be assassins of Gerald Ford and Ronald Reagan, together singing a heartfelt '70s soft-rock love song to their idols they did it for, Charles Manson and Jody Foster. "The Ballad of Guiteau" embraces three musical traditions: Charles Guiteau — President Garfield's assassin and erstwhile preacher, among other things — sings a sort of spiritual (part of which is the historical Guiteau's own words); the Balladeer fills in the narrative in folksong tradition; and Guiteau does a song-and-dance routine up the gallows steps to an authentic-sounding cakewalk. Even "The Gun Song," set more in limbo than reality and mostly in Sondheim's own musical voice, contains moments of the purely American art of barbershop quartet singing. *Assassins's* deliberately fragmented format thus comes together with its disjunct musical styles to form a single, organic piece of theatre: in a word, another instance of *Gesamtkunstwerk*.

But why? People kept asking — including nearly every New York and national critic. André Bishop observed, "The chief criticism we heard was that the show had no point of view; how could you write a show about people who kill Presidents and not have a point of view?" (Preface x). But the *Times*' Frank Rich saw and expressed well its point of view:

Without exactly asking that the audience sympathize with some of the nation's most notorious criminals, this show insists on reclaiming them as products, however defective, of the same values and traditions as the men they tried to murder.... [T]hese killers want to grab headlines, get the girl, or see their name in lights.... These are the lost and underprivileged souls who, having been denied every American's dream of growing up to be President, try to achieve a warped, nightmarish inversion of that dream instead. (NYTCR 1991 362)

*Assassins* opened during the Persian Gulf War in the winter of 1991. Because many Americans were feeling patriotic for the first time in years, André Bishop speculated that they "might not want to see something that presented a darkly comic vision of the killing off of a number of American Presidents" (Preface vii). But Stephen Sondheim disagrees, saying, "It has generally been accepted that the hostile reaction to *Assassins* was largely due to the outbreak of the Persian Gulf War. There's no way to know, but my guess is that the reaction would have been hostile anyway" (Sondheim letter 5/24/00). The Roundabout Theatre was to have mounted the first Broadway production of *Assassins* with previews beginning in November 2001. But, with grim irony, because of the terrorist attacks on September 11 of that year, the project was "postponed indefinitely."

Too controversial for New York critics and audiences, *Assassins* garnered an appreciatively perceptive review in the April 1992 issue of the British magazine *Gramophone*. Reviewing the original cast recording, the writer remarked that Sondheim

has taken on the "American Dream," challenged its validity, exposed its falsehood; he has taken on the assassination of Presidents, the rule of the gun, the laws that make it possible; he has taken on the promises, and the lies and the deceit of politicians, the social injustices, the anger of the losers and the deprived . . . In nine short songs he has taken on issues that some in the U. S. would rather forget . . . Every single word is an indictment; the musical means could hardly be pithier, or wittier, or sadder. (qtd. in Secrest 363)

Despite its short life off-Broadway, the show continued to speak to Americans nationwide. Figures from Music Theatre International show that *Assassins* had 1,138 separate regional productions between 1991 and August 31, 2000.

None of the musicals that depicted alienation — person from person, or person from the larger society — offered solutions to those feeling and experiencing such isolation, except perhaps to remind them that they were not alone. But in those same years and on into the 1990s, the musical theatre offered audiences other kinds of shows designed to provide temporary relief of the symptoms if not a cure for the disease.

# ❈ 9 ❈

# "A Recycled Culture," Nostalgia, and Spectacle

## Nostalgia and Its Causes in the Late Twentieth Century

America's nostalgia epidemic began in the 1970s. Social historians Douglas Miller and Marion Nowak offer a comprehensive diagnosis of the onset of the disease:

> Periods of intense longing for an earlier era indicate that people are discontented with the present. Excessive, sentimental nostalgia generally occurs during times of perceived crisis. . . . The rise of fifties enthusiasm [in the '70s] coincided with widespread disillusionment and a growing conservatism. For many people the 1950s came to symbolize a golden age of innocence and simplicity, an era supposedly unruffled by riots, racial violence, Vietnam, Watergate, assassinations. (5)

As evidence of the '50s nostalgia that "first became evident about 1971 and 1972," Miller and Nowak point out that by February 1976 "the fifties rock-and-roll parody *Grease* began its fifth season" (4). And *Grease* (2/14/72) was just the first of numerous musicals to respond to or capitalize on feelings of nostalgia that would last until the end of the century. Jim Jacobs and Warren Casey wrote *Grease* largely in the spirit of unsentimental parody of the days of sock hops, proms, and poodle skirts, of drive-ins, ducktails, and dating the right girl or guy. Yet the parody was so gentle that in addition to laughter the show evoked nostalgic longings. Spectators who were former mid-'50s teeny-boppers, but now were the ostensibly "grown-up" thirty-somethings of the '70s, could return to what was, for them, an idyllic past. This nostalgia for what seemed like an innocent world compared to the troubled days of Watergate and beyond explains in good part *Grease*'s record-breaking run of 3,388 performances.

If nostalgia was strong in the 1970s, it intensified in the '80s and '90s. The prime precondition for widespread nostalgia is severe discontent with the present. The first definition of nostalgia in both the *Oxford English Dictionary* and *Webster's Third* is "homesickness," with *Webster's* defining it as "a wistful or excessively sentimental sometimes abnormal yearning for return to or return of some real or romanticized period or irrecoverable condition or setting in the past" (1542). Implicit in "return to" and "irrecoverable" is the idea that the person experiencing nostalgia has in the past actually been in the place or time he or she longs to return to. True nostalgia is a desire to return to an earlier time *during one's own life*, making it in fact a kind of homesickness for one's personal past. Hence, central to nostalgia's pull is the desire to return to being the person one once was — younger, more innocent, less jaded.

Writing in 1977, Miller and Nowak confined their remarks to why people in the mid-1970s longed for the '50s, but, as later historians demonstrate, nostalgia continued to persist in American culture. During the eight Reagan years, domestic troubles gave people plenty of reasons for wanting to retreat to almost any other time or place. Reagan himself actually endorsed a return to an earlier, more innocent America without, of course, making such a return possible. According to Pulitzer Prize–winner Haynes Johnson, Reagan gave Americans the impetus for nostalgia by his own "evoking of nostalgia for a national past supposedly simpler and more pleasant, for presenting illusions that easy solutions to complicated problems existed." And the public, "in the mood for the resurrection of old myths," bought it (166).

During Reagan's two terms, Americans increasingly lost faith in everything from the government to Wall Street to Christian evangelism. Reagan's presidency stands out as the most scandal-ridden since Harding's, although Reagan himself emerged unblemished. Starting in 1981, from the Wedtech affair through the Pentagon procurement scams, the HUD scandal, and up to the cloak-and-dagger Iran-Contra fiasco near the end of his second term, one public embarrassment followed another. By the time Reagan left office, 138 administration officials were convicted, indicted, or investigated for misconduct and/or criminal acts.

Voracious Wall Street sharks like Ivan Boesky and Michael Milken equally shook the public's confidence in the world of high finance. Variously arbitrageurs, insider traders, leveraged buyout operators, or junk bond dealers, these men made lots of money for themselves and were widely admired for it — until they got caught. So enticing was The Pursuit of Money to countless Americans that new adult board games appeared with names like "Stocks & Bonds," "Arbitrage," "Trump" (devised by "The Donald" himself), and, most unashamedly, "Greed" (239). Then the biggest sharks fell. Boesky pleaded guilty to reduced charges for his insider trading and was packed off to prison (H. Johnson 215, 217). Mike Milken, a billionaire before forty, was jailed, paid fines and restitutions of $650 million dollars for his junk bond dealings, and single-handedly caused the collapse of his firm, Drexel Burnham Lambert (H. Johnson 222, 431). Then on October

19, 1987, the bottom dropped out of the stock market as never before on one day—508 points on the Dow Jones. Only quick intervention by New York's ten major banks and the Federal Reserve Board prevented a repeat of something like the Crash of '29. Even more Americans suffered losses by the Savings & Loan debacle at the end of Reagan's second term. Ultimately the government bailout of the failed S&Ls was about $500 billion. Haynes Johnson vividly, but accurately, sums up these years as "a self-indulgent and imitative age when entertainers became public leaders and when celebrities, not pioneers, scientists, or artists, became cultural heroes. . . . In the eighties few scientific eminences were produced . . . It was more a time when deal makers, money managers, and paper shufflers flourished" (461).

Other events shattered American complacency. The United States had been duly proud of the first successful space shuttle launch in 1981, and Dr. Sally Ride was the first woman in space in 1983. But that pride instantly shattered on January 28, 1986, when the shuttle *Challenger* exploded seventy-three seconds after lift-off, killing all on board including school teacher Christa McAuliffe, the first civilian in space. The catastrophe traumatized millions of school children watching the launch on TV and forced adults to question the very necessity of our space program (Kallen, *1980s* 100–103). On November 5, 1982, unemployment stood at 10.4 percent, the highest percentage since 1940, and the number of Americans living in poverty continued to increase sharply during the Reagan years (Marty 267; Kallen *1980s* 114; H. Johnson 242–43). In April 1986, the nuclear disaster at Chernobyl made Americans wary of our own nuclear power stations. And starting around 1987, America's faithful—especially those of the Religious Right—watched televangelists Jim Bakker, Jimmy Swaggart, and Jerry Falwell brought low by sex scandals and/or the egregious mishandling of other people's money (H. Johnson 213).

Did Americans' outlook improve in the 1990s? Not according to Johnson, who believes a mood of public passivity still enveloped the nation, along with "a further tendency of people to withdraw from public affairs and distance themselves from public questions" (463, 468). Voters were apathetic. George Bush beat Michael Dukakis in 1988 with only 50 percent of eligible voters exercising their right, the lowest percentage since Coolidge won in 1924 (H. Johnson 407). Even fewer—less than 50 percent—voted in Bill Cinton's reelection year of 1996 (Kallen, *1990s* 24).

In October 1990, George Bush ate his "Read my lips: No new taxes" spiel as he signed into law the single largest tax increase in U.S. history, just three months after a "deep recession" had begun (Kallen *1990s* 10, 115; *1980s* 60). The patriotism stirred by the brief, successful, and almost casualty-free Gulf War early in 1991 gave the country a lift, but troop deployments in places like Bosnia and Kosovo had most Americans more perplexed than proud. Nor could the public have been proud of allegations of money and sex scandals that dogged the Clinton White House. The World Trade Center bombing in 1993, the Branch Davidian conflagration the same year, and the bombing of the Oklahoma City Federal Building in 1995 were frightening. But the rash of indiscriminate shootings by teens and pre-teens that began in 1997 and climaxed in 1999 with the Columbine High School massacre in Littleton, Colorado, terrified the public. Perhaps more than anything else, such random and senseless acts of violence, capped by the terrorist attacks of September 11, 2001, profoundly affected American sensibilities.

How did ordinary Americans in the '80s and '90s react to such wide-ranging social and moral breakdown? Badly. The 1980s saw a significant rise in compulsive gambling, partly spurred by more states legalizing gaming and lotteries as a quick fix to economic distress. Cases of clinical depression and attention deficit disorder (ADD), real or imagined, increased sharply, with prescriptions for Prozac and Ritalin skyrocketing as respective treatments (Marty 195–96). Despite warnings about the deleterious effects of tobacco, cigarette smoking increased, and despite the AIDS epidemic that ushered in "safe sex" practices among the concerned and the cautious, carelessness, if not promiscuity, remained a problem among most of the sexually active population (Marty 299). Teenage alcohol abuse went through the roof, and teen drug use expanded from pot to cocaine to crack, though marijuana remained the drug of choice. Among the adult population heroin use rose "in the middle and upper classes of U.S. society" (Marty 300).

So much substance abuse suggests the public was primed to escape, to get away from it all, to succumb to nostalgia, the psychic equivalent of comfort food. Broadway producers were more than ready to offer the public legal doses of nostalgic and other escapist entertainments. In the last quarter of the twentieth century, Broadway presented a variety of nostalgia-based productions, including revivals and retrospective revues. In addition, the advent of totally mindless spectacles provided another kind of relief. Neither kind of show had content of any social relevance. Nonetheless, the plethora of such shows remains an important barometer of the times.

### Collectibles Off-Stage and On: Revivals and Nostalgia

The signs and symptoms of nostalgia were manifest everywhere in the '80s and '90s. Mass media promoted nostalgia with films and TV shows set in prior decades and endless reruns of defunct TV series. Nostalgia lay behind Americans' passion for collectibles — not antiques per se, but baseball and other trading cards, 78 and 45 r.p.m. phonograph records, comic books, and action figures of motion picture characters from the past. The vogue for retro clothing styles — whether the genuine articles from resale shops or newly minted imitations — can also be traced at least in part to nostalgia, as can radio's incessant broadcasting of so-called Golden Oldies, some stations devoting their entire music programming to the rock and pop of the '70s and before. In a very real sense these Golden Oldies of the FM airwaves are the pop music world's equivalent of musical theatre revivals. Although live theatre audiences continued to be an ever-shrinking entertainment market compared to film, television, and, starting in the 1990s, the Internet, recycled older musicals helped satisfy the nostalgia cravings of many.

At times during the 1980s and '90s, Broadway looked more like a revival house than a venue for new musicals. Some years produced so few new shows that the Tony Committee had to drop certain award categories or change the rules to reduce the number of nominees required in a category from four to three or even fewer. The committee also created the new category of Best Revival, so prevalent were recycled shows. Excluding limited-run revivals by the likes of the New York City Opera and The City Center, as well as concert performances of older shows, between fall 1979 and spring 2000 Broadway revived at least forty-four musicals, far more than in any comparable period. Appeal to nostalgia aside, one reason for the rash of revivals was strictly commercial.

By the 1980s, the days of the big time gamblers like David Merrick were gone. Whether a corporation or an individual, few producers would take a chance on a new musical unless it was by an established giant of the musical stage like Stephen Sondheim, or it had already proven itself commercially viable in a major market outside New York — frequently London — or off-Broadway. Safe and conservative became the watchwords of the day, words often synonymous with "revival." This does not mean, of course, that every revival produced in expectation of critical, popular, and financial success met all of those expectations. Some revivals closed almost before they opened, while others outstripped the runs of their original productions.

Although musicals from the 1950s had a slightly higher success rate than the rest, what is most striking about the era's revivals is the randomness of what attracted sizable audiences and what did not. A few notable examples: the musical version of *Peter Pan* (9/6/79) starring Sandy Duncan played 551 times, far outstripping its 1954 run of 152 performances. On the other hand, *My Fair Lady*, a runaway success from its opening in 1956, came back twice toward century's end, first on August 18, 1980, again with Rex Harrison, now seventy-three years old, but eking out only 119 showings, while thirteen years later Richard Chamberlain played Professor Higgins starting December 9, 1993, for just slightly more, 165. Starting on January 7, 1985, Yul Brynner recreated for the final time the role he originated in another '50s hit, *The King and I*, but for only 191 performances plus a national tour (he died shortly thereafter). Yet on April 11, 1996, another revival opened, starring Donna Murphy as Anna and Lou Diamond Phillips as the King, achieving an impressive 807 performances. *Damn Yankees*, which first stepped up to the plate in 1955, came out slugging again on March 3, 1994, for 533 innings. The longest run among '50s revivals was that of arguably the best-crafted diversionary musical comedy of all time, Frank Loesser's 1950 *Guys and Dolls*. The new production directed by Jerry Zaks (4/4/92) played a staggering 1,144 times.

But no one decade's musicals had the corner on successful revivals or appeal to Americans' nostalgia. A couple of shows did very well that were too old for most people to have seen. Rodgers and Hart's dance-centered *On Your Toes* was originally a star vehicle for Ray Bolger in 1936 for 315 performances; in its second Broadway revival (3/6/83; it played sixty-four times in 1954), Lara Teeter danced his way through the Bolger role 505 times, bettering the original run. Similarly, *Show Boat* had been revived in New York numerous times before its monumental reappearance on October 2, 1994, in Hal Prince's staging. Never before, including its original run, had it achieved anything like the 949 performances of its late-century incarnation.

From the 1940s, Rodgers and Hammerstein's *Carousel* (1945) came back on March 24, 1994, to run 337 times in the striking production mounted by Britain's Royal National Theatre. Close to century's end, also from the '40s was a return of Irving Berlin's *Annie Get Your Gun* (3/3/99), which logged 1,046 performances, closing well into the twenty-first century, as did the revival of Cole Porter's *Kiss Me, Kate* (11/18/99), playing 881 times. The revival of another 1940s musical not only appealed to nostalgia but was of some significance as a barometer of much of the country's mood in 1980. As noted in chapter 5, during the final month of Ronald Reagan's presidential campaign the first and only open-ended Broadway revival of Alan Jay Lerner's 1947 *Brigadoon* (10/16/80) still portrayed a desirable isolationist utopia, and it ran for 133 performances. Like the release of the Hollywood film, it seems no coincidence that the Broadway revival surfaced during a period of growing conservatism, and indeed isolationism, at the very time Reagan was beginning "to lull us into retreating into the myth of a simpler America of yesteryear" (H. Johnson 166).

Revivals from the 1960s and '70s were fairly prevalent but almost always obeyed an unspoken rule that no show gets revived with less than a twenty-year turnaround between its original opening date and its revival. From the 1960s, *Cabaret* was revived (10/22/87) with Joel Gray recreating his role as the Emcee for 262 performances. (The 1998 revival was so reconceived that it is considered with other socially significant musicals in chapter 10.) *Man of La Mancha*, which originally preceded *Cabaret* by exactly a year in 1965, fared less well in revival on April 24, 1992, managing only 108 performances. Also from the '60s, Harnick, Bock, and Masteroff's *She Loves Me* (6/6/93) bettered its original run of 301 performances with 355 precisely thirty years later. And while that ultimate piece of 1962 silliness, *A Funny Thing Happened on the Way to the Forum*, could not match its original outing, still, first with Nathan Lane and then later with (extreme silliness!) Whoopi Goldberg as the slave Pseudolus, the revival hauled in 715 performances starting April 18, 1996. To cite just two from the '70s, illustrating how ever more recent nostalgia seems to be getting, *The Rothschilds* (1970) came back exactly twenty years later at Circle in the Square Downtown on February 25, 1990, in a very respectable off-Broadway run of 435 showings; and what became the runaway hit revival of two revival-filled decades, the 1975 Bob Fosse–choreographed *Chicago* returned on November 14, 1996, with Ann Reinking recreating the dances in the style and spirit of the master. By the end of the century's last full theatre season, *Chicago* had played 1,474 times, with no indications of closing several seasons into the twenty-first century, thereby making the show the all-time longest-running revival.

The revival whose numbers *Chicago* passed in the summer of 2000 is significant because of the nature of the beast. In great part, nostalgia drove the lengthy revival of *Grease*, a show that had also appealed largely to nostalgia the first time around, beginning February 14, 1972. What's singular about the return of *Grease* on May 11, 1994, is that the revival began a mere fourteen years and one month after the original production closed on April 13, 1980, something unheard of in the annals of revivals. And, until *Chicago* broke its string, *Grease* held the revival longevity record with 1,503 performances. What in fact was so successfully revived was nostalgia itself, rather like Goodwill reselling secondhand clothes from the Salvation Army racks. Have Americans become so disenchanted with the present that they want to retreat into the *same* past again, and again, and again? Stephen Sondheim certainly thinks so, as he describes the habits of many late-century theatre-goers: "a family comes as if to a picnic, and they pass on to their children the idea that's what theater is—a spectacular musical you see once a year, a stage version of a movie. It has nothing to do with theater at all. It has to do with seeing what is familiar. We live in a recycled culture" (qtd. in Rich 40).

## Manufactured Nostalgia

What Jim Jacobs and Warren Casey intended in *Grease* was parody—but it was also manufactured nostalgia, and it continued to be such during its second life in the '90s. The songs weren't actual '50s songs but pastiche numbers—words and music faithfully imitating the styles, genres, and sounds of the songs sung by the girl-groups, guy-groups, and hip-swiveling solo-performing heart-throbs in the golden age of early rock and roll. Similarly, the musical's scenes—the sock hop, the slumber party, cruisin' the drive-in—were expertly engineered to engender those powerful personal feelings that accompany viewers' recollections of their own years of acne, poodle skirts, and ponytails. In a word, *Grease* was a piece of popular culture consciously crafted in the 1970s to capitalize on (dare we say exploit?) America's endemic nostalgia for the '50s. Later, as recycled nostalgia itself in the mid-1990s, *Grease* had its originally intended effect all over again. In the meantime *Grease* inspired a handful of other musicals that were also manufactured nostalgia, some wildly successful, some not.

That *Grease* partly inspired three of the four other manufactured nostalgia musicals, all in the 1980s, is suggested by their subject matter: high school—not a specific time period but a shared experience of virtually all potential audiences. *Is There Life After High School?* (5/7/82), based on Ralph Keyes's book, was written by Jeffrey Kindley with music and lyrics by Craig Carnelia; it used a revue format resembling fragmented musical form. Four women and five men played various characters in high school and years later at a reunion and elsewhere. The show originated at the Hartford Stage Company and after its brief stint in New York had some success in regional, college, and community theatres but not on Broadway. *Is There Life* died after twelve performances, possibly because Carnelia doesn't write nostalgically sentimental, uncritical lyrics. In *Working* he had been responsible for such edgy songs of self-exploration as "Just a Housewife," "The Mason," and "Joe," and nearly everything else Carnelia has written has an angular or ironic spin. The revue's first-act closer, "Diary of a Homecoming Queen," is such a song. Sung by a woman who had had her fifteen minutes of fame on the fifty yard line her senior year, it is crammed with Carnelia's device of making deceptively matter-of-fact, even mundane lyrics pack an emotional wallop. But a married-with-child woman realizing that her one moment of true happiness and self-definition was as high school homecoming queen is not what 1980s nostalgia-seekers wanted. Such self-critical nostalgia, even anti-nostalgia, is not comfort food for the soul.

The next nod to school-days nostalgia is peculiar in that the show did very well everywhere except New York. A musical flashback to parochial school, *Do Black Patent Leather Shoes Really Reflect Up?* opened its doors to the New York public on May 27, 1982, and closed them on May 30. Prior to that, the show had had long, popular, and financially successful runs in Chicago (where it originated), Birmingham, Michigan, and Philadelphia. Based on his own book, John R. Powers's script, with music and lyrics by James Quinn and Alaric Jans, combined gentle satire of the rigors and seeming absurdities of parochial school education with an equally gentle nostalgic affection for the experience. Although New York didn't buy it, *Patent Leather* contributed to America's mid-'80s nostalgia fix in other major-market theatrical centers.

But not the way *Nunsense* contributed, and not just in the regions where, like *Patent Leather*, it began. *Nunsense* was born in Boston and ultimately blanketed the nation, including the Big Apple. After a stint off-off-Broadway, this small show wisely settled in at the equally small Cherry Lane Theatre off-Broadway on December 12, 1985, for a run of 3,672 performances, proving again that nostalgia is a profitable business. *Nunsense* is essentially a revue with a premise (not a plot). A funny gaggle of nuns, The Little Sisters of Hoboken, put on a fundraising show to bury the last four of fifty-two sisters who dropped dead of botulism from vichyssoise prepared by the convent cook, Sister Julia, Child of God. (As a temporary measure, the "Blue Nuns," as the surviving sisters call them, have been stashed in the convent freezer.) This set-up for the revue numbers was very funny, made funnier yet by where the singing nuns were performing their benefit—from the gymnasium stage at Mount Saint Helen's, their convent school, the stage bedecked with scenery for the eighth grade production of *Grease*—a funny, splendid tribute to *Nunsense's* spiritual progenitor in nostalgia. Yet, while the show's composer/lyricist/writer/director Dan Goggin had crafted a musical whose success depends on provoking laughter, he confesses in the published script that the comedy of *Nunsense* had its origins in nostalgia: "I spent a great deal of my life around nuns. And most of my experiences left wonderful memories. I wrote 'Nunsense' because I wanted to share what I knew to be 'the humor of the nun'" (8). Goggin implies that much enjoyment of the show for Catholic audiences came from fond, nonjudgmental recollections of their own parochial school days. Yet the show's humor was universal enough to keep general audiences coming in almost improbable numbers, as well as strong if not *as* strong audiences for Goggin's several sequels to the original. Such capitalizing on one's past success almost defines the concept of manufactured nostalgia.

The remaining manufactured nostalgia musical has no thematic connection to the schooldays motif of the other three. Nevertheless it owes some debt to *Grease*, since it too played upon '50s nostalgia. In *Little Shop of Horrors* (7/27/82), nostalgia operated on three distinct levels. First, there was the nostalgia of the event itself for some spectators — watching a musical rendering of the 1960 Roger Corman low-budget horror flick they had gotten hooked on either as a first-run film or as a "B" movie cult classic. Second, Alan Menken's musical score with lyrics by Howard Ashman (who also wrote the book) is as faithfully imitative and emotionally evocative of the genres and styles of the 1950s as anything in *Grease*; perhaps even more so, since *Little Shop*'s songs go beyond the styles of the teen-faves of the time to include what adults were still listening to in the waning days of pop that wasn't rock. Finally, there is the show's potent (and, for all its lunacy, at times genuinely touching) nostalgic evocation of the simpler — if cookie-cutter conforming — lifestyle of the Eisenhower years. While Ashman in his "Author's Note" to the acting edition never mentions nostalgia, he comes very close in pointing out that for the show to work as intended, the actors must "play with simplicity, honesty, and sweetness." Those qualities give emotional depth to the show's greatest moment of nostalgic evocation, Audrey's song "Somewhere That's Green." She prefaces her lyrical dream of suburban living by addressing her listeners with such ingenuousness that tacky clichés lose their tackiness and become part of a sincere idyllic vision: "It's just a day-dream of mine. A little development I dream of. Just off the Interstate. Not fancy like Levittown. . . . The sweetest, greenest place — where everybody has the same little lawn out front and the same little flagstone patio out back. . . .":

> A MATCHBOX OF OUR OWN
> A FENCE OF REAL CHAIN LINK
> A GRILL OUT ON THE PATIO
> DISPOSAL IN THE SINK
> A WASHER AND A DRYER AND
> AN IRONING MACHINE
> IN A TRACT HOUSE THAT WE SHARE
> SOMEWHERE THAT'S GREEN.
> (Ashman 34–35)

Sadly, Audrey doesn't live to see her dream realized; she is eaten by a carnivorous plant. Still, a case can be made and in fact *was* made by Frank Rich in his *Times* review (NYTCR 1982 219–20) that the '50s nostalgia may bear more centrally on what *Little Shop* is all about than first appears on the surface of the horror-flick spoof. *Little Shop* stayed off-Broadway for its entire successful New York run, playing an impressive 2,209 times.

### Retro Revues

More than manufactured nostalgia, more even than the glut of revivals, another type of musical virtually dominated the nostalgia market in the '80s and '90s. Not new, but certainly endemic to those decades, I like to call this kind of show the "retro revue." Such revues don't contain new songs and topical material (as did, say, Ziegfeld's productions early in the century or Ben Bagley and Julius Monk's "intimate revues" in the '50s and '60s). Instead, they were "deja-revues," retrospectives of popular, jazz, or theatre songs from the past. A retro revue may celebrate the work of one songwriter or team of writers or be a compendium of songs by various hands from a particular period or performance venue, thematically, historically, or otherwise coherently tied together. Some '80s and '90s retros went beyond being revues to become book shows with stories and characters, but the emphasis remained on songs by composers and lyricists of the past.

Whatever their content, retros always look backward, appealing to audience nostalgia. Most impressive about them is their sheer number—at least thirty-one between 1980 and 1999, including the black retro revues treated in chapter 6. In some way, all of these were retros, but their impetus was more often the celebration of black musical heritage than audience nostalgia. Also, retro revues were popular. Of the thirty-one, eighteen ran more than one hundred performances (a fair measure of some success off-Broadway at least), seven of those over five hundred, and four of those over one thousand. In order to bring some clarity to the retros other than the black ones already discussed—and also to explore why some worked and others didn't—I have divided the shows into two categories based on their exclusive or predominant content: revues of theatre and/or film songs, and revues of popular music of any kind.

### Broadway (and Sometimes Hollywood) in Revue

Generally speaking, retro revues of theatre and, occasionally, film music fared poorly. Examination of the individual members of the species reveals that their failure rate can often, though not always, be attributed to the problems inherent in transporting what in book musicals were "context songs" into the very different revue format.

Just as the 1970s were ending, Martha Schlamme and Alvin Epstein— intelligent and gifted interpreters of Kurt Weill's theatre songs—tried for a long run of their two-person *A Kurt Weill Cabaret* (11/5/79), but they had two strikes against them. First, while Weill's compositions had always been on the artistic cutting edge of theatre music, most never achieved widespread popularity with the general theatregoing public in the United States. His was always something of a coterie audience. Second, Weill's songs were first and foremost *theatre* songs, but what Schlamme and Epstein offered was more concert than theatre, their "cabaret" even billed and mounted as a concert on the road before coming to New York. A few years earlier, the staged and scripted revue *From Berlin to Broadway with Kurt Weill* (10/1/72) had placed the composer's songs in theatrical contexts and played 152 times; Schlamme and Epstein's concert, 72.

Given the quality and popularity of the songs in the Frank Loesser revue *Perfectly Frank* (11/30/80), the revue's seventeen-performance lifespan seems simply inexplicable. Conceived and written by Kenny Solms, this retro appeared to have everything going for it, including Loesser's charming and talented widow, Jo Sullivan, as the revue's guide and narrator, surrounded by a cast of talented young performers like Wayne Cilento, Virginia Sandifur, and Jim Walton. And with more than sixty of Loesser's songs for stage, film, and Tin Pan Alley as the real stars of the show, hit status would have seemed inevitable, especially since Loesser's career spanned the very decades ripe for early-'80s nostalgia seekers — the 1930s through the early 1960s. But such good fortune was not to be, nor was there a critical consensus as to what did in *Perfectly Frank*. Gerald Bordman, however, isolated a problem inherent not just in this show but in most revues of theatre songs. He suggests that as a careful craftsman of songs for integrated musicals, Loesser "may be the hardest to take out of context" in a revue (704–705). As viable as Loesser's context songs were in book musicals and films, they could not survive as isolated numbers in a revue without especially intelligent conceptualization and staging.

On the flip side, two retrospectives of sorts proved that theatre songs could remain viable (and the shows become smash hits) if those songs were put into theatrical contexts, even if not their original ones. There is, however, some irony in this, since both productions showcased the songs of George and Ira Gershwin, which, given the character of musicals and films in their day, often had but slight connection to the script. Peter Stone and Timothy S. Mayer wrote the first of these retros with a plot that embraced two acts full of some seventeen songs by the Gershwins gleaned from ten of their stage and film musicals. In essence, then, *My One and Only* (5/1/83) was a retro revue tribute to the Brothers Gershwin, even though it had a plot. Not all of the tunes were standards (while others like "He Loves and She Loves," " 'S Wonderful," and "Nice Work If You Can Get It" absolutely were), but complete familiarity isn't entirely necessary for nostalgia to succeed. Tommy Tune, Twiggy, and Co. tapped their little hearts out 767 times.

The second Gershwin "book-retro" came along about nine years later and ran even longer. *Crazy For You* (2/19/92) was a great big retro with a great big book by Ken Ludwig, inspired by Guy Bolton and John Mc-Gowan's script for *Girl Crazy*, the operative words being "inspired by" in the loosest possible sense. While a few songs came from that classic musical, most were from any Gershwin show the creators thought could be cannibalized for good material. More on the strength of its nostalgia-driven score than on its book or large cast of Broadway's relative unknowns or lesser lights, *Crazy For You* brought Gershwin buffs and others into the Shubert Theatre 1,622 times.

In contrast to these hit Gershwin retros, Jerome Kern took a tremendous beating twice within about seven months. Since much of Kern's repertoire has passed into the annals of standard popular song, one would think the familiarity of his timeless melodies would have attracted audiences to a revue of them. But with no evidence of specific disasters, one can only conclude that these retros fell to weak concepts, staging, and/or performances, or again to the problem of wrenching theatre songs out of their contexts. *Ladies and Gentlemen, Jerome Kern* (6/10/85) and British import *Jerome Kern Goes to Hollywood* (1/23/86) sank into theatrical oblivion after twenty-two and thirteen performances, respectively.

Perhaps more inevitable was the failure after fifty-two performances of *It's a Grand Night for Singing* (11/17/93), the Rodgers and Hammerstein retrospective conceived by Walter Bobbie. Bordman's theory about reconceiving contextual songs for a revue format has even greater weight here than for the Frank Loesser retro. Every song Rodgers and Hammerstein wrote in perfecting the integrated musical was a context number. A revue has the unenviable choice of either ignoring songs' original contexts at the risk of confusing the audience or devising new revue contexts for the numbers to give them a semblance of theatricality and sense, which risks muddying their original dramatic intent and meaning. *It's a Grand Night for Singing*'s meagre run again suggests that songs written for book musicals, especially integrated musicals, have less viability in revues than do non-theatre songs that originally had *no* contexts but that are theatricalized by a revue's visionary creator and/or director. This supposition is borne out by the generally greater success of the popular song retros in the following section.

Before the century's end, one more retro of theatre songs appeared, one that reinforces Bordman's theory by showing what could happen to George Gershwin in a straight revue format rather than the book-revue context of the hits *My One and Only* and *Crazy for You. The Gershwins' Fascinating Rhythm* (4/25/99) was conceived by Mel Marvin and Mark Lamos and directed by Lamos, late artistic director of the Hartford Stage Company and a director of cutting-edge ingenuity. The components and credentials seemed to be in order for a hit with an apparently Gershwin-hungry public. Not so: seventeen performances and the show was gone. Even beyond the problems inherent in taking theatre songs out of context, the best explanation for this retro's quick demise is suggested by *Best Plays'* brief annotation, "Contemporary musical styles and tastes applied to the Gershwin classics" (98–99 259). It's far easier in a supper club or concert to buy into Bobby Short or Barbara Cook's purely personal postmodern take on "Someone to Watch Over Me" or "I've Got a Crush on You;" in such settings, the focus is on a unique performer's special idiom. Such restyling of show tunes in the theatre proved far less effective. Most theatre audiences anticipate not updates but nostalgic recreations (at least to some degree) of those tunes' original presentations or styles. Its very effort to be "modern" — as opposed to retro — probably doomed this Gershwin revue.

### Pop Goes the Retro

With a few exceptions, the retrospective revues of American popular song were the most successful, longest running retros in the 1980s and '90s. Added to the argument that theatre songs generally lose their effectiveness and appeal in revue format, the mere fact that greater numbers of Americans have always listened to popular music than regularly attend the musical theatre explains the tremendous drawing power of retro revues of popular song. Their sheer number underscores how nostalgia, or at least musical nostalgia, gripped the country in the last two decades of the century.

The earliest pop retro also contained the earliest songs in any such show, songs too old to have sparked the true nostalgia of personal recollection in any but an octo- or nonagenarian. *Tintypes*, the brainchild of Mary Kyte, Mel Marvin, and Gary Pearle, showcased American song before 1917. Along with less familiar pieces, it included standards like "Stars and Stripes Forever," "Yankee Doodle Boy," "You're a Grand Old Flag," "Meet Me in St. Louis," and "Shine On, Harvest Moon." Since such songs remained timeless and often sentimental standards through the entire twentieth century, this revue tapped into a kind of historical nostalgia in viewers of almost any age. Each of *Tintypes'* five cast members portrayed the essence or persona of an historical figure or character type from the period: Theodore Roosevelt, Broadway star Anna Held, social reformer Emma Goldman, a male working-class Eastern European immigrant, and an African American working-class woman. To see and hear the songs presented by the period's typical personalities created a vivid picture of the socio-ethnic-economic mix in the United States between the Spanish-American War and World Wars I. *Tintypes* first saw the light of day at the Arena Stage in Washington and the Asolo Theatre in Sarasota, Florida. The American National Theater and Academy presented it off-Broadway on April 17, 1979, for 134 performances, after which it moved to Broadway's John Golden Theatre on October 23, 1980, for another ninety-three. The larger venue for a small review may account for its short life on Broadway, but the show went on to many regional theatres.

*The 1940's Radio Hour* (10/7/79) was the first of three retro revues to focus on swing and the big band sounds of the 1940s and was, with its 105 performances, the least successful of them. Creator Walton Jones's book for the revue replicated a live radio broadcast from New York's Algonquin Hotel on December 21, 1942. During commercial breaks and other hiatuses, viewers watched the off-air lives and loves of the broadcast's personnel and on-air personalities. But the main feature of *Radio Hour*, and its source of nostalgic appeal, was its array of Hit Parade–type tunes of the early '40s.

*Leader of the Pack* (4/8/85) was something of a landmark. *Grease* and *Little Shop of Horrors* had featured pastiche numbers that cloned the musical styles, genres, and sounds of the 1950s. But *Leader of the Pack* was destined to become just what its title said—the vanguard pop retro in a generally long-running line of revues that brought back the actual songs of the Great Days of Doo-Wop. *Leader* honored the mostly '60s "girl-group" songs of composer/lyricist Ellie Greenwich and her numerous collaborators. Ms. Greenwich herself was central (though uncredited) in shaping the show and even briefly appeared in the original production as her contemporary 1980s self. Dinah Manoff played the mostly '60s Ellie during the bulk of this retro, held together by a transparently autobiographical book. Greenwich had been something of a phenomenon in her day as a female songwriter, selling over 100 million records (Greenwich 14). This retro of her biggest hits some twenty years after the peak of her career played 120 times.

Much more wildly successful was *Beehive* (3/30/86). Named for a characteristic hairdo of the day, the retro celebrated such female vocalists of the 1960s as Petula Clark and Aretha Franklin. This unabashed exercise in pop music nostalgia performed by a six-woman cast caught on and didn't let go for a full 600 performances off-Broadway, more evidence that nostalgia specifically for the '50s and '60s had an especially strong pull.

The title *Stardust* (2/19/87) would seem to signal a revue tribute to legendary tunesmith Hoagy Carmichael, composer of that enduring classic—

but it wasn't. Instead this retro honored "Stardust" lyricist Mitchell Parish, far less of a household name than Hoagy but still a writer of impressive credentials. The retro included songs by Parish and such collaborators as Duke Ellington, Sammy Fain, Glenn Miller, Leroy Anderson, and, of course, Hoagy Carmichael. Whether or not audiences were surprised (or disappointed) to find the revue was not what its title seemed to suggest, *Stardust* still gave 102 Broadway performances after fifty-nine previous outings off-off-Broadway.

February 9, 1964, was a sad night for the aspiring Four Plaids, a guy-group driving to their first professional gig at the Fusel Lounge of the Harrisburg (Pa.) Airport Hilton. They met their untimely end colliding with a busload of Catholic schoolgirls heading for the Beatles' breakthrough appearance on "The Ed Sullivan Show." A preposterous scenario for reality but not as the set-up for *Forever Plaid* (5/4/90), the nostalgia-cum-comedy flashback of the late '40s through '60s guy-groups. The retro allows the Plaids to return from dead-guy-group limbo to do the act they never had the chance to perform in life. It took a full five years for writer/creator Stuart Ross and musical arranger James Raitt to create this outlandish bit of fluff plus four-part harmonies. Their aim was to exactly replicate the sounds, styles, and even minutiae of body language that typified such squeaky-clean boy-quartets as The Four Aces, The Four Lads, the Hi-Lo's, and the Crew Cuts—and they succeeded. Such groups' close harmony renditions indelibly emblazoned into the national consciousness such icons of pop-sentimental song as "Catch a Falling Star," "Heart and Soul," "Love Is a Many Splendored Thing," "Magic Moments," "Moments to Remember," "Perfidia," and "Three Coins in the Fountain." Their songs and style spoke of an innocent musical past that in fact was effectively snuffed out forever that night in February 1964 when the Beatles introduced another way to sing. For the older-style guy-groups, that was truly the night the music died. But their songs and the guys' more preposterous idiosyncrasies came to life again harmonically and comically in this revue, which skillfully fused laughs with nostalgia 1,811 times.

The auto crash that gave the Plaids a second chance at success was, of course, a fiction. Not fiction but all too real was the disastrous plane crash on February 2, 1959, that killed Ritchie Valens, The Big Bopper, and Buddy Holly. Their untimely deaths in part provided the impetus for *Buddy: The Buddy Holly Story* (11/4/90). Written by Alan Janes and featuring songs by Holly and others, this was another retro revue with a book chronicling Holly's life. Story aside, it was the classic rock and roll of Holly and his compatriots that kept audiences coming 225 times to hear such numbers as "That'll Be the Day," "You Send Me," "Well All Right," and "Johnny B.

Goode," as well as the Big Bopper and Valens's respective signature tunes, "Chantilly Lace" and "La Bamba."

After the string of retros with runs of a hundred performances or more dating back to *Beehive* in 1986, 1993 saw one clear failure. Burt Bacharach's songwriting heyday had been 1963 to 1969—period. His special brand of slick, breezy tunes coincided with the rise of that dubious entertainment phenomenon, the Las Vegas lounge lizard, a breed of singer especially suited to Bacharach's songs. Perhaps the very time-specific nature of Bacharach's collaborations with lyricist Hal David precluded success for the retro *Back to Bacharach and David* (3/25/93) three decades after their initial popularity. Whatever the reason it failed, audiences had but sixty-nine chances to hear once again such typical Bacharach/David tunes as "Do You Know the Way to San Jose," "Close to You," and "I'll Never Fall in Love Again." Perhaps it would have done better in Vegas than NYC.

Conversely, two years later *Smokey Joe's Cafe* (3/2/95) must have struck the right nostalgia chord at the right time to become the all-time record-breaking retro revue, finally checking out with 2,036 performances. This was pop at its most pop but presented in the theatrically supercharged concept and staging of director Jerry Zaks. The songs were "Yakety-Yak" and "Hound Dog," "Dance with Me" and "Searchin' " and "Fools Fall in Love," "There Goes My Baby" and "Spanish Harlem" and "Love Potion #9"—and dozens more like them. In short, *Smokey Joe's* brought back the '50s and '60s words and music of Jerry Leiber and Mike Stoller, two guys who perhaps more than any others helped define the early sounds of rock and roll.

Meanwhile, back to World War II—almost always surefire musical bait for the nostalgia hook, since so many songs of the time outlasted the war in the active musical memory of generations of Americans. The thin book of *Swingtime Canteen* (3/14/95) by Linda Thorsen Bond, William Repicci, and Charles Busch was simple: some rather ill-assorted ladies join forces to form a kind of Andrews Sisters act in order to entertain our GIs abroad. Once rehearsed, they belted out most of the big ones from "Don't Sit Under the Apple Tree" to "Boogie Woogie Bugle Boy," in a concert for the Eighth Airforce in London in 1944, and for nostalgia-hungry audiences 294 times.

*Swinging on a Star* (10/22/95) was a retro packed with such familiar tunes as "Pennies from Heaven," "Irresistible," "Imagination," "Like Someone in Love," "Misty," "Moonlight Becomes You," and the show's title song. The revue's subtitle, "The Johnny Burke Musical," underscored what linked these songs. Burke wrote the lyrics for them all. But with the songs more familiar to the public than Burke himself, the revue played only ninety-seven times. The next retro revue was also lyricist (and occasional tunesmith) specific. But Johnny Mercer was much more familiar than either

Mitchell Parrish or Johnny Burke. Conceived by Louise Westergaard and
Jack Wrangler, *Dream* (4/3/97) ran for 109 performances. Its sixteen-member
cast and full orchestra—large for a retro—took a roughly chronological trip
through forty-two of the prolific Mercer's songs, from "Lazybones" to "Moon
River." And nearly every title in between was just as familiar.

The last of century-end's pop retros came along on the coattails of the
swing dance revival in the late 1990s. *Swing!* (12/9/99), a revue of swing
dancing styles featuring great tunes from the Big Band Era of the '30s and
'40s as well as some original compositions by members of the company.
Getting off on the right foot to essentially positive revues, *Swing!* swung 461
times.

### Broadway as Theme Park—Lloyd Webber, Disney, and the Technomusical

Conventional diversionary musicals (see appendix G) and musicals responding to America's mass nostalgia were not the only purely escapist entertainments the musical theatre offered audiences in the 1980s and '90s. Another
phenomenon, the technomusical, evoked no thoughts of the past; indeed,
it engendered little or no thinking at all. Looking back from the 1990s to
the televising of Ronald Reagan's extravagant inaugural display in 1981,
Haynes Johnson wrote, "Public appetite for the new and dramatic, fed by
the increasing ability of television networks to record everything from lunar
landings to distant wars and coronations in splendid daily isolation, made
such intensive coverage inevitable. It virtually ensured that spectacle would
triumph over substance" (32). And writers of musical theatre—bereft of real
ideas, and perhaps taking their cue from this revolution in telecommuni-
cations—turned to spectacle to attract audiences. Between Reagan's first
inauguration and the end of the twentieth century, Broadway audiences
would applaud about ten such shows that owed their longevity largely to
awestruck viewers oohing and aahing at elaborate and seemingly miraculous
technical effects. The usual term for such entertainment is "megamusical,"
but I prefer "technomusical" as more fully descriptive of a show that relies
upon theatre technology rather than real content. In technomusicals, it's
spectacle, not substance, that brings in the bucks.

It all started with *Cats* (10/7/82). Andrew Lloyd Webber set to music T. S.
Eliot's poems in *Old Possum's Book of Practical Cats*, with some of the
poems' texts tinkered with by Richard Stilgoe and Trevor Nunn, the show's
director. *Cats* had no plot. The songs and dances in the two acts were
essentially in a revue format; each song, each dance existed in isolation, as
performed by a huge cast in admittedly spectacular pussycat suits. The num-

bers did not forward a dramatic story or even coalesce with each other into a thematic whole. And the dances existed only to show off choreographer Gillian Lynne's conceptual brilliance and the talents of the terpsichores. The entire stage radiated spectacle. Designer John Napier's set was as superb as his cat costumes, offering a cat's-eye view of a back-alley junk heap with everything in properly enormous proportions. And, as in all spectacle, nothing just sits still. Napier's trash pile could transform itself into a locomotive or a sailing ship; and, when needed, a giant junked tire rose up like the Mother Ship in *Close Encounters of the Third Kind* to transport the chosen Grizabella to the "Heavyside Layer" and immortality. Spectacle can be breathtaking, although whether it alone can constitute or sustain genuine theatre is another matter. When I first saw *Cats*, my immediate reaction was, "I've never seen and heard such incredible lighting and sound design!" But that praise also tacitly expresses the lack of substance in *Cats*.

Those who write of megamusicals would slip *Les Misérables* (3/12/87) into the chronology at this point, and in the sense that "mega-" means either "large" or "million" (as in the bucks they cost to produce), I have no problem calling *Les Miz* a megamusical. But a technomusical it is not. Its visual component relies mainly on John Napier's revolving stage and what amounts to a single, massive scenic unit that virtually turns itself upside down and inside out to fill the visual needs of each scene — most famously, the barricades during the Parisian student revolt of 1832. But this mechanical marvel exists not just to get applause. It elegantly serves the visual requirements of the musical as one of many collaborating elements that together communicate a plot and characters of engaging and moving complexity. Napier's design harmonizes with Trevor Nunn's clean, economical staging for this French import by librettists Alain Boublil and Jean-Marc Natel and composer Claude-Michel Schönberg, its English version by Herbert Kretzmer and James Fenton. *Les Miz* illustrates how the visual/technical production meshes with text, music, and performers in both concept and execution. But in technomusicals, spectacle exists to be the cause of the audience's gratuitous thrills; an imbalance between effects and content turns the theatrical experience into carnival.

With the opening of *Starlight Express* on March 15, 1987, Andrew Lloyd Webber had two musicals running simultaneously on Broadway. With lyrics by Richard Stilgoe, *Starlight* was an original concept, though ultimately the plot of this sung-through railroad extravaganza smacks greatly of the *The Little Engine That Could*. The master of spectacle for both sets and costumes was John Napier of *Cats*, again supported by David Hersey's lighting and Martin Levan's sound designs. Each performer was fancifully costumed as a kind of railroad engine, freight or passenger car, or caboose, and each was also on roller skates, careening around Napier's setting of tracks, trestles, and bridges while singing Lloyd Webber and Stilgoe's score. The entire show was spectacle, the plot too thin to claim it was supported by the design elements. On the contrary, the plot was an excuse for the visual spectacle. By normal Broadway standards, *Starlight Express* had a more than respectable run, chugging along for 761 performances. But for the show's producers, *Starlight* was a failure; it had been the most expensive musical to mount up until then, capitalized at an unheard of eight million dollars—most of which it lost.

Lloyd Webber's third technomusical was *The Phantom of the Opera* (1/26/88). Even to those who haven't actually seen the show, "*Phantom*" and "chandelier" are practically synonymous. Specifically, the gargantuan chandelier suspended above the orchestra seats that descends to the stage, "*swinging more and more madly*," at the close of act 1 (Perry, *Complete* 154). This has to be the single most famous lighting fixture in the history of theatre. Even with no other spectacular effects, the descending chandelier alone qualifies *Phantom* as a technomusical, because that's what people came to see, even though *Phantom*, unlike the earlier examples of the genre, has a recognizable plot and characters, even if out of the stock-in-trade of melodrama.

Maria Bjornson's spectacle-filled production design effectively swamps *Phantom*'s story. In scene 1 there's a lumbering, life-size mechanical elephant in a rehearsal of the opera *Hannibal*. In scene 3 the Phantom reaches out to Christine from her dressing room mirror, and as she takes his icy hand she "*disappears through the mirror, which closes behind her*" (145). Next to the chandelier, probably the best-known visual spectacle is the candlelit underground boat ride in scene 4, as the Phantom ferries Christine to his lair. Their arrival in scene 5 is marked by yet another effect, when "*the candles in the lake lift up revealing giant candelabra outlining the space. The boat turns into a bed, there is a huge pipe organ*" (146). Rapidly shifting displays of gorgeous scenery fill scenes 6 through 9, and scene 10 closes with the crashing of the chandelier. Act 2 contains fewer effects (how do you top a tumbling chandelier, after all?), but they are not entirely absent. Most notably, in the mausoleum sequence, the Phantom's pike keeps hurling fireballs at Christine's fiancé Raoul. In the final scene, chased by a mob and resigned to the loss of Christine, the Phantom vanishes into thin air. In many ways, *Phantom* is more magic show than musical.

If *Phantom* is synonymous with chandelier, then Alain Boublil and Claude-Michel Schönberg's *Miss Saigon* (4/11/91; English lyrics by Richard Maltby Jr. with Boublil) is equally synonymous with "helicopter." Although John Napier designed a number of splendid scenic elements for the musical—the enormous Ho Chi Minh statues, and the Cadillac centerpiece of the "American Dream" sequence, to name just two—musicals have always been filled with splendid scenic elements. It's the landing of the chopper—a triumph of theatre technology and the key drawing card for audiences—that qualifies *Miss Saigon* as a technomusical. Virtually everyone I spoke to who has seen the show says they mostly went to see the helicopter. Yet this is a musical with a strong plot and characters, updating Puccini's *Madama Butterfly* to modern Vietnam. Both pieces tell of an American serviceman's affair with and abandonment of an Asian woman. When technical effects—not the story, musical score, or performances—are ticket-buyers' main reason for swarming to a show, we are definitely in technomusical territory.

It's one thing when a technomusical employs concealed devices of stage mechanics and theatre technology to create astonishing spectacle. It's quite another when a show exposes the instruments of the technology as a featured part of its design; then the technomusical becomes the high-technomusical, epitomized in *The Who's Tommy* (4/22/93; Pete Townshend and Des McAnuff book; Pete Townshend, John Entwistle, and Keith Moon music and lyrics). *Tommy* makes some pretension to social relevance, attempting to depict how dysfunctional families produce dysfunctional children, but the story and its telling were so murky—and there was so much else going on—it's doubtful many spectators got the social message. And that wasn't why they flocked to *Tommy* nine hundred times, anyway. The show not only employed the latest innovations in theatre electronics and technology, it showed them off in full view of the audience. Take, for example, the Vari-light, a computer-driven lighting instrument programmed to instantly change color, directionality, and the size and shape of its beam of light. *Tommy* had these gizmos visibly hanging all over the place in full view so spectators could watch them do their thing. Filmed and still projections on twenty-seven screens across the back of the stage, plus banks of strategically placed TV monitors, brought the latest in cinema and video technology into a production that seemed as much light show or rock concert as Broadway musical (see *NYTRC* 1993 158). Designer John Arnone also used conventional, concealed devices of stage mechanics and electronics for moments such as when "a psychedelic [pinball] machine rises from the stage, twists, turns, writhes in the air and then explodes" (158), or when "Arnone transforms the entire St. James Theater into a spinning, flashing, ringing pinball machine," the audience made to feel as if they're inside it (163).

In the perception of most casual observers, the technomusical was strictly an imported British genre, and if just those productions from the early 1980s through 1991 are considered, their perception would be correct. Even the French *Les Misérables* and *Miss Saigon* arrived on Broadway via their London stagings. But after 1991, things definitely swung stateside, with only one more English techno in the roster. Even though *The Who's Tommy* originated with the concert album by the British rock group, the high-tech event on Broadway was the product of American ingenuity, masterminded by director Des McAnuff at California's La Jolla Playhouse and his team of imaginative designers and technicians. But only when the Walt Disney Company entered into the field did this formerly British denizen of the New York stage become completely naturalized.

With the squadrons of animation artists, special effects experts, and computer specialists that the Disney studios employ for both animated and live-action films, not to mention the legions of designers and technicians who make the magic happen in the Disney theme parks, no American outfit was ever better equipped to mount Broadway technomusicals than the Disney Company. And mount them they did, starting with *Beauty and the Beast* (4/18/94), with a book by Linda Woolverton, music by Alan Menken, lyrics by Howard Ashman, and additional lyrics by Tim Rice, once upon a time of the Lloyd Webber–Rice combo but now lured by the lucrative prospect of writing for "Team Disney." The challenge for the team's design-tech staff was to transform an animated feature film into a stage musical with living, breathing actors. *New York Times* critic David Richards points out that whereas much of the movie's charm was in having inanimate objects look and behave like people, translating it to the stage was a sort of reverse anthropomorphism wherein "the musical prides itself on how cleverly people can be made into objects" (D. Richards). The stage is often populated with all-singing, all-dancing teacups, candelabra, feather dusters, spoons, spatulas, and, in Richards's priceless expression, other "housewares." These characters are a technomusical feat of what might be called meta-costuming, but the transformation didn't stop there. Stan Meyer's "scenery . . . is almost always on the move. . . . No apparition, disappearance, thunderbolt, rainstorm or swirling fog is beyond the capabilities of the show's special effects engineers." And it's all topped off by the Beast's mid-air whirling-dervish transformation back into handsome prince. In its sheer number and variety of effects, *Beauty and the Beast* closely rivals *Phantom* as the apotheosis of the technomusical. The big difference is that with the first of Disney's forays into Broadway, adults and children alike flocked to the musical to see how their favorite moments from a favorite film could possibly happen on stage—another variation of technomusical audience attraction in action, and a perfect example of Sondheim's "recycled culture."

Before Disney returned—twice before century's end—there was one more British and one more American entry into the world of the techno-musical. After a run at London's Adelphi Theatre and an American premiere in Los Angeles mostly for nostalgic reasons, *Sunset Boulevard* (11/17/94) again showed Broadway how a motion picture could be transformed into a stage musical. This transformation was from a live-action film, not an animated cartoon, and was achieved, like other successful technomusicals, through the design brilliance and technical wizardry of John Napier and his crew. Napier was working again with composer Andrew Lloyd Webber, who was working with new librettists and lyricists Don Black and English playwright Christopher Hampton. Again Trevor Nunn directed. A perceptive director, Nunn understood the theatre's limitations compared to what can be done on celluloid, and his goal was to avoid "film" techniques or solutions in his stage production: "It's a matter of sheer practicality. . . . In a film script anything is possible. [In the theatre] Solutions have to involve technology, but not to overwhelm things" (qtd. in Perry, *Sunset* 92). Napier echoed Nunn when he spoke specifically about the show's most spectacular effect, the movie-palace-baroque living room of faded movie queen Norma Desmond's mansion levitating above the stage floor, often with actors on it, for another scene to be played underneath. Napier claimed the Adelphi Theatre had forced this effect, because there was not enough wing space for sets of simultaneous scenes to be placed side by side; one had to be above the other "and that produced the split-screen effect. But I didn't want it seen as a high-tech show, nor as a fantasy, like *Cats*. . . . I very much wanted for the audience not to be distracted by elaborate effect" (qtd. in Perry, *Sunset* 99, 100).

Given the show's other moments of spectacle, this seems like a hopelessly ingenuous remark. Some of those other effects turned out to be precisely of the filmic variety Nunn had wanted to avoid, including actual clips of the car chase in the original Billy Wilder movie to help simulate Joe's flight from the repo man on stage. The stage version of Joe's murdered body floating in Norma Desmond's pool as seen from below with police and press photographers looming above closely replicated the scene in the film, but it was engineered through devices of the theatre (see Perry, *Sunset* 99–100). Yet while Napier doth protest too much about the presence of spectacular effects in *Sunset*, he is correct that this techno offered audiences a real story with real characters. All things considered, both the number and kinds of effects in *Sunset* are comparatively modest for shows of this genre. It is even possible that the relative paucity of effects, together with a less than distinguished score, helped account for the New York run of just 977 performances, far fewer than the other major runs in Lloyd Webber Land.

Like *Sunset Boulevard*, the technomusical *Titanic* (4/23/97) had a story to tell. With a book by Peter Stone and music and lyrics by Maury Yeston, here was no translation from cinema to living theatre but a carefully re-searched, slightly fictionalized recreation of an historical disaster of monu-mental proportions. Countless spectators were prepared to pay big bucks just to see the mega-liner sinking at a very precarious angle. That audience motive alone of wanting to see the ship go down qualifies *Titanic* as a technomusical. And, in fact, the sinking is one of the few spectacular effects in the production. Most of the musical is a rather affecting portrait of the ship's passengers and crew that succeeds in personalizing for the audience at least a fraction of them. This rare combination of strong original book, music, and lyrics with the devices of the technomusical kept the stage *Ti-tanic* afloat for 804 performances.

What gave Disney's *The Lion King* (11/13/97) a degree of class and style unusual in a technomusical was director/designer Julie Taymor's breathtak-ingly beautiful but decidedly low-tech puppet, mask, and costume design and technology. Which is not to say that Richard Hudson's scenic design didn't participate in the show's spectacle; the Pride Rock alone is quite spectacular as it rises out of the stage floor. *The Lion King* was of course another translation from animated cartoon to live stage musical. The stage production was adapted from the screenplay by Irene Mecchi, Jonathan Roberts, and Linda Woolverton, with a book by Roger Allers and Mecchi, music by Elton John, and lyrics by Tim Rice, with additional music and lyrics by Lebo M [sic], Mark Mancina, Jay Rifkin, Hans Zimmer, and Julie Taymor herself. But *The Lion King* was vastly different from *Beauty and the Beast* in that its visual production did not attempt to replicate the film. What audiences saw was very much Taymor's personal, somewhat impres-sionistic and even mystical vision of the tale. In most cases the actors were quite visible as they manipulated their animal puppet personae. This kind of symbiosis of performer and low-tech machine is nearly as ancient as theatre itself, especially in East Asian civilizations—yet withal, still a kind of techno-theatre, albeit at an elemental level. Ben Brantley of the *Times* recognized the technological underpinnings of *The Lion King* but correctly implied that it was a technology of a different order from that in most technomusicals, saying that the show was "a refreshing and more sophisti-cated alternative to the standard panoply of special-effects that dominate most tourist-oriented shows today" (Brantley, "Cub").

Toward the close of the 1999–2000 season, Disney brought *Aida* (3/23/00) to Broadway—not Verdi's *Aida*, but Tim Rice and Elton John's *Aida*, stylistically worlds apart. All things considered, Disney kept the legend of the doomed Nubian princess and Egyptian captain pretty much intact, not even sentimentalizing or "happy-ending" the story as so many animated Disney features were wont to do. True to the original, the Disney *Aida* even concludes with the death of the lovers. And according to critical consensus, if not for Heather Headley's electrifying performance in the title role, it likely would have been death for the show itself. *Aida* was minimally a technomusical, the Broadway version not nearly so high-tech as during the show's period of development and previews in Atlanta. There a lot of the glitz was scrapped, and so were its creators, with a new team brought in to clean up the act. Among them was stage designer Bob Crowley, who still produced enough shape-changing splendor that the Broadway version qualifies as a technomusical; Ben Brantley could thus remark that without Headley's performance "there would be nothing for grown-ups to focus on once they get past the visual jolt of the Las Vegas arcade that is passing for ancient Egypt" (Brantley, "Destiny"). The progressive scaling down of technological wizardry in the three Disney shows suggests a trend, and, indeed, thus far no new technomusicals have opened in the twenty-first century.

Attitudes toward technomusicals vary. The shows' creators are of course very positive, but critics range from ambivalent to downright hostile. And ticket-buying tourists (and others) adore them and made technos as a group the single biggest box office draw in the last two decades of the century. From the ranks of the techno creators, John Napier, sounding a bit defensive, says of *Miss Saigon*'s helicopter, "Nothing is gratuitous, or 'special effects' only; I hate that. Everything happens with a purpose, because the story requires it" (qtd. in Behr and Steyn 131). Peter Stone, *Titanic*'s librettist, perhaps is more honest in acknowledging the role of the show's technical effects. In his eyes, the small *Titanic* model "steaming her way across a mirror-smooth sea, her lights blazing, her funnels smoking, oblivious of the iceberg which lies immediately ahead — closes the First Act and turned out to be one of the most breathtaking effects ever seen on stage, equal, in our minds, to the helicopter in *Miss Saigon* and the chandelier in *Phantom of the Opera*" (Stone, *Titanic* 31). And talking about Stewart Laing's design, Stone made no apologies for the show *having* to be a technomusical: "Attempting to present a spectacle the size of *Titanic* . . . demanded, not only an impressionistic concept, but an engineering miracle. We were determined to show the ship actually sinking on stage — and Stewart's success in creating this mechanical marvel has been cheered at every performance" (26).

As would be expected, negatives about technomusicals have come both from theatre critics and from writers and directors of other kinds of plays and musicals. Howard Kissel's *Miss Saigon* review categorized the show with others of its ilk, pointedly capitalizing the central techno-feature of each: "As everyone knows, British musicals are less about music than they are about scenery. "Les Miz" was about The Barricades, "The Phantom of the Opera" was about The Chandelier, and "Miss Saigon," theoretically about the consequences of America in Vietnam, is really about The Helicopter. . . . Whether it's worth $100 for premium seats or $60 for orchestra locations depends on how intense your craving for novelty is" (*NYTCR 1991* 317). Kissel's repeated "about" underscores the fact that for most tourist-audiences, these scenic effects were centrally what the shows were *about*.

Writing of *Beauty and the Beast*, David Richards used an apt analogy in remarking, "Nobody should be surprised that it brings to mind a theme-park entertainment raised to the power of 10" (D. Richards). As do all tech-nomusicals. Frank Rich, interviewing Stephen Sondheim, used the same analogy in stating that he shared Sondheim's "alarm that Broadway was turning into a theme park" (Rich 40). Sondheim prefaced his earlier-quoted lament about stage versions of movies and recycled culture by observing that "[y]ou have two kinds of shows on Broadway—revivals and the same kind of musicals over and over again, all spectacles" (Rich 40).

Playwright Albert Innaurato traces the origin of such spectacles and de-scribes their effect on spectators: "In the '70s and '80s, financial pressures pushed the industry to forsake medium-size productions in favor of gigantic spectacles. As a result, medium-size backers—central to the culture of Broadway—threw in the towel, leaving the field wide open for Disney. . . . Meaning is a phantom; a chandelier falls and we go home happy—minus a hundred shekels and 10,000 brain cells" (Innaurato 28). Playwright and director George C. Wolfe also had a few choice words to say about tech-nomusicals, getting to the heart of what authentic theatre has traditionally been about: "The conventional Broadway wisdom is 'When in doubt give 'em spectacle,' . . . But a human being going through emotions is the best sort of event you can witness" (qtd. in Lahr ix).

To which I can only add an historical note to put things in perspective. It is demonstrable that from the late days of Attic Greece (fourth century B.C.) at least to the late 1920s in America, whenever theatre, musical or otherwise, featured spectacle and style over genuine substance, there was a corresponding decadence and decay of values in that culture. But lest we declare too soon the end of civilization as we know it, numerous musicals of rich and varied social content shared the stage with the technos and the retros of the '80s and '90s. These are the subject of chapter 10.

# New Voices, New Perspectives

T he diversionary musicals, nostalgia-driven shows, and technomusicals of the 1980s and '90s shared New York's musical stages with over fifty musicals containing serious social themes. Nearly all of these issue-oriented musicals — including those discussed in earlier chapters — have the same approach to their subject matter. Eschewing the overt biases and agendas of the '70s "in your face" message-musicals, most socially meaningful shows of the '80s and '90s simply tell it like it is, letting audiences reach their own conclusions. At the same time, their varied subject matter mirrors the emphasis on diversity that characterized the last two decades of the century. The very fact that some of the most successful musicals in this period were socially relevant shows about women, homosexuals, blacks (dealt with earlier), and other often marginalized persons is evidence that again the musical theatre was keeping pace with the most significant issues in the nation.

### Women's Issues in Musicals

Between 1981 and 1984, six musicals appeared on and off-Broadway that focused specifically on women's issues. The first women's-oriented show — written by all men — was the only one to achieve long-running Broadway success, with 770 performances. Based on the 1942 M-G-M Katherine Hepburn/Spencer Tracy film, *Woman of the Year* (3/29/81) had a book by Peter Stone and music and lyrics by John Kander and Fred Ebb. The musical centers on prominent TV morning talk-show host Tess Harding, a work-obsessed career woman, whose second husband, Sam Craig, is an equally successful cartoonist. The pair struggle to balance their careers and personal lives.

Stone, Kander, and Ebb created in Tess a multifaceted individual. About to receive an award near the beginning of act 1, Tess sings her feelings in a feminist manifesto:

> WHAT YOU NEED IS BRAINS
> WHAT YOU NEED IS PUSH
> WHAT YOU NEED IS ENERGY
> TO GET OFF YOUR TUSH
> BUT YOU DON'T NEED MEN,
> WHEN YOU COME TO BAT
> NO YOU DO NOT NEED A MAN,
> I'M THE PROOF OF THAT!
> (Stone, *Woman* 13–14)

Yet seconds later Tess wishes her estranged husband were with her. Throughout, *Woman of the Year* presents women's options in all their complexity; the hilarious show-stopping second-act duet "The Grass Is Always Greener" sharply contrasts homemakers with career women. *Woman of the Year* even looks at the consequences of female careerism from the male perspective. After Tess announces on TV that she's quitting to be a full-time wife, Sam says to her, "I don't want you to stop being you. All I ever wanted was for you to leave some room in your life for me" (102). How Sam and Tess strike a balance between their careers and marital life illustrates the methods of most socially relevant musicals toward century's end. These shows presented well-rounded characters, laid out issues, and offered dramatically viable solutions but rarely preached a particular party line.

Following *Woman of the Year*, off-Broadway's *I Can't Keep Running in Place* (5/14/81; 208 performances) focused on the female psyche. The show was written and staged by women: book, music, and lyrics by Barbara Schottenfeld, direction by Susan Einhorn, and choreography by Baayork Lee. *Running in Place* depicted six sessions of six women in "group" with their female psychiatrist. Through song and dialogue they explored their innermost concerns, sometimes explicitly feminist, sometimes not. While such self-analysis and introspection grew from the previous decade's fragmented musicals, the salient difference is that here the characters share their self-exploration with each other.

Next up was Betty Comden and Adolph Green's musical sequel to Ibsen's *A Doll's House*. *A Doll's Life* (9/23/82) picks up where *A Doll's House* left off, speculating on what Nora did after slamming the door on her husband, children, and repressive Norwegian society. Harold Prince jumped at the chance to produce and direct the show:

I like shows that are about something. I particularly like them if they are political and yet, at the same time entertaining. *A Doll's Life* touches on an important issue;

it was an important issue 100 years ago and it's still an issue. . . . It isn't about a woman's rights any more than *A Doll's House* was. . . . Ibsen didn't intend that. He intended it to be about people standing on their own feet—in this case, not only Nora but her husband as well. Nora's story forces you to examine the issues. . . . What I like about *A Doll's Life* is that *we* don't have to force those issues on the audience—the mere fact that the story is being told causes those issues to be raised. (qtd. in Ilson 315).

Prince had high ideals for the show, but he and his collaborators never got it right. Prince teamed old hands Comden and Green with little-known composer Larry Grossman because he liked Grossman's score for *Minnie's Boys* (3/2/70). But Grossman had as little name-recognition as the musical's star, Betsy Joslyn. *A Doll's Life* would have to stand or fall on its merits alone. It fell. Although the story of Nora "working for pay, attaining power, having love affairs and concluding with her next major decision about her life" (Ilson 314) resonated with contemporary relevance, the show simply lacked entertainment value. *A Doll's Life* was scheduled for a ten-week tryout in Los Angeles that was cut to eight because of horrendous reviews and financial losses. The creative team had more than enough time in L.A. to tinker with the show's problems, but once Prince brought *A Doll's Life* into New York, the reviews drove him to post a closing notice the day after it opened. After just five performances, Broadway slammed the door on Nora.

*Baby* (12/4/83) was less political than gynecological. With a book by Sybille Pearson and music and lyrics by David Shire and Richard Maltby Jr., it dealt with a very private matter: pregnancy. The musical follows the stories of three couples. Two unmarried college undergraduates sort out their options when the young woman gets pregnant; a thirtysomething married couple learn to deal with the macho husband's low sperm count being responsible for the wife's "infertility"; and an older couple looking forward to *being* a couple again, now that their grown children have moved away, suddenly discover the wife is pregnant. *Baby* explores nonjudgmentally how each pair deals with their options and alternatives. The show played a respectable if not spectacular 241 times.

*A . . . My Name Is Alice* (2/24/84) dealt with a myriad of women's concerns. A product of the American Place's Women's Project, the revue was conceived and directed by Julianne Boyd, who had masterminded the Broadway tribute to Eubie Blake, and Joan Micklin Silver, best known for her films *Hester Street* and *Crossing Delancy*. More than half of the show's twenty-eight writers were men. The numbers range tremendously in approach and intention. Commentary is implicit in "All-Girl Band," "Welcome to Kindergarten," and Anne Meara's "Hot Lunch," a screamingly funny putdown of construction workers' sexual heckling. Other pieces, like

"At My Age," "The Portrait," and "Friends," are candid and psychologically perceptive presentations of women's dilemmas, problems, or reflections. Still others are just flat-out hilarious entertainment. In all, *Alice* was a wide-lens kaleidoscopic picture of American women in the mid-'80s, as entertaining as it was insightful, explaining its 353 performances at off-Broadway's Village Gate.

Perhaps *Quilters* (9/24/84) deserved better than it got in New York; it had done better elsewhere and went on to have a life beyond its brief stay in Manhattan. *Quilters* had succeeded at the Denver Center for the Performing Arts, where it originated, followed by strong runs in Washington and Los Angeles. But on Broadway the stitches came apart after just twenty-four showings. Based on *The Quilters: Women and Domestic Art* by Patricia Cooper and Norma Bradley Allen, the musical had a book by Molly Newman and Barbara Damashek, with the latter supplying both music and lyrics. Inspired by the symbolic or metaphoric significance of quilting patterns, the musical told of pioneer women struggling and surviving in the American West and offered a strong, dramatic statement of women's resilience and self-reliance. But the show's format irritated some critics. In Frank Rich's view, "the authors have given their libretto a patchwork structure. 'Quilters' is a static mélange of skits, monologues and songs unified by a theme rather than a sustained plot or characters." Ron Cohen in *Women's Wear Daily* echoed Rich with "its fragmented structure takes away from its overall impact" (*NYTCR* 1984 206–207). Just a decade earlier, fragmented musicals were generally well received, but now both Rich's and Cohen's remarks fault the fragmented approach *generally*, not just in *Quilters*. As *Quilters* marks the end of the specifically women-oriented musical, it was also— with only *Assassins* to follow in 1991—the penultimate fragmented musical as well.

### Homosexuality in Musicals

Mart Crowley's 1968 *The Boys in the Band* was the first overtly gay-oriented play on Broadway. A year later, in June 1969, Greenwich Village's Stonewall Riots raised national consciousness about the rights of homosexuals, marked the origin of the modern gay and lesbian movement, and spurred an increase in gay rights groups nationally from 100 in 1969 to 2,500 two years later (see "Gay-rights"; Marty 95). Still, acceptance for homosexuality and homosexual issues in musicals would be long in coming. Despite the success of *The Boys in the Band*, only one musical depicted a gay male relationship prior to the 1980s. *Sextet* (3/3/74) was a one-act show with book by

Harvey Perr and Lee Goldsmith, lyrics by the latter, and music by Lawrence Hurwit. Two gay men, Kenneth and David, give a dinner party for David's widowed mother, her middle-aged divorced boyfriend with a fear of commitment, and David's old college roommate and his wife, whom he cheats on with alarming regularity. Throughout the party, the six explore their sexuality and takes on monogamy, all concluding they're stuck being who they are. Almost every critic compared this self-searching to Sondheim and Furth's *Company*, usually not flatteringly (*NYTCR* 1974 352–54). Nonetheless, it can be said that *Sextet* pioneered by many years, if for only nine performances, musicals like *March of the Falsettos* and *La Cage aux Folles*.

## March of the Falsettos *and* Falsettoland

*March of the Falsettos* (5/20/81) was the first successful musical to depict a gay male relationship. *March* was born at Playwrights Horizons, later moving to the Chelsea Westside Theatre, both off-Broadway; it achieved wide critical acclaim and audience popularity with 268 performances between its two venues. This one-act musical deals with a gay male relationship and other human relationships with a sensitivity that resonates for people regardless of sexual preference. Indeed, the homosexual relationship between Marvin and Whizzer is categorically *not* the center of the show. Marvin is its center, just as he's the center of his own universe until he slowly learns better. Composer/lyricist William Finn also put Marvin at the center of two companion pieces, *In Trousers* (workshopped at Playwrights Horizons in 1979) and *Falsettoland* (6/28/90). So focal is Marvin that Finn refers to his trilogy as "the 'Marvin' musicals" (Bishop, liner notes).

Marvin is a thirtysomething Jewish guy formerly married to Trina, with whom he had a son, the precocious Jason. Realizing that he was gay, Marvin divorced Trina and "ran off with a friend" (Finn, *March* 2), neither of whom, by the way, is ever portrayed as a gay stereotype. Marvin exposes his me-centered universe right from the top of the show in "A Tight-Knit Family," as he tries to make his former family harmonize with his new male lover, the song concluding with Marvin's self-defining catch-phrase, "I want it all."

Marvin's self-absorption is the musical's core, accounting for the show's most powerful dramatic and thematic statement. A musical about a man leaving his wife for another woman would be fairly conventional; for him to leave his wife for a man is less so, and Finn uses that to make a major point. While Marvin and Trina accurately say that he divorced her and not she him, Trina makes it equally clear in "This Had Better Come to a Stop" that she was getting fed up with his self-centered behavior:

> I was supposed to make his dinner—
> Kippered salmon on his plate—
> Every wife should pull her weight:
> Clip the coupons, check for specials,
> And love him.
>
> (Finn, *March* 4)

Later in the show, when Marvin's male lover, Whizzer, rebels at certain traits in his partner just prior to leaving him, he sings to the same melody as Trina,

> Whizzer's supposed to make the dinner.
> Be a patsy, lose at chess;
> Always bravely acquiesce.
> Clip the coupons, make the dinner
> And love him.
>
> (7)

Had Marvin simply gone from heterosexual to heterosexual relationship, all we would see is a traditionally chauvinistic man making egocentric demands on each female partner. But when Marvin alienates Whizzer by the same kind of behavior, he demonstrates that his selfishness does not depend upon his partner's gender. Marvin's demanding egocentricity is displayed as a fault endemic to certain males of the Me Generation—those with unreasonable role expectations for their partners *regardless of their sexual orientation*.

*March* contrasts Marvin's outlook and behavior with Trina's remarriage to Mendel, nearly everyone's psychiatrist. Theatrically, Mendel is a workaholic bundle of comic neuroses, but for Trina he's a husband in a marriage that's a partnership—as demonstrated in their duet "Making a Home," which should have dispelled the notion at the time that *March* advocated gay above straight relationships. Not at all. For Finn, the dynamics of individual personalities, regardless of gender, make relationships viable or not.

Finn explored relationships very widely in *March*. In "I Never Wanted To Love You," all the characters expose their feelings about whether or not to risk loving someone. Mendel is most comic, fretting over his strong feelings for Trina. As he sees it, "In my profession one's love stays unexpressed. / . . . God, I'm distressed how I love you" (Finn, *March* 7). More seriously, Trina reveals to Marvin her ambivalent and conflicted feelings for him, both when they were married and now, post-divorce:

> I never wanted to love you.
> I only wanted to love and not be blamed.
> Let me go.
> You should know
> I'm not ashamed to have loved you.
>
> (7)

Whizzer argues that his love for Marvin was never meant to imply monogamy:

> I never wanted " 'til death do we two part."
> Condescend.
> Stay my friend.
> How do I start not to love you?
>
> (8)

Unlike the other adults, Marvin aims his remarks at more than one person. He attacks Trina for remarrying ("It really killed me when you took those vows"), and in a brilliant Freudian-slip lyric he exposes his mixed feelings for Whizzer,

> I never wanted
> I wanted
> I never never never never never
> Never wanted to love you.
>
> (8)

The string of six "never"s tries to deflect from the accidental "I wanted." And in one of the most painfully realistic moments, Marvin sings to Jason: "I never wanted to love you. / I only wanted to see my face in yours" (8), a feeling symptomatic of his narcissism.

Throughout, Jason expresses feelings relating to yet another of the musical's concerns—the status and feelings of children of divorce (and, not incidentally, of an out-gay parent). Jason's lyric in this song at least equals Marvin's to him for its pain quotient (other characters' interjected lines omitted): "I hate the world. / I love my dad. / I love the things I've never had" (7), equating those never-had things with his absent father. This precocious kid also comes up with lines like "I'm too smart for my own good, / And I'm too good for my sorry little life" (4). And in "Everyone Tells Jason to See a Psychiatrist," when the adults gang up on him to see a shrink, Jason counters with, "If intelligence were the only criterion, / Then I really wouldn't need a psychiatrist, / Would I? . . . Would I? / Just because you've failed as parents" (4). In the quietly moving finale "Father To Son," Marvin, having lost both ex-wife and lover, tries to re-establish contact with Jason.

Nearly a decade passed before Finn completed the third of his "Marvin musicals," this one in collaboration with James Lapine, who had directed *March of the Falsettos*. *Falsettoland* opened at Playwrights Horizons on June 28, 1990, and was transferred to the newly restored Lucille Lortel Theatre on September 16, playing a total of 215 times between the two theatres. The new show brought back all the characters from *March* plus two new ones, Dr. Charlotte (an internist) and Cordelia (a kosher caterer), who refer to themselves collectively as "the lesbians from next door" (Finn and Lapine 170). But the nearly ten-year hiatus between shows did not mean that the characters in *Falsettoland* were ten years older. Finn wisely ignored the lapse in "real time" between the musicals, choosing instead to continue chronologically where *March* had left off, since, as Mendel explains in *Falsettoland*'s opening, "This story needs an ending" (Finn and Lapine 98). While the precise time of the sequel was not made explicit in the 1990 production, once Finn and Lapine revised both *March* and *Falsettoland* for Broadway in 1992, it became clear they take place in 1979 and 1981, respectively. Under the truncated title *Falsettos* (4/29/92), that production linked the two distinct one-acts as the two acts of a full-length musical. Each remained essentially the same as originally, with only minor alterations in some lyrics for continuity and occasional clarification but no substantive changes in the characters, story, or themes. Its 487-performance Broadway run enabled Finn and Lapine to present the artistry and issues of the Marvin musicals to a considerably wider audience than before.

By setting the sequel just two years after the original, Finn assured strong continuity in the action. Alone since Whizzer walked out on him and aching from loneliness, Marvin is thrown back into the bosom of his former family (and Trina's new husband, Mendel) as they go through the comic convolutions of planning Jason's bar mitzvah. At a Little League game to which Jason invites Whizzer, he and Marvin renew their relationship. Shortly thereafter, Whizzer collapses during a racquetball game with Marvin. If making *Falsettoland*'s dramatic continuity was easy, Finn's choices of what to dramatize presented some difficult challenges. Overall the themes and storylines of *Falsettoland* are few and simple compared to the intricacies of *March*. Aside from simply portraying the warmly comic lesbians as a devoted couple, Finn broke no new ground exploring relationships as he had earlier, although the appearance of both gay and lesbian couples occasioned the creation of a rare, moving, and beautiful serious same-sex love song for four voices, "Unlikely Lovers." But having Whizzer fall victim to a disease that in 1981 didn't even have a name entailed some very skillful writing. Finn rose to the challenge admirably, in the process writing and composing the first professionally produced musical to treat the subject of AIDS. And, other than *Rent*, this was the only successful musical to do so through the end of the century, even though the number of non-musical AIDS plays is considerable.

Appropriately, only Dr. Charlotte even gets close to saying anything specific about the unnamed disease, first through her observations at the hospital:

> Bachelors arrive sick and frightened.
> They leave weeks later unenlightened.
> We see a trend, but the trend has no name.
> (141)

and later in the historical context that in 1981 the still unnamed AIDS was considered almost exclusively a "gay disease":

> Something very bad is happening.
> Something that kills.
> Something contagious.
> Something that spreads
> From one man to another.
> (162)

The stories of Marvin and Whizzer and of Jason's bar mitzvah come together late in the musical. Jason doesn't want to have the ceremony until Whizzer gets well enough to attend. Coming to realize that may never be, Jason suggests holding a small bar mitzvah in Whizzer's hospital room. They do, just before Whizzer dies. Distraught as he is over Whizzer's death, Marvin grows up in the show's closing moment as he accepts the support of friends (former spouse and son included) to help him through the loss of his lover.

## La Cage aux Folles

A little over three months before the hit *La Cage aux Folles* (8/21/83) opened, another show opened that had no run at all but is historically significant as the first mainstream Broadway musical to depict a gay male love affair. Alan Jay Lerner loosely adapted *Dance a Little Closer* (5/11/83) from *Idiot's Delight*, Robert E. Sherwood's 1936 Pulitzer Prize–winning apocalyptic and, not incidentally, isolationist drama. Sherwood's play took place on the brink of World War II, but Lerner reset *Dance a Little Closer* on the eve of a projected World War III. With music by Charles Strouse,

*Dance a Little Closer* was librettist/lyricist Lerner's final (and failed) bid for one more hit; the show closed the night it opened. Yet Lerner's open depiction of homosexuality in a Broadway musical for general audiences cannot go unremarked. Lerner transformed what had been the heterosexual honeymoon couple of Sherwood's subplot into two gay male airline stewards and gave them their special moment in a sincere love duet called "Why Can't the World Go and Leave Us Alone?" The eighty-three-year-old Lerner said he risked doing this because "I wanted to make a statement about love being essential to all lifestyles. I have to admit some people have been critical of my including the two boys in the story, but I've found you have to write something because you believe in it" (qtd. in Citron 378).

Gay librettist Harvey Fierstein and composer/lyricist Jerry Herman's musical adaptation of Jean Poiret's French play *La Cage aux Folles* had a long life of 1,761 performances. Yet the musical ultimately fell short of its creators' goals by largely failing to make any serious statements about gay relationships and lifestyles. Their source material—"a bevy of sight gags, wildly drawn characters and sexual rompery. Truly the fabric of a farce" (Herman, *La Cage* 10)—combined with their own (mis)treatment of it in the show's book, music, and lyrics finally defeated Fierstein and Herman's good intentions.

In "A Note from the Author" in the published text, Fierstein discusses how he, Herman, and director Arthur Laurents sought to give the French original "heart" by fleshing out the love story of Georges and Albin as it comes into conflict with Georges's son, Jean-Michel. Although Albin had been more a mother to Jean-Michel than the boy's biological one, Jean-Michel views him as an embarrassment and wants him to disappear for the duration of his fiancée's homophobic father Dindon's visit. This plotline has the potential to treat some serious issues, but *La Cage* doesn't acknowledge them. Apart from such sensitive numbers as "Song on the Sand," and Albin's impressive yet heartbreaking paean to gay pride, "I Am What I Am," the musical remains, like the French original, a gaggle of gags in the fabric of farce. Nothing is more farcical than *La Cage*'s slapdash ending, during which Dindon is blackmailed into accepting his daughter's engagement to Jean-Michel and the boy's gay father and "mother." If *La Cage* intended to promote heterosexuals' acceptance of gays, the coercion of Dindon was not the way to do it.

More problematic even than the slapstick action is the musical's retention of the play's "wildly drawn characters" purely through Fierstein and Herman's choice to retain them, even though they wanted to give the show more "heart." With the lone exception of Georges, who appears as straight as Marvin in the *Falsettos* musicals, the gay characters in *La Cage*, from the nightclub's chorus boys and Jacob the butler (who prefers being called the maid) to Albin himself, aren't just drag performers in the club but drag queens off-stage, whose dialogue and mannerisms consistently portray them as homosexual stereotypes. Thanks to this unbalanced portrayal, audiences may have left the theatre entertained, but they left with their prejudices largely intact. Moreover, Jerry Herman's music seemed to be in a 1960s timewarp, which led me to conclude my *Boston Herald* review of the tryout by noting that, overall, *La Cage* looked and sounded like *Hello, Dolly!* in drag.

## The Gay '90s

In the 1990s, musicals expanded upon homosexual relationships and issues. *Kiss of the Spider Woman* (5/3/93) is a same-sex love story. But it is equally a critical depiction of government-sanctioned human rights violations. One view of *Spider Woman* does not obviate the other; the storylines are inseparable. Adapted from Manuel Puig's novel (later a play and film) by Terence McNally, with music and lyrics by John Kander and Fred Ebb, *Spider Woman* traces the shifting relationship of two mismatched prisoners deliberately put in the same cell in an unnamed Latin American country. The cell's first occupant is Molina, a homosexual arrested for corrupting a minor. His new cellmate, Valentin, was arrested for passing travel documents to political fugitives (*Best Plays* 92–93 211). This pairing of prisoners immediately sets up the political focus of the musical—the worldwide parallels between human rights violations against political dissidents and hate crimes against gays. From Valentin's initial homophobia, through Molina and he becoming lovers, right up to Valentin's torture and the Warden's cold-blooded killing of Molina in front of Valentin, not for a moment does *Spider Woman* let an audience forget its concern with atrocities against all who dare to be different, politically or sexually. Fundamentally serious, often brutally so in depictions and descriptions of torture, yet theatrically glamorous in the "movie" sequences, *Spider Woman* lured customers into her web 906 times.

Following *Spider Woman*, two gay-oriented satirical revues opened just about three years apart. Working out of The Glines, one of off-Broadway's oldest and most respected gay theatre companies, a large group of collaborators put together *Howard Crabtree's Whoop-Dee-Doo!* (6/29/93). The show spoofed the format and production values of spectacular revues, at the same time that it topically satirized aspects (and not just gay aspects) of contemporary society. That formula netted the show a run of 258 performances. Named for the creator of the show's outlandish costumes, *Whoop-Dee-Doo!* was the product of many hands: conceived, created, and developed by Charles Catanese, Crabtree, Dick Gallagher, Phillip George, Peter Morris, and Mark Waldrop; songs and sketches by Gallagher, Morris, and Waldrop, with additional material by Brad Ellis, Jack Feldman, David Rambo, Bruce Sussman, and Eric Schorr. It was so successful that three years later Crabtree and two of his original collaborators created a second revue, *When Pigs Fly* (8/14/96). Crabtree and Waldrop conceived the show, with sketches and lyrics by Waldrop, and music again by Gallagher. Once more featuring Crabtree's goofy costumes and based on the premise of "a man named Howard putting on an extravagant show under many difficulties," *Pigs* featured "numbers dealing with sundry aspects of modern American life and times" (*Best Plays 96–97* 262). Although the writers and performers were gay, the revue's wide-ranging material drew audiences from beyond the gay community, helping to account for the show's success. Indeed, *When Pigs Fly* defied the impossibility of its title, ignored the myth that sequels never succeed like the originals, and played 840 times. Sadly, Crabtree died from an AIDS-related illness on June 28, 1996, five days after finishing work on *Pigs* (*Theatre World 96–97* 118). He never saw his greatest success come to fruition.

## Cabaret

The Roundabout Theatre Company's *Cabaret* (3/19/98) was a revival of the 1966 musical (see chapter 7). But author Joe Masteroff, composer John Kander, and lyricist Fred Ebb so extensively altered the original, and British director Sam Mendes so radically reconceived the venue, staging, and overall thrust of the show, that this *Cabaret* is more a new show than a revival of an older one. One of the most significant changes is the centrality given to homosexuality, present in the musical's sources but absent from the 1966 original. In fact, all varieties of sex and sexuality are much more upfront in the 1998 version than in the 1966 one. Still, for 1966, Hal Prince's *Cabaret* was a pretty sexy show. But apart from the androgynous look and mannerisms of Joel Gray's Emcee, it was strictly heterosexually sexy, as exemplified by the tawdry costumes of the Kit Kat Girls, the slightly naughty lyrics of Sally's "Don't Tell Mama," and the still naughtier ones of "Two Ladies."

But the heart of Christopher Isherwood's stories, *Cabaret's* primary source, was Sally Bowles's relationship with a *homosexual* writer, the actual author of *The Berlin Stories* Christopher Isherwood using his own name in that story. The revisionist *Cabaret* was quite faithful to the letter and spirit of the Isherwood original: "Mendes and Masteroff clarified the story by allowing all the characters—young, old, straight, gay, bisexual, and undecided—their sexuality" (Sunshine 13). By the fourth scene of act 1, Cliff's homosexuality is outed when he agrees to go backstage at the Kit Kat Klub with Bobby, a "cabaret boy" he had previously met in a London bar. Moments later a stage direction states that "*CLIFF and BOBBY have a real kiss*" (Masteroff, *Cabaret* 1999, 37). When Sally asks Cliff, "Are you homosexual in any way? Bobby says you are" (47), Cliff neither confirms nor denies, but the audience knows a kiss is worth a thousand words.

And the Emcee is now clearly bisexual. In Mendes's staging of "Two Ladies," one of the alleged femmes is a boy in drag (Bobby, in fact), and during what was a dance-break in 1966, in the delicate words of Clifford A. Ridley of *The Philadelphia Enquirer*, "the trio shortly retires behind a scrim to perform a shadow play not to be described in a family newspaper" (qtd. in Masteroff, *Cabaret* 1999, 56). Factoring in such other things as the hyper-sleazy costumes, make-up, and behavior of the Kit Kat Girls, the almost continual sexual charge of the Roundabout production made the play's sexuality much more central to both its story and to what *this Cabaret* was all about.

The intention of each *Cabaret* was conveyed through its director's very different stagecraft. Prince worked primarily through metaphor and analogy. While he admired the 1972 film's frank treatment of homosexuality, Prince also regretted it did not make "metaphoric use of the MC" (Prince 135). In his 1966 production, Prince used the Emcee and his grotesque deterioration as an emblem of Germany's creeping decadence. Through analogies, his production pointed to the frightening parallels between 1930s Germany and the contemporary United States. The 1966 version of *Cabaret* asked Americans to remember the past in order to prevent like atrocities from happening not only now, but *here*. On the other hand, there is an odd discrepancy between Mendes's stated intention and what he actually achieved. Mendes declared his *Cabaret* was "really about the central mystery of the twentieth century—how Hitler could have happened. And it's important that we go on asking the question whether or not we can find some sort of answer" (qtd. in Masteroff, *Cabaret* 1999 99). Mendes never suggests that he intended to draw any parallels between what happened in Germany and anything current in the United States or elsewhere.

But Sam Mendes's *Cabaret* is much more than what he claimed. There are three major differences between the 1966 and 1998 *Cabaret*: alterations in the score; the performance venue; and the new focus on alternative sexualities. According to Joe Masteroff, both in Hal Prince's 1987 revival and the 1998 production, almost all changes in the musical program were made for pragmatic, not thematic reasons (Masteroff interview). If three of the songs cut from the Mendes production had been retained, they would have expressed the director's vision of the show as a reminder of "how Hitler could have happened": Herr Schultz's little Jewish parable "Meeskite," which elicits a chilly reception from his increasingly Nazi-sympathizing neighbors; the Emcee's "The Money Song," with its allusions to the decadence and money woes of crumbling Weimar Germany, replaced by the film's "Money Makes the World Go Around," which just generically says it's better to have money than not; and Cliff's first-act "Why Should I Wake Up?" and its companion dialogue in act 2 (see chapter 7). Two songs written for Liza Minelli in the film largely to beef up her role's singing part entered the Roundabout production, for similar pragmatic reasons. "Mein Herr" is a slick, sexy number Sally performs in the club, while "Maybe This Time" is a book song when pregnant Sally contemplates a permanent relationship with Cliff—a song growing from plot and character but in no way related to the show's thematic concerns. Of all the ways in which Mendes reworked the 1966 *Cabaret*, the altered musical program did least to sharpen and focus the musical's social import.

Mendes's choice of performance venue was much more effective. In 1966, *Cabaret* was mounted in a conventional Broadway theatre, with considerable distance between the audience and the show. It wasn't easy for the metaphor of the mirror and similar devices to reach an audience over such a distance to make clear the terrifying parallels between 1930s Berlin and the United States in the '50s and '60s. The 1998 *Cabaret*, however, was performed in an actual cabaret setting, the stage intimately close to the audience, the majority of spectators sitting at little café tables; the audience thus *became* the cabaret's patrons (food and drinks available). They were not even given theatre programs until they left. Much of the impact of Mendes's show was due to the immediacy of the setting, not to metaphor.

According to both Masteroff and Mendes, the cabaret seating had a visceral impact on the audience. During the first act, cabaret numbers and the "love stories" of Cliff and Sally and Herr Schultz and Fraulein Schneider entertained the happy spectators. Only early in act 2, from the Emcee's line "She wouldn't look Jewish at all" about the dancing gorilla (*retained* in this production—see chapter 7), "the musical turns into a black-as-pitch play. The audience is a willing participant in the first part of the evening, but then the doors lock from the outside and they become prisoners" (Mendes qtd. in Sunshine 14).

While the 1998 *Cabaret* retained the 1966 depiction of the Nazi party's anti-Jewish violence, the then-peripheral depiction of sex and sexuality stepped up in 1998 to share center stage with the Jewish persecution motif.

Mendes's confrontational staging drove the parallel themes home through a horrific revelation in the show's closing moments. This *Cabaret* proclaimed its contemporary relevance when the Emcee took off his coat to reveal him in concentration camp clothing emblazoned with both the yellow star designating Jews and the pink triangle marking homosexuals. The revised *Cabaret* thus used the Third Reich's incarceration of homosexuals as well as Jews (and other ethnic minorities) to remind contemporary audiences that hate crimes and human rights violations still persist worldwide, including but not limited to recent outbreaks of homophobia, gay-bashing, and gay murders in the United States. *Cabaret* conveyed its theme directly and dramatically with no comment of any kind, and it did so in the context of supercharged entertainment from opening to curtain call. This helped account for its 879 performances by the end of the last twentieth-century theatre season, with many more to come in the twenty-first.

## Divisiveness, Decadence, and Diversity

In the century's closing decades a number of significant (though not uniformly successful) musicals tried to address various ills current in American society. Mostly these were the ills that divide not just person from person, but people from people—poor from rich, black from white, homosexual from homophobic, and so on. Appearing as they did in commercial musicals, these themes validate Haynes Johnson's neat summary of the period: "American life grows increasingly fragmented and divisive." Most such musicals are set in the past and communicate through historical analogy and the dramatic presentation of complex issues. Further, while all portray a divisive or decadent America, only *Rent* offers any kind of healing inclusiveness in its acceptance of Americans' diversity.

## Grind

*Grind* (4/16/85) was a fascinating flop. In 1975, two producers at Universal Studios asked Fay Kanin for a screenplay about a tacky biracial burlesque theatre in 1933 Chicago. The project never materialized. Years later Kanin brought her script to old friend Hal Prince, who saw its affinity to *Cabaret*. Both shows used, in the words of *Newsweek*'s Jack Kroll, "showbiz as a metaphor for the dislocations of reality" (qtd. in Ilson 328). Prince brought back Larry (*A Doll's Life*) Grossman to do the music, the virtual unknown Ellen Fitzhugh for the lyrics, Lester Wilson to choreograph, and a charismatic biracial cast led by Ben Vereen, Stubby Kaye, Joey Faye, Leilani Jones, and Timothy Nolen. Prince then watched his venture bump and grind into musical theatre obscurity after seventy-nine performances.

Grind depicts the lives of black and white burlesque performers in Chicago during the World's Fair. Segregation still ruled Chicago show biz in 1933. The Caucasian and African American "artistes" had separate dressing rooms and could not appear together on stage. Yet some black performers, like the stripper Satin (Leilani Jones), were the stars of the show. In the course of the action, Satin has a relationship with an Irish radical. Enraged by the biracial affair, a handful of neighborhood toughs crash a performance, only to be beaten back by the whole burlesque company, black and white acting in concert. Yet Prince didn't see racial tension and harmony as central: "What Fay Kanin and the rest of us had in mind was a show about violence — every conceivable kind of violence, which sadly we come to accept as part of our everyday lives. That would have worked fifteen years earlier; it would have had a run" (qtd. in Ilson 331). Prince may have been right; perhaps mid-'80s audiences had had enough of violence or had become too inured to it to appreciate Grind.

## Grand Hotel

Grand Hotel (11/12/89) was an indictment of greed, wheeling and dealing, and social decadence. When it opened, the Wall Street scams and other national embarrassments had been airing for a couple of years. Americans watched the greed of Boesky and Milken, the scheming of Ollie North and Admiral Poindexter, and the fiscal and sexual transgressions of televangelists Bakker, Swaggart, and Falwell drag them down to defeat, disgrace, and/or prison. But what should have been an object lesson failed to squelch many Americans' belief that they too could and would strike it rich. Getting and spending characterized the Reagan '80s at a pace not seen since the 1920s. Haynes Johnson observed that if the $60 million price tag of George Bush's 1989 inauguration doubled the cost of Reagan's in 1981, "there should have been no surprise. Public excess had become the standard. . . . Bush took office against a backdrop of an America conditioned during the Reagan years to think of addressing personal opportunities instead of national problems" (439, 441).

Accordingly, when Luther Davis crafted the book for Grand Hotel from Vicki Baum's 1928 novel Menschen im Hotel, it was no accident that the milieu of grasping, high-living, decadent 1928 Berlin was a metaphor (if not a cautionary tale or warning shot) for the decadence of fin de siècle America some sixty years later. Davis doesn't state the parallels outright in his notes to the published text, but he unambiguously hints at them when writing of how everyone from the highest-paying hotel guests to the lowest-paid hotel employees believe somehow, someday, they'll make a financial killing: "In 1928 most people suffered from an excess of hope and optimism. . . . The scullery workers in the musical are angry because they're not getting in on the action. . . . [But] perhaps they'll all hear about a 'hot, hot stock,' and move upstairs as hotel guests. In 1928, people believed in things like that— unlike today?" (L. Davis [12]).

The symptoms of greed, spending, and decadence pervade composer/lyricists Robert Wright and George Forrest's lyrics, as well as Maury Yeston's additional songs. One song proclaims the have-nots' desire to emulate the haves, right down to their skill at illegally maneuvering money for their own gain:

> IF ONLY I WERE SMARTER
> I WOULDN'T HAVE TO SWEAT SO MUCH!
> TO HAVE THAT FELLOW'S BANKROLL
> I COULD WHEEL AND DEAL,
> CHEAT, STEAL, WHATEVER
> HE DID TO GET SO MUCH!
>
> (30)

Also paralleling pre-Crash Berlin with the United States in the '90s, another song depicts the gulf between each society's affluent and impoverished, a gulf that widened drastically during the Reagan years. The upstairs hotel staff and disgruntled below-stairs scullery crew sing:

> SOME HAVE, SOME HAVE NOT! WHY?
> THEY'RE HERE SPENDING MONEY:
> A MILLION MARKS A DAY!
> WE'RE JUST ONE STEP FROM THE STREET,
> MAKING JUST ENOUGH TO EAT
> FOR A DAY,
> WEEK,
> MONTH,
> YEAR . . .
> WITH A THOUSAND BILLS TO PAY!
>
> . . . . . . . . . . . . . . . . . . . .
> AND WE PRAY FOR TIPS OF A MARK,
> FRANC,
> DOLLAR,
> POUND!
>
> (L. Davis 20)

This image of a society deeply divided between rich and poor is reinforced with bitter humor later on. Flaemmchen, the nineteen-year-old typist and wannabe film star, naively asks a black American entertainer, "Are the streets really paved with gold?" to which he retorts sardonically, "Honey, where I come from they ain't even paved!" (38).

The frayed threads of human lives that Davis, Wright, Forrest, and Yeston weave into the tapestry of *Grand Hotel* unravel to reveal shreds of humanity with dreams or schemes for making it, bailing out, or pulling themselves back together. Corporate magnate General Director Preysing of Saxonia Mills could have stepped back into 1928 from the '80s world of leveraged buy-out operators. He's a desperate man in need of a deal: "If we don't get the Boston merger our company's down the drain!" (27). The Baron, an impoverished young nobleman who resides at the hotel on the strength of his dubious credit, is a wired creature who gets his kicks from living dangerously close to the edge:

> GIVE ME THE THRILL
> OF A CARELESS EXISTENCE!
> GIVE ME THE HEAT
> AND THE PASSION TO WIN!
> I WANT THE HEIGHT
> AND ROMANCE OF ADVENTURE,
> COOLED BY THE CHILL
> OF THE DANGER I'M IN!
>
> (20–21)

In hock to an Algerian loan shark from the start of the show, the Baron is in danger of bodily harm from the goon sent to collect. But, calling from a hotel pay phone, the Baron tries cutting another deal with his shady creditor: "Hello, I'll be able to pay you back in full—but to do so I'd have to borrow another five thousand more—Why?—I have a tip on a stock on the New York Stock Exchange!—a hot, hot stock which is sure to go right through the roof!" (25). His desperate lifestyle leads the Baron to increasingly desperate means of supporting it. Finally, as if a deathwish had driven him all along, he is killed in a bungled robbery attempt to help finance his reckless style of living.

Similarly, other characters are exemplars of people in decadent cultures who will do whatever they must to live the high life. Despite appearances and what later decades would call being "sexually active," little Flaemmchen is quite naive and fairly conventional in her morality. Yet out of desperation she comes close to prostituting herself to Preysing for a thousand marks, later explaining, "Well, people come to that. When you've been without a job, and your clothes are all out of date, and you can't bear where you live—" (103). And Grushinskaya, the washed-up prima ballerina, so aches for admiration that she willingly lets herself be duped by the Baron, who is only coming on to her to purloin her jewels.

The one life-affirming story in *Grand Hotel* is Kringelein's, the fortyish terminally ill Jewish bookkeeper for Preysing's firm who has been nothing but a slave to his ledgers. Kringelein quits his job, withdraws all his savings, and comes to the hotel to spend whatever it takes in search of "Life" before he dies. Not satisfied with what he finds, at the musical's end he's off to Paris to look for it there with, of all people, Flaemmchen in tow, not after his money but actually having fun. What's uplifting is that all the while Kringelein continues to look for "Life," he is depicted as robustly *living* it, every moment he's still alive. Whether or not audiences recognized in *Grand Hotel* the analogy to the avaricious and decadent early 1990s, they kept checking in 1,077 times.

Rent

*La Boheme* is a love story. So too, in most essentials, is *Rent* (4/29/96), Jonathan Larson's pop-rock musical more than inspired by the Puccini opera. In the main plot of *La Boheme*, Rodolfo, a poet, falls in love with the frail Mimí; she dies of consumption. *Boheme*'s subplot about Musetta and Marcello also is a love story. Although Musetta carries on with her older sugar daddy Alcindoro, she and the painter Marcello end up together. *Rent*, on the other hand, has numerous subplots, only some of which, like *its* main story of Roger and Mimi, are also love stories. Others are not, such as landlord Benny's (Puccini's Benoit) rotten treatment of the homeless, his plan to build a multimedia studio on his East Village property, and his padlocking the artist-residents out of their lofts. Here *Rent* depicts a side of the "Bohemian life" Puccini never gave his audience in *Boheme*—direct or implicit social commentary. And Benny's landlord-tenant escapades (he ultimately relents, by the way) are just the tip of the proverbial iceberg.

Granted, Puccini's Mimí was dying and indeed finally did die of consumption, but the medical issues in *Rent* are deadlier and more widespread. Not just Larson's Mimi but three other characters are HIV-positive, some with full-blown AIDS. And that number doesn't include Roger's former girlfriend, who, Mark tells the audience, "left a note on the mirror telling Roger 'We've got AIDS' and then slit her wrists" (*Best Plays* 95–96 168). Roger and Mimi declare at first sight that they have two things in common—they're in love with each other and they're HIV-positive (she, a drug addict, from bad needle habits; he presumably from his former girlfriend). The others infected (in roles wrenched unrecognizably from their Puccini originals) are Tom Collins (Colline) and the transvestite street drummer Angel Schunard (Schaunard). These two also have an instant attraction and immediately tell one another they are gay and have AIDS. Another same-sex love story (without any lethal disease) spins off of the Marcello-Musetta-Alcindoro triangle, but here it's Mark's ex-girlfriend, Maureen, entering into a stormy on-again-off-again lesbian affair with Joanne, an attorney, rather than Musetta toying with her aging government official.

*Rent's* composer/librettist Jonathan Larson didn't live to see his musical produced or received so enthusiastically; the thirty-five-year-old Larson died suddenly of an aortic aneurysm the day before workshop productions of *Rent* began. Some of the press's initial enthusiasm, however, didn't transfer to Broadway with the musical, even when a single critic saw both productions. It's possible that Larson's untimely death at first masked the shows flaws, or that reviewers of the off-Broadway original simply chose to ignore them. But once the show moved, the critics' assessments were peppered with phrases like "the cop-out ending," "the puzzling muddle of the story," "pretentiousness that is not backed up by culture," and one that frankly helps explain its status as a runaway hit because of Larson's death, "a sentimental triumph" (*NYTCR* 1996, 249–51). Still, whatever one may say about the problems in the plot, characterizations, and, yes, the absurd ending of *Rent*, it is greatly to Larson's credit as a musical playwright that the social, sexual, and medical issues in the show are never mere background. Everything is personal and part of the stories, whether it's a lucrative TV offer challenging Mark's artistic integrity as a video artist, or, most centrally, how best to live with or (in, Angel's story, die with) AIDS or being HIV-positive. Themes and stories are inseparable. And, too, Larson let his characters' stories tell themselves, without comment or judgment. All of this netted Larson a posthumous Pulitzer Prize for drama for 1996 and netted *Rent* 1,705 performances as of the close of the last theatre season wholly in the twentieth century, with the show continuing long past that date.

### Solemnity and Somnolence in Five Late '90s Musicals

Writers from William Finn in the early 1980s through Jonathan Larson in the mid-1990s strove for an objective-seeming, definitely non-editorializing presentation of their socially conscious material; and, more often than not, that approach was successful and effective. Yet in the final years of the twentieth century this dispassionate approach to the subject matter in musicals backfired in a number of shows. In these musicals, dramatizing without judgment or agenda either tied a musical too closely to its historical setting without clearly connecting to the present, or too narrowly confined the theme (if theme there was) to its equally narrow milieu without offering larger social ramifications. Two such shows had some measure of success because of their entertainment value, but the remaining three had disappointingly brief runs despite their well-intentioned social relevance.

Advance press, ads, and "word on the street" make some musicals seem to have "social consciousness" written all over them even before they open. And once they do, the tiny shards of meaningful moments remaining suggest that the writers once *did* have something significant to say but were lured away by the commercial temptations of a conventionally melodramatic story, glitzy production values, and some Fosse-esque choreography — all things that spell success, socially relevant or not. In this case, for *The Life* (4/26/97) they spelled 446 performances. This musical tale of Times Square streetwalkers was largely the brainchild of composer Cy Coleman, with his music, Ira Gasman's lyrics, and a book by the two of them plus David Newman. The three set out to portray "the life" of the hookers and hustlers, pimps and prostitutes that peopled the Times Square area in the early '80s, before Disney started scrubbing up 42nd Street and environs; that *The Life* in an earlier life may have been socially relevant was picked up by Ben Brantley of the *New York Times* when he observed that "Mr. Coleman and his associates seem to have hoped to create something with the brusque social impact of 'West Side Story,' 'Rent,' or even 'The Threepenny Opera.' (It evokes elements from all three)" (Brantley, "Lively"). If in fact that was their aim, they failed. A bloody face-pounding here, a veiled AIDS reference there, the cliché brutality of bad-guy pimps toward their really-good-girl-at-heart hookers — these do not social relevance make. About all that was left was a song-and-dancical about "ho"s, johns, and mean dudes in bad hats. But is that the stuff of upbeat, diversionary entertainment? Or, as Clive Barnes pointedly asked, "Is anyone, by the way, nostalgic for 42nd St. when it was a human sewer?" (qtd. in *Theatre World* 96–97 43).

Similarly, one would think that the musicalization of E. L. Doctorow's *Ragtime* (1/18/98) would offer analogies and parallels to matters of contemporary relevance, since it is set in Teddy Roosevelt's America and peopled on its periphery with such historical figures as Booker T. Washington, Harry Houdini, Emma Goldman, and J. P. Morgan. In fact, however, *Ragtime* never breaks out of its historical time and place. Supported by Stephen Flaherty's music and Lynn Ahrens's lyrics, Terence McNally trimmed down Doctorow's epic novel into something manageable for the musical stage, but the scope and convolutions of the musical still make *War and Peace* look like *Dick and Jane*. In the last analysis, what *Ragtime* became was an historical novel turned into an historical musical of epic proportions, perhaps enlightening as to the way things *were* just after the turn of the century but in no way elucidating or remarking on the way things *are* in the late twentieth century. An historian friend of mine accurately characterized *Ragtime* as a conventional musical melodrama in which an Irishman is the villain, a Jew is the hero, and a black man gets crucified. What little social muckraking the show does contain—as in the Emma Goldman sequence and when Coalhouse Walker turns militant terrorist—remains firmly rooted in the story's historical period. But the black man's vendetta is not for a social cause, it is purely personal; he wants to avenge his wife Sarah's death and get his car back. At the end the Jewish Tateh marries the WASP Mother and the two adopt the orphaned black child of Sarah and Coalhouse. For 861 performances, any social relevance in *Ragtime* was limited by the confining treatment of its historical setting.

*The Capeman* (1/29/98) also seemed to have the ingredients for socially significant musical theatre: music by Paul Simon, book and lyrics by Simon and Derek Walcott, the setting a Puerto Rican enclave in New York, and a story based on an actual street-gang murder in 1959. In some respects the story was deterministic, indicting society for allowing the conditions of poverty to create the environmental deprivation that bred a young killer like the Capeman. The subject and its implications were clearly contemporary, but Simon and Walcott never found the means to turn what was essentially a sociological essay into a musical theatre entertainment. According to the reviews and knowledgable theatregoers, for all his pop artistry Simon had no feel for writing theatre music, and Walcott's kind of dramatic writing did not suit a Broadway musical. Even with numerous rewrites, personnel changes, and previews, *The Capeman* closed after sixty-eight performances.

*Parade* (12/17/98)—set in pre–World War I Georgia—told a moving, anger-provoking story. Yet the show seemed to exist more to educate audiences about early twentieth-century ethnic and religious intolerance than (like *Cabaret*) to parallel or shed new light on current persecutions of marginalized minorities. Co-conceived and directed by Harold Prince, *Parade* was written by Georgia-born Jewish playwright Alfred (*Driving Miss Daisy*) Uhry, with music and lyrics by Jason Robert Brown. *Parade* musicalized the Leo Frank case, a grim bit of Georgia history in which a Jewish man from the North, married to a Southern Jewish woman, is accused of murdering a thirteen-year-old girl in the factory he manages in Atlanta. Frank—forced to accept perfunctory, biased legal counsel—is convicted and sentenced to death, but the governor, on reviewing the trumped up evidence, commutes the sentence to life imprisonment. This decision further incenses the community's anti-Jewish feelings, and a lynch mob drags Frank from jail and hangs him.

*Parade* makes a great display of anti-Semitic sentiments and actions throughout the pretrial period, the trial, and the appeal. Nathan Rosenblatt, the Jewish attorney Frank engages for his defense, sends instead an incompetent redneck lawyer on the grounds that "A Jew shouldn't defend another Jew." Rosenblatt clearly wants to save his own neck in every way (*Best Plays 98–99* 134). Leo sums himself up as a victim of multiple prejudices: "I'm a Yankee, and I'm college educated, and I have an extensive vocabulary. Oh, and I'm a Jew of course! And you know what us Jews are, don't you? Smart!" (142). It's hard to argue with *Parade*'s powerful depiction of deep-seated bigotry, but it's equally unclear how its treatment of the issue resonates with any specific contemporary relevance beyond the general and obvious irrationality of prejudice and its often horrific consequences. The critics liked the show more than the public; *Parade* came to a halt after eighty-five performances.

Whatever *Parade* had to say about prejudice and bigotry, Alfred Uhry, skillful playwright that he is, was always careful to dramatize, not sermonize. The same cannot be said for John LaChiusa's words and music for *Marie Christine* (12/2/99), the last of the twentieth-century's socially relevant musicals. According to Ben Brantley of the *New York Times*, the stunning vocal and dramatic performance of Audra McDonald swamped the interesting and at times even powerful material of the musical itself. Theatre folk during and after its short forty-four-performance run humorously but accurately labeled *Marie Christine* "Medea on the bayou." Marie Christine is a mixed-race Louisiana Creole woman in the late nineteenth century who has inherited her mother's capacity for casting spells. Like Medea, she is wooed, married, and betrayed by a man (here a sea captain), triggering a string of grisly murders. Brantley saw in this "solemn, sometimes somnolent musical tragedy" a frequently "baldly didactic quality to the show's book and lyrics, as it considers the socially oppressive climate of its time" (Brantley, "Promises"). Brantley's "of its time" explicitly indicates that the social commentary stayed within the time period of the musical rather than expanding to suggest some contemporary meanings or associations. The potential for that was certainly there, since the status and treatment of racially mixed individuals and couples in the United States has never been completely or happily resolved.

## The Tone of Social Relevance

The last few attempts at socially relevant musicals near the end of the twentieth century were all very earnest, or, in Ben Brantley's word, "solemn." Frank Rich observed that Stephen Sondheim was also "discouraged that recent musicals confuse his and Hammerstein's idea of the 'serious' musical with mere solemnity: 'They're so eager to make what they write important that they start with themes instead of stories and characters'" (Rich 88). While that's not precisely true of Alfred Uhry's *Parade*, like the rest it is relentlessly solemn in its approach. What is missing from shows like *The Capeman*, *Parade*, and *Marie Christine* is the theatrical art's fundamental component of playfulness, going back to antiquity. No matter how "serious" a work may be, there has almost always been an element of playfulness in music theatre pieces. This playfulness need not be equated with humor or comedy. In *Homo Ludens*, his monumental study of the concept of "play" in Western culture, Johan Huizinga aligns the activity of "play" with the feeling of "fun." He argues convincingly that "fun" virtually defies any definition except by the very word itself. Huizinga further notes that a fundamental requirement of "fun" is that both participants and spectators must be having it, even in events that are in no way "funny," such as a football game or any other sporting event (2–3). Such activities arouse that indefinable feeling of fun in both the doers and viewers, as has musical theatre ever since the ancient Athenians mostly sang (and even danced) their tragedies.

It is precisely this sort of fun or playfulness that was nearly or wholly absent from a number of late-twentieth-century musicals, whereas earlier (and in a few isolated cases quite recently), such playfulness abounded, no matter how serious the show's ideas. *West Side Story* is playful, and not just during "America," "I Feel Pretty," and "Officer Krupke." Playfulness informs the way the Jets and Sharks interact with their fellow gang members, and, frequently, the way they back-talk to the adults as well. Yet the overall seriousness of *West Side Story* is undeniable. *Sweeney Todd* is playful in its characterizations of Mrs. Lovett and even Todd himself through most of the show, not just during "A Little Priest." The playful approach to depicting serious social statements in both versions of *Cabaret* goes without saying. For all its relentlessly serious subject matter, the entirety of *Assassins* is fun, imbued with a playfulness in Weidman's theatrical approach to the material and Sondheim's wry composition of pastiche numbers for most of the score. And, perhaps at the most extreme, William Finn, composer/lyricist of the *Falsettos* musicals, wrote *A New Brain* (6/18/98) with a pervasive playfulness, despite the show fancifully recreating Finn's own bout with what was thought to be a life-threatening brain tumor. If fun can pervade that kind of intimately personal subject matter, it can enter into anything. Indeed, until the 1990s, when some younger writers' quest for significance led them into unsmiling earnestness, it is hard to find any American musical where the theatre's perennial staple of playfulness does not creep in, if only occasionally (*Street Scene*, *Lost in the Stars*, and Sondheim's own uncompromisingly serious *Passion* included). And if writers of late-century musical solemnity had only looked back to *Finian's Rainbow*, they would have seen a musical with the most serious of intentions—a satiric attack on racial bias—promoting its message entirely through fantasy, romance, and fun.

That such solemn musicals ended the twentieth century on a gloomy note is, depending on one's point of view, either a truism or an understatement. That Broadway continued to dish up revivals unabated—some, like *The Music Man*, very successfully—suggests that the American public was still caught in the grip of nostalgia and/or yearning for Sondheim's "recycled culture." But on the upside, the fact that no blockbuster technomusicals have opened since *The Lion King* in 1997 suggests that perhaps Broadway has gotten out of its theme-park mentality in favor of again presenting musicals with content, not just spectacle.

To some extent, *The Full Monty* and *The Producers* prove this point. While social relevance isn't key to either show (but not entirely absent, either), neither one relies on stage mechanics and electronics for its "fun." Instead, both musicals fall back on the content and writing of their scripts and songs, the staging thereof, and the performers, just the way musicals used to do. One wants to interpret the appearance and success of these two shows as a harbinger of more rich diversionary entertainment to come, of the sort we look for in musical theatre. On the other hand, *The Producers* and *The Full Monty* both represent a kind of show that Sondheim lamented—"a stage version of a musical"—even though the film originals of these shows were not movie musicals. One reason such shows have become so popular is that audiences have become attuned to "seeing what is familiar" rather than engaging in the challenges of a truly innovative theatrical event.

And what of socially relevant, issue-driven, and often provocative—as well as entertaining—musicals? Did the solemnity of shows like *Parade* and *Marie Christine* drive such musicals out of the theatre entirely? It certainly seemed so, until on September 20, 2001, when—following an overture whose opening shamelessly spoofs Kurt Weill's for *The Threepenny Opera*—our friendly neighborhood narrator first greeted a Broadway audience with, "Well, hello there and welcome to *Urinetown*. Not the place, of course.

The musical." And thereby hangs a very good clue to both the content and method of this outrageous musical satire. The product of Mark Hollmann's music, Greg Kotis's book, and lyrics by the two of them, *Urinetown* appropriately first burst upon an unsuspecting world in the New York Fringe Festival and went on to a successful off-Broadway run before moving to Broadway. Since then, *Urinetown* has proved two things: |that a socially conscious musical need not be solemn but can be preposterously, even absurdly hilarious; and that this kind of *playful, entertaining* socially meaningful musical can be a hit. |

*Urinetown* is satire and parody at once. The show satirically raises serious questions about individual freedoms vs. monopolistic or totalitarian control, while it parodies socially relevant musicals, and, more generally, musical theatre styles of writing, performance, and choreography. The result is a wildly funny show punctuated by some pointed, provocative, and even scary "moments of truth." Odd as it may seem, the combination works—the humor providing a context for the seriousness, the seriousness puncturing the hilarity to dramatically thrust home its points.

In its plot and premise, *Urinetown* is a darkly comic, surrealistic, and even parodic descendent of *The Cradle Will Rock*. A city is in the grip of a devastating drought. It is also in the grip of Mr. Caldwell B. Cladwell, the nattily dressed but ruthless c.e.o. of UGC (Urine Good Company). Cladwell not only owns everyone who is anyone in town, from the police to a senator, he owns all the pay toilets and urinals as well. People unwilling to use these official and costly conveniences and caught relieving themselves elsewhere pay a high price. They are taken off to "Urinetown," which, as it turns out, is not a place but a code word for the police to surreptitiously hurl the prisoner from a high building to his death.

In this respect alone, the musical is a brilliant satire on efforts to curtail individual freedoms. A young man named Bobby Strong leads a people's revolt against the monopolistic, totalitarian ways of Cladwell and the UGC, and Bobby also falls in love with Cladwell's dewy-eyed, idealistic daughter, Hope—and she with Bobby. After Bobby meets a bad end in "Urinetown," Hope successfully carries on the revolution against her own father, until the common people of the town win the good fight. But then, in the chillingly ironic ending, we learn that the populace has no clue shout how to conserve and manage the water supply during the drought, so that things go to wrack and ruin once again. That situation prompts this exchange of dialogue between the wise-beyond-her years street urchin Little Sally and the crooked cop but friendly narrator Officer Lockstock:

LITTLE SALLY:     I don't think too many people are going
                  to come and see this musical.

| | |
|---|---|
| LOCKSTOCK: | Why do you say that, Little Sally? Don't you think people want to be told that their way of life is unsustainable? |

(J.B.J. notes from seeing the show)

If all this seems unrepentantly grim, trust me, it is not. Except for a chilling moment here and there, it is riveting, highly theatrical, and wildly comic throughout. Perhaps even its seeming grimness is another way the show is spoofing those too-solemn musicals that were its immediate predecessors.

In other ways, *Urinetown* parodies the entire tradition of Broadway (and off-Broadway) musicals of just about every variety. Bobby Strong and Cladwell are blood brothers to *Cradle's* Larry Foreman and Mr. Mister, and, in John Cullum's Cladwell, a good bit of *Damn Yankees'* devilish Mr. Applegate is thrown in. Little Sally is a composite of every streetwise (or wise-ass) street girl from *West Side Story's* Anybodys through Annie to Eponine from *Les Miz*. And speaking of *Annie*, Penelope Pennywise, the mistress of the urinals (and, we later learn, Cladwell's former mistress too) sounds and behaves like Miss Hannigan reincarnated. More broadly, these comically generic, almost allegorical, names are in the tradition of musical theatre satire from the early *Of Thee I Sing* and *The Cradle Will Rock* to the later *How To Succeed in Business without Really Trying*.

In the midst of this happy nonsense, *Urinetown* zings its powerful sociopolitical points right at the audience. Cladwell, for example, tells Hope that he did not send her to "the most expensive university in the *world*" to become a soft-hearted do-gooder but to learn "how to manipulate great masses of people" and to control people "wherever people learn to live in fear." In a word, at the same time *Urinetown* is a send-up of the *methods* of musicals with a social conscience, its own messages are very serious indeed.

But for all the import of its ideas, the happy nonsense abounds and undoubtedly caused the great success of the show. Almost no corner of the Broadway musical tradition is left unremarked, and hilariously so. If bits of the overture and other songs owe their existence to Kurt Weill, other composers do not escape unscathed. Several big brassy production numbers could have been penned by Cy Coleman or Jule Styne, and Hope and Bobby's sweetly innocent love duet "Follow Your Heart" sounds like an escapee from *The Fantasticks*, right down to its charming piano accompaniment. Broadway dance takes a couple of whacks as well, in two screamingly funny (because very recognizable) parodies of Jerome Robbins and Bob Fosse's styles of choreography.

Above all, *Urinetown* never lets the audience forget they are watching a musical, from Officer Lockstock's opening greeting noted above to his reply when Little Sally asks if Hope is going to fall in love with Bobby: "He's the hero of the show, she has to love him." Never are we led to believe this is reality; it is always a musical, no matter how many ideas it might contain. Which, I think, is ultimately what makes *Urinetown* work so well and accomplish its goals so brilliantly. The show, like, let us say, *Finian's Rainbow* before it, never loses sight of "fun" and "playfulness," those two magical mediums through which audiences can absorb even the most serious of messages.

I would like to think those too-solemn musicals were just a passing symptom of their time. One can understand them as a logical extension of the introspectiveness of the American people in the 1970s, followed by their nostalgic longings in the '80s and '90s; such inward-turning and backward-turning are solemn and serious almost by definition. Add to this that it seems no accident that the cluster of solemn musicals came right at the end of the century. Among serious and thoughtful creative people, the ends of centuries have often provoked a lot of serious and thoughtful thinking and the production of works of literature, art, or in our case, musical theatre of especially unsmiling seriousness.

But now the old century has "turned" into the new, such turnings always suggesting new beginnings. Which is why, following the return of almost purely diversionary comic musicals with *The Producers* and *The Full Monty*, I would like to believe that *Urinetown* is heralding a return to those kinds of shows from past decades in which "serious musical" and "entertaining musical" were not contradictions in terms.

# APPENDIXES

# Broadway Musical Production, 1919–1929

The figures below are compiled primarily from Bordman (either calculations appearing in his text, or my own counting of the shows he mentions, figures that do not always coincide; his figures are sometimes approximations, and they include revues, foreign imports, and what few revivals there were). Still, exact numbers are not as important as these approximations, which reveal the enormous number of shows mounted on Broadway each season in the 1920s. The shows listed in the third column, along with the names of their composers (and occasionally lyricists as well), are those that were not only long-running hits in their day but still have real interest or significance in the history of the American musical. Other shows not named here, primarily the annual editions of the spectacular revues, were also substantial money-makers in the 1920s.

| Season | Number of shows | Hit musicals |
| --- | --- | --- |
| 1919–1920 | 41 | *Apple Blossoms* (Fritz Kreisler)<br>*Irene* (Harry Tierney) |
| 1920–1921 | 44 | *Sally* (Kern)<br>*Shuffle Along* (Eubie Blake) |
| 1921–1922 | 35 | *Blossom Time* (Franz Schubert/Romberg) |
| 1922–1923 | 41 | *Little Nellie Kelly* (Cohan) |
| 1923–1924 | 40 | |
| 1924–1925 | 42 | *Rose-Marie* (Friml)<br>*Lady, Be Good!* (Gershwin)<br>*The Student Prince* (Romberg)<br>*The Garrick Gaieties* (Rodgers and Hart) |
| 1925–1926 | 42 | *No, No, Nanette* (Youmans)<br>*Dearest Enemy* (Rodgers and Hart)<br>*The Vagabond King* (Friml)<br>*Sunny* (Kern)<br>*The Cocoanuts* (Berlin)<br>*Tip-Toes* (Gershwin)<br>*The Girl Friend* (Rodgers and Hart) |
| 1926–1927 | 49 | *Oh, Kay!* (Gershwin)<br>*The Desert Song* (Romberg)<br>*Hit The Deck!* (Youmans) |

| | | |
|---|---|---|
| 1927–1928 | 51 or 53* | *Good News* (DeSylva, Brown and Henderson)<br>*My Maryland* (Romberg)<br>*A Connecticut Yankee* (Rodgers and Hart)<br>*Funny Face* (Gershwin)<br>*Show Boat* (Hammerstein and Kern)<br>*Rosalie* (Gershwin/Romberg)<br>*The Three Musketeers* (Friml)<br>*Present Arms* (Rodgers and Hart)<br>*Blackbirds Of 1928* (Jimmy McHugh) |
| 1928–29 | 42 | *The New Moon* (Romberg)<br>*Hold Everything* (DeSylva, Brown and Henderson)<br>*Whoopee* (Walter Donaldson)<br>*The Little Show* (Schwartz and Dietz) |
| 1929–30 | 34 | *Hot Chocolates* (Fats Waller)<br>*Sweet Adeline* (Hammerstein and Kern)<br>*Bitter Sweet* (Noel Coward)<br>*Fifty Million Frenchmen* (Porter)<br>*Strike Up The Band* (Gershwin)<br>*Flying High* (DeSylva, Brown and Henderson) |

* 51 according to Burns Mantle, 53 according to *Variety*.

# Long-Running Diversionary Musicals, 1929–1938

The following chronology lists those Depression-era diversionary musicals and revues with two hundred or more performances; each entry includes the opening
date, book musicals' composers and subject matter, revues' principal song writers,
and the length of the Broadway run. Here and throughout, general information is
from Bordman, with length-of-run figures from the *Best Plays* annuals. (Some of
the socially conscious musicals and revues also had impressively long runs, which
are taken up in chapter 3, where these show are treated individually.)

*Fifty Million Frenchmen* (11/27/29): Cole Porter score; wealthy Americans in Paris.
254 performances.
*Fine and Dandy* (9/23/30): Kay Swift score; slapstick vehicle for comic Joe Cook.
255 performances.
*Girl Crazy* (10/14/30): George Gershwin score; wealthy New Yorkers at dude ranch.
272 performances.
*Three's a Crowd* (10/15/30): Schwartz and Dietz revue. 272 performances.
*The Band Wagon* (6/3/31): Schwartz and Dietz revue. 260 performances.
*Earl Carroll Vanities of 1931* (8/27/31): Last successful edition of the revue. 278
performances.
*George White's Scandals of 1931* (9/14/31): Brown and Henderson (minus DeSylva)
revue. 202 performances.
*The Cat and the Fiddle* (10/15/31): Kern/Hammerstein score; sophisticated love story.
395 performances.
*Music in the Air* (11/8/32): Kern/Hammerstein virtual operetta set in Bavaria. 342
performances.
*Take a Chance* (11/26/32): Nacio Herb Brown score, Youmans interpolations; show
biz show. 243 performances.
*Gay Divorce* (11/29/32): Cole Porter score; sophisticated "French bedroom farce."
248 performances.
*Murder at the Vanities* (9/8/33): Earl Carroll revue with a plot. 207 performances.
*Roberta* (11/18/33): Jerome Kern/Otto Harbach score. Americans and high fashion
in Paris. 295 performances.
*Life Begins at 8:40* (8/27/34): Harold Arlen, E. Y. Harburg, Ira Gershwin revue. 237
performances.
*The Great Waltz* (9/22/34): Operetta using music of Johann Strauss Sr. and Jr. 298
performances.
*Anything Goes* (11/21/34): Cole Porter score. Shady Americans, classy Brits on a boat.
420 performances.
*Sketch Book* (6/4/35): The last of Earl Carroll's "other" revues. 207 performances.

*Jumbo* (11/16/35): Rodgers and Hart score; Billy Rose–produced circus spectacular. 233 performances.

*May Wine* (12/5/35): Romberg/Hammerstein operetta. 213 performances.

*On Your Toes* (4/11/36): Rodgers and Hart score for George Abbott dance musical. 315 performances.

*The White Horse Inn* (10/1/36): Adaptation of a German operetta (hard to believe!). 223 performances.

*Babes in Arms* (4/14/37): Rodgers and Hart's kiddy summer camp/show biz show. 289 performances.

*I Married an Angel* (5/11/38): Rodgers and Hart score for sophisticated fantasy. 338 performances.

*Hellzapoppin* (9/22/38): Revue for comics Olsen and Johnson; "puerile escapism." 1,404 performances.

*The Boys from Syracuse* (11/23/38) Rodgers and Hart's *The Comedy of Errors*. 235 performances.

# Long-Running Diversionary Musicals, 1939–1945

The following list of only hit book shows demonstrates that long runs were indeed getting longer, with shows passing the three hundred- and even five hundred-performance mark becoming more and more common. I have also included some shows with runs under three hundred performances only because of the particular importance of their writers or performers.

*Too Many Girls* (10/18/39). Rodgers and Hart college football musical. 249 performances.

*DuBarry Was a Lady* (12/6/39). Cole Porter score. Ethel Merman/Bert Lahr romp. 408 performances.

*Louisiana Purchase* (5/28/40). Irving Berlin score, Morrie Ryskind book. Vaguely (but not very) satiric look at Louisiana politics, but mostly just comic fun. 444 performances.

*Hold On to Your Hats* (9/11/40). Burton Lane, E. Y. Harburg score. Al Jolson as a radio cowboy. 158 performances.

*Panama Hattie* (10/30/40). Cole Porter score, Herbert Fields book. Ethel Merman as a Canal Zone barmaid who falls for a Main Line Philadelphia gent. 501 performances.

*Best Foot Forward* (10/1/41). Hugh Martin and Ralph Lane (far better known for the score for the film *Meet Me in St. Louis*). College prom show whose hit song, "Buckle Down Winsocki," "had a second vogue with revised lyrics, as 'Buckle Down Buck Private' " (Bordman 525). 326 performances.

*Let's Face It* (10/29/41). Cole Porter score, Herbert and Dorothy Fields book. Vaguely contemporary farce starring Danny Kaye, in that three wives latch on to three soldiers, convinced their husbands are cheating on them, while the husbands have improbably latched on to the same soldiers' girls. 547 performances.

*By Jupiter* (6/3/42). Rodgers and Hart's last collaboration, a sophisticated Greek myth affair (in every sense), starring Ray Bolger. 427 performances.

*Something for the Boys* (1/7/43). Cole Porter score, Herbert and Dorothy Fields book. Three cousins inherit a ranch in Texas. 422 performances.

*One Touch of Venus* (10/7/43). Kurt Weill score, S. J. Perelman and Ogden Nash book, Nash lyrics. Literate, romantic, Pygmalion-like fantasy. 567 performances.

*Mexican Hayride* (1/28/44). Cole Porter score, Herbert and Dorothy Fields book. A silly romp in Mexico for Bobby Clark and June Havoc. 481 performances.

*Song of Norway* (8/21/44). Robert Wright and George Forrest's book and lyrics set to Edvard Grieg's music to spin a romanticized biography of the Norwegian composer. 860 performances.

*On the Town* (12/28/44). Music by Leonard Bernstein, book and lyrics by Betty Comden and Adolph Green, choreography by Jerome Robbins. Remotely relevant to the war years only in that its story is of three sailors on twenty-four-hour shore leave in New York City. 463 performances.

*Up in Central Park* (1/27/45). Score by Sigmund Romberg, book by Herbert and Dorothy Fields, lyrics by Dorothy Fields. Nostalgic operetta of New York City's earlier days. 504 performances.

# Long-Running Diversionary Musicals, 1946–1960

Here a long-running show is again one that achieved, minimally, close to three hundred performances, although in the postwar and cold war years many such musicals, popular enough to sustain a run of nearly a year, were not commercial successes, failing to make back their investments or barely break even.

*Call Me Mister* (4/18/46). Harold Rome score included "South America, Take It Away." 734 performances.

*Annie Get Your Gun* (5/16/46). Irving Berlin score, Herbert and Dorothy Fields book. 1,147 performances.

*High Button Shoes* (10/9/47). Jule Styne music, Sammy Cahn lyrics. 727 performances.

*Where's Charley* (10/11/48). George Abbott book, Frank Loesser words and music. 792 performances.

*As the Girls Go* (11/13/48). Jimmy McHugh/Harold Adamson words and music. 420 performances.

*Kiss Me, Kate* (12/30/48). Cole Porter score, Samuel and Bella Spewack book. 1,070 performances.

*Miss Liberty* (7/15/49). Irving Berlin score, Robert Sherwood and Moss Hart book. 308 performances.

*Gentlemen Prefer Blondes* (12/8/49). Joseph Fields and Anita Loos book, Leo Robin lyrics, Jule Styne music. 740 performances.

*Call Me Madam* (10/12/50). Irving Berlin score, Howard Lindsay and Russel Crouse book. 644 performances.

*Guys and Dolls* (11/24/50). Frank Loesser score, Jo Swerling and Abe Burrows book. 2,000 performances.

*A Tree Grows in Brooklyn* (4/19/51). George Abbott and Betty Smith book, from her novel, Dorothy Fields lyrics, Arthur Schwartz music. 270 performances.

*Top Banana* (11/1/51). Hy Craft book, Johnny Mercer songs. 350 performances.

*Pal Joey*, revival (1/3/52). Vivienne Segal repeating the role she originated, Harold Lang as Joey. Ran longer than its original run. 540 performances.

*Wish You Were Here* (6/25/52). Joshua Logan and Arthur Kober's adaptation of Kober's *Having Wonderful Time*. Words and music by Harold Rome. 598 performances.

*Wonderful Town* (2/25/53). Joseph Fields and Jerome Chodorov's adaptation of their own play *My Sister Eileen*, music by Leonard Bernstein, lyrics by Betty Comden and Adolph Green. 559 performances.

*Can-Can* (5/7/53). Cole Porter score, Abe Burrows book. 892 performances.

*Kismet* (12/3/53). Robert Wright and George Forrest book and lyrics adapted from the play by Edward Knoblock, score adapted by them from the music of Alexsandr Borodin. 583 performances.

*By the Beautiful Sea* (4/8/54). Herbert and Dorothy Fields book, Dorothy Fields lyrics, Arthur Schwartz music. 270 performances.

*The Pajama Game* (5/13/54). George Abbott and Richard Bissell's adaptation of Bissell's novel *7 1/2 Cents*. Music and lyrics by Richard Adler and Jerry Ross. And, no, it is not a serious, satirical, or in any other way socially relevant treatment of union and management problems; it is all entirely too silly and good-natured, especially in its plot resolution, to be considered so. The proof of this lies in producer Hal Prince's story of director George Abbott being persuaded by co-director Jerome Robbins to try moving the strike-demands song "7 1/2 Cents" from the end of the musical, where it "had been affectionately humorous," to the beginning of the show for one of the New York previews. But, as it turned out, the song "was serious business in front. It scared the hell out of Abbott, and he refused to try it for a second performance" (Prince 136). Despite Robbins as co-director, *The Pajama Game* is historic as the first Broadway musical choreographed by Bob Fosse. 1,063 performances.

*The Boy Friend* (9/30/54). Sandy Wilson book, music, and lyrics, parodying by almost exact replication the musicals of the 1920s. Julie Andrews's Broadway debut. 485 performances.

*Fanny* (11/4/54). S. N. Behrman and Joshua Logan book, Harold Rome score. 888 performances.

*Plain and Fancy* (1/27/55). Joseph Stein and William Glickman book, Albert Hague and Arnold B. Horwitt music and lyrics. 461 performances.

*Damn Yankees* (5/5/55). George Abbott and Douglass Wallop adaptation of Wallop's *The Year the Yankees Lost the Pennant*. Richard Adler and Jerry Ross score, their second and last smash hit together; Ross, only twenty-nine, died of a lung problem on November 11, 1955. 1,019 performances.

*My Fair Lady* (3/15/56). Alan Jay Lerner book and lyrics, Frederick Loewe music. 2,217 performances.

*Mr. Wonderful* (3/22/56). Joseph Stein and Will Glickman book, Larry Holofcener and George Weiss lyrics, Jerry Bock music. 383 performances.

*The Most Happy Fella* (5/3/56). Frank Loesser libretto, lyrics, and music, adapted from Sidney Howard's 1924 play *They Knew What They Wanted*. 676 performances.

*Bells Are Ringing* (11/29/56). Betty Comden and Adolph Green book and lyrics, Jule Styne music. 924 performances.

*Happy Hunting* (12/6/56). Howard Lindsay and Russel Crouse book, Matt Dubey and Harold Karr score. 412 performances.

*New Girl in Town* (5/14/57). George Abbott adaptation of Eugene O'Neill's *Anna Christie*. Music and lyrics by Bob Merrill. 431 performances.

*Jamaica* (10/31/57). Fred Saidy and E. Y. Harburg book and lyrics, Harold Arlen music. 555 performances.

*The Music Man* (12/19/57). Meredith Willson book, lyrics, and music. 1,375 performances.

*Say, Darling* (4/3/58). Abe Burrows, Marian Bissell, and Richard Bissell's adaptation of Richard Bissell's novel of the same name that fictionally recounted turning his own novel *7 1/2 Cents* into his own (with collaborators) musical *The Pajama Game*. Got that? Betty Comden and Adolph Green lyrics, Jule Styne score. 332 performances.

*Redhead* (2/5/59). Herbert and Dorothy Fields book, with Sidney Sheldon and David Shaw, Dorothy Fields lyrics, Albert Hague score. 452 performances.

*Destry Rides Again* (4/23/59). Music and lyrics by Harold Rome, book by Leonard Gershe. 473 performances.

*Gypsy* (5/12/59). Book by Arthur Laurents, music by Jule Styne, lyrics by Stephen Sondheim. 702 performances.

*Take Me Along* (10/22/59). Joseph Stein and Robert Russell adaptation of Eugene O'Neill's *Ah, Wilderness!* Music and lyrics by Bob Merrill. 448 performances.

*Little Mary Sunshine* (11/18/59). Rick Besoyan book, music, and lyrics, all parodying the types of operettas popular earlier in the century. 1,143 performances.

*Bye, Bye, Birdie* (4/16/60). Michael Stewart book, Charles Strouse music, Lee Adams lyrics. 607 performances.

# Long-Running Diversionary Musicals, 1960–1969

With shows having to run longer to make back their investments, and increasingly longer runs becoming the criteria of critics and the editors of *Variety* for a show to be considered a hit, a long-running show is now defined as one that achieved, minimally, something at least approaching five hundred performances. Yet, as in the previous decade, while popular enough to be considered hits for sustaining runs of well over a year, many of these shows were not commercial successes.

*The Unsinkable Molly Brown* (11/3/60). Meredith Willson music and lyrics, Richard Morris book. 532 performances.

*Carnival* (4/13/61). Bob Merrill music and lyrics, Michael Stewart book. 719 performances.

*A Funny Thing Happened on the Way to the Forum* (5/8/62). Stephen Sondheim music and lyrics, Burt Shevelove and Larry Gelbart book. 964 performances.

*Hello, Dolly!* (1/16/64). Jerry Herman music and lyrics, Michael Stewart book adapted from Thornton Wilder's *The Matchmaker*. 2,844 performances.

*What Makes Sammy Run?* (2/27/64). Ervin Drake music and lyrics, Budd and Stuart Schulberg book adapted from Budd Schulberg's novel of the same name. 515 performances.

*Funny Girl* (3/26/64). Jule Styne score, Bob Merrill lyrics, Isobel Lennart book. 1,348 performances.

*Sweet Charity* (1/29/66). Cy Coleman music, Dorothy Fields lyrics, Neil Simon book. 556 performances.

*Mame* (5/24/66). Music and lyrics by Jerry Herman, Jerome Lawrence and Robert E. Lee book adapted from their own play *Auntie Mame* in turn adapted from Patrick Dennis's book. 1,508 performances.

*The Apple Tree* (10/18/66). Sheldon Harnick lyrics, Jerry Bock music, Harnick and Bock book with additional material by Jerome Coopersmith, adapted from stories by Mark Twain, Frank Stockton, and Jules Pfeiffer. 463 performances.

*I Do! I Do!* (12/5/66). Tom Jones book and lyrics based on Jan de Hartog's *The Fourposter*, Harvey Schmidt music. 560 performances.

*You're a Good Man, Charlie Brown* (3/7/67). Clark Gesner book, lyrics, and music. 1,597 performances.

*Curley McDimple* (11/22/67). Robert Dahdah music and lyrics, Mary Boylan and Dahdah book. 931 performances.

*Your Own Thing* (1/13/68). Hal Hester and Danny Apolinar music and lyrics, Don Driver book. Musical updating of Shakespeare's *Twelfth Night*. 933 performances.

*Jacques Brel Is Alive and Well and Living in Paris* (1/22/68). English lyrics and

additional material by Eric Blau and Mort Shuman. 1,847 performances off-
Broadway; fifty-one more in limited Broadway run.

*Promises, Promises* (12/1/68). Burt Bacharach music, Hal David lyrics, Neil Simon
book. 1,281 performances.

*Dames at Sea* (12/20/68). Jim Wise music, George Haimsohn and Robin Miller
book and lyrics. 575 performances.

# Long-Running Diversionary Musicals, 1969–1979

For the criteria for including musicals in this list, see headnote to Appendix E.

*Applause* (3/30/70). Betty Comden and Adolph Green book, Charles Strouse music, Lee Adams lyrics. 896 performances.

*Grease* (2/14/72). Jim Jacobs and Warren Casey book, music, and lyrics. 3,388 performances.

*Sugar* (4/9/72). Peter Stone book, Jule Styne music, Bob Merrill lyrics. 505 performances.

*A Little Night Music* (2/25/73). Stephen Sondheim music and lyrics, Hugh Wheeler book. 600 performances.

*Candide* (3/8/74). Music by Leonard Bernstein, revised book by Hugh Wheeler, lyrics by Richard Wilbur and John Latouche, new lyrics by Stephen Sondheim. 740 performances.

*The Magic Show* (5/28/74). Stephen Schwartz music and lyrics, Bob Randall book. 1,920 performances.

*The Wiz* (1/5/75). Charlie Smalls music and lyrics, William F. Brown book. 1,672 performances.

*Shenandoah* (1/7/75). James Lee Barrett, Peter Udell, and Philip Rose book, Udell lyrics, Gary Geld music. 1,050 performances.

*Chicago* (6/3/75). Adaptation of Dallas Watkins's 1926 play of the same name by Bob Fosse and Fred Ebb. Ebb lyrics, John Kander music. 898 performances.

*On the Twentieth Century* (2/19/78). Betty Comden and Adolph Green book and lyrics, Cy Coleman music. Robin Wagner sets, of which *Variety* wrote, "It's ominous when an audience leaves a musical whistling the scenery." 453 performances.

*Dancin'* (3/27/78). A dance revue conceived and choreographed by Bob Fosse. 1,774 performances.

*Ain't Misbehavin'* (5/9/78). Revue of songs by and made famous by Fats Waller, conceived and directed by Richard Maltby Jr. 1,604 performaces.

*The Best Little Whorehouse in Texas* (6/19/78). Carol Hall music and lyrics, Larry L. King and Peter Masterson book. 1,639 performances.

*They're Playing Our Song* (2/11/79). Neil Simon book, Marvin Hamlisch music, Carole Bayer Sager lyrics. 1,082 performances.

# Long-Running Diversionary Musicals, 1979–2000

For the criteria for including musicals in this list, see headnote to Appendix E. For most musicals still running as of the end of the 1999–2000 theatre season, the last theatre season fully in the twentieth century, the number of performances is shown as of May 28, 2000, *Variety*'s "official" closing date for that season.

*Scrambled Feet* (6/11/79). Revue, mostly on show biz themes, by John Driver and Jeffrey Haddow, played by four performers and a duck. Off-Broadway, at the Village Gate Upstairs. 831 performances.

*Sugar Babies* (10/8/79). Salute to Minsky's burlesque conceived by Ralph G. Allen and Harry Rigby; sketches by Ralph G. Allen based on traditional material. With Mickey Rooney and Ann Miller. 1,208 performances.

*Barnum* (4/30/80). Mark Bramble book, Cy Coleman score, Michael Stewart lyrics. 854 performances.

*A Day in Hollywood, A Night in the Ukraine* (5/1/80). Dick Vosburgh book, music by Frank Lazarus and others, lyrics by Vosburg and others. 588 performances.

*42nd Street* (8/25/80). Book by Michael Stewart and Mark Bramble. Stage version of 1933 Warner Bros. classic. Music and lyrics by Harry Warren and Al Dubin from that film and others; other lyrics by Johnny Mercer and Mort Dixon. 3,486 performaces.

*The Pirates of Penzance* (1/8/81). The Joseph Papp/New York Shakespeare Festival rendition of the comic opera with book and lyrics by W. S. Gilbert, music by Arthur Sullivan, and featuring Rex Smith, Linda Ronstadt, George Rose, Kevin Kline. 772 performances.

*Pump Boys and Dinettes* (2/4/82). Music and lyrics by Jim Wann, John Foley, Mark Hardwick, John Schimmel, Cass Morgan, and Debra Monk. 573 performances.

*Cats* (10/7/82). Based on T. S. Eliot's *Old Possum's Book of Practical Cats*; additional lyrics by Trevor Nunn and Richard Stilgoe; music by Andrew Lloyd Webber. 7,485 performances; closed 9/10/00.

*Big River: The Adventures of Huckleberry Finn* (4/25/85). William Hauptman book, Roger Miller music and lyrics. 1,005 performaces.

*Song & Dance* (9/18/85). Andrew Lloyd Webber music. Don Black lyrics; American adaptation and additional lyrics by Richard Maltby Jr. 474 performances.

*The Mystery of Edwin Drood* (12/12/85). Rupert Holmes book, music, lyrics. Musicalized Dickens. 608 performances.

*Me and My Girl* (8/10/86). Revival of a British import originally produced in London 12/16/37 for 1,646 performaces. L. Arthur Rose and Douglas Furber book and lyrics, Noel Gay music. Book revised by Stephen Fry with contributions to revisions by Mike Ockrent. 1,420 performances.

*Les Misérables* (3/12/87): Original French text by Alain Boublil and Jean-Marc Natel. Claude-Michel Schönberg music. English book and lyrics by Herbert Kretzmer and James Fenton, along with Boublil and Schönberg. 5,439 performances through 5/28/oo.

*Starlight Express* (3/15/87). Andrew Lloyd Webber music, Richard Stilgoe lyrics. 761 performances.

*Into the Woods* (11/5/87). Stephen Sondheim music and lyrics, James Lapine book. 765 performances.

*The Phantom of the Opera* (1/26/88) Andrew Lloyd Webber music. Richard Stilgoe and Lloyd Webber book, Charles Hart lyrics; additional lyrics by Richard Stilgoe. 5,150 performances through 5/28/oo.

*City of Angels* (12/11/89) Larry Gelbart book, Cy Coleman music, David Zippel lyrics. 878 performances.

*Miss Saigon* (4/11/91). Alain Boublil and Claude-Michel Schönberg book, Claude-Michel Schönberg music, Richard Maltby Jr. and Alain Boublil lyrics, adapted from Boublil's original French lyrics. 3,816 performances through 5/28/oo.

*The Secret Garden* (4/25/91). Marsha Norman book and lyrics, Lucy Simon music. 706 performances.

*The Will Rogers Follies* (5/1/91). Peter Stone book, Cy Coleman music, Betty Comden and Adolph Green lyrics. 983 performances.

*The Who's Tommy* (4/22/93) Pete Townshend and Des McAnuff book, Pete Townshend music and lyrics. Additional music and lyrics by John Entwistle and Keith Moon. 900 performances.

*Blood Brothers* (4/25/93). Willy Russell book, music, and lyrics. 839 performances.

*Beauty and the Beast* (4/18/94). Linda Woolverton book, Alan Menken music, Howard Ashman and Tim Rice lyrics. 2,480 performances through 5/28/oo.

*Sunset Boulevard* (11/17/94). Andrew Lloyd Webber music, Don Black and Christopher Hampton book and lyrics. 977 performances.

*Victor/Victoria* (10/25/95). Blake Edwards book, Henry Mancini music, Leslie Bricusse lyrics. Additional musical material by Frank Wildhorn. 734 performances.

*Jekyll & Hyde* (4/28/97). Leslie Bricusse book and lyrics, Frank Wildhorn music. 1,287 performances through 5/28/oo.

*The Scarlet Pimpernel.* (11/9/97). Nan Knighton book and lyrics, Frank Wildhorn music. Divided run finally totalling 772 performances.

*The Lion King* (11/13/97). Adapted from the screenplay by Irene Mecchi, Jonathan Roberts, and Linda Woolverton. Roger Allers and Irene Mecchi book, Elton John music, Tim Rice lyrics. Additional music and lyrics by Lebo M [sic], Mark Mancina, Jay Rifkin, Julie Taymor, and Hans Zimmer. 1,062 performances through 5/28/oo.

*Footloose* (10/22/98). Adapted from the original screenplay of Dean Pitchford by Pitchford and Walter Bobbie; Tom Snow music, Dean Pitchford lyrics. Additional music from the film score. 737 performances.

*Fosse* (1/14/oo). Dance review of Bob Fosse's choreography conceived by Richard Maltby Jr., Chet Walker, and Ann Reinking. 581 performances through 5/28/oo.

# Sources Cited

This book uses the system of parenthetical documentation detailed in the second edition of the *MLA Style Manual and Guide to Scholarly Publishing* by Joseph Gibaldi (New York: Modern Language Association of America, 1998). Most often the author's last name and relevant page number(s) are sufficient to locate the item in the "Sources Cited" section. In the list below, however, I have added to some entries a notation in square brackets indicating how that item is cited in the text to differentiate it from other works by the same author, a work by another author with the same last name, a specific volume in a multivolume annual series, and so forth.

Allen, Frederick Lewis. *Only Yesterday: An Informal History of the 1920's*. New York: Harper & Row, 1931; rpt. New York: John Wiley, 1997.

Allen, Frederick Lewis. *Since Yesterday: The Nineteen-Thirties in America, September 3, 1929–September 3, 1939*. New York: Harper, 1940. [Allen, *Since*]

Anderson, Maxwell. *Knickerbocker Holiday*. New York: Anderson House, 1938.

Ashman, Howard. Music by Alan Menken. *Little Shop of Horrors*. New York: Samuel French, 1985.

Baily, Leslie. *The Gilbert & Sullivan Book*. London: Cassell, 1952.

Baral, Robert. *Revue: The Great Broadway Period*. New York: Fleet Press Corporation, 1962.

Behr, Edward, and Mark Steyn. *The Story of* Miss Saigon. New York: Arcade, 1991.

Berkowitz, Gerald. "The Metaphor of Paradox in Sondheim's *Company*." *Philological Papers* 25 (1979), 94–100.

Berlin, Gerald. Telephone interview. 8 February 2000. [Berlin interview]

Berlin, Irving. *The Songs of Irving Berlin: Broadway Songs*. Milwaukee: Hal Leonard, 1991.

Bernstein, Leonard. *Trouble in Tahiti: An Opera in Seven Scenes*. New York: Schirmer, 1953.

*Best Plays of 1899–1909* through *1998–1999*. Ed. Burnes Mantle and Garrison P. Sherwood, 1899–1909 and 1909–1919. New York: Dodd, Mead, 1943–1944. Ed. Burns Mantle, 1920–21 through 1946–47. New York: Dodd, Mead, 1930–1947. Ed. John Chapman, 1947–48 through 1951–52. New York: Dodd, Mead, 1947–1952. Ed. Louis Krononberger, 1952–53 through 1960–61. New York: Dodd, Mead, 1953–1961. Ed. Henry Hewes, 1961–62 through 1963–64. New York: Dodd, Mead, 1962–1964. Ed. Otis L. Guernsey Jr., 1964–65 through 1984–85. New York: Dodd, Mead, 1965–1985. Ed. Otis L. Guernsey Jr., and Jeffrey Sweet, 1985–86 through

1995–96. New York: Dodd, Mead, 1987–1988; Applause, 1989–1992; Limelight Editions, 1993–1996. Ed. Otis L. Guernsey Jr., 1996–97 through 1998–99. New York: Limelight Editions, 1997–1999. [*Best Plays* and abbreviated designation of covered theatre season, as *Best Plays 63–64*]

Bishop, André. Liner Notes. *March of the Falsettos.* LP. DRG Records, 1981. [Bishop Liner]

Bishop, André. Preface. *Assassins.* By Stephen Sondheim and John Weidman. New York: Theatre Communications Group, 1991. vii–xi.[Bishop Preface]

Blitzstein, Marc. *The Cradle Will Rock: A Play in Music.* New York: Random House, 1938.

Blitzstein, Marc. *Marc Blitzstein Discusses His Theatre Compositions.* New York: Spoken Arts 717/Westminster Records, 1956. [*Marc*]

Blum, John Morton. *V Was for Victory: Politics and American Culture During World War II.* New York: Harcourt Brace Jovanovich, 1976.

Bordman, Gerald. *American Musical Theatre: A Chronicle.* 2nd ed. New York: Oxford UP, 1992.

Brantley, Ben. "Cub Comes of Age: A Twice-Told Cosmic Tale." *New York Times* 14 November 1997: E1+. [Brantley, "Cub"]

Brantley, Ben. "Destiny and Duty, Nile Style." *New York Times* 24 March 2000: E1+. [Brantley, "Destiny"]

Brantley, Ben. "Lively Women, But Very Tired." *New York Times* 28 April 1997: C12. [Brantley, "Lively"]

Brantley, Ben. "The Promises of an Enchantress." *New York Times* 3 December 1999: E1+. [Brantley, "Promises"]

Brockett, Oscar G., with Franklin J. Hildy. *History of the Theatre.* 8th ed. Boston: Allyn and Bacon, 1999.

*Byrne v. P.B.I.C., Inc.* 398 U. S. 916.

Campbell, A.E. *America Comes of Age.* New York: American Heritage Press, 1971.

Charnin, Martin. Telephone interview. 14 March 2000.

Citron, Stephen. *The Wordsmiths: Oscar Hammerstein 2nd and Alan Jay Lerner.* New York: Oxford UP, 1995.

Churchill, Allen. *Over Here!: An Informal Re-creation of the Home Front in World War One.* New York: Dodd, Mead, 1968.

Colker, Jerry. Music by Michael Rupert. *3 Guys Naked from the Waist Down.* New York: Samuel French, 1986.

Cooper, John Milton Jr. *Pivotal Decades: The United States 1900–1920.* New York: Norton, 1990.

Crane, David, Seth Friedman, and Marta Kauffman. Music by William K. Dreskin, Joel Phillip Friedman, Seth Friedman, Alan Menken, Stephen Schwartz, and Michael Skloff. *Personals.* New York: Samuel French, n. d. [c. 1987].

Cryer, Gretchen. Music by Nancy Ford. *I'm Getting My Act Together and Taking It on the Road.* Garden City, N.Y.: Nelson Doubleday, 1980.

Davis, Luther. Songs by Robert Wright and George Forrest. Additional music and lyrics by Maury Yeston. *Grand Hotel—The Musical.* New York: Samuel French, 1992.

Davis, Ossie, Philip Rose, and Peter Udell. Lyrics by Peter Udell. Music by Gary Geld. *Purlie.* New York: Samuel French, 1971.

De Mille, Agnes. *America Dances.* New York: Macmillan, 1980.

Doherty, Thomas. *Projections of War: Hollywood, American Culture, and World War II*. New York: Columbia UP, 1993.

Else, Gerald, trans. *Aristotle: Poetics*. Ann Arbor: U of Michigan P, 1967.

Emigh, John. Telephone interview. 19 May 2000.

Faircloth, Tara. Non-Equity Licensing Agent, Music Theatre International. Telephone interview. 31 August 2000.

Finn, William. Libretto. *March of the Falsettos*. LP. DRG Records, 1981. [Finn, *March*]

Finn, William, and James Lapine. *Falsettos*. New York: Plume, 1993. [Finn and Lapine]

Fishman, Sylvia Barack. "American Jewish Fiction Turns Inward, 1960–1990." *American Jewish Yearbook 1991*. New York: American Jewish Committee, 1991. 35–69.

Fishman, Sylvia Barack. Personal interview. 14 February 2000. [Fishman interview]

Flanagan, Hallie. *Arena*. New York: Duell, Sloan, and Pearce, 1940.

Frum, David. *How We Got Here: The 70s: The Decade That Brought You Modern Life (For Better or Worse)*. New York: Basic Books, 2000.

Frye, Northrop. *Anatomy of Criticism*. New York: Princeton UP, 1957; rpt. Atheneum, 1966.

Gänzl, Kurt. *The Musical: A Concise History*. Boston: Northeastern UP, 1997.

"Gay-rights birthplace named historic landmark." *The Providence Sunday Journal*, 19 March 2000: A10.

Goggin, Dan. *Nunsense*. New York: Samuel French, 1986.

Goldberg, Isaac. *The Story of Gilbert and Sullivan, or The 'Compleat' Savoyard*. New York: Simon and Schuster, 1928.

Goldman, Eric F. *The Crucial Decade: America, 1945–1955*. New York: Knopf, 1956.

Goldstein, Malcolm. *The Political Stage: American Drama and Theater of the Great Depression*. New York: Oxford UP, 1974. [Goldstein, *Political*]

Goldstein, Malcolm. *George S. Kaufman: His Life, His Theater*. New York: Oxford UP, 1979. [Goldstein, *Kaufman*]

Gordon, Eric A. *Mark the Music: The Life and Work of Marc Blitzstein*. New York: St. Martin's, 1989.

Goren, Arthur A. "A 'Golden Decade' for American Jews: 1945–1955." *Studies in Contemporary Jewry; An Annual: Vol. VIII: A New Jewry? America Since the Second World War*. Ed. Peter Y. Medding. New York: Oxford UP, 1993. Rpt. without original footnotes in *The American Jewish Experience*. 2nd ed. Ed. Jonathan D. Sarna. New York: Holmes & Meier, 1997. 294–311.

Gottfried, Martin. *Sondheim*. Rev. and updated ed. New York: Abrams, 2000.

Green, Stanley. *The World of Musical Comedy*. 4th ed., rev. and enlarged. San Diego and New York: A. S. Barnes, 1980.

Greenwich, Ellie. Book by Anne Beatts. Additional material by Jack Heifner. *Leader of the Pack*. New York: Samuel French, c. 1987.

Hamlisch, Marvin. Book by James Kirkwood and Nicholas Dante. Lyrics by Edward Kleban. *A Chorus Line*. New York: Applause, 1995.

Hammerstein, Oscar II. *Carmen Jones*. New York: Knopf, 1945.

Harburg, E. Y., and Fred Saidy. *Finian's Rainbow*. New York: Random House, 1947.

Harnick, Sheldon. Telephone interview. 8 February 2000.

Hart, Dorothy, and Robert Kimball, eds. *The Complete Lyrics of Lorenz Hart*. New York: Knopf, 1986. [Hart and Kimball]

Hart, Moss, with lyrics by Ira Gershwin and music by Kurt Weill. *Lady in the Dark.* New York: Random House, 1941.

Hellman, Lillian, Leonard Bernstein, Richard Wilbur, John Latouche, and Dorothy Parker. *Candide.* New York: Random House, 1957.

Henderson, Amy, and Dwight Blocker Bowers. *Red, Hot, & Blue: A Smithsonian Salute to the American Musical.* Washington: The National Portrait Gallery and the National Museum of American History in association with the Smithsonian Institution Press, 1996.

Herman, Jerry. Book by Don Appell. *Milk and Honey.* Vocal score. New York: Edwin H. Morris, 1963. [Herman, *Milk*]

Herman, Jerry. Book by Harvey Fierstein. *La Cage aux Folles.* New York: Samuel French, 1987. [Herman, *La Cage*]

Hirsch, Foster. *The Boys from Syracuse: The Shuberts' Theatrical Empire.* Carbondale and Edwardsville, IL: Southern Illinois UP, 1998.

Hirson, Roger O. Music and lyrics by Stephen Schwartz. *Pippin.* New York: Drama Book Specialists, 1975.

Holt, Will. Gary William Friedman, music. *The Me Nobody Knows.* Vocal selections. Milwaukee: Hal Leonard, 1970.

Houseman, John. *Run-Through: A Memoir.* New York: Simon and Schuster, 1972.

Huber, Eugene R. *Stephen Sondheim and Harold Prince: Collaborative Contributions to the Development of the Modern Concept Musical, 1970–1981.* Diss. NYU. Ann Arbor: UMI, 1990. 9025177.

Huizinga, Johan. *Homo Ludens: A Study of the Play Element in Culture.* London: Routledge & Kegan Paul, 1949.

Ilson, Carol. *Harold Prince: From* Pajama Game *to* Phantom of the Opera. Ann Arbor: UMI Research P, 1989.

Innaurato, Albert. "Today, the Musical Dies." *The New York Times Magazine* 26 September 1999: 27–28.

Isherwood, Christopher. *The Berlin Stories.* New York: New Directions, 1954.

Jablonski, Edward. *Alan Jay Lerner: A Biography.* New York: Holt, 1996.

Johnson, Haynes. *Sleepwalking through History: America in the Reagan Years.* New York: Norton, 1991.

Johnson, John C. "Gerald Berlin and Defending Hair." Compiled information of Johnson's interview with Attorney Gerald A. Berlin. Available at <hair-list@lists.jabberwocky.com>.

Jones, John Bush. "DeSylva, B. G." *American National Biography* Ed. John A. Garraty and Mark C. Carnes. Vol. 6. New York: Oxford UP, 1999. 489–90. [Jones, "De Sylva"]

Jones, John Bush. "From Melodrama to Tragedy: The Transformation of *Sweeney Todd.*" *New England Theatre Journal* 2 (1991), 85–97. [Jones, "From Melodrama"]

Jones, John Bush. "Maxwell Anderson, Lyricist." *Maxwell Anderson and the New York Stage.* Ed. Nancy J. Doran Hazelton and Kenneth Krauss. Monroe, N.Y.: Literary Research Associates, 1991. 97–111. [Jones, "Maxwell"]

Jones, John Bush. "Musicals of the 'Me Generation.'" *Brandeis Review* 3 (1982), 16–19. [Jones, "Musicals"]

Jones, Tom. Telephone interview. 17 March 2000. [T. Jones interview]

Jones, Tom. *Celebration*. Director's script. New York: Music Theatre International, n.d. [T. Jones, *Celebration*]

Jones, Tom. Music by Harvey Schmidt. *The Fantasticks*. New York: Drama Book Shop, 1964. [T. Jones, *Fantasticks*]

Kallen, Stuart A. *The 1980s*. San Diego: Lucent Books, 1999. [Kallen, *80s*]

Kallen, Stuart A. *The 1990s*. San Diego: Lucent Books, 1999. [Kallen, *90s*]

Kaufman, George S., and Moss Hart, with lyrics by Lorenz Hart. *I'd Rather Be Right*. New York: Random House, 1937. [Kaufman and Hart]

Kaufman, George S., and Morrie Ryskind, with lyrics by Ira Gershwin. *Let 'Em Eat Cake*. New York: Knopf, 1933. [Kaufman, *Let*]

Kaufman, George S., and Morrie Ryskind, with lyrics by Ira Gershwin. *Of Thee I Sing*. New York: Knopf, 1932. [Kaufman, *Of Thee*]

Kennedy, David M. *Over Here: The First World War and American Society*. New York: Oxford UP, 1980.

Kinkle, Roger D. *The Complete Encyclopedia of Popular Music and Jazz, 1900–1950*. New Rochelle: Arlington House, 1974.

Kopit, Arthur. Music and lyrics by Maury Yeston. *Nine — The Musical*. Garden City, N.Y.: Doubleday, 1983.

Kreuger, Miles. *Show Boat: The Story of a Classic American Musical*. New York: Oxford UP, 1977.

Lahr, John. Introduction. *Jelly's Last Jam*. By George C. Wolfe. Lyrics by Susan Birkenhead. Music by Jelly Roll Morton. Additional music and musical adaptation by Luther Henderson. New York: Theatre Communications Group, 1993. [vii]–xiii.

Leaming, Barbara. *Orson Welles*. New York: Viking, 1985.

Leigh, Mitch. Lyrics by Joe Darion. *Man of La Mancha*. Vocal score. Port Chester, N.Y.: Cherry Lane Music, n.d.

Lennart, Isobel. Music by Jule Styne, lyrics by Bob Merrill. *Funny Girl*. New York: Random House, 1964.

Leonard, Neil. "Morton, Ferdinand Joseph." *Dictionary of American Biography: Supplement Three 1941–1945*. New York: Scribner's 1973. 541–42.

Lerner, Alan Jay. Music by Frederick Loewe. *Camelot*. New York: Random House, 1961. [Lerner, *Camelot*]

Lerner, Alan Jay. *Paint Your Wagon*. New York: Coward-McCann, 1952. [Lerner, *Paint*]

Lerner, Alan Jay. *The Street Where I Live*. New York: Norton, 1978. [Lerner, *Street*]

Leuchtenburg, William E. *The Perils of Prosperity 1914–32*. Chicago: U of Chicago P, 1958.

Leuchtenburg, William E. *A Troubled Feast*. Boston: Little, Brown: 1973. [Leuchtenburg, *Feast*]

Lingeman, Richard R. *Don't You Know There's a War On?* New York: Putnam's, 1970.

Loesser, Frank. *How To Succeed in Business without Really Trying*. Vocal Score. New York: Frank Music, 1961. [Loesser, *How To*]

Loesser, Frank, Jo Swerling, and Abe Burrows. *Guys and Dolls: (A Musical Fable of Broadway)*. London: Frank Music, 1951. [Loesser, *Guys*]

Lord, Walter. *The Good Years: From 1900 to the First World War*. New York: Harper & Brothers, 1960.

Marty, Myron A. *Daily Life in the United States, 1960–1990: Decades of Discord.* Westport, Conn.: Greenwood Press, 1997.

Masteroff, Joe. Telephone interview. 28 February 2000. [Masteroff interview]

Masteroff, Joe. Music by John Kander, lyrics by Fred Ebb. *Cabaret.* New York: Random House, 1967. [Masteroff, *Cabaret*]

Masteroff, Joe. Music by John Kander. Lyrics by Fred Ebb. *Cabaret: The Illustrated Book and Lyrics.* New York: Newmarket Press, 1999. [Masteroff, *Cabaret* 1999]

Matlaw, Myron. "Alan Paton's *Cry, the Beloved Country* and Maxwell Anderson's/ Kurt Weill's *Lost in the Stars*: A Consideration of Genres." *Arcadia* 10 (1975): 260–72.

Matusow, Allen J. *The Unraveling of America: A History of Liberalism in the 1960s.* New York: Harper, 1986.

McCabe, John. *George M. Cohan: The Man Who Owned Broadway.* Garden City, N.Y.: Doubleday, 1973.

Meltzer, Milton. *Brother, Can You Spare a Dime?: The Great Depression, 1929– 1933.* New York: Knopf, 1969.

Michener, James A. *Tales of the South Pacific.* 10th printing. New York: Macmillan, 1949.

Miller, Douglas, and Marion Nowak. *The Fifties: The Way We Really Were.* Garden City, N.Y.: Doubleday, 1977.

Molnar, Franz [Ferenc Molnár]. *Liliom: A Legend in Seven Scenes and a Prologue.* English text and introduction by Benjamin F. Glazer. New York: Liveright, 1921.

Mordden, Ethan. *Better Foot Forward: The History of American Musical Theatre.* New York: Grossman, 1976.

Mordden, Ethan. *Make Believe: The Broadway Musical in the 1920s.* New York: Oxford UP, 1997.

Morgan, Edward P. *The 60s Experience: Hard Lessons about Modern America.* Philadelphia: Temple UP, 1991.

"Musical Theatre and the American Dream." A panel discussion with Martin Charnin, Sheldon Harnick, Galt MacDermot, and Andrea Most; John Bush Jones, moderator. Archival videocassette. Spingold Theatre Center, Brandeis U, Waltham, Mass.: 21 April 1999.

*New York Theatre Critics' Reviews.* New York: Critics' Theatre Reviews, 1940–. [NYTCR and year of included reviews, as *NYTCR* 1987]

O'Hara, John. Lyrics by Lorenz Hart. Music by Richard Rodgers. *Pal Joey.* New York: Random House, 1952.

*P.B.I.C., Inc. v. Byrne.* 313 F. Supp. 757. D. C. Mass., 1970.

*P.B.I.C., Inc. v. District Attorney of Suffolk County.* 357 Mass. 770. MA Supreme Judicial Ct., 1970.

Perrett, Geoffrey. *Days of Sadness, Years of Triumph: The American People 1939– 1945.* New York: Coward, McCann & Geoghegan, 1973.

Perry, George. *The Complete Phantom of the Opera.* New York: Holt, 1988.

Perry. George. Sunset Boulevard: *From Movie to Musical.* New York: Holt, 1993.

Prince, Hal [Harold]. *Contradictions: Notes on Twenty-Six Years in the Theatre.* New York: Dodd, Mead, 1974.

Ragni, Gerome, and James Rado. Music by Galt MacDermot. *Hair: The American Tribal Love-Rock Musical.* New York: Pocket Books, 1969. [Ragni and Rado 1969]

Ragni, Gerome, and James Rado. Music by Galt MacDermot *Hair: The American Tribal Love-Rock Musical (Revised)*. Prompt book. New York: Tams-Witmark Music Library, 1995. [Ragni and Rado 1995]

Rice, C. Duncan. *The Rise and Fall of Black Slavery*. New York: Harper & Row, 1975. [C. Rice]

Rich, Frank. "Conversations with Stephen Sondheim." *The New York Times Magazine* 12 March 2000: 38+.

Richards, David. "Disney Does Broadway, Dancing Spoons and All." *New York Times* 19 April 1994: C15.

Richards, Stanley, ed. *Great Musicals of the American Theatre*. 2 vols. Radnor, Penn.: Chilton, 1973, 1976. [Richards 1] and [Richards 2]

Richards, Stanley, ed. *Great Rock Musicals*. New York: Stein and Day, 1979. [Richards, *Rock*]

Riggs, Lynn. *Green Grow the Lilacs*. New York: Samuel French, 1931.

Rodgers, Richard. *Musical Stages: An Autobiography*. New York: Random House, 1975. [Rodgers, *Stages*]

Rodgers, Richard, and Oscar Hammerstein II. *6 Plays by Rodgers and Hammerstein*. New York: Random House, 1955. [Rodgers, *6 Plays*]

Rodgers, Richard, and Oscar Hammerstein, 2nd. *The King and I*. New York: Random House, 1951. [Rodgers, *King*]

Rodgers, Richard, and Oscar Hammerstein II. *Pipe Dream*. New York: Viking, 1956. [Rodgers, *Pipe*]

Rodgers, Richard, Oscar Hammerstein, 2nd, and Joseph Fields. *Flower Drum Song*. New York: Farrar, Straus and Cudahy, 1959. [Rodgers, *Flower*]

Rodgers, Richard, Oscar Hammerstein II, Howard Lindsay, and Russel Crouse. *The Sound of Music*. 14 printing. New York: Random House, 1978. [Rodgers, *Sound*]

Rodgers, Richard, Oscar Hammerstein, 2nd, and Joshua Logan. *South Pacific*. New York: Random House, 1949. [Rodgers, *South*]

[Rome, Harold.] *New "Pins and Needles" Lyrics*. Printed broadside; n. p., n. d. In John Hay Library, Brown University. [Rome, *New Pins*]

Rome, Harold. *Pins and Needles*. Piano-vocal score. New York: Florence Music/ Chappell & Co., n.d. [Rome, *Pins*]

Russell, Francis [author of the narrative sections]. *The American Heritage History of the Confident Years*. New York: American Heritage, 1969.

Sarna, Jonathan D. Telephone interview. 7 February 2000.

Schwartz, Stephen, Craig Carnelia, Micki Grant, Mary Rodgers, Susan Birkenhead, and James Taylor. *Working*. Director's script. New York: Music Theatre International, n. d.

Secrest, Meryle. *Stephen Sondheim: A Life*. New York: Knopf, 1998.

Shannon, David A. *Between the Wars: America, 1919–1941*. Boston: Houghton Mifflin, 1965.

Shull, Michael S., and David Edward Wilt. *Hollywood War Films, 1937–1945: An Exhaustive Filmography of American Feature-Length Motion Pictures Relating to World War II*. Jefferson, N.C.: McFarland: 1996.

Silver, Joan Micklin, and Julianne Boyd. *A . . . My Name is Alice*. New York: Avon, 1985.

Slatta, Richard W. *Cowboys of the Americas*. New Haven and London: Yale UP, 1990.

Smith, Cecil, and Glenn Litton. *Musical Comedy in America*. New York: Theatre Arts Books, 1981.

Sondheim, Stephen. Letter to the author. 24 May 2000. [Sondheim letter 5/24/2000]

Sondheim, Stephen. Letter to the author. 14 July 2000. [Sondheim letter 7/14/2000]

Sondheim, Stephen. "The Musical Theater: A Talk by Stephen Sondheim." *The Dramatists Guild Quarterly* 15 (1978), 6–27. [Sondheim, "The Musical"]

Sondheim, Stephen. Book by George Furth. *Company*. New York: Random House, 1970. [Sondheim, *Company*]

Sondheim, Stephen. Book by James Goldman. *Follies*. New York: Random House, 1971. [Sondheim, *Follies*]

Sondheim, Stephen. Book by James Lapine. *Sunday in the Park with George*. New York: Dodd, Mead, 1986. [Sondheim, *Sunday*]

Sondheim, Stephen. Book by John Weidman. *Assassins*. New York: Theatre Communications Group, 1991. [Sondheim, *Assassins*]

Sondheim, Stephen. Book by John Weidman. Additional material by Hugh Wheeler. *Pacific Overtures*. New York: Dodd, Mead, 1976. [Sondheim, *Pacific*]

Sondheim, Stephen. Book by Hugh Wheeler. *Sweeney Todd: The Demon Barber of Fleet Street*. New York: Applause, 1991. [Sondheim, *Sweeney*]

*Southeastern Promotions, Ltd. v. Conrad*. 420 U. S. 546.

Stagg, Jerry. *The Brothers Shubert*. New York: Random House, 1968.

Stearns, Marshall, and Jean Stearns. *Jazz Dance: The Story of American Vernacular Dance*. New York: Macmillan, 1968.

Stein, Joseph. Telephone interview. 5 July 2000. [Stein interview]

Stein, Joseph. Music by Jerry Bock, lyrics by Sheldon Harnick. *Fiddler on the Roof*. New York: Crown, 1964. [Stein, *Fiddler*]

Stein, Joseph. Music by Charles Strouse. Lyrics by Stephen Schwartz. *Rags*. Rev. Production Script. New York: Rodgers & Hammerstein Theatre Library, 1993. [Stein, *Rags*]

Stillman, Edmund [author of the narrative sections]. *The American Heritage History of the 20's & 30's*. New York: American Heritage, 1970.

Stone, Peter. Music by John Kander. Lyrics by Fred Ebb. *Woman of the Year*. New York: Samuel French, 1981. [Stone, *Woman*]

Stone, Peter. Music and lyrics by Sherman Edwards. *1776: A Musical Play*. 1970. New York: Penguin, 1976. [Stone, *1776*]

Stone, Peter. Music and lyrics by Maury Yeston. *Titanic: The Complete Book of the Musical*. New York: Applause, 1999. [Stone, *Titanic*]

Sunshine, Linda. Introduction. *Cabaret: The Illustrated Book and Lyrics*. By Joe Masteroff. Music by John Kander. Lyrics by Fred Ebb. New York: Newmarket Press, 1999. 11–14.

Swados, Elizabeth. *Runaways*. New York: Samuel French, 1980.

Taylor, Samuel. Music and lyrics by Richard Rodgers. *No Strings*. New York: Random House, 1962.

*Theatre World 1986–1987* through *1996–1997*. Ed. John Willis. New York: Crown, 1988–1991; Applause, 1992–1999. [*Theatre World* and abbreviation of covered theatre season, as *Theatre World 86–87*]

Toll, Robert C. *Blacking Up: The Minstrel Show in Nineteenth-Century America*. New York: Oxford UP, 1974.

"Too Many Okinawans Western, Say Pickets." *New York Times* 29 December 1970: 38.

Wagenknecht, Edward. *American Profile 1900–1909*. Amherst: U of Massachusetts P, 1982.

Wasserman, Dale. Telephone interview. 25 March 2000.

Wasserman, Dale. Lyrics by Joe Darion. Music by Mitch Leigh. *Man of La Mancha*. New York: Random House, 1966.

Wecter, Dixon. *The Age of the Great Depression 1929–1941*. New York: Macmillan, 1948.

Weidman, Jerome, and George Abbott. Music by Jerry Bock. Lyrics by Sheldon Harnick. *Fiorello!* New York: Random House, 1960.

White, Richard. *"It's Your Misfortune and None of My Own": A History of the American West*. Norman: U of Oklahoma P, 1991.

Wilk, Max. *OK!: The Story of Oklahoma!* New York: Grove, 1993.

Wilk, Max. *Overture and Finale: Rodgers & Hammerstein and the Creation of Their Two Greatest Hits*. New York: Back Stage Book, 1999. [Wilk, *Overture*]

Wolfe, George C. Lyrics by Susan Birkenhead. Music by Jelly Roll Morton. Additional music and musical adaptation by Luther Henderson. Introduction by John Lahr. *Jelly's Last Jam*. New York: Theatre Communications Group, 1993.

Woll, Allen. *Black Musical Theatre: From* Coontown *to* Dreamgirls. Baton Rouge: Lousiana State UP, 1989.

Zadan, Craig. *Sondheim & Co.* 2nd ed. New York: Harper & Row: 1986.

Ziegfeld, Richard and Paulette. *The Ziegfeld Touch: The Life and Times of Florenz Ziegfeld, Jr*. New York: Harry H. Abrams, 1993.

# Index

Because of the range of time discussed in this book, dates are designated in the index in two ways: two digits in the year column indicate the twentieth century; four digits represent the nineteenth or the twenty-first.